# FAMILY THERAPY IN BRITAIN

**Open University Press**
Psychotheraphy in Britain series
*Series Editor*: Windy Dryden

TITLES IN THE SERIES
**Individual Therapy in Britain**
Windy Dryden (ed.)

**Marital Therapy in Britain: Volumes I and II**
Windy Dryden (ed.)

*Forthcoming*

**Innovative Therapy in Britain**
John Rowan and Windy Dryden (eds.)

**Group Therapy in Britain**
Mark Aveline and Windy Dryden (eds.)

**Sex Therapy in Britain**
Martin Cole and Windy Dryden (eds.)

*Related titles*

**Cognitive-Behavioural Approaches to Psychotherapy**
Windy Dryden and William Golden

**Therapists' Dilemmas**
Windy Dryden

# FAMILY THERAPY IN BRITAIN

*Edited by*
Eddy Street and Windy Dryden

Open University Press
Milton Keynes · Philadelphia

*To our colleagues*

Open University Press
Open University Educational Enterprises Limited
12 Cofferidge Close
Stony Stratford
Milton Keynes MK11 1BY
and
242 Cherry Street
Philadelphia, PA 19106, USA

First Published 1988

*British Library Cataloguing in Publication Data*

Family therapy in Britain.
   1. Great Britain. Medicine. Family therapy
   I. Street, Eddy   II. Dryden, Windy
   III. Series
   616.89'156'0941

   ISBN 0-335-09841-X
   ISBN 0-335-09831-2 Pbk

*Library of Congress Cataloging-in-Publication Data*

Family Therapy in Britain / edited by Eddy Street and Windy Dryden
P. CM. — (Psychotherapy in Britain Series)
Includes bibliographical references and index
1. Family psychotherapy — Great Britain.   I. Street, Eddy.
   II. Dryden, Windy.   III. Series.
RC 488. 5. F3399   1988
616.89'156'0941 — DC 19        88–12454
ISBN 0-335-09841-X
ISBN 0-335-09831-2 Pbk

Typeset by Inforum Ltd, Portsmouth
Printed in Great Britain by Biddles Ltd., Guildford and Kings Lynn

# CONTENTS

**Part 2  Special issues**

# PREFACE

This book follows the pattern of presentation established in other volumes in the series 'Psychotherapy in Britain'. Thus its overall aim is to present to the reader those theoretical models that inform the activities of British family therapists as well as to discuss issues which bring to the fore themes central to the practice of family therapy in Britain. The text is thus divided into two sections, 'Theoretical Approaches' and 'Special Issues', to meet these twin aims.

By way of introducing the reader to the general area of 'family therapy thinking', in Chapter 1 Ian Bennun outlines the development of family therapy and pays particular attention to its relationship to systems theory. The subsequent six theoretical chapters all follow the same structure thereby enabling the reader to compare and contrast the models. These chapters are not organized in any set way and may be read in any order. Chris Dare outlines the psychoanalytic approach in Chapter 2; John Burnham and Queenie Harris present the systemic approach in Chapter 3. The structural approach is described by Ruth Reay in Chapter 4. Family therapy from a behavioural perspective is presented by Ian Falloon in Chapter 5; Harry Procter and George Walker write about the Brief Therapy (strategic) model in Chapter 6 and finally Paul O'Reilly and Eddy Street outline the experiential/historical approach. Some of these models readily find their echo in individual and marital therapy (behavioural and psychoanalytic), while other approaches are specific to family therapy (structural and systemic). We believe that these models cover the basic principal influences on the practice of family therapy in Britain. We are aware however that it has not been possible to present a detailed account of the British contribution to family therapy theory; indeed that would have been well outside the scope of this work. The reader, however, will find such contributions and developments well referenced throughout the book. The theoretical section is completed by Andy Treacher (Chapter 8) with an account of an integrated approach that in some way makes links with all the models outlined previously. It may well be that all therapists need to develop their own integration in order to develop their practice and this chapter presents just one way of undertaking that task.

The second section opens with Dave Dungworth examining the question of context to the practice of family therapy (Chapter 9). He begins from the position that the theory and application of systems thinking need be applied not only to families but also to the agencies in which therapists work. Arnon Bentovim and Brian Jacobs examine how family therapists can approach the problem of helping children who have been abused in their families (Chapter 10). By discussing this the authors deal with important ethical issues and additionally present another example of an integrated theoretical model. In Chapter 11 Jan Walker reviews problems that can beset parents and children when divorce occurs and she outlines strategies family therapists can adopt to help families struggling with this. The next two chapters seriously question the conceptions which family therapists have of families and therapy; in Chapter 12 Annie Lau discusses how different cultures view the family and how this therefore should affect how a therapist behaves. Jennie Williams and Gilli Watson in Chapter 13 critique the theory and practice of family therapy from the perspective that in the past it has been prejudicial to women and offer suggestions as to how this can be remedied. In Chapter 14 Erica De'Ath shows that in modern-day Britain the family is not a unitary social institution but includes a variety of social groupings with differing needs; she is then able to ask whether family therapists are effective in achieving all that they are capable of. Furthermore, she questions whether family therapists should take on a more active and influential role in framing social policy. Finally in Chapter 15 Arlene Vetere reviews the research on family therapy that is taking place in Britain; although this research is not extensive by virtue of its infancy the value of its contribution augurs well for the future development of the field.

*Eddy Street, Cardiff*
*Windy Dryden, London*

# THE EDITORS

## EDDY STREET

Eddy Street works as a clinical psychologist within the children's section of the Department of Clinical Psychology, South Glamorgan Health Authority, being based at Preswylfa Child and Family Centre.

After his first degree at the University College, Swansea, he pursued professional training in South Wales. Following qualification he undertook his training in psychotherapy in Birmingham. His interest soon focused on working with families and since that time his clinical practice, research and teaching have reflected this.

His particular research interest is on the training of family therapy skills. He has presented many workshops on family therapy throughout the country. He has contributed articles and chapters to several publications. He is a member of the Board of Assessors of the *Journal of Family Therapy*. At present he lives with his two children in Cardiff.

## WINDY DRYDEN

Windy Dryden is Senior Lecturer in Psychology at Goldsmiths' College, University of London. He is the author of *Rational-Emotive Therapy: Fundamentals and Innovations* (Croom Helm 1984) and *Therapists' Dilemmas* (Harper & Row 1985) and is editor of several books including *Key Cases in Psychotherapy* (Croom Helm 1987). He is series editor of the *Psychotherapy in Britain* series published by Open University Press and series editor of the forthcoming *Counselling in Action* series to be published by Sage Publications. He is a Fellow of the British Psychological Society, serves on the editorial boards of several international journals including the *British Journal of Guidance and Counselling* and is co-editor of the *Journal of Cognitive Psychotherapy: An International Quarterly*. At present he practises part-time as an honorary psychotherapist in the Department of Psychiatry, St Thomas's Hospital, London, and part-time for the Raphael Counselling Centre in London.

# THE CONTRIBUTORS

**Ian Bennun,** Principal Clinical Psychologist, Torbay Health Authority and University of Exeter.

**Arnon Bentovim,** Consultant Child Psychiatrist, Hospital for Sick Children, London.

**John Burnham,** Senior Social Worker and Family Therapist, Charles Burns Clinic, Birmingham.

**Christopher Dare,** Consultant Psychiatrist, Department of Children and Adolescents, Bethlem Royal and Maudsley Hospitals.

**Erica De'Ath,** Social Policy Officer, The Children's Society, London.

**Dave Dungworth,** Assistant Unit General Manager, Community Services Unit, Frenchay Health Authority, Bristol.

**Ian Falloon,** Associate Professor, University of Southern California, Los Angeles. Consultant Physician (Mental Health), Buckingham Hospital, Buckingham.

**Queenie Harris,** Consultant Child and Family Psychiatrist, Charles Burns Clinic and Dudley Road Hospital, Birmingham.

**Brian Jacobs,** Consultant Child Psychiatrist, Queen Mary's Hospital, Carshalton.

**Annie Lau,** Consultant in Child and Adolescent Psychiatry, Redbridge Child and Family Consultation Centre and King George Hospital, Ilford.

**Paul O'Reilly,** Principal Clinical Psychologist, District Department of Clinical Psychology, Exeter Health Authority, Exeter.

**Harry Procter,** Principal Clinical Psychologist, Tone Vale Hospital, Taunton.

**Ruth Reay,** Principal Lecturer, Department of Social Work and Social

Policy, Faculty of Social Sciences, Newcastle upon Tyne Polytechnic.
**Andy Treacher,** Clinical Tutur, MSc Course in Clinical Psychology, District Department of Clinical Psychology, Exeter Health Authority, Exeter.
**Arlene Vetere,** Clinical Psychologist, District Psychology Service, Branksome Clinic, Poole.
**George Walker,** Senior Clinical Psychologist, Southmead Hospital, Bristol.
**Janet Walker,** Co-Director, Conciliation Project Unit, University of Newcastle upon Tyne.
**Gilli Watson,** Senior Clinical Psychologist, District Department of Clinical Psychology, Exeter Health Authority, Exeter.
**Jennie Willaims,** Senior Clinical Psychologist, District Department of Clinical Psychology, Exeter Health Authority, Exeter.

# PART 1
# THEORETICAL APPROACHES

CHAPTER 1

# SYSTEMS THEORY AND FAMILY THERAPY

## Ian Bennun

## INTRODUCTION

Family therapy, like most psychotherapeutic approaches, developed from the general field of psychiatry. In tracing this development one observed the progress of various theorists, their research and the crystallization of diverse ideas. Prominent influences in Britain have been Bowlby's (1949) conjoint interviews as an adjunct to individual therapy, Bell's (1961) monograph on a family group therapy and the debate at the Tavistock Clinic, Howells's (1963) account of the development of the family psychiatry, Laing's (1964) study of schizophrenic families and the initial seminars led by Skynner from the Institute of Group Analysis and the later establishment of the Institute of Family Therapy.

The development of family therapy in Britain can also be traced in terms of how the early practitioners defined their approach and formulated problems compared with more recent accounts. Howells (1963) defined family psychiatry as a clinical approach where the patient is referred for some emotional disorder indicating family pathology. Within the family psychiatric approach, the family was accepted as the patient with the presenting person known as the prepositus, the indicating patient or the manifest patient. These ideas were refined within the British context as illustrated by Walrond-Skinner (1976) and Skynner (1976). All these accounts describe the shifting focus from the individual to the family and the dilemma of describing and conceptualizing what was previously seen as individual psychopathology in family relational terms.

Marital and family therapy have been influenced through the

development of social psychiatry, psychoanalysis and the psychosocial effects of the Second World War. Family case work, as practised by social workers, moved away from working with individual patients and extended to counselling couples and later to counselling these couples about difficulties presented by their children. The establishment of child guidance clinics gave further impetus to the family psychiatry movement, essentially because the family treatment approach was becoming the appropriate treatment for child-centred disorders. This was later extended to convening family meetings where one of the parents presented with difficulties.

Walrond-Skinner (1976) defined family therapy as the psychotherapeutic treatment of a natural system using the medium of conjoint interpersonal interviews. The focus on family systems rather than on individuals highlights the conceptual shift within systems theory as applied to the treatment of human groups. Interventions and information gathering are directed towards understanding individual behaviour patterns, the family matrix and the reciprocal relationship that exists between the two. It can be distinguished from other psychotherapies by its conceptual focus on the family as a whole with a major emphasis being placed on understanding individual behaviour patterns as arising from and influencing the general family system.

In this introductory chapter, the main concepts and terms in current use will be described. The shift from an individual-centred approach to a family system interactional approach has necessitated a more contextual framework for viewing the individual as part of a wider system. The concepts described will be elaborated further in the specific chapters dealing with the different theoretical approaches.

## SYSTEMS AND INDIVIDUALS: THE EPISTEMOLOGICAL CONTRAST

It is not surprising that the development of family therapy was influenced by individual psychotherapeutic approaches. Not only did psychoanalysis predate family therapy, but also it has shaped much of its practice. In this country both individual psychoanalysis and group analysis influenced the early practice and supervision of family therapy and, to an extent, still continue to do so (see Chapter 2 and Cooklin 1979; Dare 1979; Skynner 1981). Holmes (1983; 1985) has argued that psychoanalysis and family therapy should not be seen as alternative theories of psychopathology, but rather as competing paradigms so as to avoid the false polarization between the two approaches. Other writers (Kerr 1981) note that the distinction between individual and systemic theory is so marked that any attempts to mix them would reflect a failure to appreciate their difference.

The one-to-one situation within individual therapy presents the therapist with a unique view of the patient and his or her conceptualization of the world. Classical psychoanalysis conceptualizes psychological difficulties as maladaptive and unsuccessful resolutions of instinctual childhood conflicts which are rooted in real or fantasized involvements with significant others. The conflicts, being too painful or unacceptable to the child's ego, are defended against but emerge in adult life as their psychic consequences of earlier repression. The goals of psychoanalysis are to undo the repressions through the analysis of the unconscious, thereby relieving the patient of his or her difficulties. By helping the patient discover the unconscious meanings of repetitive and self-defeating behaviours and by helping to gain insight into their infantile origins, the therapist enables the patient to participate in the full development of the personality.

The epistemological basis of the systems approach is in marked contrast to individual approaches. One can picture a different configuration. In the room are not only the therapist and patient, but also other people who are central to the (identified) patient's life. Each has his or her own view of 'self' and 'other' and each has a specific view of the relationship and differences between them. The contrast between the two approaches extends beyond the participants in the therapy situation (system) and differs in the formulation of the presenting problem and the mechanisms of change. A fundamental premise within systems theory is that the problems that bring individuals into treatment persist only if they are maintained by the ongoing current behaviour of the patient and others with whom he or she interacts. If the problem-maintaining behaviour configuration can be altered, the nature of the problem too will change. These two basic assumptions underlie the essence of systemic thinking and intervention.

It is not my intention to contrast in detail the two approaches but rather describe the systemic context and how this directs the systemic therapist. Most family therapists see systemic thinking as the basis of their work. System implies the relationship between mutually independent units: thus systems can be defined as a set of objects together and the relationship between them and between their attributes. Systems theory emphasizes that the family represents a functioning operational system or unit comprising a set of collected interrelated parts, all of which combine to influence its total functioning. Furthermore, systems theory conceptualizes the relationship system as the functioning positions of the people who comprise that system. It still considers the individual, but in an entirely different way. Events are studied within the context in which they occur, with attention being placed on the connections and relationships rather than on individual characteristics. This formulation when applied to the family places it within a social context and the interdependence takes place within the context. The activation of the system can be effected by any constituent unit, or by an external force.

This view is in marked contrast to the individual formulation described earlier. Within the individual (intrapsychic) model, the emphasis remains with internal processes and does not consider in any detail the interpersonal processes operative in individual functioning. Holmes (1985), for the sake of clarity, uses the unconscious and the system as a way of comparing the two paradigms. As such the unconscious rather than the family system is the arena of therapy and the transference rather than the relationship between family members is the vehicle of change. Although both approaches provide a wider context within which symptoms are understood, the unconscious-system duality illustrates their difference.

Palazzoli's illuminating account of anorexia offers one clinician's epistemological shift from an intrapsychic to a transpersonal focus (Palazzoli 1974). By offering an object-relation theory of anorexia, Palazzoli describes how the body becomes an incorporated object, threatening the patient's ego: the symptom represents an intrapersonal process where badness is projected into the body. After studying the family interaction literature, Palazzoli began to view forms of mental illness as 'logical adaptions to a deviant and illogical transpersonal system' (1974 : 193). From this, the contrast between the intrapsychic and interpersonal approach is documented culminating with a systems account of anorexia: 'the patient is engaged in a vicious battle on two fronts, namely against her body and the family system' (Palazzoli 1974 : 233).

# THE INFLUENCE OF FAMILY INTERACTION RESEARCH ON THE DEVELOPMENT OF FAMILY THERAPY

The development of systems thinking as applied to the family was also initially encouraged by family interaction research (Mishler and Waxler 1968). In the same way that there is no unitary view of family therapy, there have been divergent avenues of research on family interaction. Much of the early work on family interaction patterns was associated with the aetiology and development of schizophrenia. Lidz (1963) extended and applied psychoanalytic concepts to studying the family triad and emphasized how the blurring of age, sex and role boundaries were precursors in the development of schizophrenia. In interactional terms, Lidz distinguished two schizogenic family patterns, both of which interfered with normal developmental processes. The 'marital schism' described the family triad as being in a constant state of disequilibrium through repeated threats of parental separation. Communication consisted of either attempts to avoid and mask conflict or were defiant and coercive in nature. Within this particular family pattern, the parents disqualified each other and sought collusions with the children thereby excluding their partner. The second pattern, the 'marital skew' described the family equilibrium being achieved through a distorted parental relationship. Characteristically one particular feature of their interaction was the psychopathology of one parent being excessively powerful and thus dominant in determining family functioning. A major distinction between the two interaction patterns was that in the latter the marriage was not under constant threat.

Wynne was another pioneer who investigated family interaction as a contributing factor in schizophrenia (Wynne *et al.* 1977). Rather than focus on dyads and triads, emphasis was placed on the social organization of the family as a whole. Like the formulation proposed by Lidz, Wynne and his co-workers described family communication patterns as styles of relating which led to perceptual and thought disorders. The overall family structure was characterized by shared manoeuvres that served to deny or reinterpret the reality of feelings and the underlying meaninglessness of relationships. Two concepts used to describe these phenomena are integrally linked to Wynne's formulation. Pseudo-hostility and pseudo-mutuality describe the lack of family complementarity where the structure is either too loose or too rigid, communication is disjointed or fragmented with the continuity of interaction being disrupted by irrational shifts in the focus of attention. The child therefore feels pressured to maintain this façade to avoid recognition of the meaninglessness of family relationships: as a result the child is isolated from forming other social relationships. It is these disordered patterns of social interaction that Wynne believes leads to schizophrenic thought disorder.

The double-bind theory (Bateson *et al.* 1956; Sluzki and Ransom 1976) has been a seminal account in the evolution of family therapy. In the early 1950s Bateson embarked on investigating the communication patterns evident in families containing a schizophrenic member. The double-bind described a context of habitual communication impasses imposed on one person by others in their relationship system (Hoffman 1981). In essence, the double-bind is a communication sequence whereby the different levels of communication are contradictory. It is a special type of learning context of conflicting injunctions from which the recipient (usually the child) cannot escape and therefore cannot comment on the messages being expressed. An example of the transaction is a mother who requests affection from her child and then freezes when the child approaches. The mother's communication puts her child in an impossible dilemma. In order to maintain a tie with the mother, the child must show that he or she loves her; at the same time, the mother's response is unreceptive. The child then needs to resolve the dilemma by responding to the mother's quest for affection and withstand the mother's seemingly rejecting posture. The originators of the theory hypothesized that the impact of the contradictory communication sequences would lead to a breakdown in the individual's capacity to discriminate between the different levels of communication provoking behaviour characteristic of schizophrenia.

There are a number of accounts which describe the link between interaction research and therapy. Brown *et al.* (1972) noted that the recurrence of florid schizophrenic symptoms was related to particular factors in the patient's social (familial) environment. The interaction pattern within families containing a schizophrenic member once again became the focus of investigation with the major research being carried out in this country. Various accounts of this research appeared (Vaughn and Leff 1976; Leff *et al.* 1982) and it will be described more fully in Chapter 15. Relapse in schizophrenic patients was linked to particular interactions occurring within the family. In particular these families were described as having a high incidence of critical comments, increased hostility or a generalized criticism with a frank dislike of the patient and an over-protective or self-sacrificing emotional response in relation to the patient.

A second example of this interaction research–therapy link is the work of Alexander (1973a; Alexander and Barton 1980) who became aware of the different styles of communication evident in families presenting to the clinic and those who did not. The families could be differentiated along two communication dimensions: deviant families showed higher levels of communication defensiveness which was characterized by threat and punishment. The non-deviant intact families showed a supportive style of communication characterized by attempts to seek and give genuine information, spontaneously solve problems and show empathic understanding and equality. Based on the distinction between the two groups of families, an intervention programme was developed emphasizing the functional aspects of the non-distressed families. Minuchin's work with families containing an anorexic (psychosomatic) member (Minuchin *et al.* 1978) has led to the development of a descriptive profile of these families (see Chapter 4). Minuchin and his colleagues suggest that these families characteristically avoid conflict, the members are over-involved with each other, they are typically child-oriented and the identified patient's autonomy is curtailed by the intrusive concern of others.

## FAMILY ORGANIZATION

Systemic therapists invariably construct a map defining the organization, roles and rules of the families they treat. The theoretical position equating the family as a system will determine among other things how competently it serves each member.

Differentiation or separateness within the family is usually conceptualized in terms of sub-systems. These represent the constituent components that comprise the family. For example the usual sub-systems are the parental sub-system, the sibling sub-system and the sub-system defined by sex (mothers and daughters, fathers and sons). These sub-systems may in turn have their own sub-systems: an individual is made up of a complex of various sub-systems (physiological, cognitive, psychological and somatic). Sub-systems can also represent hierarchies which illustrate the executive functions that the family conduct. The parental and sibling/child sub-systems are arranged such that the parental sub-system has executive power which determines the rules imposed upon the family. Sometimes hierarchies are less clear when there is constant movement of some members between systems, for example when a child goes to school, or a parent goes to work. The executive positions are constantly shifting so that different hierarchies exist, depending on which system and sub-system is operative.

Both sub-systems and hierarchies are differentiated from each other by boundaries. They control the emotional exchanges and functions that each undertakes. Boundaries are categorized by the extent to which they are permeable: some families have relatively impermeable boundaries so that they are fairly isolated from the social or external environment. In these families for example, there is a limited flow of information, decisions are taken unilaterally and family members seem unaware of internal or external changes. Others have readily permeable boundaries and are thereby susceptible to changes in their wider social environment. Permeable or semi-permeable boundaries allow for exchanges between sub-systems: however when the boundary fails to differentiate between sub-systems, they become confused (or enmeshed) such that their functions become chaotic or dysfunctional. An example of the enmeshed boundary may be the confusion that both the child and family experience when he or she oscillates between different sub-systems and may constitute 'the parental child' on one occasion and then be relegated back into the child sub-system.

Communication is clearly necessary within and between sub-systems. Boundaries therefore define the flow of communication within the system. They exist around both sub-systems or hierarchies and individuals. A child who is enmeshed with his or her parents has little opportunity for individuation and growth because all attempts to develop independently will be thwarted.

Finally, when moving towards a systemic approach, the question of causality and aetiology must be addressed. The family or the individual does not 'cause' the problem: the genesis or development of family problems arises from the interrelationship between the various systems and sub-systems. The genesis and maintenance of problems are viewed in a circular way and as such feedback becomes critical in understanding family pathology.

In contrast to linear models of causality, the principle of circularity emphasizes mutual causality. Since each part of this system continually influences all the other parts, the overall pattern of relationships is the focus, rather than just one segment.

To complete the analysis of the family as a system, it is possible to list some of the systemic characteristics of the family.

1 Families, like other social groups, are systems having properties which are more than the sum of their attributes or their parts.
2 The family system is made up of sub-systems which together constitute the relationships within the family.
3 Each system and sub-system has a boundary, the properties of which define the flow of information between sub-systems and the individuation of each member. Communication between the various parts of this system is important in the functioning of the system.
4 The family as a system stands in relation to a supra-system which represents the external environment within which a family operates.
5 Circular rather than linear models of causality apply in understanding the genesis and maintenance of family problems.
6 Any tendency of the system to move away from equilibrium is corrected through negative feedback; changes in the system's functioning (as opposed to stability) are achieved through positive feedback.

## FURTHER TERMS WITHIN FAMILY SYSTEMS THEORY

Like most therapeutic approaches, family therapy has generated a specific vocabulary of its own. To some degree it is shared across family theoretical orientations, therefore what follows should be seen in the context of broadly introducing the terminology.

In a preceding section, mention was made of Howells's (1963) view of the presenting patient. This is generally also referred to as the identified patient (IP), although some use this abbreviation as meaning identified problem. In a sense, this is the pivotal view of systemic approaches. In general terms the IP is that member who becomes symptomatic and who is subsequently labelled as 'bad' or 'sick'. Rather than seeing the symptom as residing in one identified family member, this individual is often thought of as being indicative of disturbance within the whole family. The symptomatic family member may be the family scapegoat and may have the family difficulties placed on him or her. In addition, he or she may be the youngest, weakest or most sensitive and thus be unable to cope with the wider family disturbance.

If family disturbance or family dysfunction is seen to be represented by the

IP, then the meaning of the dysfunctional family requires elaboration. Dysfunctional families appear to lack a healthy sense of interaction and involvement in a differentiating group. These families lack the competence to negotiate interpersonal distress and are characterized as often having an extreme lack of cohesion or being excessively involved with each other. The extent to which family members are differentiated from one another is often used as a fundamental family description. Those families who have difficulty in dealing with the changes and developments of family life are unable to communicate satisfactorily and show poor problem-solving competency. Within a developmental framework, when the family goes through a natural transition, the nature of the relationships within the system has to be negotiated. Family dysfunction then typically arises from a failure to make these transitions properly.

Family therapists are particularly interested in the relationships between family members, their communication and interaction. Communication on one level can be seen as who says what to whom, how it is understood, whether the impact of the exchange matches its intent and the sequential responses that follow the initial interaction. Ultimately in a sequence of exchanges, information is fed back to the initiator indicating the dynamic processes involved. This feedback (either positive or negative) is incorporated into successive sequences creating a series of spiral or circular transactions.

Walrond-Skinner (1976) describes three patterns of communication breakdown. First, communication can be blocked thus reducing the flow of communication; this could result in prolonged silence, withdrawal or isolation. As a consequence of blocked communication, the capacity for development and growth is greatly reduced, non-verbal communication becomes prominent and secrets are generated or maintained. Second, communication can be displaced through the development of symptoms. What becomes important is who becomes symptomatic and which symptom becomes evident. Third, communication can be damaged, manifest by double-binds, levels of expressed emotion or defensive exchanges.

At a different level of analysis, therapists may address communication by clarifying distortions, facilitating open exchanges or just eliciting information. The distinction between analogic/'non-verbal' and digital/'verbal' communication (Bateson 1972) becomes operative when interventions are primarily focused on understanding the family's communication style and hypothesizing how language relates to psychopathology. Verbal language is more or less digital and provides a sense of order to communication whereas language described as analogic is paralinguistic including gestures, tone and pause, all of which describe discourse. The correspondence of these two forms of language is critical in understanding intrafamilial communication.

Successive chapters within this volume will show the variations in the terms that have been developed from family (systems) therapy. Some of the different approaches are best differentiated by their respective emphasis on different foci and it is in this context that general definitions and concepts should be viewed.

# THE FAMILY AS AN OPEN SYSTEM

The view of the family as a system suggests that as a functioning unit family members depend on each other for appropriate functioning and adaptation. The individuals within the family each have particular relationships with one another and as such are interdependent. Any changes that the individual members experience influence how they will be perceived by others and any family effects will have consequences for each member.

This introduces the idea of the family's relationship to the external world or supra-system. In systemic terms this describes the extent to which the family is an open or closed system. Brody (1975) has described the closed system family as one which is unresponsive to the changes that may occur within one member or to alterations in the wider environment. These closed system families have predetermined expectations of each member and fail to respond to the vicissitudes of the environment which do not fit with expectation, thus the evolutionary power of the family is limited. Brody further compares these families to automated factories where all patterns and responses are pre-programmed and cannot change except in predetermined ways. The family cannot resolve double-binds and is intolerant of any form of resistance to the status quo.

Whereas closed systems have impermeable boundaries which limit their interaction with the environment, open systems are constantly interacting with the environment whenever energy or information is exchanged. This interaction can be either dangerous or advantageous for the family depending on how it calibrates to environmental contingencies. Appropriate family functioning as an open system would demand a balance in responsiveness to the external forces that are operative. If the responsiveness is restricted, the family will become rigid, if it responds too readily chaos and insecurity may ensue. The external changes that may demand a family system response, may include the arrival or loss of a family member, a change of circumstance of one member (for example illness, unemployment, leaving home), individuation, political or socio-economic pressure, influences from schools, churches and the like. Essentially the family or an individual member confronts a different reality that exists outside the family and brings this information back to the system, thereby demanding some response (Koman and Streckler 1985).

## FAMILY STABILITY AND CHANGE

The preceding discussion has been based within the context of viewing the family as a responsive system. Within this theoretical framework, the functioning or stable family has a number of characteristics or mechanisms which maintain and promote its vitality and growth.

The notion of homeostasis describes the quality of the system that enables it to maintain a steady or same state throughout time. When a system is put under stress, the usual balance of forces is disturbed and the system is inclined towards imbalance. Homeostasis is determined by the extent to which information can be incorporated into the system through the various means of feedback sources that are available. The feedback operates as a regulator of the system maintaining its steady state. As a self-correcting mechanism, it is essentially concerned with the preservation of the status quo against the stress that emanates from the external environment.

It is important to note that homeostasis does not imply a stagnant or static characteristic of the family. In fact it may be the most dynamic and sensitive characteristic in its responsiveness to the minutiae of stress effects. Further, homeostasis is not an 'object' that each family conceptually possesses; rather it represents the responsiveness of each sub-system, hierarchy and boundary to changes in the environment.

Although family stability is seen as a necessary prerequisite for healthy family functioning, the dynamic nature of family systems suggests that within the homeostatic operation, it remains stable rather than experience disruption. This stability is in part determined by the capacity of the family to withstand change, but failure to remain stable will inevitably indicate stress. Kerr (1981) has noted that when the balance of forces impinging on the family is disturbed, symptoms are not far behind; this however demonstrates the negative qualities of change. Homeostasis was originally defined as a regulator of change, but there is the functional side of change.

Two further processes have been linked to the models of homeostasis. Morphostasis describes the capacity of the system to maintain constancy while it is being impinged upon by environmental forces. The dynamic of negative feedback ensures this constancy is perpetuated. Morphogenesis, on the other hand, describes the inevitable process that on occasions the system must change its basic structure: this involves positive feedback. In both these cases, the system is attempting to resist moving to a state of randomness or chaos. Wertheim (1973) has described these two processes as the family's steady-state tendency (morphostatic) and rule-changing capacity (morphogenetic) and has discussed them within a grid model of system typologies. It is suggested that a family's response to treatment will in part be determined by these two processes. Development and change are indicative of functioning family systems. Each family member is subject to lifespan changes and challenges for which individuation is the healthy response. This represents one side of positive change. The other is the change that is brought about through the process of treatment. The notion of change poses a curious dilemma as there are many different views on what constitutes change. A two-level model for change was proposed by the researchers at the Mental Research Institute (Watzlawick *et al.* 1974) that took into account behaviour/symptom change or a systemic/setting change.

Within the systemic context, change extends beyond an alteration of the presenting symptom. This group's two-level model postulates levels of change that describe different change processes. In one, the system remains unaltered and the nature of change involves symptom removal or corrective responses which is known as first order change. The other level of change or transformation is that whose occurrence changes the system itself, the second order change. Second order change is applied to what in the first order perspective appears to be a solution. The commonly used analogy of the thermostatic mechanism illustrates distinction between the levels of change. First order changes are the automatic shift it makes to maintain particular room temperature: in order to make a second order change, for example when the outside temperature drops, the occupier needs to alter the setting of the thermostat. The two-level model of change is both empirically and conceptually difficult to identify; there are a number of discussions which have attempted to clarify these complex issues (Lask 1980; Hoffman 1981; Papp 1983; Bennun 1986).

If one considers the idea of change and its relation to homeostasis, it is possible to assume that an intervention which alters the family's homeostasis will, by definition, lead to change. This would be reflected in the family's attempt to recalibrate to the change in their current functioning. Haley (1962) illustrated the relationship between homeostasis and change by describing the sequence that occurs when change takes place. 'When an organism indicates a change in relation to another, the other will act upon the first to diminish and modify that change' (Haley 1962 : 277). Critics of this view (Speer 1970; Dell 1982) have suggested that a theory of change cannot be based on a theory of how systems resist change. It might be that the self-regulation that homeostatic processes are proposed to fulfil, limits the range of spontaneous change and thus minimize the potential of systemic chaos. Dell (1982) argues that homeostasis is the nature of the systemic organization and not just one aspect of it. He describes the problem as follows: homeostasis

> was sometimes construed to be an end (of constancy in the face of change) and sometimes as a means to that end. Homeostasis as a means (i.e. the homeostatic mechanism) is a causal dualism. . . . Any description of a system as resisting the changes proposed by environmental inputs must explain how or why that resistance occurs.

> (Dell 1982 : 25)

Homeostasis cannot be both constancy and a means of attaining stability. This according to Dell describes the problematic dualism with the concept.

## THE FAMILY LIFE CYCLE

The life cycle paradigm has had a major impact on the way family therapists view family functioning (Solomon 1973; Hughes *et al.* 1978; Carter and McGoldrick 1980; Breulin 1983). Some suggest that family psychopathology is the result of disruption in the unfolding of the life cycle of the family (Haley 1973). Families pass through critical stages within their evolution and each stage presents developmental tasks that need to be negotiated. Within the life cycle perspective, a problem is viewed as a developmental impasse which occurs when the family is struggling to negotiate developmental transition.

The family life cycle can be seen as a sequence of characteristic stages beginning with the formation of the family through to its dissolution. Hughes *et al.* (1978) describe a seven-stage life cycle and give an account of the tasks and functions of each.

1 Beginning families include courtship and marriage prior to the couple's starting a family.
2 Child-bearing families begin with the birth of the couple's first child and continue until this child begins school.
3 Child-rearing families are a continuation of the previous stage until the oldest child becomes a teenager.
4 Families with teenagers begin with the first teenage child and continue until the oldest child leaves home.
5 Families as launching centres comprise the duration of time during which the first and last child leave home and commence their more independent living.
6 Families in the middle years span the time when the parental couple are together without their children until one or both retire.
7 Ageing families incorporate the remaining portion of the couple's lives.

These seven stages provide a framework for studying family relationships and conflict. One can develop a matrix of life cycle stages on one axis and family needs on a second. The physical, social, interpersonal and intra-psychic needs of each member and sub-system pose specific family dilemmas which, if not resolved, will result in family problems.

The needs described are not independent and the conflicting needs may not always be compatible. To take a simple example, parents may simul-taneously be supporting one child leaving home, while at the same time providing nurture and comfort for another. As the younger child observes his or her oldest sibling's emerging independence, he or she may experience envy or anxiety both of which need to be negotiated.

Those therapists using the life cycle conceptually may apply a stage model to guide their interventions within the course of therapy. Haley (1980) and Hughes *et al.* (1978) both provide accounts of this in terms of stages of therapy that to some degree match the family life cycle stages. Haley describes four stages; the first involves engaging families so as to prepare them for the eventual effects of intervention. The second stage, unbalancing the family, is based on the idea that one of the causes of the difficulties is the family's rigid organization and their thwarted attempts to progress developmentally. The intervention (solution) needs to be powerful enough to unbalance the system and so free it from its impasse. The next stage is dealing with the consequences of change given that it often produces some negative effects. Finally the therapist needs to disengage and leave the family functioning within its appropriate life cycle stage.

In concluding this section it is important to note Liddle and Saba's (1983) cautionary remarks about applying the family life cycle model. They suggest that the model is useful in understanding and assessing the family but may be limited in the specific therapist behaviour it suggests. They argue that the framework should be used within a clearly articulated approach to therapy and so avoid the possibility of an overly reductionist approach to complex family problems. The approach, if seen in systemic terms, must incorporate both the system's life cycle and the developmental changes of each individual member: the family life cycle model does not indicate that the life stages of each individual should be ignored and similarly does not preclude the definition of individuals as systems.

> Any family life cycle paradigm must include clear statements about precisely how change occurs through the life cycle; it must define whose change is being discussed and what kind of change is being considered.
>
> (Liddle and Saba 1983 : 170)

# THE APPLICABILITY OF FAMILY THERAPY

In attempting to identify the indications and contra-indications for family therapy, one immediately begins to grapple with the problems that face family therapy. One cannot assume that failures (Coleman 1985) contra-indicate family therapy. Holmes (1985) identifies two issues affecting choice of treatment: change and context. In his analysis Holmes sees change as helping families find healthy patterns from within their range of functioning: by context, one considers the process of referral. Here the issues are who is asking for help, is this occurring on behalf of another, whether the individual is usually accompanied by others, has the patient adopted a sick role for the family, and so on.

The contra-indications for family therapy are best described by Ackerman (1966). However, just as there is debate about whether family therapy is indicated, so there is disagreement about it as the treatment of choice. It is true that what might be contra-indicated for one therapist presents as a challenge for another. Ackerman (1966) listed the following contra-indications for family therapy twenty years ago, many of which would be challenged today:

1 The presence of an irreversible trend towards the break-up of the family.
2 The dominance within the group of destructive motivations.
3 One parent who has a paranoid condition or who has psychopathic destructiveness or is a confirmed criminal or pervert.
4 Parental dishonesty.
5 The existence of a valid family secret.
6 The existence of cultural or religious prejudices against this form of treatment.
7 The existence in some members of extremely rigid defences which, if broken, might induce a psychosis.
8 The presence of organic disease or other disabilities that would preclude the participation of one or more members.

In her discussion of the topic, Walrond-Skinner (1976; 1978) notes some of the above but in addition includes those families who contain such emotionally deprived individuals that they may not be able to share the therapist. In situations where outside agencies have particular undeclared reasons for requesting family therapy, Walrond-Skinner suggests that the therapist may choose to resist seeing the family together.

Walrond-Skinner (1976; 1978) following others has suggested that family therapy should be the treatment of choice when intrafamilial relationship difficulties are in evidence. Further clinical situations that present transactionally rather than individually are usually appropriate for family work as is the circumstance when one member is attempting to differentiate him or herself from the family. While intuitively some would see this as an individual difficulty it may be that the family is impeding this individual's attempts towards independence. Another instance indicating family work is where the family members are inappropriately being used to relieve family stress. One member may present symptomatically even though the difficulty is more appropriately placed in the family system. Finally Walrond-Skinner suggests that families who are 'hard to reach' where the individual is opposed to seeking help for him or herself but who would come with others are appropriate for family therapy.

Clarkin *et al.* (1979) describe the instances where family therapy would be the treatment of choice by way of a three-stage decision-tree model. Taking the first two stages together which address whether a family evaluation is indicated, the authors suggest the following criteria as appropriate indicators: when a child or adolescent is the presenting patient; when the presenting problem jeopardizes family relations; when there has been a recent disruption in the family caused by a family crisis; and when the family themselves define the problem as a family issue. In discussing the choice between marital or family therapy, Clarkin and his colleagues suggest the latter when the symptom is identified as being within the child or parent–child sub-system, when cross-generational relationships are currently reinforcing symptomatic behaviour in a child or adolescent and when marital therapy has reached an impasse due to the over-involvement of one partner's parents.

There are constrasting views as to whether family therapy is a total orientation or just a type of treatment. Clarkin *et al.* (1979) are cautious about wholeheartedly accepting the view that family therapy is an orientation and is therefore always appropriate. They suggest just as there are occasions when it is preferable to see one partner rather than the couple, one must not be myopic about seeing families because they are available and intact. An opposing view was presented by Haley in his discussion of family therapy as a method or an orientation. He described family therapy as an 'orientation to human problems, (Haley 1970 : 234). Further, Haley suggested that a family therapist should be puzzled by the question about the applicability of family therapy since all interventions are directed at a family systems level and all psychopathology represents relationship problems. Since these views were first presented, 'systemic' in some senses has replaced 'family'. When reviewing Ackerman's contra-indicated list, one now sees the development of systemic methods to address for example divorce (see Chapter 11), cultural or religious minorities (see Chapter 12), marital or family secrets and working with families containing a member with a disability or handicap.

## THE FAMILY AND THE INDIVIDUAL

Systemic thinking does not mean a rigid adherence to always working with the total system. Rather the systemic approach implies an attitude and conceptualization of the problem in a way that extends beyond separate units and their intrapsychic dimensions. Those theorists who adopt a strictly based systems approach (e.g. Haley 1976) tend to ignore individual psychopathology as necessarily needing individual treatment; others have described the appropriate place of individual therapy when necessary and stressed the importance of individual development in the psychopathology of family members (Ackerman 1966; Skynner 1976; Minuchin *et al.* 1978).

What necessarily distinguishes family therapists from others is the view that the family unit is one direct focus for treatment albeit through an alliance with one member. This is in marked contrast to the position adopted by Fisher and Mendell (1958) who described the spread of psychotherapeutic effects from the individual to his or her family following individual psychotherapy.

In describing the family life cycle stages, the changes that are experienced can be seen as both developments within the family and the individual. A family moving through the various developmental stages comprises individuals who themselves are proceeding through their own developmental stages (Erikson 1963). A focus on the former should not be at the expense of the latter. The effect of individual changes on the family is paramount as is the capacity of the individual to cope with evolutionary changes within the family. The reciprocal changes also provide the context for the systemic view but do not preclude the effect of family change on individuals. Indeed the brief therapy model (Weakland *et al.* 1974) specifically addresses the effects of systemic interventions on the individual as well as on the family as a whole (see Chapter 6).

There is now a growing literature on the place of marital and family therapy with one family member (Sauer 1980; Bennun 1985; Wells and Giannetti 1986). In the field of marital therapy, the examination of 'the marriage' is sometimes best undertaken as a task of uncovering each spouse's marital reality (Gurman and Kniskern 1986). This reality will be influenced by both dyadic/relational effects and individual/intrapsychic effects. On their own, neither is sufficient but both are necessary in order to gain an accurate and objective view (see Chapter 8). In a somewhat different way, Sauer (1980) notes that sometimes family members either refuse to participate in treatment with the IP or their participation is thwarted by their presence. The report describes how the therapist worked systemically through one individual when the more traditional approach was blocked. The major differences between the marital and family accounts are that in the former there is a specific systemic emphasis by choice when only one partner attends, whereas in the family therapy example, this was by default. However in both instances the focus remained on both the individual and the system.

Family therapy in Britain is at the state where diversity rather than a monolithic tradition exists. Practitioners are making their philosophies explicit and the application of technique is extending beyond the traditional arena. The ideas contained in this chapter represent a summary of systems theory as applied to family therapy. It introduces the language of family therapy and provides a model for applying a systemic analysis of family functioning. The remaining chapters within this volume will focus on two aspects of the diversity within British family therapy. The theoretical models

(Chapters 2–8) describe how the systemic approach to viewing families fits into a specific theoretical framework; while the various issues and contexts (Chapters 9–15) provide good evidence that the debate will continue as to whether this is a type of treatment or a total orientation. Nevertheless the process of changing families and helping them search for a different reality will be maintained and refined.

# REFERENCES

Ackerman, N. (1966). *Treating the Troubled Family*. New York, Basic Books.

Alexander, J. (1973a). Defensive and supportive communication in normal and deviant families. *Journal of Consulting and Clinical Psychology*, 40, 223–31.

—— (1973b). Defensive and supportive communication in family systems. *Journal of Marriage and the Family*, 35, 613–17.

Alexander, J. and Barton, C. (1980). Systems-behavioral intervention with delinquent families: clinical, methodological and conceptual considerations. In J. Vincent (ed.) *Advances in Family Intervention Assessment and Theory*. Greenwich, JAI.

Bateson, G. (1972). *Steps to an Ecology of Mind*. St Albans, Paladin.

Bateson, G., Jackson, D., Haley, J. and Weakland, J. (1956). Towards a theory of schizophrenia. *Behavioral Science*, 1, 251–64.

Bell, J. (1961). *Family Group Therapy*. Public Health Monograph, US Dept of Health, Education and Welfare.

Bennun, I. (1985). Unilateral marital therapy. In W. Dryden (ed.) *Marital Therapy in Britain*, vol. 2. London, Harper & Row.

—— (1986). Evaluating family therapy: a comparison of the Milan and problem-solving approaches. *Journal of Family Therapy*, 8, 225–42.

Bowlby, J. (1949). The study and reduction of group tensions in the family. *Human Relations*, 2, 123–8.

Breulin, D. (1983). Therapy in stages: a life cycle view. In H. Liddle (ed.) *Clinical Implications of the Family Life Cycle*. Rockville, Md, Aspen.

Brody, W. (1975). A cybernetic approach to family therapy. In G. Zuk and I. Boszormenyi-Nagy (eds) *Family Therapy and Disturbed Families*. Palo Alto, Science and Behavior Books.

Brown, G., Birley, J. and Wing, J. (1972). Influence of family life on the course of schizophrenic disorders: a replication. *British Journal of Psychiatry*, 121, 241–58.

Carter, E. and McGoldrick, M. (1980). *The Family Life Cycle*. New York, Gardner.

Clarkin, J., Frances, A. and Moodie, J. (1979). Selection criteria for family therapy. *Family Process*, 18, 391–403.

Coleman, S. (1985). *Failures in Family Therapy*. New York, Guilford.

Cooklin, A. (1979). A psychoanalytic framework for a systemic approach to family therapy. *Journal of Family Therapy*, 1, 153–65.

Dare, C. (1979). Psychoanalysis and systems in family therapy. *Journal of Family Therapy*, 1, 137–51.

Dell, P. (1982). Beyond homeostasis: toward a concept of coherence. *Family Process*, 21, 21–41.

Erikson, E. (1963). *Childhood and Society*. Harmondsworth, Pelican.

Fisher, S. and Mendell, D. (1958). The spread of psychotherapeutic effects from the patient to his family group. *Psychiatry*, 21, 133–40.

Gurman, A. and Kniskern, D. (1986). Individual marital therapy: have reports of your death been somewhat exaggerated? *Family Process*, 25, 51–62.

Haley, J. (1962). Family experiments: a new type of experimentation. *Family Process*, 1, 265–93.

—— (1970). Family therapy. *International Journal of Psychiatry*, 9, 233–42.

—— (1973). *Uncommon Therapy: The Psychiatric Techniques of Milton Erickson*. New York, Valentine.

—— (1976). *Problem-Solving Therapy*. New York, Harper Colophon.

—— (1980). *Leaving Home*. New York, McGraw-Hill.

Hoffman, L. (1981). *Foundations of Family Therapy*. New York, Basic Books.

Holmes, J. (1983). Psychoanalysis and family therapy: Freud's Dora case reconsidered. *Journal of Family Therapy*, 5, 235–51.

—— (1985). Family and individual therapy: comparisons and contrasts. *British Journal of Psychiatry*, 147, 668–76.

Howells, J. (1963). *Family Psychiatry*. London, Oliver & Boyd.

Hughes, S., Berger, M. and Wright, L. (1978). The family life cycle and clinical intervention. *Journal of Marriage and Family Counseling*, 5, 33–40.

Kerr, M. (1981). Family systems theory and therapy. In A. Gurman and D. Kniskern (eds) *Handbook of Family Therapy*. New York, Brunner/Mazel.

Koman, S. and Streckler, G. (1985). Making the jump to systems. In M. Mirkin and S. Koman (eds) *Handbook of Adolescence and Family Therapy*. New York, Gardner.

Laing, R. (1964). *Sanity, Madness and the Family*. Harmondsworth, Pelican.

Lask, B. (1980). Evaluation – why and how? (A guide for clinicians.) *Journal of Family Therapy*, 2, 199–210.

Leff, J., Kuipers, L., Berkowitz, R., Eberlein-Fries, R. and Sturgeon, D. (1982). A controlled trial of social intervention in families of schizophrenics. *British Journal of Psychiatry*, 131, 241–58.

Liddle, H. and Saba, G. (1983). Clinical use of the family life cycle: some cautionary guidelines. In H. Liddle (ed.) *Clinical Implications of the Family Life Cycle*. Rockville, Md, Aspen.

Lidz, T. (1963). *The Family and Human Adaptation*, New York, International Universities Press.

Minuchin, S., Rosman, B. and Baker, L. (1978). *Psychosomatic Families*. Cambridge, Mass., Harvard University Press.

Mishler, E. and Waxler, N. (1968). *Interaction in Families: An Experimental Study of Family Processes and Schizophrenia*. London, Wiley.

Palazzoli, M. (1974). *Self-Starvation*. New York, Jason Aronson.

Papp, P. (1983). *The Process of Change*. New York, Guilford.

Sauer, R. (1980). Family therapy with the individual patient. *Family Therapy*, 7, 125–30.

Skynner, A. (1976). *One Flesh: Separate Persons*. London, Constable.

—— (1981). An open-system group-analytic approach to family therapy. In A. Gurman and D. Kniskern (eds) *Handbook of Family Therapy*. New York, Brunner/Mazel.

Sluzki, C. and Ransom, D. (1976). *Double Bind: The Foundation of the Communicational Approach to the Family*. London, Grune & Stratton.

Solomon, M. (1973). A developmental conceptual premise for family therapy. *Family Process*, 12, 179–88.

Speer, D. (1970). Family systems: morphostasis and morphogenesis, or is homeostasis enough? *Family Process*, 9, 259–78.

Vaughn, C. and Leff, J. (1976). The influence of family and social factors on the course of psychiatric illness: a comparison of schizophrenic and depressed neurotic patients. *British Journal of Psychiatry*, 129, 125–37.

Walrond-Skinner, S. (1976). *Family Therapy: The Treatment of Natural Systems*. London, Routledge & Kegan Paul.

—— (1978). Indications and contra-indications for the use of family therapy. *Journal of Child Psychology and Psychiatry*, 19, 57–62.

Watzlawick, P., Weakland, J. and Fisch, R. (1974). *Change: Principles of Problem Formation and Problem Resolution*. New York, Norton.

Weakland, J., Fisch, R., Watzlawick, P. and Bodin, A. (1974). Brief therapy: focused problem resolution. *Family Process*, 13, 141–68.

Wells, R. and Giannetti, V. (1986). Individual marital therapy: a critical reappraisal. *Family Process*, 25, 43–51.

Wertheim, E. (1973). Family unit therapy and the science and typology of family systems. *Family Process*, 12, 343–76.

Wynne, L., Singer, M., Bartko, J. and Toohey, M. (1977). Schizophrenics and their families: recent research on parental communication. In J. Tanner (ed.) *Developments in Psychiatric Research*. London, Hodder & Stoughton.

# CHAPTER 2

# PSYCHOANALYTIC FAMILY THERAPY

*Christopher Dare*

## INTRODUCTION

Many of the pioneers in family therapy were trained as psychoanalysts or as psychoanalytic psychotherapists (for example Nathan Ackerman, Mara Selvini-Palazzoli, Lyman Wynne, Salvador Minuchin, Don Jackson, Ivan Boszormenyi-Nagy, Carl Whitaker). A small number of family therapists have made overt connections between psychoanalysis and family therapy (for example Boszormenyi-Nagy and Spark 1973; Bowen 1978; Dare 1979; 1981a; Framo 1982; F.M. Sander 1979; Shapiro *et al.* 1975; Skynner 1976; Slipp 1984; Stierlin 1977) but there has been a strong tendency to disavow the psychoanalytic roots within the mainstream of the subject. For those who espouse the view, psychoanalytic thinking is an essential ingredient in their approach to all clinical problems and processes. It is particularly preoccupied with people as family participants both in the creation of the personality and in the aspirations of the individual. For others, psychoanalysis represents an outmoded, hopelessly unscientific, individually oriented and awkward mass of ideas and theories. By these opponents, psychoanalysis is seen as either passively irrelevant or actively obstructive in the development of family therapy. In this chapter I will try to show the utility of psychoanalytic ideas for the creation of a psychodynamically oriented family therapy.

Unfortunately there are many difficulties in describing what precisely is meant by psychoanalysis as a general phrase or, in particular, what psychoanalytic family therapy might be. The word psychoanalysis has two broad meanings, the one usage describing a psychology (see Sandler *et al.*

1973) and the other that of clinical practice, a dominant and diverse psychotherapy. In addition to the confusion that comes from the dual meaning of the word there are complexities that derive from the historical and geographical development of psychoanalysis. Over nearly a century psychoanalysis both as a general psychology and a clinical practice has changed in innumerable ways. There are many schools of psychoanalysis, which are divergent in their theoretical propositions and their clinical activities.

This chapter can present only a personal view. In it I will describe some of the links between the two fields of thought and activity that I have found useful.

## THEORETICAL ASSUMPTIONS

### Major theoretical concepts

There are two major theoretical constructs of psychoanalytic family therapy. First, there are the concepts utilized to describe the family organization. Second, there is the theory of clinical practice. This section will be concerned with the theoretical framework whereby the family is understood. Later sections will address the clinical concepts of psychoanalytic family therapy.

A family is defined by its socio-historical context; its specific cultural and genealogical origins; its location on the family life cycle and the crises of loss and addition it has sustained and by its interactional or transactional structure (see Dare 1985a; 1985b). Although psychoanalysis has contributed to the theory of society, history and culture, these contributions are not of immediate, practical value in the clinical theory of the family. The psychoanalytic theories of the personality and personality development and the theory of personal relations are central concepts for the psychoanalytic family therapist. They provide understanding of the intergenerational (genealogical) life cycle and transactional structure of the family as a system.

### Psychoanalytic theories of personality

In modern psychoanalysis the word personality seems to be used relatively rarely, but it is used here in place of the related and currently more often used notion of *self*. Psychoanalytic theories of the personality are as diverse as psychoanalysis itself. However they all have in common a view of a person as having mental structures that transport personal history with them as important organizers of present and future personal relationship. This chapter presents a schematic and essentially idiosyncratic view of the psychoanalytic theory of the personality as it is relevant to the psychoanalytic family therapist (Dare 1986).

Commentators unfamiliar with contemporary psychoanalysis still suggest that it is predominantly a drive psychology. According to this view, the person was seen as governed by the need to 'tame' imperious and basically selfish demands, deriving from constitutionally determined biological sources. It is this classical theory that is so rightly criticized as portraying the person as a 'closed system'. Initially sexuality and later aggression were portrayed as the well-springs of human nature and of motivation. Private and confidential psychotherapy will, broadly speaking, be much taken up with these two topics. However, over time, psychoanalytic theories of the personality changed from seeing the mind as dominated by the need to manage these drives, to formulating it as overwhelmingly concerned with psychological derivatives of personal relationships. Personal relations in psychoanalysis are called *object relations* in order to emphasize that the concept is to do with psychological processes in the mind of the person and not just the interpersonal processes going on between people. The word object is used because the important people in the life of the individual were originally described as the 'object' of the drives, in relation to whom drive discharge and personal satisfaction were achieved. The theory of the person and object relations have come to be conceived of as totally intertwined.

Originally Freud formulated a 'traumatic theory' of neuroses and a parallel 'affect-trauma' model of the mind (Sandler *et al.* 1972). Always the traumas shaping the personality were interpreted to have been seductions – family events. When the role of such traumas was exchanged for drive theory (Freud 1900), family structure was more firmly installed within the person as the famous Oedipus complex. This was stated in terms of sexual and aggressive wishes: of jealous wishes for sole possession of the opposite sex parent and rivalrous, murderous hatred for the same sex parent deriving solely from the child. Freud later (1923) brought into psychoanalysis the idea of the superego, an internalized watchdog of the mind, setting ideals for the self and inspiring a sense of conscience, as a lifelong mark of the passing of the phase of the Oedipus complex. The superego was and is described as the establishment of internalized representations of the parents and their own ideals, rules and prohibitions. Such representations are a mixture of the actual demands and injunctions of the parents as experienced by the growing child. The superego is seen as containing elements which were the products of the child's imaginations concerning the parents (fantasies) and, also, as formed by elements of the parents' own superegos (by identification).

I have followed a number of psychoanalysts in seeing the concept of the Oedipus complex as an interactive one (see Pincus and Dare 1978). The growing child has at a certain time, to accommodate to a developing and passionate attachment to each parent separately. The child also has to take into account the realization that each parent has a continuing, potential or past relationship to the other parent. (Psychologically there can rarely be said to be a 'one-parent family'.) However, the parents are not passive, immutable and disinterested partners. A parent, whether or not in co-habiting partnership with another person, has a dynamic internal world within which his or her own experience of the Oedipus triangle, of the family of origin, leaves him or her with a combined predilection for and fear of repeating certain experiences. The way that these internalized attributes of the parent or parents are actually played out is determined by the role of the actual present or past other parent and of the sibling configuration of the family. Parents may in day-dream or unconscious fantasy seek to set a child up as of equal or more importance than the co-parent in conflict with the inter-parental relationship.

The superego, as heir to a complex piece of development and family relationship experiences, is an elaborate structure in modern psychoanalytic theory and serves as a model for the whole concept of object relationships and their link to the personality. The superego is a paradigm for the intergenerational organization of families. It is a structure in the present, deriving from family experiences of the past, and having an important effect on the creation of the present-day family.

The multiple, elaborately emotionally charged patterns of internalized relationships, like those described under the rubric of the superego, are known as the *internal world* of the person. The complex sets of relationship patterns within the person are built up in the course of all phases of childhood, and soon take in personages outside the immediate family. In psychoanalytic thinking, the core relationships are family relationships which then extend into the outside world. The child, in development, draws upon expectations of family relationships as the prototypes of all other relationships. Other bonds then, in turn, modify the internal world of the child, usually by addition of fresh relationship possibilities, not by the elimination of established patterns. The internal world, the sets of relation-ship patterns are 'templates' (Boszormenyi-Nagy and Spark 1973). They make up the particular intergenerational and cultural inputs of individuals when they come to be family makers.

## The life cycle

It is one of the recurrent features of many different schools of psychoanaly-sis, but not of all, that development is seen as taking place in discrete phases. The above account traces an historical line in Freud's theory of the roots of neurosis and character structure from sexual seduction by a family member, to the idea of an intrinsic libidinal drive leading to an inevitably sexual form of oedipal rivalries and longings, to a mental structure, the superego, built up from family relations. It has been given first place because it represents a fact in the history of psychoanalysis. (The family is so central in these propositions that it is possible to ask the question why Freud developed an individual psychotherapy and not family therapy.) Freud's first theory of childhood sexuality was of oedipal longings. Later, and in collaboration with early psychoanalytic colleagues (Abraham 1924; Ferenczi 1952; Jones 1948), he devised a scheme of a sequence of nuclei for sexual development (*libidinal phases*), the well-known oral, anal, phallic, oedipal, genital series. This progression is not of great clinical interest to the psychoanalytic family therapist except in understanding certain symbolic aspects of family communication when, by identifying the 'libidinal mode' of the content of discussion, the therapist may use phrases associated with the mode, to enhance the metaphorical potency of an intervention (see later section on technique). However the importance of the theory of phases of development has a central part to play in the psychoanalytic theory of the family.

Freud (1905) and his co-workers came to see the mind itself (and hence the personality) and not just sensual behaviour as having qualities which could be envisaged as having a date label. Earliest life is dominated by feeding and was postulated as an oral phase and the infant's mental functioning was dominated by that oral organization of sensual life (Sandler and Dare 1970). The phase of orality gives way to anality with its different preoccupations (for example with dirtiness and cleanliness; with giving or withholding; with autonomy or submission to outside control). The phallic phase (now no longer thought of as an identical model of sexuality for boys and girls) was seen as an essentially exhibitionistic and masturbatory interest. The oedipal phase was originally, but no longer, thought to inaugurate an orientation of sexuality towards another person (and has been described above). With the move out of the house into schooling, the tumultuous nature of the little child's relationships with parents does tend to calm. There is an increased need and engrossment in peer relationships and a wish for some privacy from other family members. This is called the 'latency' period. Adolescence was and is seen as a mixture of a recapitulation of the preceding phases and a further move away from the family under the impact of biological pubescence. The genital phase refers to what can be thought of as 'mature' sexuality in which altruistic and compassionate manifestations of sexuality are expressed, characteristic of adults relatively freed from too many relics of the preceding phases and who are in a position to create their own new families.

This progression is the prototype for the psychoanalytic account of an individual life cycle. It involves the person in sequences of tasks, appropriate to the stage of development and requiring reasonably satisfactory accomplishment of the maturational tasks to ensure optimal capability in the next phase. Each stage enables the person to develop specific personality and relationship qualities. In turn, each phase requires and evokes specific responses from those close to them. This is a central aspect of the psycho-analytic view of the family life cycle. The baby and then the developing child dictate different environments for optimal development. The infant has the same capacity as all people to provoke the response from others that will meet, in part, the needs of the stage of life. A baby trains the mother to the rhythms of its own physical and emotional needs as much as the parents try to structure the timetable of the baby's life to their wishes (see L. Sander 1980). The individual moving through the differing phases of the life cycle has differing needs, appropriate to the phase he or she is in, and has the ability to communicate those needs in such a way as to gain a relationship pattern that fits the needs. This is an additional description of the internal world.

In the interaction between the specific desires of the individual and that which actually happens to him or her in his or her family of origin rela-tionships, there is a tension. This is internalized as patterns of self and other in interaction in which there is a contrast between what actually happened and what was longed for. The extent of the differences between the ideal (what was longed for) and the actual is associated with strong feelings negatively or positively coloured according to the proximity of the actual to the longed for. So that if the person's wishes are largely met, then feelings of contentment, safety, satisfactory self-esteem, and so on ensue. If the gap between the longed-for ideals and the actual state becomes large then depression, a sense of pain, so-called 'narcissistic injury' and discomfort follow. Because of the persistence of such patterns of satisfactions and frustrations, and because the patterns are always linked to family experi-ences, then the unfolding life cycle leaves innumerable traces within the structure of the adult mind. When the children of the adult go through their own life cycle, there is a tendency for the adults to re-experience, by identification, aspects of their own life at the comparable stage. An intricate process is continued from the preceding stage. The children and all the other family members are seeking relationships which enable them to sustain the developmentally appropriate needs and tasks of their own particular phase of the life cycle. This results in a negotiation to reach compromises whereby there is mutual acceptance and compliance with the needs of others in return for some meeting of the needs of the self. The fact that the parents and older children are having earlier aspects of their lives re-evoked by the younger children's qualities not only adds to the understanding of each family member for the other but also complicates the negotiations. To some extent, a parent or older child may wish to try to correct special frustrations in the past, or to re-experience especially gratifying aspects of their own life cycle in their identification with the younger family members. The structure of the family in the present is therefore being dominated by the urgent life cycle tasks of its individual members. Transitions through life cycle phases require psychological work and reciprocal responses from others. The transitions are therefore rightfully called 'crises' (Erikson 1950; Solomon 1973), requiring the formation of new ways of family organization relevant to the developing and changing needs of the family members. At the same time the structure is given particular form by the continued re-evocation of past family experiences, in the present through the agency of the internal worlds of the family members.

## The transactional structure of the family

Transactional features of the family are evolved in the interplay of the different internal worlds of the family members and in the negotiations around the development of mutually fitting patterns of relationships to secure fulfilment of life cycle needs. However there is an additional way to describe the transactional processes in the psychoanalytic model of the family. This comes from the special techniques of individual, psychoanalytic psychotherapy.

Originally psychoanalytic treatment was based upon the assumption that 'cure' would follow from the communication to the patient of the psychoanalyst's understanding of the contents of the patient's unconscious mind (as revealed by following the track of the patient's thought processes – see Sandler *et al*. 1973). This produced what were seen to be partial cures however, and eventually psychoanalytic treatment came to be based on the idea that there was something special about the relationship between the analyst and patient. The patient has come to be seen as developing feelings, attitudes and beliefs about the psychoanalyst which are not determined by the reality of the therapy nor by the true qualities of the analyst, but are acquired because the psychoanalyst is relatively anonymous and unforthcoming to the patient. In the dearth of real information about the therapist, the patient can use only what comes from his or her own life and ultimately that means family life. Technically this is described as the development of a *transference*. The practice of psychoanalytic psychotherapy of the individual is now dominated by the investigation of the transferences that the patient has to the analyst, while at the same time the analyst keeps an extremely close watch on the parallel process, that is the feelings, attitudes, ideas and beliefs that the analyst gets about the patient (countertransferences). By monitoring the extent to which what the patient and analyst feel and think are distortions of reality, the psychoanalyst gains a crucial source of data, about the internal world of relationship expectations, wishes and fears of the patient. The analyst's own feelings in response to the patient provide information about what it might be like to be one of the figures in the patient's internal world.

The investigation of transference and countertransference between patient and therapist has little part to play in the *technique* of family therapy, but is central to the conceptualization of the transactional patterns of family life. As Sandler (1976) has pointed out, the psychoanalytic setting reveals the pressure that both patient and therapist put into their relationship to 'actualize' inner derived relationship needs, that is the patient appears to be trying to get the therapist to repeat parental or sibling patterns, or rather to enact the versions of such relationships that are represented in the patient's inner world. Likewise, the analyst may detect similar wishes in his or her thoughts and wishes about the patient.

All the features of the internal world described so far are potential patterns of relationships that persistently influence real personal ties. Each person in the family can be seen as relating to each other in some ways as do patient and therapist, trying to get an aspect of their internal world, made real, actualized, in the external world. In the therapeutic setting of psychoanalysis these processes can become visible because all real activity other than talking is largely prohibited. In family life the reverse applies: people do not usually become conscious of the family of origin wishes being represented in the current family, precisely because they are being enacted. The family therapist, trained to perceive the unconscious patterns and communications, can see the multiple layering of relationship needs displayed between spouses, between spouses and children, and children and parents.

## The nature of healthy family functioning

Although psychoanalysis was at one time concerned with definitions of health and disturbance, the considerations are not particularly relevant to family therapy. Indeed I would be very hesitant in propounding any firm ideas as to what constitutes either normality or health, in regard to family functioning. First, any such statements must always be extremely dependent upon the socio-cultural context. Second, it is, in my view, unnecessary for family therapists to have views about normality and health. There is no particular reason why we should believe that our interventions, even when they are effective in reducing or eliminating the presenting problems, are 'normalizing'. For example, the very fact of calling the family together in order to convene a family therapy session might be taken to imply that a whole family discussion was a 'healthy' or normal aspect of family life. But this is not necessarily so. Likewise the encouragement of discussion of problems and of direct conversation between family members that occurs in psychoanalytic family therapy is not necessarily the fostering of a healthy or normal mode of communicating. It is simply the mobilization of a possibly useful therapeutic technique. Interpretation, the favourite mode of intervention in psychoanalytic psychotherapy with highly motivated, co-operative and verbally skilled adults, is not a normal mode of communication but a therapeutic device. In this section, therefore, I am going to make some tentative observations, without claiming any general validity for them.

The outline in the previous section implied that family structure is formed out of the manifold negotiations around individual, self-derived needs, and the accompanying needs and wishes to fit in with the other family members. This embodies one normative notion which is that a family has to provide a balance within which individual demands and the cohesion of the family as a whole are both heeded. There is also a view of the family as being a changing structure. It evolves through phases, starting with the couple or pre-parenting phase, to a parenting of infants and toddler phase, to the pre-school preparation for allowing the boundaries of the family to become more penetrable by the outside world (a process greatly extended when children are at school), to a phase of domination by adolescence, to a leaving home phase and a post-parenting and grandparental phase. All these phases can be complicated by crises of loss or threat of loss (serious illness, death, separation, divorce, and so on) or crises of addition (birth, re-marriage, accession of stepchildren). The moves from each succeeding phase to the next demand psychological change and so do the crises of loss and addition. In this way a 'healthy' family is defined as one that undergoes transitions. 'Health' can also be defined in terms of the maintenance of appropriate boundaries: internal boundaries between parents and children and an external boundary between the family and the outside world.

The family is usually the context that provides a secure milieu within which the people of the family can develop their own clear identity without feeling they lose the safety and comfort of the family support. This is known technically, within psychoanalysis, as the provision of age-adequate separation-individuation experience (Mahler 1968) for all family members and is an especially important function at the toddler and adolescent times.

A family must also establish age-appropriate and effective control, nurturance and communication systems. Although these are not essentially psychoanalytic concepts, they are readily integrated into the psychoanalytic understanding of the organization of the family.

## The nature, development and maintenance of family disturbance

As caution has to be deployed in the use of the concept of family health so too must care be taken with the idea of family 'disturbance' or 'abnormality'. Family therapy may be shown, by empirical means, to be an effective intervention, but there are extremely few studies of any form of family therapy whereby specific targets of family interaction have been identified, changes in which have been shown to predict resolution of the presenting problems (Dare 1985a; 1985b). The lack of such studies means that little can be said with any certainty about the nature, origins and maintenance of disturbance in family function. There are theoretical concepts, which are used in order to organize thinking, but it is important to realize that these are abstractions, important devices that facilitate practice in helping families change.

The main psychoanalytic proposition upon which I draw is the definition of disturbance in terms of block or delay in development. Originally these ideas were described in the language of mental energies as fixations and regressions.

Excessive frustration or gratification of a libidinal drive, at a particular stage, was thought to create 'fixation' points, inclining the individual to manifest modes of thought and relationship tendencies coloured by the qualities of that stage. This notion is not used in psychoanalytic family therapy in relation to libidinal development, but as an extension of the concept into consideration of unmet or painful relationship experiences which tend to be repeated in subsequent phases of life, it is very relevant. Family life can be seen to represent many attempts by the parents and children to repeat aspects of past life, in an effort to re-create areas of distress for the purposes of mastery. For example, it is common to see children who have had difficult separation experiences, challenging the ability of the parents to maintain the family unity. Likewise, parents who have been separated from their own parents in their childhood find themselves reproducing gaps in their lives with their children. Families, in their balance of control and chaos, of closeness or disengagement (Olson *et al.* 1979) are expressing repetitions of or reactions to family of origin experiences which can be likened to fixation points in the organization of the internal worlds of the family members.

Regression was a word with neurological origins, and implied a return to a more primitive mode of thinking and a retreat from a more advanced stage. It came to be applied more to overall behaviour rather than simply to patterns of thought. In the family, regression can be seen to be operating when the family makes some move into the next phase of the life cycle and then falters, and moves back to earlier styles.

Disturbance in family life is defined using these concepts, although the words themselves may not be used. Troubled families are seen as being stuck in a particular phase of the life cycle, failing to move beyond it, or, having begun some changes, as having fallen back to the preceding phase. The sequence of the family life cycle given above was given to emphasize those points at which difficulties arise: difficulties for a couple to become parents; problems in allowing a family to recover parental intimacy after the stage of preoccupation with infancy; problems of allowing increased permeability through the boundary with the outside world when the children become of school age; blocks on the acceptance of the independence and incipient adulthood of adolescence; obstruction in achieving separation and the new stage of the primacy of the couple in the leaving home time. The aims of psychoanalysis were defined, underlining the importance of the notions of fixation and regression. Therapy endeavours to facilitate the move from a phase of life in which the person was stuck into the age-appropriate stage (A. Freud 1945). Likewise the aims of family therapy are similarly defined (Haley 1973) as aspiring to help the family overcome difficulties in moving through a particular phase of the family life cycle.

## THE THERAPEUTIC PROCESS

### The setting of therapy

The major emphasis in this chapter has been upon the theoretical framework offered by psychoanalysis to family therapy. The practice of psychoanalytic family therapy can be diverse and will have essential similarities to other forms of family therapy, for two reasons. First, psychoanalysis as a covert influence has had a part to play in the formation of the practice of family therapy as a whole. Second, the context of treatment determines, to an important extent, the features of the treatment, effacing the therapist's theoretical tendencies. Many of the qualities characterizing the activity of the family therapist are determined by the task of engaging with a whole family and override behaviourism, psychoanalysis, general systems theory or whatever.

The paradigm for psychoanalytic psychotherapy has been the training analysis. This is undertaken as a central part of psychoanalytic training. It is designed to facilitate the overcoming of blindspots in the therapist's psychological sensitivity by undoing neurotic conflicts. By its nature, such a therapy is undertaken with a person who is usually a young adult, who is highly motivated, verbal, interested in the development of personal problems and in long-term training. The training clinics, selecting patients for such candidates, choose subjects who resemble, in important ways, the trainees. This has coloured the nature of the usual features of psychoanalytic psychotherapy towards being intensive, verbal, utilizing insight and requiring some therapeutically induced regression in the patient for its conduct.

All these features are irrelevant to the conduct of family therapy, in which the motivation is for symptomatic change, not self-understanding, where the verbal fluency will vary considerably and in which regression is inappropriate. Family therapy tends to be brief, seeking to take advantage of existing family qualities in order to mobilize rapid change in the face of the pressure of the symptom and the life cycle crisis. The usual level of motivation, in my own practice, sustains something between three and fifteen sessions over two to four months, with a mean of six sessions. Some cases, for example anorexia nervosa, child abuse, marital problems in a childless couple, tend to require longer treatments, perhaps fifteen to thirty sessions over the course of a year.

Early on, psychoanalytic family therapy used a two-person therapeutic team. (In the Tavistock Clinic this was justified using an *obiter dictum* of Ronald Laing: 'It takes a team to meet a team'.) Now, most psychoanalytically informed family therapists would use one-way screen, closed circuit television and video-recording for supervision, for training in technique and the identification of countertransference. The techniques of live supervision have made the practice of domiciliary family therapy less popular. The 'diagnostic' information derived from a home visit can be extraordinarily revealing, but the domestic environment is not one within which it is easy to establish a clear therapeutic relationship.

## The nature of change

The theory of change in family therapy is of great theoretical interest. In summary, psychoanalysts tend to insist that change in underlying structures is the main aim of psychoanalysis. Family therapists of most persuasions have likewise said that change in basic family structure is the aim of family therapy. I am sceptical of the possibility of demonstrating such propositions. My aims in therapy are the alleviation of symptomatic problems by the alteration of overt family interactional characteristics. If the presenting problem is serious, for example life threatening or severely disrupting relationships with the outside world, then the first aim of family therapy is to change family interactions so that the symptomatic state is reversed. Then, and from the start in less florid circumstances, the aim of family therapy is to alter the overt aspects of family life so that relapse of symptom is made more difficult. From my observations, I also perceive psychological changes occurring in family therapy, of the same nature as those that occur in individual psychoanalytic psychotherapy. Family therapy interventions of the sort described in this chapter can, symbolically and metaphorically, convey a complicated message to the family. The 'message', if expressed completely in language, would embody an interpretation, in the psychoanalytic sense. It is largely accepted within psychoanalysis that the setting and non-verbal aspects of the therapy are also meaningful and potentially helpful interventions containing, in effect, interpretations in actions rather than words.

## THE ROLE OF THE THERAPIST

In the following sections I will apply to the family therapy setting some of the theoretical considerations which describe clinical psychoanalysis (Sandler *et al*. 1973).

## The creation of the therapeutic context

Psychoanalytic treatment is regarded as being sustained by the establishment and maintenance of a therapeutic or working alliance. This is one aspect of the feelings and attitudes of the patient towards the therapist and contains both conscious and unconscious elements. It constitutes those ideas and wishes that make it possible for the patient to attend and work in the therapy, even when beset by uncertainty or hostility towards the project. The establishment of a therapeutic alliance implies that whatever else the patient may believe from time to time, there is a core belief in the nature and process of the treatment, sufficient for the patient to stay the course.

The therapeutic alliance, in psychoanalytic family therapy, is achieved by the process of *engagement*. The differences between the engagement of varying patient or client groups must always be taken into consideration. Because, as summarized above, the paradigm of psychoanalytic treatment appears to be the training analysis, a rather one-sided view as to the essential nature of the therapy is sometimes presented. If the paradigm had been work with 'poorly motivated', highly disturbed people, then the usual model of engagement and treatment would have looked very different. I have been very strongly influenced in the development of treatment models by the practice of child psychotherapy and child consultations in a child and adolescent psychiatric setting (Winnicott 1971a). There are a number of features of such a practice:

1 The family will not give the clinician the opportunity for a large number of contacts.
2 The presenting problems tend to be strident, that is serious and disruptive.
3 An agency other than the family may be making the main complaint and may be the chief source of pressure for attendance.
4 The level of verbal fluency will show wide variation.

These constraints parallel those documented by Minuchin, and which led him in his path from psychoanalytic psychotherapy to family therapy (Minuchin *et al*. 1967; Minuchin 1970). They regulate the process of engagement and the whole construction of the therapy. It is no use the therapist having a mental model of what therapy is like, if it is too discrepant with the life-style and expectations of the client or patient population. The family meeting the therapist must soon begin to recognize that they are being involved in a process that accords with their sense of the occasion. This is not at all the same as saying that the therapist must do what the family wants or expects. In fact the reverse is the case, for if the family knew how to solve their problem they would not need the therapist. Therefore the task of creating the therapy has contradictory properties. The therapist has to help the family extend their usual repertoire while maintaining the family's sense of being in sufficiently safe and helpful surroundings. This is achieved by paying great attention to the social qualities whereby the therapist first meets the family. This has to be accomplished quickly and with apparent informality. On seeing the family for the first time, for example in a waiting-room, the therapist must assess the order and style of approaching the family members. Each person must be met in a different way, according to their perceived ages and status in the family. The therapist must squat to the level of little children and judge how close to and what physical contact can be made with them. Adults and adolescents should be held long enough in a handshake to feel reassured about the therapist's beneficence. Each family member should feel personally attended to and that they have left an impression on the therapist.

This attention to the needs and qualities of individuals must remain a focus throughout the therapy *for the purposes of engagement*. Families attend because a majority force in the family see coming as likely to be advantageous. The therapeutic alliance is firmly established by the focus the therapist develops in the enquiry as to the nature of the problems that bring the family. The family members must all contribute to giving an account of the difficulties. The therapist listens, reflecting back to the family a view of their problems that resembles what they say enough to sound authentic, and yet which subtly reorganizes what the family actually say and also implies that change is possible. The reorganization takes two forms. First, complaints are likely to have been put in terms of the individual family member *possessing* the symptom. When this occurs, the therapist speaks back to the family as though the problem exists between people. Hence:

THERAPIST: Well, what's the problem then?
MOTHER: We went to our doctor, to another hospital, they said Emma had anorexia nervosa.
THERAPIST (looking at the daughter kindly): How long has your mum had difficulty in getting you to eat?

Or (with another family):

FATHER (looking angrily at his wife): We don't know why we've had to bring our daughter, *she* doesn't stay in her room all the time like *him* (glowering at the son).
THERAPIST (warmly to father): I agree with you that you must protect your daughter and I certainly will refuse to see any of you if I think there is any risk of harming anyone by coming. How do you try to get him out of his room without upsetting her (smiling sweetly at the daughter)?

Second, the therapist tries to effect the emotional tone of the conversation about the problems. There is a tendency for families to play down the seriousness of the difficulties they are experiencing. Usually some realistic increase in worry is useful to facilitate commitment to therapy. This can be the case only if the therapist, at the same time, has a rigorously non-blaming attitude. Arousing anxiety can facilitate therapy; instigating guilt is detrimental. It hardly needs emphasizing that all this requires the therapist to be active and directive. This is true for the engagement process in all forms of family therapy.

## Methods of intervention

The activities undertaken by the therapist to establish a treatment alliance are interventions. They will not necessarily achieve any specific therapeutic change (but the non-specific improvements arising from the convening of family meetings can be underestimated). In psychoanalytic family therapy, interventions are mobilized as an outcome of a two-stage process. First, a formulation has to be evolved, at some level of the therapist's consciousness. Second, an intervention carrying the meaning of an aspect of the formulation is devised. We have described (Szmukler *et al.* 1985) an orderly method for the organization of observations of a family into a psychodynamic, systemic formulation which is likely to have some measure of reliability. In summary, we advocate making careful statements about interactional processes at a level of observable words and actions, proceeding to make higher-level interpretations putatively underlying these observations; noting the life cycle and identifiable intergenerational features of the family; describing the way the family involves the therapist and building all these elements into an overall formulation. This portrays:

1 The structural qualities of the family (coalitions and alliances; family hierarchy; distances of family members from each other; quantity, quality and direction of communication; boundaries within and around the family; control organization and affective tone).
2 Some identifiable 'functions' for the symptoms (usually the protection of aspects of the family organization from the change consequent on life cycle developmental and other crises of loss or addition).
3 Thoughts about what might be the 'risk' to the family of losing the symptoms (fear of dissolution of the family; pain at the loss of special closeness; dread of responsibility having to be taken for past disasters) (see Bentovim and Kinston 1981).

In the psychoanalytic psychotherapy of the adult, the major mode of intervention, based on the therapist's explicit or implied formulation, is interpretation supported by working through. In the earliest days of psychoanalysis an interpretation was simply the therapist telling the patient his or her formulation as to the underlying, unconscious meaning of the patient's communications. Over time, the range and formulation of interventions became subject to what can only be called *strategic* considerations (although few psychoanalysts would accept the phrase). Matters of timing, tact, the state of the transference (positive, negative, infantile or oedipal, and so on) and the level of the therapeutic alliance became acknowledged as determining the mode and content of interpretative interventions. The idea of having a focus for therapy guiding and structuring moment-to-moment choice of interpretative intervention evolved in the writings and practice of Malan (1963; 1976).

All these developments were evolved in the expectation that verbal interpretation was the main therapeutic ingredient in psychoanalysis. However there was another line of growth in thoughts about the nature of psychoanalysis. It was realized that the psychotherapeutic setting itself constituted a communication to the patient that had meaningful and therapeutic aspects (Balint 1968; Stone 1967). The notion of the activities of the therapist having symbolic or metaphorical meaning is of central importance in brief, focal therapies with people who are not interested in discovering the workings of their mind and who do not have a lot of time to devote to therapy. The development of child psychotherapy, especially following Winnicott (1958; 1965; 1971a; 1971b), enlarges our understanding of how quite specific interpretations could be made in symbolic rather than verbal form. The principles whereby formulation is translated into intervention are difficult to summarize but will be demonstrated in the brief case presentation.

Interventions in psychoanalytic family therapy must be designed to have more 'impact' qualities than those of individual therapies. Families, having intimate and important people in the room, other than the therapist, do not feel impelled to heed what the therapist says unless it has a certain force. That force is achieved by activity and directiveness, by humour and playfulness, by a paradoxical and intriguing quality and by colourful metaphor. The therapist should be not only friendly and admiring of the family but also enigmatic and opaque. The directives that can be in the form of suggested diagnostic 'experiments', ideas to change patterns of care, tasks for the family to take on in the outside world, and so on, will not reveal the focal formulation explicitly, but if 'unravelled', have a meaning that pertains to the formulation.

For example, one of a pair of adolescent daughters is perceived as handicapped by the family, with a label such as food allergy, hyperactivity or school phobia. The effect is to allow the family to have a 'successful' daughter, moving into the world, and an 'ill' daughter, requiring the attentiveness appropriate to a younger child and enabling the family to prolong the pre-adolescent style of family relationships. The intergenerational history may show that one parent had a rather disengaged style of parenting while the other is seen as having come from a very close family, which is idealized. The direction of the therapist's interventions will be towards reinforcing the sibling dyad, talking for example of the daughters of children losing contact with the parents, going too far away from the family, and advising the parents to set target distances for the girls to travel at weekends, 'so that they can learn how risky the world is, *safely*'. The metaphorical and literal use of the concept of distance, the acceptance of the fears about separation, the implication of leaving the parents alone together, are all contained in the intervention, but all wrapped in a somewhat opaque package.

The psychoanalytic notion of *working through* is especially important. It underlines the need to reiterate interventions in different forms, to facilitate the eventual effectiveness and achievement of the focus of treatment. It is central to the practice of brief family therapy. It is crucial that the therapist sticks to one focus, making all the interventions congruent with it, to encourage change in that area of family life. Brief therapy requires the therapist to start therapeutic interventions as soon as possible and to concentrate on one area, in the expectation that there will be insufficient motivation to sustain a prolonged assessment phase. There is always a risk of having made a mistake and chosen an inappropriate focus but that risk is less than that of losing a family from any therapy whatsoever by squandering their available motivation in attendances for detailed diagnostic evaluation.

## Family response to the process of change

Therapy with families, like individuals, proceeds on the assumption that the symptom has a 'function'. Though troublesome and disabling, it is, for the time being, an acceptable adaptation. Change would implicate the family in a phase of the life cycle or an overcoming of a crisis of loss or addition. Loss of the symptom can be thought to be feared as creating more problems than its loss would solve. This means that there is no treatment without resistance (see Sandler *et al.* 1973). The assumption that the symptom has both meaning and function for the family means that straightforward interpretation of the symptom is ineffective. If the interpretation is accurate and shows the psychological advantages of the presenting problem, the family is likely to resist the implication. This is what can be seen in the opening sessions of family therapy conducted by someone wishing to make verbal and explicit communication of the therapeutic 'insights' as to the nature of the problem. The family act as though the information is hostile while appearing to use it to enhance the rigidity of the family processes maintaining the symptoms. It is for this reason that therapy has to be focused, active and metaphorically conducted and why repetitive working through of interventions is necessary.

So-called 'paradoxical' shaping of the intervention can be helpful, for such interventions usually acknowledge the family need for the symptom. They can be thought of as following the psychoanalytic method of interpreting the defences maintaining conflicts before interpreting the unconscious meaning and nature of the problem.

Although the aim of psychoanalytic family therapy is not the evolution of insight as a primary agent of change, successful therapy is often accompanied by an alteration of the family members' beliefs and attitudes towards themselves and these affective/cognitive changes can sustain the therapeutic gains. Later in therapy, some open and direct reporting of the therapist's understanding of the problem can constitute an interpretative intervention and can be helpful. In general it can be said that therapeutically advantageous change tends to produce some insight while insight can, under favourable circumstances and especially further on into therapy, produce change.

## Assessment of change

We have undertaken some experimental studies to investigate the reliability of observers' observations about the changes in family interactional patterns that occur in family therapy. So far the results suggest that small groups, achieving a consensual agreement, can make reliable statements as to observed changes in a family in treatment. The relation between family changes and symptomatic change is unexplored and therapists should, on the whole, set low-level goals for change in family therapy and be content if relatively small movement in symptomatic presentation is achieved.

## EFFECTIVE THERAPISTS

There is no empirical evidence as to the efficacy of psychoanalytic family therapy, except in the treatment of anorexia nervosa (Russell *et al.* 1987). This study did not provide evidence as to the specific effectiveness of individual therapists or as to what constitutes good training. The ideas that will be expressed below are hence clinically derived.

### Qualities of effective therapists

The qualities of activity, directiveness, opacity and humour have all been mentioned in the structuring of interventions. These have usually to be released rather than inculcated in the therapist and like playfulness and an inventive use of anecdote and metaphor cannot be taught to everyone. The psychoanalytic family therapist may look to be acting 'naturally' in treating a family, but in fact the spontaneous quality may be an artificially acquired therapeutic style. Just as a psychoanalytic psychotherapy with an individual may simply look like a conversation when, in fact, it is a carefully executed piece of transference-interpretative work.

The account given above as to the making of a life cycle, an intergenerational and a transactional assessment of the family, expect of the therapist an ability to think at several different levels at once, but that is true for all family therapies.

The main specific qualities of the psychoanalytic family therapist are those of a preparedness to listen to the unconscious meanings of the family communication. At the same time, therapists need to accept a reciprocal unconscious responsiveness in themselves. They also need to accept that responsiveness is likely to lead them to conform to the family pattern in such a way as to maintain rather than change the family's customary organization. This is all in keeping with the psychoanalytic concept of countertransference (see Sandler *et al*. 1973) and role responsiveness in therapists (see Sandler 1976).

## Skills required by therapists

The qualities outlined imply skills. The specific psychoanalytic skills are those of 'listening to the unconscious', and picking up metaphorical and unspoken meaning in the speech and acts of the family members. Simultaneously therapists need skills in reading the conscious manifestations of their unconscious responsiveness. This means becoming aware of traces of emotional reaction to the family and identifying whether it comes from the reality of the situation, the therapist's own life, or whether it is an 'orphan' whose origins must be traced. Likewise the therapist can become aware of a fantasy, a belief, or of wishes and attitudes, drifting into mind during therapy and not obviously connected to overt process. The therapist needs to have skills to assign such material in such a way as to use it as possible information about the family. This is what can be called the positive, helpful aspect of countertransference understanding. The more negative feature is the responsiveness that pulls the therapist into complying with the family pressure to reinforce rather than change their organization. This comes out in tendencies to take sides, to disengage, to be hostile or too loving, too active or too unresponsive. All of the therapist's attitudes and verbal and behavioural reactions must be monitored for the possibility that they constitute a countertransference enactment, continuing rather than challenging the family problem. These reactions are not only negative for, when they are perceived, they represent information about patterns of family life that are being protected.

The acquisition of familiarity with the psychoanalytic model of individual and family functioning must be acquired, for the purposes of making the family assessment. This implies the development of conceptual skills; the executive skills of engagement and of making intervention also have to be attained.

## Training model for therapists

Much of the training for psychoanalytic family therapy is the same as for other forms of family therapy. The emphasis is upon 'hands on' experience whereby trainees are required to see cases under conditions of 'live' supervision while having specific conceptual input in seminars, individual supervision and group case discussion. It is important that the trainers are seen doing the same job as the trainees so that teaching and observation of other therapists of differing amounts of experience go hand in hand.

Trainee therapists, especially early on in training, will differ from the therapy of experienced practitioners as all the skills of therapy cannot be learned at once. Initially therapists are encouraged to learn the skills of engagement. They are taught and shown how to 'meet' the family. They are taught and shown how to conduct a focused discussion around the presenting problem that will leave the family feeling attended to and believing that the therapy will be addressing matters of pressing importance to them. The observing supervisor (probably in conjunction with other trainees and possibly with one or more other staff members present as well) will take on the task of identifying the family processes to reach a formulation. At a planned intermission (thirty to forty minutes into the session) the family are asked by the therapist to return to the waiting-room and are told of the impending team discussion. In the intermission the team's observations are discussed and matched with the trainee therapist's perceptions. A formulation is reached and a first intervention devised. The trainee is encouraged, in this early stage, to rely quite heavily on observers to make interventions while focusing his or her own efforts on the engagement. As the latter skills become more effective and automatic, the therapist feels more free to observe what is going on in order to identify process and plan interventions. At this stage the trainee can be taught some of the skills of partial disengagement from the family, for example by getting them to talk to each other, or about each other, to obtain more space, within the session, for the ordering of observation and thinking up treatment measures. Later, the trainee will learn self-monitoring, and so become less reliant on observers for the conduct of sessions. Reviewing video-tapes of the trainee's treatments is essential for developing engagement and interventive technique. Above all, video review is used for the therapist to build up a repertoire of safe, 'stock' responses. These are used by experienced therapists to sustain a sturdy 'automatic pilot'. This will serve to initiate therapy quickly, and to cover the therapist when not in a live supervision setting. A therapist needs to be able to be 'abstracted' in the presence of the family while thinking through specific inputs but, at the same time, to be conducting an apparently lively and involved discussion.

There is no doubt that personal, psychoanalytic psychotherapy for trainee therapists gives them great enlightenment as to their own family of origin experience and sensitizes them to the signals of their own unconscious life. All psychoanalytic family therapists would probably recommend some such experience of therapy for all trainees, but few would make it a condition of training. If a therapist is to work with families containing young children, there is also no doubt that supervised experience of psychoanalytic psychotherapy with children is of inestimable value in learning how to read the play and drawings of children as revelations of family process.

## A FAMILY IN THERAPY

The account of this case begins quite a long way into the overall management of a case of anorexia nervosa, and at a stage when the family had a sustained experience of therapy but were now meeting with a new therapist because their previous worker had left the hospital. The preceding stages of treatment had resulted in the anorexia nervosa being no longer life-threatening and the presenting patient, Emma, was physically well. The family met the new therapist, for the first time, after a three months' gap in treatment. They had initiated the appointment because they believed that Emma still wished to diet and caused the parents despair by the extent to which she clung to her mother.

The family were all in attendance at the first of the meetings with the new therapist. They seated themselves with the males by the therapist, father to the left and Daniel (17 years) to the right. Emma (14 years) was on her brother's right, on the left hand side of mother. There was a larger gap between mother and father than elsewhere in the circle.

The therapist met with the family for thirty-five minutes, before making the usual planned break, to discuss the therapy with a small observing team. The following fragments from a transcript of the video-tape focus for a while on the sibling relationship in order to introduce the idea of development into the family. This took the form of questions about the future relationship between Emma and Daniel. This idea came from Daniel who, when asked what his mother meant by saying that Emma was disturbed, had commented and then retracted; 'Growing up'.

> THERAPIST (to Emma): In ten years' time you'll be 24 and he'll be 27. Do you think you'll be friends? What do you think you might do together with your brother when you are 24. What would you expect?
> EMMA: Nothing.

THERAPIST: You wouldn't do anything with him. You won't be friends.

EMMA: Yes, perhaps, I don't know.

THERAPIST: Think! What would you expect to be doing? How often do you think you would see your brother?

EMMA: Once a month.

THERAPIST: And that would be seeing him. How often would you phone him in between times?

EMMA: Once a week.

THERAPIST: Do you think he will be married by then?

DANIEL: I hope so.

THERAPIST: Will you be friendly with his wife, or not do you think?

EMMA: (nods)

THERAPIST: You think you will? Do you think he will have a baby by then?

EMMA: Yes.

THERAPIST: Will you baby-sit?

EMMA: (shakes her head vigorously)

THERAPIST: You won't baby-sit. Why not?

At this time the therapist became increasingly interested in why Emma would not baby-sit for her brother's child, in ten years' time. It seemed a flexible and intriguing metaphor and had a quality of playfulness and ambiguity. Emma insisted that she would not baby-sit, and quite soon Daniel, who so far had been a bit uninvolved, became puzzled as to why his sister was not going to do baby-minding for him. This led the therapist into discussion of the qualities of aunts.

EMMA: I might have my own children.

THERAPIST: I see, I see. If you don't have your own children, though, by then, do you think you would baby-sit for him?

EMMA: No.

THERAPIST: Do you think you would be a good aunt? Do you know what a good aunt is? Have you got a good aunt?

What is characteristic about this portion of the session is that the therapist is using an active, directive and quite pressurizing technique but, at the same time, allows himself to find an intuitive sense of the importance of the extended family context to focus on the future. This led to a quite unexpected revelation about the meaning of the family story of the death of the maternal grandfather.

The therapist pursued questions around the family history and then returned once more to the question as to why Emma was not going to baby-sit for her brother, why that would not be part of being an aunt. It is important to keep with a chosen topic rather than exploring too many ideas. Finally, before the break in the session, the therapist began to question when the family thought that they would give up being responsible for keeping Emma alive by feeding her. This introduced the idea that Emma had some striving for autonomy. However, she also acted in such a way as to force her parents to curtail her freedom and to control her.

## Team discussion

The discussion with the observing group of colleagues focused, first, upon the more 'behavioural' observations, which were then assembled into more theoretical, interpretative formulations. The following behavioural, interactional comments were made:

1 Mother and father disagree about the severity and emphasis of Emma's problems.
2 The rest of the family speak for Emma.
3 Mother in particular believes that she knows what Emma thinks but that she should speak for herself.
4 Emma enjoys the therapist commenting favourably upon the differences between the parents.
5 Father is annoyed at Emma 'following mother about like a shadow', but protects her from mother saying that she is 'disturbed'.
6 Father and mother get at Emma for her rather childish fidgety habits.
7 Daniel likes to point out his sister's 'misbehaviour', but is uneasy at saying that she is 'disturbed'.
8 Mother gets confused between her aunt and Emma's.
9 Emma appears to be pleased at being told that she is still a problem.
10 Emma was the least confused in recounting the family history.
11 Mother puts herself down and is not contradicted by the family in doing this.

These Level 1 statements were put together, with other inferences, to form a series of more abstract conceptualizations.

1 There is a family belief that girls have a problem growing up and that growing up may not be a good thing.
2 There is some idea that sexuality in teenagers is disgusting.
3 The family assume a lot of knowledge about each other but are in fact confused about the history of the family and what is going on at present.
4 Mothers are believed to be needy and helpless.
5 There is no expectation that the couple should agree or look after each other.

*The life cycle definition of the family* was that they were a professional, nuclear family with two children in mid-adolescence.

Unusually for a first interview with a therapist, some relevant *identifiable, intergenerational features* of the family were perceptible. First, a confusion had been revealed about mother's history (particularly around the death of her father when she was an infant). Second, the consequences of this for the family view of mothering seemed to be that mother was seen both as needy and ineffective but, contradictorily, not really requiring help.

A *diagram* of the family showed mother and father rather separated and focused upon Emma as a young child. Daniel was portrayed as moving across the family boundary with the external world and gaining a nearly adult place in the hierarchy of the family.

The family *related to and involved the therapist* in a rather flippant 'pseudo-cheerful' way. It was noted that the therapist took on Emma's mannerism of chewing a finger.

The *denoted functions for the presenting symptom* included the idea that it legitimized and desexualized father's physical interest in Emma and gave mother a continuing closeness to a little child. It provided Daniel with 'cover' to leave the family as the parents could be relied upon to be preoccupied with Emma.

## Feedback

After about twenty minutes, the therapist recalled the family from the waiting-room.

THERAPIST (to father): What's your job?
FATHER: A university teacher in business studies and a part-time building society director.
THERAPIST (to mother): What's your job?
FATHER: Feeding her.
MOTHER: Well, I actually work at a restaurant . . .
FATHER: That's only in the last few weeks.
MOTHER: Yes, the last two months.
THERAPIST: What sort of restaurant?
MOTHER: Nouvelle cuisine.
THERAPIST: Oh no . . .
MOTHER: Funnily enough.
DANIEL: I've been working there as well but I got chopped.
THERAPIST: You're not delicate enough.
DANIEL: They didn't want me.
THERAPIST: Ooo! What a cheek.
DANIEL: Yes.
MOTHER: But I didn't actually know it was nouvelle cuisine when I applied.
THERAPIST: They are such small portions! Now [changing tone and becoming serious] you have a nice family. Would you have liked three?
MOTHER: I always thought we would have more, actually. But I don't know why I wanted more.
THERAPIST: Well, you were an only child, which sometimes leaves people with feelings about the size of the family. Did it for you?
MOTHER: I think I did want three and he said: 'No, it is either two or four.' That's right, wasn't it?
THERAPIST: You didn't like three. That was a bad idea, was it?
MOTHER: Well, he's one of three.
FATHER: I suppose basically what I was thinking of was two and two, you know, with a gap. I didn't like the idea of the third one being some way behind. I mean

the three of us, the gaps, there was two and a half years and three and half years but really it didn't, you know, we were fairly evenly spaced. But it's a bit late to start now.

MOTHER: No it's not.

THERAPIST: You like babies.

MOTHER: I think you think they're a problem whatever age they are until you go on a bit. You know, when they were younger they were a problem, I never thought, uh, I always wanted a daughter.

THERAPIST: Emma's a mistake?

MOTHER: Now, at the moment. She's not always been like that. Only this last year. At the moment I feel that it is her premenstrual bit, that's getting me down as much as the other. But maybe it's not. Maybe it is all anorectic.

The therapist now explores some detail about the duration of the problem.

THERAPIST: That's three years it's been going. Look, Emma, your mother seems to set herself the task of curing you, right? And she has saved your life, but I don't know that she can cure you and you are in great danger. When you have been going for three years or more, it is getting increasingly difficult to get out of the habit of starving yourself. And you are in great danger. You won't have a baby, you will never have a baby, unless you change. You should have menstruated by now, and you haven't. The longer you go on not menstruating the less likely it will be that you will ever menstruate. If you go on starving yourself for another year or two, you can permanently make it not happen. Permanently. You may never have a baby if you don't begin to menstruate in the next three years, but you should really menstruate in the next few months to give yourself a proper menstrual cycle, a proper sexual development. Did you know that?

This is an intervention designed to raise the family anxiety and to focus on the developmental and sexual block.

EMMA: No.

THERAPIST: You can go from being a girl to being an old woman without being a woman in between times. Do you see? We know that, we know that now.

MOTHER: How can she help herself?

THERAPIST: Eat enough carbohydrate to stop thinking about food, and go on eating more carbohydrate until you stop thinking about food. And that is what I want to see you for, to see if I can help you.

MOTHER: Carbohydrate or calories?

THERAPIST: Carbohydrate. I've got to stop. I'm going to see you to try and think out how I can help you push it over to Emma. She has to take over from you, the two of you. And that will require a lot of work from you, I'm afraid. It is very serious, Emma. Because, you see, you are not ill enough for someone to have to make you stay alive and therefore get into menstruation, but you are not well enough to actually mature properly. And unless you menstruate you will never have a baby, and the longer you don't menstruate the less likely it is that you will ever menstruate. You see. So it really is a very risky business at the moment.

The form of the intervention is as though it were physiological advice from a physician. The force and direction with which it is given is designed to express the major formulation which is the extent to which the family have become habituated to seeing Emma as the unchanging baby who will keep mother preoccupied and cared for by having a baby to worry and fuss over. Men seem to believe that maternal worries threaten their development. Emma's presumed wishes and fear of autonomy are addressed.

This session inaugurated a new phase in the therapy. Weight and diet continued to be a feature of the therapeutic meetings, but gradually the parents and daughter achieved a pattern whereby the patient's weight gradually increased. Concomitantly the focus of therapy became more focused upon Emma's independent social life, upon Emma and Daniel's relationship and, openly or covertly, upon the marital relationship. Much of the work could be described as 'structural' in the sense that tasks and activities for the family were suggested. Always, the therapist could also express to himself these active, directive interventions linguistically. They had meanings that, if translated into words, would have been an account of the unconscious function of the family members' internal, feared and longed-for object relations, anxieties, guilt and defensive activities. Late in the therapy, some of the 'interpretations' were made more explicit, as verbal communications. Often such communications were put in the form of: 'It is *as if* you fear that growing up is always a loss of precious innocence'; 'Sometimes people of your age, at the back of their mind, unconsciously, for some reason or other, are frightened that their mother will think that you, Emma, would want Daddy for yourself! We don't know where such ideas came from.'

# CONCLUSIONS

Psychoanalytic family therapy utilizes the concepts of psychoanalysis to understand the psychological nature and tasks of individuals, the internal, interpersonal longings and fears and the intergenerationally transmitted myths and scripts of family life. This mainly enriches and complements other models of family organization. Interventions, of an active, directive, strategic or paradoxical nature are given in a way that characterizes most family therapies. Psychoanalytic family therapy differs from other therapies in seeking to understand the unconscious meaning of both family process *and* family therapy interventions and, late in therapy, these hypothesized unconscious meanings may be communicated in the family. In this way change in families is believed to foster the development of insight into the meaning of why change was necessary. In turn, later in therapy, insight, that is information about unconscious meaning, buttresses and enhances changes in patterns of interpersonal activity and relationships.

# REFERENCES

Abraham, K. (1924). A short study of the development of the libido in the light of mental disorders. In K. Abraham (1973) *Selected Papers on Psycho-Analysis*. London, Hogarth Press.

Balint, M. (1968). *The Basic Fault: Therapeutic Aspects of Regression*. London, Tavistock.

Bentovim, A. and Kinston, W. (1981). Brief focal family therapy when the child is the referred patient. In S. Walrond-Skinner (ed.) *Developments in Family Therapy*. London, Routledge & Kegan Paul.

Boszormenyi-Nagy, I. and Spark, G. (1973). *Invisible Loyalties*. New York, Harper & Row.

Bowen, M. (1978). *Family Therapy in Clinical Practice*. New York, Jason Aronson.

Dare, C. (1979). Psychoanalysis and systems in family therapy. *Journal of Family Therapy*, 1, 137–52.

—— (1981a). Psychoanalysis and family therapy. In S. Walrond-Skinner (ed.) *Developments in Family Therapy*. London, Routledge & Kegan Paul.

—— (1981b). Psychoanalytic theories of the personality. In F. Fransella (ed.) *Personality: Theory, Measurement and Research*. London, Methuen.

—— (1985a). Family therapy. In M. Rutter and L. Hersov (eds) *Child and Adolescent Psychiatry: Modern Approaches*. Oxford, Blackwell.

—— (1985b). The family therapy of anorexia nervosa. *Journal of Psychiatric Research*, 19, 435–85.

—— (1986). Psychoanalytic marital therapy. In N.S. Jacobson and A.S. Gurman (eds) *Clinical Handbook of Marital Therapy*. New York, Guilford.

Erikson, E.H. (1950). *Childhood and Society*. New York, Norton.

Ferenczi, S. (1952). *First Contributions to Psycho-Analysis*. London, Hogarth Press.

Framo, J.L. (1982). *Explorations in Marital and Family Therapy*. New York, Springer.

Freud, A. (1945). Indications for child analysis. *The Psychoanalytic Study of the Child*, 1, 127–49.

Freud, S. (1900). *Interpretation of Dreams. Standard Edition*, 4–5. London, Hogarth Press.

—— (1905). *Three Essays on Sexuality. Standard Edition*, 7. London, Hogarth Press.

—— (1923). *The Ego and the Id. Standard Edition*, 19. London, Hogarth Press.

Haley, J. (1973). *Uncommon Therapy: The Psychiatric Treatments of Milton H. Erickson*. New York, Norton.

Jones, E. (1948). *Papers on Psycho-Analysis*. London, Baillière, Tindall & Cox.

Mahler, M. (1968). *On Human Symbiosis and the Vicissitudes of Individuation*. New York, International Universities Press.

Malan, D. (1963). *A Study of Brief Psychotherapy*. London, Tavistock.

—— (1976). *Toward the Validation of Dynamic Psychotherapy*. New York, Plenum.

Minuchin, S. (1970). Psychoanalytic therapies and the low socioeconomic population. In J. Marmor (ed.) *Modern Psychoanalysis*. New York, Basic Books.

Minuchin, S., Montalvo, B., Guerney, B.G., Rosman, B.L. and Schumer, F. (1967). *Families of the Slums*. New York, Basic Books.

Olson, D.H., Sprenkle, D.H. and Russell, C.S. (1979). Circumplex model of marital and family systems. 1. Cohesion and adaptability dimensions, family types, and clinical application. *Family Process*, 18, 3–28.

Pincus, L. and Dare, C. (1978). *Secrets in the Family*. London, Faber.

Russell, G.F.M., Szmukler, G., Dare, C. and Eisler, I. (1987). An evaluation of family therapy in anorexia nervosa and bulimia nervosa. *Archives of General Psychiatry*, 44, 1047–56.

Sander, F.M. (1979). *Individual and Family Therapy*. New York, Jason Aronson.

Sander, L. (1980). Investigations of the infant and its care-giving environment as a biological system. In S.I. Greenspan and G.H. Pollock (eds) *The Course of Life*, vol. 1. Washington DC. National Institute of Mental Health.

Sandler, J. (1976). Countertransference and role responsiveness. *International Review of Psycho-Analysis*, 3, 43–7.

Sandler, J. and Dare, C. (1970). The psychoanalytic concept of orality. *Journal of Psychosomatic Research*, 14, 211–22.

Sandler, J., Dare, C. and Holder, A. (1973). *The Patient and the Analyst*. London, Allen & Unwin.

Sandler, J., Holder, A. and Dare, C. (1972). Frames of reference in psychoanalytic psychology. IV. The affect-trauma frame of reference. *British Journal of Medical Psychology*, 45, 265–72.

Shapiro, E., Zinner, J., Shapiro, R. and Berkowitz, D. (1975). The influence of family experience on borderline personality development. *International Review of Psycho-Analysis*, 2, 399–411.

Skynner, A.C.R. (1976). *One Flesh: Separate Persons*. London, Constable.

Slipp, S. (1984). *Object Relations: A Dynamic Bridge between Individual and Family Treatment*. New York, Jason Aronson.

Solomon, M.A. (1973). A developmental conceptual premise for family therapy. *Family Process*, 12, 179–88.

Stierlin, H. (1977). *Psychoanalysis and Family Therapy*. New York, Jason Aronson.

Stone, L. (1967). The psychoanalytic situation and transference: Postscript to an earlier communication. *Journal of the American Psychoanalytic Association*, 15, 3–58.

Szmukler, G., Eisler, I. and Dare, C. (1985). Systematic observation and clinical insight: are they compatible? An experiment in recognizing family interaction. *Psychological Medicine*, 15, 701–37.

Winnicott, D.W. (1958). *Collected Papers: Through Paediatrics to Psycho-Analysis*. London, Hogarth Press.

—— (1965). *The Maturational Process and the Facilitating Environment*. London, Hogarth Press.

—— (1971a). *Therapeutic Consultations in Child Psychiatry*. London, Hogarth Press.

—— (1971b). *Playing and Reality*. London, Tavistock.

Zinner, J. and Shapiro, R. (1972) Projective identification as a mode of perception and behavior in families of adolescents. *International Journal of Psycho-Analysis*, 53, 523–9.

—— (1974). The family group as a single psychic entity: implications for acting out in adolescents. *International Review of Psycho-Analysis*, 1, 179–86.

# CHAPTER 3

# SYSTEMIC FAMILY THERAPY: THE MILAN APPROACH

## John Burnham and Queenie Harris

## INTRODUCTION

This chapter describes some enduring features of the Milan Approach to Systemic Family Therapy as well as some recent developments. Readers wishing to explore further are referred to Hoffman (1981); Tomm (1982; 1984a; 1984b); Campbell and Draper (1985); Keeney and Ross (1985); Burnham (1986); and Gustafson (1986). These accounts, like ours, are based mainly on the observations of and contact with Luigi Boscolo and Gianfranco Cecchin, two members of the original Milan team.

In 1967 Mara Selvini Palazzoli and Luigi Boscolo created in Milan the first centre for family therapy in Italy (Boscolo 1979, personal communication). Ten psychoanalytically oriented colleagues met periodically to discuss their work with families.

In 1971 Selvini Palazzoli, Boscolo, Gianfranco Cecchin and Guilana Prata split from the psychoanalytic model to explore the interactional model. These four became known as the 'Milan Team'. They initiated a research project with a range of families presenting a variety of types of problems, including psychosis. Their work was greatly influenced by the Strategic school of family therapy (Haley 1963; Watzlawick *et al.* 1967). *Paradox and Counterparadox* (Selvini Palazzoli *et al.* 1978a) documents this period.

From 1975 the team examined and used extensively the theories proposed by Gregory Bateson (1973; 1979) and Boscolo and Cecchin began their training programme. Trainees, as well as readers of *Paradox and Counterparadox*, asked the question, 'How do you do what you do?'. The team responded by defining and describing their working principles: Hypothesiz-ing – Circularity – Neutrality (Selvini Palazzoli *et al*. 1980a).

In 1979/80 the team of four effected an amicable separation and became known as the Milan Associates. Selvini Palazzoli and Prata together de-veloped new areas of research. Boscolo and Cecchin elaborated their training programme in Milan (Boscolo and Cecchin 1982) and consultations to interested agencies abroad. Milan-type teams began to emerge in places such as New York, Cardiff, London, Calgary and Birmingham. These teams worked in different agencies from that in which the model was created, developing new applications of the approach. Hoffman (1981) declares the Milan approach as distinct from the Strategic school, naming it 'The Systemic Model'.

In 1983/4 Boscolo and Cecchin began to work separately clinically and as trainers. The reasons for this included increasing demands for training, emergence of second-generation trainers from their training programme and opportunities to free each other to develop other work. They also initiated different therapeutic patterns by working with other clinicians.

During 1986 Selvini Palazzoli and Prata separated. The four founders of the model continue to practise, train and entertain new ideas in diverse ways. Therefore the approach continues to evolve.

## THEORETICAL ASSUMPTIONS

Selvini Palazzoli (1974) describes her transition from psychoanalysis to systemic therapy being influenced by the writings of Haley (1963) and Watzlawick *et al*. (1967). This framework proposed a two-level hierarchy between the *process* and *content* of interpersonal communication. The meaning of content was seen as being determined by the process of inter-action. Symptoms were perceived as content and the interaction around the symptom as the process. When the Milan team directly examined Bateson's ideas about 'multiple levels of context' in interpersonal systems they became interested in the systemic meaning/history of a symptom as well as the current interaction.

Bateson's dictum that 'without context there is no meaning' led the Milan team to pay attention to context, context markers and to the message conveyed by behaviours within different contexts. The abstract notion of 'multiple levels of context' has been elegantly teased apart, elaborated and clarified by Pearce and Cronen (1980) and Cronen *et al*. (1982). Cronen and Pearce (1985) propose a hypothetical hierarchy of levels of context in which the meaning of any level can be understood by reference to the next higher level. The following seven-level organization is a reasonably comprehensive example: content (of a statement); speech act (the utterance as a whole);

*Figure 3.1*  Multiple levels of context

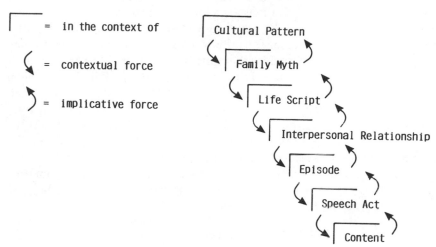

= in the context of

( = contextual force

) = implicative force

Cultural Pattern

Family Myth

Life Script

Interpersonal Relationship

Episode

Speech Act

Content

episode (the particular social encounter); interpersonal relationship; life script (of an individual); family myth and cultural pattern. This hierarchy is represented diagrammatically in Figure 3.1.

The influence of a higher-level context upon a lower-level context is referred to as the contextual force while the influence of a lower level upon a higher level is called the implicative force. It is proposed that the relationship between levels is *circular* and reflexive rather than vertical and linear. For example, just as a person's life script (I am a loser) influences the ways in which they behave during interpersonal relationships, so repetitive experiences of being involved in episodes of losing, influence the continuation of the life script. This circular relationship is also called recursion or self-reflexivity and describes the organizational relationship between the levels.

Contextual force generally exerts more influence than implicative force and appears to stabilize the organization of relationships. However the notion of reflexivity between levels means that implicative influences have the potential to generate changes in higher levels. For example, the 'loser' may engage in a relationship in which he or she experiences a series of episodes in which he or she wins, or which casts doubt on the idea that there has to be a winner and loser in every interpersonal episode. The implicative force of these experiences may well become the context for a redefinition of this person's current life script. This may lead to historical and future relationships, episodes, speech acts, and so on being given a new meaning also. Change therefore can occur in therapy due to both contextual and implicative forces.

However, Bateson's statement 'the map is not the territory' (Korzybski quoted in Bateson 1979 : 37) reminds therapists that theoretical frameworks, including ideas, principles, terminology, procedures, activities, lists of indications and contra-indications are a kind of map with which to negotiate the territory of therapy. Like any map a theory is an approximation of a territory, it is never the same. The criterion for using a particular theoretical map is whether it usefully guides therapists in their work. The Milan team's interest in maps led them to reintroduce the question: '*Why* is a problem occurring in this system at this time?' This question had apparently been outlawed by the family therapy field which had been almost exclusively concerned with the current interaction in a family. This emphasis led the Milan team to see the function of therapists as introducing new information and connections between behaviours, between behaviours and beliefs, and between beliefs and behaviours. They oriented themselves to stimulating families to generate new patterns for themselves. The therapist became more of an enzyme than an educator.

To act in this way with families therapists require information and information is viewed as 'news of a difference':

> perception operates only upon difference. All receipt of information is necess-
> arily the receipt of news of difference, and all perception of difference is limited
> by threshold. Differences that are too slight or too slowly presented are not
> perceivable. They are not food for perception.
>
> (Bateson 1979 : 29)

For there to be a difference there needs to be at least two objects that are compared. Any difference therefore necessarily involves a relationship. The significance of this led the Milan team to develop a style of therapy known as circular interviewing, which seeks to elicit information in terms of difference and relationships in the family and related systems.

The Milan team also drew on Bateson's three categories of relationships. Complementarity refers to those relationships based around the exchange of different behaviours: helper/helped, bully/coward, weak/strong and nurturer/nurtured. Symmetry describes relationships characterized by the exchange of the same type of behaviours: for example two people exchanging boasts about their performance, compliments, or tales of woe. Any relationship can be described as either complementary or symmetrical at any particular moment. Both types have the potential to be mutually satisfying for the participants in a relationship and/or to escalate towards an unsatisfactory situation. Reciprocity describes a relationship with a capacity to switch between complementarity and symmetry and in which the participants can take either position in a mutual exchange.

Systemic therapists adopt a stance that there is no single reality waiting to be discovered by an observer. Reality, it is argued, is 'co-constructed' between an observer interacting with the phenomena being observed. Reality, therefore, is not considered as separate and distinct from the observer and his or her framework and prejudices. Statements such as '*the* reality of the situation is . . .' are discouraged in favour of '*their* reality might be . . .' or 'punctuating from the point of view of . . . the mother . . . the son' and so on. Therapists must not believe that what they choose to believe is *the* truth. Cecchin (1984, personal communication) has observed that using the same conceptual posture repeatedly leads to confirmation of your ideas and thus the illusion of 'truth'. Periodically the Milan team deliberately abandon successful hypotheses in order to create other ideas and to avoid 'falling in love with their hypotheses'.

## The nature of healthy family functioning

The Milan approach accepts a wide variety of relationship styles and configurations (Boscolo 1983). Their neutral and accepting stance questions many traditional premises about what is a healthy family structure: children leaving home at a particular age, the strongest relationship must be the spouse relationship, and so on. Selvini Palazzoli *et al.* (1978a) writing about 'parental children' state:

> We should note that parentification is a universal and physiological phe-
> nomenon. . . . The parentification of a child may appear pathological upon first
> consideration, but it may be functional . . . depending on the context in which it
> occurs. . . . Parentification becomes the cause of dysfunction when it occurs in
> inappropriate situations in a context of ambiguous or incongruous transactions.

This view contrasts with that of Haley (1980), who stresses that therapists should always aim to put parents in charge of their children.

A guiding principle of this approach is that a clear definition of relationships without ambiguity is more important than what the particular definition of a relationship is. Keeney proposes that:

> A healthy family will follow a choreography of diverse interactional episodes,
> which provide a sort of ecological climax or balance. In these families, the role of
> scapegoat as well as white knight will constantly shift from person to person,
> coalitions will fluctuate between separateness and togetherness, fights and hugs
> will be given fair representation, and so on.
>
> (Keeney 1983 : 127)

Families may be considered 'healthy' if they are able to respond flexibly to changing circumstances and are able to change their rules and maps to fit the new situation. The notion of a clear definition of relationship is not comprehensive and many therapists may occasionally or consistently turn to models which provide clearer 'blueprints' of effectively functioning families (e.g. Minuchin 1974) when they are in a position of making decisions about how a family should behave (for example statutory functions). However the notion is extremely useful in steering therapists away from taking the position of prescribing a particular type of relationship. For example, where a child is expected to obey two contradictory messages simultaneously a therapist may introduce a ritual designed to introduce clarity. Successful outcomes may include various new family organizations: both parents agreeing about the message to be conveyed; the parents deciding that only one parent would discipline the child; the parents retaining separate opinions and taking turns in handling a situation.

Family therapy, like other modes of psychotherapy, exists in the context of changing cultural patterns. Traditional ways of relating are being challenged and perturbed by influences such as feminism, changes in legislation on divorce, sexuality, and so on. New patterns of forming stable relationships are emerging: single parents, stepfamilies, same gender parenting. Therefore principles and guidelines that are clear but not rigidly prescriptive are likely to be most useful to therapists during this stage of cultural transition.

## The nature of family disturbance

Family relationships tend to become disturbed around the time of significant transitional stages in their evolution. Events such as maturational development, death, members leaving, new members arriving, perturb the current patterns of relating. Relationships that were close become more distant, those that were distant become closer. It is usually a time for a reshuffling of existing relationship patterns and re-evaluation of the ideas about these patterns.

Families who become disturbed can be viewed as being at an impasse in such a transition. It may be that they develop new ideas, but have difficulty in altering their interactional patterns and/or they respond to some new behaviour according to an outmoded premise or map. As Tomm suggests:

> The tendency for 'old beliefs' to channel present behaviours into 'old' redundant patterns leaves the family appearing 'stuck' when their continuing behavioural evolution has taken them past the point where a particular map fits. . . . With increasing retention of outmoded maps over time, the degree of discrepancy, distortion and constraint grows until the system becomes increasingly symptomatic.
>
> (Tomm 1984a : 16)

Symptoms and other problematic behaviours can be viewed as a systems solution to this evolutionary impasse. For example, a couple came for help with the 'overactive' behaviour of their 6-year-old son. The behaviour seemed appropriate for his age. Further enquiry revealed that the mother had over the years experienced regular periods of depression. Such a phase was usually heralded when she became vigorously preoccupied (overactive) with cleaning the house. Thus in this couple's map, vigorous activity signalled an impending period of depression. In the context of this map their child's appropriate behaviour was given an inappropriate meaning. This led the couple to make strenuous efforts to help their son to 'relax', with predictable results.

Including a therapist or agency in this analysis permits us to imagine how a problem may arise/persist because of outmoded maps of therapist/agency therapist culture. For example, if a therapist's map includes the notion that therapy takes at least one year before real change can occur then any changes occurring before that time may be dismissed as 'flights into health'.

## THE THERAPY PROCESS

### The setting of therapy

The Milan associates created their team approach in the relative freedom of a private clinical setting. However, second-generation Milan teams and practitioners have found ways of circumventing apparently insoluble difficulties and creating systemic practices within public institutions (see Selvini Palazzoli 1983; Campbell and Draper 1985). The team approach usually involves one therapist conducting an interview while the other team members observe and supervise from behind a one-way screen. The information gained from this 'double description' (Bateson 1979) is different and complementary. The perspective gained is often referred to as a meta view and is one of the unique advantages of a team approach. Teams claim that, after a while, a 'team mind' becomes more creative than the sum of the individual contributions. To capitalize the potential of a team approach it is necessary to establish and maintain clear distinctions between the levels of therapy and supervision (Burnham and Harris 1985) as well as cultivating the working relationships between team members (Speed *et al.* 1982; Burnham 1986). Selvini Palazzoli (1980) describes the serendipitous discovery that a one-month interval between sessions yielded better results than weekly intervals. This discovery triggered a departure from other sacrosanct time periods and experiments with the 'power' of time as an intervention.

### The nature of change

Solutions to a family's dilemma are assumed to be latent within its own organization. A Milan-style therapy aims to discover and use patterns of behaviour and contextual meaning so that a family can reorganize itself and continue on a non-symptomatic evolutionary path.

Change may be triggered by introducing *clarity* into those systems which have become immobilized by confusion, and introducing *confusion* into those systems characterized by rigid scripts and beliefs. Clarity is mainly introduced through the effects of circular questioning and carefully designed rituals. Rigid beliefs may be confused by systemic reframes which propose new and often unexpected and/or provocative meanings for existing behaviour. When old patterns of behaviour and beliefs are interrupted a family can then become more free to develop new patterns of action and different systems of belief that remain consistent with but discontinuous from its preferred culture. A solution or blueprint is not imposed from outside; a family system is stimulated to create its own.

Interventions often contain statements about the 'normative' development of individuals and relationships but statements prescribing what a particular family should do are avoided. This stance is often difficult to maintain for those therapists who are accustomed to receiving requests for, and giving direct advice.

# THE ROLE OF THE THERAPIST

## Therapeutic conditions created by the therapist

Invitations are extended to those regarded by the family and/or therapist as significant to the problem. When referring professionals are included in the interview it is described as a consultation. An interview room includes at least one more seat than family members to maximize the proximal clues about relationships. A therapist takes the seat that allows for the best all-round view of family members. An explanation of the working method (see Burnham 1986) should clearly mark the particular context that is being created, for example assessment, therapy, consultation, or court report. Each session is organized according to a five-part ritual.

### 1. Pre-session discussion (15–20 minutes)
Information about the family and their involvement with other professionals is discussed including referral data; information gained from earlier sessions, and inter-session contact from the family and/or professionals. Hypotheses are created and questions selected to explore the symptom's significance/influence in family relationship patterns, changes in these patterns and the meaning attached to these changes. Specific hypotheses are indicated by general cues such as: Why does the family present to this agency now? Which relationship patterns are entering or undergoing a transition? What is the systemic significance/influence of the symptom in this transition? A hypothesis gives the therapist initiative and facilitates a purposeful interview. Hypotheses are modified or abandoned based on the circular feedback between therapist and family. Improved or new hypotheses lead to more questions, further feedback, refinement of hypotheses and so on. Systemic hypotheses eventually describe a symptom in terms of its influence in the significant relational network.

## 2. The session (50–60 minutes)

Interviews tend to consist of the therapist asking circular and reflexive questions (illustrated in the section on circular interviewing). Tomm (1987a; 1987b) distinguishes between *orienting* questions and *interventive* questions. Orienting questions are designed to elicit information *for the therapist* about the current and historical nature of family system: its interactional patterns; its belief system; its current life cycle position(s); and the significance of the symptom for the various members of the system. Interventive questions propose new beliefs or suggest different interactional patterns *for the family* and are purposefully introduced as the therapist/team's understanding of a family improves. Some rules governing a systemic interview have been described and elaborated by Viaro and Leonardi (1983).

During the session the team behind the screen note interactions, develop and refine hypotheses, and create questions for the therapist. Live supervision is at the discretion of therapist or team.

## 3. The discussion break (10–25 minutes)

The team assemble separately from the family and evaluate the session. Hypotheses leading to an adequate systemic explanation for the symptom provide the basis to create an intervention designed to trigger change at the levels of beliefs and behaviour of the relevant system. When no hypothesis has been confirmed the information from the session provides hypotheses for future sessions.

## 4. The intervention (0–5 minutes)

The family are reconvened and given the team's conclusion to the session in the form of a message. Insufficient information usually prompts the offer of another appointment. An intervention may aim to confuse rigidly held beliefs; clarify confused/chaotic systemic patterns, or generate new patterns of relating. A component addressing the family–therapy relationship includes who is convened for subsequent sessions, the time gap between sessions and the definition of future meetings.

Meticulous attention is paid to the verbal and non-verbal levels of delivery. Phrasing emphasizes relationships and is syntonic with a family's language. Details such as therapist posture, expression and expressed mood can have a significant bearing on whether an intervention is successful.

## 5. Post-session discussion (5–20 minutes)

Team discussions usually begin with analysing the immediate responses of family members to the intervention: Who spoke? What did they say? Who agreed with their view? Who disagreed? Who remained silent? How did they look and at whom? Who looked pleased, angry, or puzzled? Acceptance and an apparent understanding on the family's part do not necessarily indicate success. Alternatively rejection does not always indicate failure. In fact it may well be the reverse. A team usually proceeds with a review of the whole session which includes a critique of the therapist's performance and his or her interaction with the family and team. Each session follows this five-part ritual as closely as possible whether a therapist is working with a team or not.

## Principal methods of therapist intervention

There are two principal classes of interventions in this approach: circular interviewing and systemic interventions.

### Circular interviewing

Circular interviewing was introduced by Selvini Palazzoli *et al*. (1980a) and has been elaborated by several authors including Penn (1982; 1985); Tomm (1985; 1987a; 1987b; 1987c); Burnham (1986); Fleuridas *et al*. (1986).

A circular interview begins when a hypothesis is formulated and circular questions are selected to explore this systemic speculation. Linking questions to a hypothesis creates a purposeful and coherent interviewing pattern wherein information is revealed to the therapist and the family simultaneously. Families and clients tend to present the 'story' of their problem in one of two ways. The story may be presented as an apparently 'random' or 'chaotic' collection of actions, problems, people, emotions, events, and ideas which seem relevant but disconnected from one another. Alternatively the story may be presented as if it is 'written in stone' with actions and meanings 'welded' together into an inflexible, unchanging pattern ('We are the way we are because of X'). A circular interview recycles these stories through circular and reflexive questions into patterns which connect them into a systemic understanding. If a therapist has insufficient data circular questions can elicit general information to create specific systemic hypotheses.

There are many types of circular questions. Triadic questioning is a format that is unique to this model and underlies many circular questions. As well as asking people to comment on their own ideas, perceptions and behaviour each person is asked to comment on the thoughts, behaviour and relationships of the other members of the family. For example:

> THERAPIST (to father): Since your mother-in-law came to live with your family has the relationship between your son and his mother been better or worse?

To maintain the rule that each person should speak for him or herself, triadic questions are prefaced with phrases such as 'in your opinion'; 'from your point of view' or 'from your position what do you see'.

This method seems to make people stop and think rather than give stereotypical answers. It is common to observe the quizzical and eager anticipation of family members as they wait to hear how another person perceives their relationship. Triadic questioning may be used even when important members are absent or dead. For example, 'Suppose that your father were alive today what do you think his opinion would be about this problem?' It is extremely advantageous with families who are initially reluctant to answer direct questions about relationships. Individuals who do not respond verbally cannot help but show their non-verbal message since it is impossible not to communicate on this level.

Six basic categorics of question elicit information in terms of:

*1. Interactional sequences of behaviour.*   Sequential questions can place individual feelings into a circular context:

> THERAPIST (to mother): When your son [Frank] says that life isn't worth living, what does your husband do?
> MOTHER: He talks to him, tells him to pull himself together.
> THERAPIST (to brother): When your father tells your brother to pull himself together what does your mother do?

*2. Differences as indicated by behaviour rather than descriptions of individual characteristics.*   Descriptions such as 'he's impossible' or 'she does nothing' can be expanded as follows:

> THERAPIST: What did your mother-in-law do when your husband got admitted to hospital to dry out from alcohol?
> WIFE: Nothing, absolutely nothing, she's pathetic.
> THERAPIST: What does she do or say that makes you say she is pathetic?

*3. Ranking of responses by family members to specific behaviour or specific interactions.*   Enquiring about the differential responses (pleasure, anger, suspicion, and so on) or beliefs (optimism/pessimism, doubt, and so on) of all family members can expand the meaning of a particular transition, problem or attempted solution.

> THERAPIST (to husband): When your wife said that she was fed up with being at home and was thinking about getting a job, which of the three children, in your opinion, showed most enthusiasm towards the idea?

*4. Changes in behaviour that indicate a change in relationships before and after a specific event.*   This type of question elicits behavioural manifestations of the redefinition of relationships prompted by a transitional stage.

> BROTHER: Greg and Mommy are very close to each other.
> THERAPIST: Yes, I understand that but did they get close to each other before or after your father died?

*5. Mind-reading questions.* This type of question examines the quality of communication in a family, showing the extent to which members are aware of each other's thoughts and feelings. It also reveals differences of opinion between family members over important issues.

> THERAPIST (to mother): If your mother were still alive today, what do you think her opinion would be about the problems you are having with the children?
> MOTHER (long silence): . . . She, she would say it was inevitable, she said I'd never make a good mother.
> THERAPIST (to mother): In a moment I'm going to ask your husband if he agrees or disagrees with your mother's opinion. What do you think his answer will be?
> MOTHER (looks quizzically at the therapist, then across to husband): That's a funny question.
> THERAPIST: Yes, most people find them a bit strange to begin with but they're very useful to me. What do you think he will say?

Such enquiries often provoke spontaneous interactions, highlighting confusions, illustrating belief systems, divided loyalties and incongruencies between verbal and non-verbal levels of communcation. It is especially useful with children since they seem to find this 'guessing game' easier than direct questions.

*6. Differences of opinion with respect to hypothetical (past/current/future) situations, ideas or explanations.* Such questions release people from the concreteness of 'factual' answers and reveal hopes, fears and aspirations. Many systemic therapists (Penn 1985; Boscolo 1983; Tomm 1987b) propose that hypothetical questions have considerable potential for being interventive.

> THERAPIST (to daughter): Let's just suppose that you were able to concentrate at school, you passed exams, got a place at university and moved away from home. Which of your parents do you think would suffer the most?

Experienced therapists develop useful patterns of questions to explore particular hypotheses. Descriptions of circular questioning include: 'gossiping in the presence of others', and 'perceiving oneself and one's relationships through the eyes of another'. Families respond enthusiastically to this style of enquiry perhaps because they are stimulated to give answers that make connections between events, behaviours and beliefs that were hitherto thought to be unrelated. A good circular interview will leave the family remembering the answers they gave rather than the questions they were asked.

*Systemic interventions*
This constitutes part four of the interview ritual. It usually includes a systemic reframe, and a behavioural prescription linked to the systemic theme of the message.

*Systemic reframes.*  A systemic reframe involves a therapist retelling/ reconstructing the 'story' told by a family about its problem. It synthesizes what the family has said in a way that introduces and/or emphasizes circular connections made during the session. It presents the same events and problems in the context of a new meaning that is different from the family's previous understanding in at least three aspects. First, it connotes positively the systemic *intent* of problematic/symptomatic behaviours that have been previously cast in a negative light. Second, it proposes an altruistic and volitional rationale for the problematic behaviours/relationships. Third, it places these events, actions, thoughts and behaviour into a relational framework which emphasizes their interconnectedness with other signifi- cant family events (actual or anticipated). For example, a family might present a child who will not speak outside the home and thus does not make friends or develop peer relationships. Previous definitions of this problem might have included such negative connotations of the child as over- dependent, selfish, anti-social, immature or ill. The family too may have been described as overprotective, enmeshed or suffocating. A systemic intervention utilizing positive connotation might begin with the following reframe:

> We are impressed with the *independence* of Shirley who by *deciding* not to speak, sacrifices her opportunities to continue her social development in order to *help* her family. After many years of living in such a close and devoted family we *think* that she has developed the *idea* that if she was to grow up, make friends and spend less time at home then her parents would be lonely. Therefore by not speaking she makes sure that she will remain at home always available for them.

Systemic reframes intend to propose new and often unexpected meanings for individual behaviour, the nature of a particular relationship and the collective behaviour of a whole family system. Reframes may trigger a difference through allowing people to change without losing face; placing solutions to the problem within the interactional grasp of the family or releasing the family from their currently restricted map. Seligman (1986) gives an in-depth analysis of the organization and content of a single intervention.

*Systemic prescription.*  While systemic reframes propose new contextual meanings for problematic situations, a systemic prescription addresses the level of behaviour. These prescriptions include paradoxical injunctions, rituals and split team opinions.

Paradoxical injunctions (Selvini Palazzoli *et al.* 1978b; Cade 1984) re- quest, advise or prescribe the continuation of the symptomatic behaviours/ relationships and thus apparently align the therapist with the stability/ homeostatic tendency of a system. This unusual request is facilitated by the preceding positive connotation of the problem. It is usual to add the rider 'for the time being' and suggest some experiment which may help the family out of their dilemma. For instance the above intervention might have continued

> and so we think that, *for the time being*, Shirley should continue not to talk to outsiders, to avoid making friends and so on, so that she can continue to do this work for her family. When Shirley becomes convinced that her parents do not need her to do this work then she will decide to give up this job and continue her development. Convincing Shirley will be a difficult task for her parents and so we will meet with them next session to discuss how she might have got this idea and what they can do to convince her that they can, as we believe, manage without her.

Such a prescription introduces a paradox into the relationship between the family and the therapist: 'A therapist's job is to help us change, yet she tells us not to change.' Some families feel reassured and/or differently (more positively) about one another and change ensues at the levels of action and meaning. Families who have been encouraged to change by many professionals may respond by 'rebelling' against the therapist's requests and change in spite of the therapist. Situations which include dangerous symptoms are often dealt with by prescribing some other problematic part of the family process rather than the symptom itself.

Systemic rituals involve the prescription of a task for the family to carry out before the next session. The details of the ritual are very precise indicating who is to do what, with whom, in what order, for how long and how often. Rituals take many forms since they are usually designed to fit a particular family. A central feature of rituals seems to be that a new *process* is (mysteriously) introduced in the form of old *content*. For example, in a family where the spouses had been parents since the age of 15, producing six children, the children in turn (in various ways including symptomatic behaviour) interrupted any attempt by the parents to spend time together alone. This over-involvement was positively connoted as cohesion and closeness and the children's behaviour reframed as helping the parents to avoid the possibility of being disappointed with one another after such a long time. In front of the children the parents were requested to go to a room in their house on two specified nights of the week between 7 and 7.30 p.m. and to lock the door. Their task was to discuss ways in which they can postpone the development of their own relationship until the children had all left home. This ritual introduced new process (parents spending time with each other) in the disguise of old content (talking about how to avoid spending time with each other).

Whether the family performs the ritual or not the therapist gains new information about the family process and the family–therapist process. A ritual is not designed to become a regular part of the family life or to indicate the 'right' way to do things. Its function is to stimulate through experimentation, new ideas and processes of the family's choosing. A regular template is the 'odd day and even day' ritual (Selvini Palazzoli *et al*. 1978b) illustrated in the case example (see pp. 70–6).

*Split team message.* This may be usefully offered in a therapy which is struggling because of covert tensions, between family members, between the therapist and family or between other sub-systems (Cade 1980; Papp 1980). This can make covert issues overt through a team dispute for example: half the team think *X*, the other half think *Y* and couldn't decide. 'We'll leave it there for today and perhaps you can be thinking about which opinion you agree with or you may have a completely different idea'; (this could be introduced at the beginning of a session in order to focus the discussion and debate). Another way is to make the split between the therapist and the team behind the screen (or the support group back at the office). Usually the cautious or pessimistic opinion (it's too soon or too difficult for the family to change) is attributed to the team and the therapist takes the positive or optimistic position. A team may implicitly or explicitly criticize a therapist and stimulate the family to rescue him or her from the team.

The response to interventions depends to a large extent on the unique organization and belief system of a particular family and cannot be predicted with any certainty by the therapist. The process of therapy always involves a recursive relationship between hypothesizing (meaning); questions (action); feedback from family (at levels of action and meaning); intervention (at levels of meaning and/or action); feedback from family; hypothesizing, and so on.

Interventions may be arrived at by the end of the first or second session or may take some considerable time. Therapy may last one session or may last twenty sessions. In longer therapeutic encounters interventions tend to include wider systems than the nuclear family, and address the relationship between the family and the therapist. It is likely that original interventions will be created as 'regular/favourite' therapist patterns are exhausted. For example, when a therapy continues without change, interventions often become increasingly elaborate, inclusive and longer. A process might be observed where the therapist is noticeably the most enthusiastic member of the family-therapist system. In these situations the most novel, unexpected intervention may be 'no' intervention delivered by an apparently despondent, unenthusiastic therapist: 'Today we have nothing to report and so the next session is on . . .' A family is stimulated to ponder: I wonder what is wrong with them? I wonder how we can motivate her again?

## Family responses to the change process

Responses to the process of therapy vary between families and with the same family at different stages in therapy.

*Engagement*

Family expectations are crucial to early engagement: families who anticipate criticism and blame tend initially to be critical of therapy. Families who feel that family therapy is the last resort for difficult families tend to be harder to engage. Major disagreements between family members or within the referring agency about coming for therapy have to be addressed in the engagement phase. These speculations should be regarded as tentatively as any other hypothesis. Anticipated blame is often decreased and engagement facilitated through the rationale that family interviews are useful *for the therapist* to understand the problem experienced by the family.

*Mid-therapy*

As therapy unfolds families respond in different ways. Families may show fascination or irritation with circular questioning but many are 'relieved' that they are not criticized and become easier to work with. Interventions intended to be 'provocative' have been received in a calm, matter-of-fact way by the family. Routine, engaging interventions have provoked amazement or anger from the family.

Families who have experienced therapists who gave more advice might express impatience and ask, 'But when are you going to tell us what to do?' Some families react to live supervision with amusement and interest, eagerly awaiting the comments from the team or the end-of-session intervention. Others respond with boredom or sarcasm. As I (Burnham) was called out by my colleagues, a father asked me, 'What have you done wrong this time?', another enquired, 'How long will it be before you can sit behind the screen and think of the questions instead of just asking them?'

*End of therapy*

Therapy may be terminated at any time by mutual agreement, by the therapist, or by the family. Various ways of ending therapy have been proposed by the Milan team. A fundamental theme is to give the family the credit for any changes while the team claim responsibility for lack of progress or failure. Regular ending interventions include one when a family is on the brink of a major change or becoming dependent on the therapy: 'Any residual problems you have are ordinary difficulties of family life which we are sure you will be able to deal with on your own and do not need psychiatric or professional help'. Sometimes when there is a resolution of the presenting problem and, while the team think there are 'deeper' relationship problems, the family are reluctant to continue: 'We are undecided about offering another appointment to your family. One opinion is that to continue would undermine the degree of competence you have already achieved, another view is that to end now would deprive you of the opportunity to consider other areas of your life in which you might like to make changes. We will offer you another appointment and you can decide whether to keep it.' If the family keep the appointment it is on a different basis from the original problem. Cecchin (1986, personal communication) prefers a family to terminate therapy and suggests offering appointments until they choose not to come.

Even when the correlation between therapy and improvements is quite striking families often give no credit to therapy. Family members may say something like, 'I think it was just a stage we were going through, though it has helped to have an outsider to talk to'. Changes may be ascribed to serendipitous events, unrelated to therapy (and of course they may well be right!). Families sometimes state that they had disagreed with us and had done it their own way. Those families who do give credit to therapy say the questions helped them to think about their situations in a different way. Follow-up studies indicate that some families who choose to 'drop out' of therapy display a significant degree of change. These families sometimes display anger or annoyance at therapy and convey that they changed in spite of the therapy rather than because of it. There are also 'drop-outs' that represent therapeutic failure and indicate a lack of engagement, a misunderstanding of the problem, an insensitive interaction or some other error on the part of the team or therapist.

At any stage of therapy the behaviour of families should be analysed in terms of the developing 'dance' between family and therapist. There may be simple and plausible reasons for failed appointments, absent members, forgetting to carry out rituals, and so on. A systemic team will always consider other hypotheses for such events.

## Assessment of change

The Milan approach does not give clear guidelines about what a functional family is and so successful outcome is more difficult to gauge than it appears in other models (for example the structural model). The fact that families do not always credit therapy for therapeutic changes makes it difficult to construct a picture of successful therapy that fits traditional research criteria.

Studies have been carried out in our own centre and other institutions: the Family Institute, Cardiff; the Royal Hospital for Sick Children, Edinburgh; the Department of Clinical Psychology, Exeter are some of the British institutions undertaking outcome studies into this way of working. Speed (1985) reports Prata and Cecchin as indicating rates of improvement that compare favourably with other methods of family therapy. These results were with families presenting with severe problems. Tomm (1984b) compared his centre's earlier more directive mode of family therapy to results of using the Milan approach. Preliminary evidence suggests that while the improvement rate remains the same, the changes reported in the presenting problem occur with fewer sessions using the Milan approach. The average number of cases handled by the same number of staff increased by 25 per cent for the four years after the introduction of the Milan approach.

As yet there are insufficient studies about the use of this approach and it remains to be seen how researchers deal with the epistemological and methodological problems inherent in the evaluation of this model.

# EFFECTIVE THERAPISTS

## Qualities of effective therapists

*Process and content*
Systemic therapists need to develop an ability to listen to important content issues that are sometimes sad, frightening and disturbing and then enquire from a meta position about the process that such information triggers. Therapists would find themselves resisting any urge to be the comforter of the distressed family member and instead enquiring, 'When your mother becomes upset like this, who in the family is most successful at giving her comfort?' This is a skill that goes against the training of many therapists.

*Curiosity*
Mendez *et al.* (1987) use the term 'multiverse' to emphasize that there are many equally valid ways of perceiving the world (though not all equally desirable). Discovering a family's idiosyncratic world view requires a therapist to adopt a posture of curiosity about the family as it is and how it might be. Curiosity orientates therapists towards neutrality and facilitative enquiry rather than bias and inference (Cecchin 1988). In response, a family is more likely to question and change its own behaviour and beliefs rather than needing solutions imposed from outside itself.

*Neutrality*
Neutrality does not mean that a therapist demonstrates coldness, passivity or disregard for people's feelings. A therapist does not become 'neutered' as a human being. Neutrality requires a therapist to accept everything, challenge everything and side with no one person or view. A therapist 'accepts' by listening to a person's point of view, and then 'challenges' this view by asking other people about their opinion and posing questions that yield a different or opposite situation to that which prevails. For example a family presented a 19-year-old daughter who volunteered herself as the problem

because she 'obsessively and graphically' talked about sex and embarrassed family members by openly reading pornographic magazines around the house. Cecchin, after listening to this description, began to ask in a curious fashion: 'How come nobody else talks about sex or likes to read such magazines?' Such questions establish a therapist's neutrality in relation to contentious issues in the family. Such questions also have the potential to trigger answers which suggest the possibility of the unusual, or the flipside of the family's usual behaviour/beliefs. To do this a therapist has to be able/willing to suspend moral judgements and consider unusual possibilities in his or her own mind.

Professionals working in therapeutically restrictive environments need to develop ability to suspend, at least temporarily, their agency task/function and to think outside their usual role, i.e. what might I do or say to this family if I weren't a probation officer, social worker, educational psychologist. With this different perspective they can then step back inside their usual boundaries and translate this perspective into an action that is appropriate to their agency position.

*Teamwork*

Team members need to be able to sacrifice an uncertain amount of individual freedom to reap the rewards of the team mind and process. Therapists need to be able to consider themselves as part of the system under observation as well as accept live supervision in the knowledge that a supervisor has a meta perspective. Supervisors need to remember that their perspective is different from not better than a therapist's and to convey information in a succinct fashion enabling a therapist to proceed more usefully.

# Skills required by therapists

Conceptually a systemic therapist needs to be able to distinguish and organize data about family relationships in terms of multiple levels of meaning, action and context. This organization should include the conception of themselves as an observer/organizer who is influencing what is being observed. After drawing these distinctions a therapist needs the ability to recognize the reflexive connections between the different levels of meaning. Executively a therapist needs to be able to create competently a circular interview using the three guidelines of hypothesizing, circularity and neutrality. An ability to organize the overall process of therapy as well as each session is also necessary. Techniques such as circular questions become a therapeutic skill when a therapist is able to select from his or her repertoire of techniques those which are most useful for a particular family at a particular time, Tomm (1987a) has coined the term 'strategizing' to describe this process of selection and proposes it as a fourth guideline for interviewing.

*Family therapy in Britain*

## Training model for therapists

Boscolo and Cecchin (1982; 1985) describe an aim of their training programme as putting trainees in a position where they have to 'think not
imitate'. This helps students to become more effective in their own contexts.
This *modus operandi* has been adopted by others describing systemic
training programmes in Britain (Harris and Burnham 1985; Draper and
Lang 1985). Our training programmes typically include seminars on theory,
case presentations and extended essays. Before working with families under
live supervision trainees observe live and recorded interviews by staff
therapists and practise therapy through simulated family exercises. Other
training exercises develop individual and teamwork skills that facilitate the
application of a systemic approach to a variety of systems as well as families.
This is particularly important when students are from agencies where family
therapy is seen as 'peripheral' to the main agency task.

# A FAMILY IN THERAPY

The Milan approach is often associated with families presenting difficult,
intractable problems. Therefore it is not surprising that a myth has developed which goes something like: 'The Milan method is only for very
difficult cases which need a powerful paradoxical approach.' The following
case example demonstrates that the Milan approach can be useful in a
variety of cases.

A GP referred a family to our centre (a regional child psychiatry unit) with
a letter containing the following information:

> Mrs P is aged 36 and has three children. A boy aged 19, a girl aged 18 and a boy
> aged 14. She has been married to her present husband for the past two years
> although she has lived with him for the last eight years. There have recently been
> marked problems between the youngest child and her husband. There have
> apparently been no problems with the older children. The whole situation is not
> only causing arguments between Mr P and the youngest child but also between
> him and his wife.
>
> The family saw a counsellor last year and the situation did improve for a short
> time.

## Pre-session

A useful way to create systemic hypotheses is to identify events which can
trigger developmental transitions in the family and extended relationships
and then hypothesize about the influence which the problem may have in
organizing or shaping the changing nature of relationships.

The team made three hypotheses:

1 *Trigger*: the adolescence of the two older children. *Transition:* leaving home. *Influence*: the fighting between the other three members slows down the process of separation by the elder two children.
2 *Trigger*: the marriage two years ago after six years of living together. *Transition*: change from lovers to parents, from co-habitee to stepfather. *Influence*: fighting may be an attempt;
   (a) by new father and son to make mother choose between her husband and her children;
   (b) to end this relationship and reunite the old family;
   (c) to influence whether this couple have a child of their own.
3 *Trigger*: the termination of the relationship with the counsellor. *Transition*: the loss of a helpful outsider means family have to deal with each other directly over difficult issues without an outside peacemaker. *Influence*: fighting may serve to engage another professional who would become peacemaker or solution creator.

Questions were developed to explore and test these hypotheses and will be illustrated by extracts from the session. Readers may like to develop some questions before continuing.

## Interview

The first part of the session provided the information illustrated in Figure 3.2.

The children had chosen not to see their natural father some time ago.

*Figure 3.2*

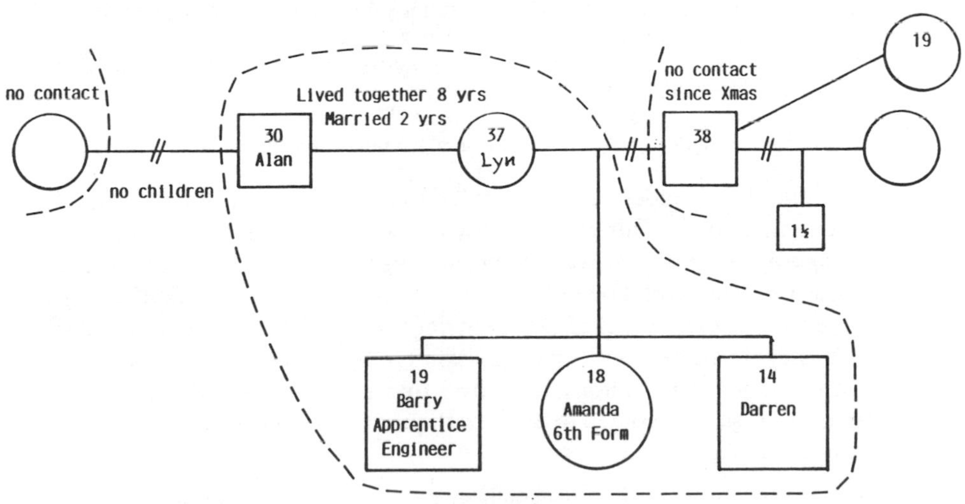

They disapproved of the way he had handled his life and relationships over the past few years. The stepfather had no children from his previous marriage and had no contact with his previous wife. Hypothesis 2b seemed implausible and directed the therapist to explore others.

### Problem exploration

Everyone agreed that the fighting between Darren and the stepfather presented the main problem. Mr P added that he lacked support from his wife and felt that he lacked credibility in the family. Amanda added that it seemed as though everybody was unhappy, not only Dad and Darren.

Different explanations were offered about why the problem was happening. Mrs P stated, 'My husband doesn't share the same sense of humour as the rest of the family. We four can be sat round having a laugh and he comes in and puts a damper on it all.' (The stepfather is a fireman!) Darren agreed with his mother. Barry added, 'Maybe Dad just doesn't know what kids of this age are like'. Dad disagreed: 'Nobody seems to pull their weight around the house, except me and Lyn. It makes me angry when they take advantage of her.' Amanda: 'I'm not sure but I think that Darren takes a few liberties with Dad and then Dad gets really annoyed'.

This next piece of transcript occurred about twenty minutes into the session. It indicates how hypothesis 2 was explored and the conclusions that were reached:

> THERAPIST: You married recently. What was the date of your marriage?
> MOTHER: The 14th of February.
> THERAPIST (to Mandy): Was the friction more noticeable before or after your mother and father got married?
> MANDY: More noticeable after they got married.
> THERAPIST: After they got married. Do you think they were surprised at what happened? Do you think they were expecting that when they got married things would get even better? Do you think it was a surprise?
> MANDY: I don't know. I don't think they got married to sort out the problems. I think they got married just for themselves.
> THERAPIST: What do you think made them decide to get married?
> MANDY: I think they just wanted to be a real man and wife, be a real family.

Enquiry into the extended family revealed that every marriage in the family had ended in divorce. This was the only remaining marriage in the family.

During a live supervision break the following ideas related to hypothesis 2 emerged. Everybody had been in favour of this marriage. The family *map* contained the romantic belief that marriage would improve relationships because they would become a *real* family. Traditionally however the *territory* of marriage in the family indicated that marriages usually ended in divorce. The session resumed to explore the contradiction between map and territory in relation to marriage.

> THERAPIST (to Darren): My colleague is interested to know – when your dad got

married to your mom, what do you think he expected would be different for him?

DARREN: He probably thought we would become more of a family . . . like.

THERAPIST: More of a family – that means different things to different people. What do you think it meant to him?

DARREN: Oh . . . Well that . . . he was actually part of us . . . you know. Before he was just going out with Mom. Now he'd be part of us all.

THERAPIST: So before, you think he felt that he was just going out with your mom and now he'd be part of you all. What kind of things do you think he expected to happen, how would that show itself?

DARREN: I think he thought we would respect him more . . . like.

THERAPIST: Do you think he's more pleased or more disappointed with the way things have gone?

DARREN: More disappointed.

THERAPIST (to Darren): What do you think your mom hoped for?

DARREN: Same sort of thing really, that we'd be more of a family.

THERAPIST (to Mandy): Do you agree?

MANDY: I agree, they've both put a lot into it to make us more of a family.

THERAPIST: Your dad mentioned credibility, that he thought he was more credible before they got married than afterwards.

MANDY: I think so, we all knew it wasn't a permanent position . . .

THERAPIST: You *all* knew it wasn't . . .

MANDY: So he didn't *have* to stay, if he didn't want to, if he didn't like it. Because of that I think he had a lot more authority over us.

THERAPIST: Ahh, you thought you had to please him more before [they got married]?

MANDY: Yes, because we *wanted* him to *stay*.

(At this stage the non-verbal communication was: wife looking at husband, Mandy looking at father, positive looks towards each other.)

THERAPIST: 'cos you *wanted* him to *stay*.

MANDY: Yes.

BARRY: Yes, that's true, that is.

THERAPIST: Now you treat him like a *real* dad . . . a dad that doesn't count (humorously).

BARRY:
DARREN: } No that's not true (laughing).
MANDY:

Mother looks at father and both are laughing.

MANDY (continuing): . . . it's just we think we can push him a lot further.

THERAPIST: You know you can push him a lot further because he says 'I'm staying now'. . . . What do you think Barry?

BARRY: I think she's right, she's a bit of a philosopher actually.

THERAPIST: So for five years you were on your best behaviour, they got married and . . . (everyone is laughing in a good-humoured way) . . .

FATHER (shaking his head and smiling): That's shocked me that has.

BARRY: I think . . . oh god . . . I had a load of things to say there I've forgotten them . . . I must admit it was a lot different before they got married.

THERAPIST: So you got married hoping to be more of a family and found that you were more of a family before than after.

BARRY: That's true.

THERAPIST (to father): Are you surprised at what they've said?

FATHER: Yes, especially what Mandy said. I was really surprised.

MOTHER: Yes, especially Mandy, I've never heard her say that before.
BARRY: It's right though.
BARRY (laughing, to Mandy): You've dropped a bomb there!

**** This exploded the family myth! ****

## Team discussion

This lasted about fifteen minutes and it can be noted that there did not seem to be any immediate plans by the eldest children to leave home; the relationship with the counsellor did not seem to have become a significant part of the family system in the way described by Selvini Palazzoli *et al.* (1980). The most important transition seemed to be the changing nature of relationships following the marriage two years ago. The friction between Darren and the stepfather involved the triangulation of the mother and seemed to be influencing whom she gave her firmest loyalties to. As she stated: 'I feel torn in two'. An intervention based on this hypothesis was delivered:

## Intervention

We meet and work with many stepfamilies. What has impressed us most about yours is the commitment on everybody's part to make this family work. Often there are two factions – one part that wishes to stay together and one faction that doesn't – usually there is a great battle. We don't see that in your family, we see everybody committed to making it work. We can see how surprised you all were when you two got married, expecting things to get even better, instead they seemed to get worse!

What we see happening is that before you got married people were treating each other like house guests [nods all round] politely, pleasantly, taking a lot of time and trouble to make people feel welcome and *credible*. Then you got married and the fighting began. The two older ones had grown up and had benefited from the relationship that you [looking at stepfather] had with them. When you became an official family Darren was the child in the family who you both [looking at mother and stepfather] could be a 'real' family with.

The fighting is a sign that you are a 'real' family – you don't treat each other like house guests any more. Children have become stroppy, father's become strict, and mother's often caught in between. So in some ways the fighting is evidence that you are a 'real', official family.

Our first thought was that you could get divorced and just live together again [hilarity all round] – but we thought that was going too far.

NOW, how are you going to work out how *your* family will be? I guess you both have different ideas and rules and I wonder how you are going to blend these differences.

The next appointment we can offer you is in two weeks' time at 9.30 am. Before then we suggest that you carry out the following experiment to help clarify how you want things to be in your family.

For the time being we recommend that you both [stepfather and Darren] continue to fight and argue. Darren, you continue to appeal to your mother to take your side and Mr P, you continue to appeal to your wife to side with you.

Mrs P, on Mondays, Wednesdays and Fridays we suggest that you side with your husband whether you agree with him or not. On Tuesdays, Thursdays and Saturdays take your son's side, whether you think he is right or wrong. On Sundays you can take a holiday and be spontaneous!

Meanwhile, Mandy and Barry, you can become observers of what happens, don't comment at the time, take notes and we will discuss what happens next time.

Some family members smiled, some looked puzzled, others smiled and looked puzzled. I asked if I had made the instructions clear and if there were any questions. Mrs P said, 'So on Mondays, Wednesdays and Fridays?' giving the therapist a quizzical look while smiling. The therapist repeated the instructions until everyone seemed clear about what they were being asked to do.

## Post-session discussion

The family seemed engaged and the interview process seemed to have prompted the revelation of new information, of positive feelings when they had been assuming negative ones. The most noticeable current pattern of interaction was fighting between Dad and Darren during which they both turned to mother for support, who felt 'torn in two'. The intervention built on the information gained through circular questioning and emphasized the implicative connections between the episodes of fighting and the changes in the definition of the interpersonal relationships (that is marriage). It also revealed and commented on the contradictions between the levels of family mythology (marriage = a real family) and behaviour (marriage = taking people for granted). Hypothesis 3 had been explored only superficially and may require further investigation.

## Session 2

The whole family attended the next session. The therapist chose to begin by asking how the ritual had gone. The stepfather responded that 'it hadn't really worked'. It hadn't 'suited' their family. Furthermore he felt, '. . . it was a bit of a ploy on your part by setting that task, in that umm . . . to make us look for our own answers'.

The therapist listened, resisting the temptation to defend or justify the ritual. Sometimes 'doing nothing' is the most difficult skill to 'do'.

The mother agreed that 'it hadn't worked' but went on to say, '. . . on the other hand, the last couple of weeks, things have gone a lot better for various reasons. I think a lot of it is just coincidence, I may be wrong. . . . But then again it may slide back to square one again unless we do come up with THE solution.'

The therapist explored the family's hesitancy regarding the durability of their improvement through questions such as: 'If the improvements between Father and Darren continue what might be the disadvantages for Barry, for Mandy, for Mother, for the marriage and so on?' Mandy commented, perceptively, that family life would become boring without any fighting and it was unrealistic to expect always to be laughing and harmonious.

The intervention emphasized the apparently 'contradictory' developmental stages that the family were at simultaneously: a young marriage with teenagers; the possibility of having their own children and/or grandchildren! It continued by normalizing the conflicts and tensions and concluded with a metaphor in the form of a story which seemed to encapsulate the family's situation. An appointment was set for three months hence at the suggestion of the family.

The father rang on behalf of the family to cancel the next session, reporting that things were going well and that they did not require any further appointments. Improvement was maintained at one year later.

# CONCLUSIONS

Many practitioners in Britain have successfully adopted and adapted the Milan approach. Some of them have closely matched the Milan approach in agencies that are designated as therapeutic. Others have looked beyond therapy to comprehend systemic thinking *per se*, and have then become competent as systemic practitioners within their agency context. These innovators have developed systemic approaches to their agency tasks rather than concentrating on creating family therapy units in agencies where therapy is sometimes regarded as a peripheral activity. These practitioners have found ways of using the concepts, methods, skills and techniques of the Milan approach while still operating as a coherent part of their professional system.

The Milan approach to family therapy offers therapists a clearly defined method of therapy which includes conceptual postures and technical skills. The approach enables practitioners to interview efficiently and intervene effectively in significant family relationships. The model continues to evolve with further refinements and elaborations. Recent theoretical influences include the ideas proposed by Maturana (Maturana and Varela 1980; Mendez *et al.* 1987) on the nature of reality. Technical developments include confirmation and clarification of how the process of circular interviewing can be interventive as well as informative (Tomm 1987a; 1987b; 1987c). Advances in application (Selvini Palazzoli 1983; 1984; Campbell and Draper 1985) indicate that the approach is useful for a wider range of systems than first envisaged by the original Milan team when they initially described their work with families in Selvini Palazzoli *et al.* (1978a).

# REFERENCES

Bateson, G. (1973). *Steps to an Ecology of Mind*. St Albans, Paladin.
—— (1979). *Mind and Nature: A Necessary Unity*. London, Fontana.
Boscolo. L. (1983). Proceedings of 'The Process of Change', a conference organized by the Institute of Family Therapy, London.
Boscolo, L. and Cecchin, G. (1982). Training in systemic therapy at the Milan Centre. In R. Whyffen and J. Byng-Hall (eds) *Family Therapy Supervision: Recent Developments in Practice*. London, Grune & Stratton.
—— (1985). Twenty more questions: selections from a discussion between the Milan Associates: Luigi Boscolo and Gianfranco Cecchin and the editors: David Campbell and Rosalind Draper. In D. Campbell and R. Draper (eds) *Applications of Systemic Family Therapy: The Milan Approach*. London, Grune & Stratton.
Burnham, J.B. (1986). *Family Therapy: First Steps Towards a Systemic Approach*. London, Tavistock.
Burnham, J.B. and Harris, Q. (1985). Therapy, supervision, consultation: different levels of a system. In D. Campbell and R. Draper (eds) *Applications of Systemic Family Therapy: The Milan Approach*. London, Grune & Stratton.
Cade, B.W. (1980). Resolving therapeutic deadlocks using a contrived team conflict. *International Journal of Family Therapy*, 2, 253–62.
—— (1984). Paradoxical techniques in therapy. *Journal of Child Psychology and Psychiatry*, 25, (4), 509–16.
Campbell, D. and Draper, R. (1985). *Applications of Systemic Family Therapy: The Milan Approach*. London, Grune & Stratton.
Cecchin, G. (1988). Hypothesizing – circularity–neutrality revisited: an invitation to curiosity. *Family Process*, 3–14, 26:1.
Cronen, V. and Pearce, B. (1985). Toward an explanation of how the Milan method works: an invitation to a systemic epistemology and the evolution of family systems. In D. Campbell and R. Draper, (eds) *Applications of Systemic Family Therapy: The Milan Approach*. London, Grune & Stratton.
Cronen, V., Johnson, K.M. and Lannamann, J.W. (1982). Paradoxes, double binds and reflexivle loops: an alternative theoretical perspective. *Family Process*, 21, 91–112.
Draper, R. and Lang, P. (1985). Training in systemic thinking for professional workers. In D. Campbell and R. Draper (eds) *Applications of Systemic Family Therapy: The Milan Approach*. London, Grune & Stratton.
Fleuridas, C., Nelson, T. and Rosenthal, D. (1986). The evolution of circular questions: training family therapists. *Journal of Marital and Family Therapy*, 12, (2), 113–27.
Gustafson, J. (1986). *The Complex Secret of Brief Psychotherapy*. New York, Guilford.
Haley, J. (1963). *Strategies of Psychotherapy*. New York, Grune & Stratton.
—— (1980) *Leaving Home: The Therapy of Disturbed Young People*. New York, McGraw-Hill.
Harris, Q. and Burnham, J. (1985). A training programme in systemic therapy: the problem of the institutional context. In D. Campbell and R. Draper (eds) *Applications of Systemic Family Therapy: The Milan Approach*. London, Grune & Stratton.
Hoffman, L. (1981). *Foundations of Family Therapy*. New York, Basic Books.
Keeney, B. (1983). *Aesthetics of Change*. New York, Guilford.
Keeney, B. and Ross, J.M. (1985). *Mind in Therapy: Constructing Systemic Therapies*. New York, Basic Books.

Maturana, H. and Varela, F. (1980). *Autopoiesis and Cognition*. Dordrecht, Holland and Boston, Mass., D. Reidel.

Mendez, C., Coddou, F. and Maturana, H. (1987). The bringing forth of pathology. *Family Process* (forthcoming).

Minuchin, S. (1974). *Families and Family Therapy*. London, Tavistock.

Papp, P. (1980). The Greek Chorus and other techniques of paradoxical therapy. *Family Process*, 19, 45–57.

Pearce, B. and Cronen, V. (1980). *Communication Action and Meaning: The Creation of Social Realities*. New York, Praeger.

Penn, P. (1982). Circular questioning. *Family Process*, 21, (3), 267–80.

—— (1985). Feed-forward: future questions, future maps. *Family Process*, 24, (3), 299–310.

Seligman, P. (1986). A brief family intervention with an adolescent referred for drug-taking. *Journal of Adolescence*, 9, (3), 231–42.

Selvini Palazzoli, M. (1974). *Self-Starvation: From the Intrapsychic to the Transpersonal Approach to Anorexia*. London, Chaucer.

—— (1980). Why a long interval between sessions. In M. Andolfi and I. Zwerling (eds) *Dimensions of Family Therapy*. New York, Guilford.

—— (1983). The emergence of a comprehensive systems approach. *Journal of Family Therapy*, 5, 165–77.

—— (1984). Behind the scenes of the organization: some guidelines for the expert in human relations. *Journal of Family Therapy*, 6, 299–308.

Selvini Palazzoli, M. and Prata, G. (1982). Snares in family therapy. *Journal of Marital and Family Therapy*, 8, 443–50.

Selvini Palazzoli, M., Cecchin, G., Prata, G. and Boscolo, L. (1978a). *Paradox and Counterparadox*. New York, Jason Aronson.

Selvini Palazzoli, M., Boscolo, L., Cecchin, G. and Prata. G. (1978b). A ritualized prescription in family therapy: odd days and even days. *Journal of Marriage and Family Counseling*, 4, 3.

Selvini Palazzoli, M., Cecchin, G., Prata, G. and Boscolo, L. (1980a). Hypothesizing – circularity – neutrality. *Family Process*, 19, 3–12.

—— (1980b). The problem of the referring person. *Journal of Marital and Family Therapy*, 6, 3–9.

Speed, B. (1985). Evaluating the Milan Approach. In D. Campbell and R. Draper (eds) *Applications of Systemic Family Therapy: The Milan Approach*. London, Grune & Stratton.

Speed, B., Seligman, P., Kingston, P. and Cade, B. (1982). A team approach to therapy. *Journal of Family Therapy*, 4, 271–84.

Tomm, K. (1982). The Milan Approach to family therapy: a tentative report. In D. Freeman (ed.) *Treating Families with Special Needs*. Ottawa, Candian Association of Social Workers.

—— (1984a). One perspective on the Milan systemic approach. 1. Overview of development, theory and practice. *Journal of Marital and Family Therapy*, 10, 113–23.

—— (1984b). One perspective on the Milan systemic approach. 2. Description of session format, interviewing style and interventions. *Journal of Marital and Family Therapy*, 10, 253–71.

—— (1985). Circular interviewing: a multifaceted clinical tool. In D. Campbell and R. Draper (eds) *Applications of Systemic Family Therapy: The Milan Approach*. London, Grune & Stratton.

—— (1987a). Interventive interviewing. 1. Strategizing as a fourth guideline for the therapist. *Family Process*, 3–14, 26:1.

—— (1987b). Interventive interviewing. 2. Reflexive questioning as a means to enable self-healing. *Family Process*, 5–17, 26:2.

—— (1987c). Interventive interviewing. 3. Reflexive questioning: analysis and choice, guidelines for the therapist. *Family Process* (forthcoming).

Viaro, M. and Leonardi, P. (1983). Giving and getting information: an analysis of a family interview strategy. *Family Process*, 22, 27–42.

Watzlawick, P., Jackson, D.D. and Beavin, J. (1967). *Pragmatics of Human Communication: A Study of Interactional Patterns, Pathologies and Paradoxes.* New York, Norton.

CHAPTER 4

# STRUCTURAL FAMILY THERAPY

## Ruth Reay

## INTRODUCTION

Structural family therapy was developed initially by Salvador Minuchin and his colleagues in the 1960s as they worked with disadvantaged youngsters and their families at the Wiltwyck School, New York (Minuchin *et al*. 1967). Subsequently the model was refined and extended in work at the Philadelphia Child Guidance Clinic (Minuchin 1974) and with families with a psychosomatic child (Minuchin *et al*. 1978). In his most recent publication Minuchin (1984) adopts the metaphor of the kaleidoscope which captures the essence of the structural model. Looking through a kaleidoscope you see a colourful pattern usually with some symmetrical or repeating sequences. With a slight movement this vivid arrangement is transformed into an equally clear but different pattern which may nevertheless have some of the same sequences as the first pattern. At the point of transformation the regular structured forms dissolve, and momentarily it is difficult to recognize any pattern. Thus the viewer sees in succession a series of clearly defined structures which are changed, almost imperceptibly, by the slightest movement which rearranges the same elements into a new pattern. Looking through the kaleidoscope the interface between structure and process is apparent but because the process is glimpsed so fleetingly the eye tends to be drawn to the structure of each pattern. Similarly in structural family therapy the focus is the structure of the family and the family with therapist, but it is recognizable as a structure in constant process of forming and re-forming.

## THEORETICAL ASSUMPTIONS

The structures of families are delineated by boundaries into components called sub-systems which relate to each other to form different patterns. The boundaries are the rules which govern who belongs to which sub-systems and determine the shape and characteristic pattern of each unique family structure. The character of these boundaries is determined by two processes; the way in which decision-making is carried out, and how intimacy levels between members are managed.

There are several key sub-systems in families which relate to the different needs and tasks of different generations. For example, adults in families with children carry a parental function and form a parental sub-system. In order to carry out daily living activities families need an executive sub-system which makes decisions and ensures they are carried out. It can be formed by the adults, or by an adult and an older child. The adults have sexual affectional needs which are met by a spouse or partner sub-system. The children have play and companionship needs which are usually met in the sibling sub-systems. Each person in the family will belong to more than one sub-system; thus a rich matrix of sub-systems is created, and as with the kaleidoscope clear boundaries between them are essential if a workable pattern is to emerge. As Minuchin points out, 'the composition of subsystems . . . is not nearly as significant as the clarity of the subsystem boundaries' (Minuchin 1974 : 54).

Through his work with delinquent youngsters and their families at Wiltwyck School he developed the concepts of enmeshment and disengagement to describe the quality of these boundaries. He observed in the families characterized by enmeshed boundaries that it was difficult to distinguish a clear executive sub-system and so decision-making was problematic. If decisions were taken they were not carried out or subsequently undermined or vetoed by others. Individuals were not free to express independent opinions or to take autonomous decisions. Because of the inattention to individual wishes and needs, members, especially the children, engaged in a constant clamour for attention, but without any confident expectations of being heard. Often family members were stuck in endless, sometimes acrimonious and boisterous, arguments which never reached closure. There was frequently a lot of affection expressed but it was difficult for family members to have private space or time. Boundaries between adults and children were blurred and both generations were unable to relate to peers without experiencing intrusion from other generations. Thus, children constantly involved their parents and relied on them to sort out sibling rivalries. Lack of private space made it difficult for adults to develop satisfying partner relationships. The main characteristic of enmeshed families is that they are 'tightly interlocked' (Minuchin *et al.* 1967 : 358).

In contrast families described as disengaged were loosely interconnected with distant and often rigid boundaries. In these families it was also difficult to elicit satisfying responses from other family members but for different reasons. Because of the extreme distance between members affectional needs could not be met and even severe distress in one person remained unnoticed. Members failed to connect with each other in meaningful interactions and often with defeated outside helpers who tried to reach them. Each person seemed to be moving in 'isolated orbits' (Minuchin *et al.* 1967 : 254) and any actions failed to elicit responses from others.

In well-functioning families these extremes of enmeshment and disengagement are not present. Instead, the boundaries in the family are clear and firm with a capacity to change in response to developmental life stage events. For example it is usually functional for mothers and infants to be relatively enmeshed and for parents and young adults to be relatively disengaged. So it is important for boundaries to be clear and firm but also flexible and adaptable; they have dual needs to be rigid and elastic, to change while staying the same, to maintain coherence while constantly shifting.

Enmeshment and disengagement are useful concepts for understanding family relationships but the structure created by these different types of boundaries is more complex. For example both types of boundaries may be present in one family; a mother and children can be enmeshed while the father is disengaged. Additionally, the composition of the sub-systems in relation to the clearness of the boundaries produces different constellations. Relationships always involve two people and these two are usually relating to each other in the light of other relationships in which they are involved. Thus the young adults forming a new partnership relate to each other within the matrix of their relationships with their families of origin. In order for their new relationship to develop they need a clear boundary between them and their respective parents. Yet they relate to each other in the light of their relationship to their parents. So, even if they are physically distant from their parents they carry beliefs from their past which impinge upon the new relationship; also they continue as an adult child to their parents and need to negotiate the inclusion of their new partner in that relationship. There are many possibilities for the boundaries between these relationships to become unclear and a variety of ways have been evolved for dealing with their renegotiation. In traditional Chinese families the new wife joins the man's household and the primary position of the mother is preserved. In many western societies, especially in the more geographically and socially mobile sections, the young couple establish a clearly defined new unit to distance themselves from both sets of parents who often remain relatively apart until the arrival of grandchildren which signals the resumption of a closer bond between the generations. However, if, for example, a young man is overly enmeshed with his mother he may find it more difficult to forge a close bond with his new partner, and his mother may find it difficult to allow this to happen.

As both women compete for his primary affinity the situation may be resolved in unhelpful ways; either one person may become triangulated, or a detouring coalition may be formed. The man could become triangulated as he struggles to meet the women's demands by alternatively siding with one then the other. This arrangement is likely to persist if a higher level rule is implicitly agreed which disallows any comment upon it. As the two rivals compete and the third party struggle to satisfy contradictory demands considerable strain is usually experienced by all three. Sometimes the triangulated person finds the only way out of the dilemma is to become symptomatic by for example abusing alcohol, having psychosomatic pains, or psychiatric problems.

An alternative to this solution is for two people in the triad to form a detouring coalition against the third. For example, the young couple may unite in their criticism and hostility towards the man's mother and thus create a rigid boundary. If their attention is absorbed in maintaining this boundary they may have insufficient resources with which to build their own dyad. Furthermore, if this boundary remains impermeable the many possibilities for mother/son, mother-in-law/daughter-in-law, grandmother/mother, grandmother/father, grandmother/grandchildren relationships become blocked. These blockages may result in the development of further unhelpful coalitions such as the grandmother/grandchild against one parent.

The way in which detouring coalitions between parents can affect the development of children is well documented in the book *Psychosomatic Families* (Minuchin *et al.* 1978). In this type of constellation the parents avoid confronting their own issues, and especially any threat of conflict, by becoming preoccupied by a symptomatic child. A variation on this triadic arrangement is when parents join together in a coalition against a child who becomes a scapegoat. Coalitions are usually formed against another party and any number of people can join a coalition; for example a mother and two children can scapegoat a father, or a third child.

All families have to find ways of organizing these triadic relationships. Haley (1976) has calculated that in a three-generation family with four grandparents, two parents and two children, there is the possibility for fifty-six triads to form and that each person belongs to twenty-one triads. The relationships formed in these matrices tend to become dysfunctional when four characteristics are present:

1 The boundaries become rigid and impermeable, or diffuse and unclear.
2 Coalitions are formed against a third party.
3 The coalitions cross generational boundaries.
4 The coalition is denied or concealed.

In well-functioning families alliances between dyads are tolerated, and in many cases encouraged or enjoyed, because they do not have these characteristics. Rather they are characterized by permeability, flexibility and openness, and when generational boundaries are crossed shared activities are age appropriate and executive functions are maintained.

In families where the boundaries are too rigid or unclear there is often a breakdown in the executive functions. So in the first example, of the mother, son and his partner, as long as the mother is allowed to intrude, the decision-making powers of the partnership will be eroded: Haley (1976) and Madanes (1981) have emphasized the importance of the decision-making function which is dependent upon the existence of a hierarchy within the family structure. In their view many problems are caused and maintained when the hierarchy is in disarray. For example a parent's executive ability may be undermined by a coalition between the other parent and a child, or between a grandparent and a child. Alternatively the executive sub-system can abdicate decision-making and allow outside professionals to take over, or be tyrannized by a child's symptomatic or delinquent behaviour. A variation on these constellations is when a child is drawn into the executive sub-system and takes on parenting functions. Such a structure could be said to have a parental child. In some situations this can be functional; for example an older child may assist a single parent and learn some executive skills. The arrangement becomes dysfunctional when the child is expected to carry responsibilities beyond his or her years, becomes overburdened, sacrificing normal childhood development tasks.

Transitional stages in the life cycle are nodal points for the recalibration of boundaries. Families also have life events which do not arise from these usual transitions. Unemployment, sickness, unexpected death, chronic disability, separation of parents and children, and divorce are some examples. Each will require some renegotiation of boundaries; failure to create new clear boundaries can produce problems. For example, with a couple where the man becomes unemployed and the woman takes on the wage-earning role, if the new boundaries created by the role reversal are not redefined clearly they may experience difficulties; when divorce takes place multiple new boundaries are created and it is often difficult to synchronize the development of each new boundary.

Just as the composition of each kaleidoscopic image is dependent upon clear repetitive patterns, so is the functioning of the family dependent upon clear structural organization. The lines creating the kaleidoscopic patterns epitomize precision, but they are capable of apparently infinite change. Likewise the boundaries in a family are the key to its organization; while being crystal clear they also need to be flexibly responsive to change. The number of elements is limited but the patterns which can be formed are many.

# THE THERAPY PROCESS

When families come to therapy usually the process of their daily transactions have become bound by rules which create and maintain ill-defined and chaotic structures or rigid and unresponsive structures. The aim of therapy is to redefine the rules so that the structural pattern is unblocked and transformed. To restructure the family the therapist works at the interface of the new family boundaries encouraging shifts towards different, more functional, boundary definition. In families where the boundaries are too blurred and chaotic, efforts will be made to create firmer, more consistent rules governing decision-making and intimacy regulation. Where the boundaries are inflexible and unresponsive to individual needs, closer, more permeable boundaries will be encouraged. Where the hierarchy is in disarray the generational boundaries will be restored with executive functions more clearly defined.

Two types of therapeutic activity are needed; first, unhelpful transactions need to be blocked, and second, unused repertoires of transactions need to be activated. For example, in a family where the stepfather and mother are constantly bickering about the behaviour of the 13-year-old daughter the bickering may be blocked by asking the stepfather to withdraw from parenting functions for a while. The mother can then be in sole charge of her daughter and they can establish a clear generational boundary without interference from the parental quarrelling. As the subject of the parents' bickering is withdrawn they are released to spend time together as spouses. Thus, new more clearly defined boundaries are drawn between the generations and hitherto unused transactions between the spouses, and between mother and daughter, can be brought into play. There are often several stages in the restructuring process and it may be necessary to activate transitionary structures which in turn require changing before an optimum constellation is achieved.

The aim of therapy is to create a structure with clear and flexible boundaries which enables family members to carry out age-appropriate life tasks in a way which is congruent with their family's cultural context. Families are offered opportunities to experience different transactional patterns within the relative safety of the therapy session. Frequently they are given tasks to do between sessions which will reinforce these transactions.

The aim is to identify the structural properties of the family which are creating and maintaining the problem behaviour. Using the problem behaviour as a medium for the work the therapy seeks to change the structure which is perpetuating the problem behaviour. For example, in a family where the son's difficult behaviour is being maintained by an alliance between mother and son which undermines the parental authority, the therapy would be concerned with how the parents could unite together to create a firm generational boundary in order to help him to overcome his difficulties. The content of the therapy sessions would be change in the son's behaviour but the process of therapy would be concerned with changing the family structure.

The goals agreed with the family will be concerned with changes in behaviour often expressed in interactional terms but the structural changes will usually remain implicit. Although the structural changes may not be included overtly in negotiated agreements they quickly become apparent in the therapy sessions as the therapist seeks to block malfunctional structures and activate new ones.

The model recognizes that there is a complex interactional process mediating behaviour and beliefs. Consequently the family's belief system becomes an integral part of the therapy process, being alternatively challenged or used as a lever by the therapist.

Usually therapy begins when all members living in the family home are invited to a meeting with the therapist. The presence of everyone ensures that a comprehensive assessment of the family structure can be made. Where other professionals, extended kin or members of an immediate social network appear to be closely involved they can be usefully included in the early sessions. It is especially important to invite people, such as influential grandparents or enmeshed professionals, with whom it may be necessary to make clearer boundaries. As therapy progresses it is often useful to include and exclude different sub-systems in the sessions to create or reinforce new boundaries. For example, older children who have usurped parental functions can be excused from some sessions when the parents are being helped to negotiate directly with younger children.

Therapeutic change is accomplished when a more functional structural pattern has become relatively well established. This can be observed in the secure repetition of functional boundary maintenance within the sessions and in the reported transactions which occur between sessions.


# THE ROLE OF THE THERAPIST

## Hypothesizing

Just as the family requires an organizational framework so does the process of therapy. This is provided by generating a series of hypotheses which focus on the structure of the family and how this may be creating and maintaining the problem behaviour which has brought the family into therapy. These hypotheses form the boundaries of the therapy and like family boundaries they need to be clear but capable of changing. The referral information is used to develop a few hypotheses which can be tested, elaborated and if necessary discarded as the therapy proceeds.

The questions which need to be asked are

1 What is the quality of the boundaries?
2 Is the balance between enmeshment and disengagement enabling individuals to carry out life tasks appropriate for their age?
3 Are boundaries sufficiently clear without producing either too much confusion or too much rigidity?
4 How are the triadic structures organized?
5 How are executive functions carried out?

It is possible to generate hypotheses on sparse information by taking note of the constitution and developmental stage of the family, and the nature of the problem.

With childhood behavioural problems it can be hypothesized that the parental sub-system is in some way malfunctioning. With a single-parent family it may be that the parent has an insufficient support network, or is experiencing interference from another sub-system such as the grandparents or the professional network, or there may be an overburdened parental child. With a two-parent family some of the same factors may apply and in addition it may be that there are unresolved issues between the parents which can be avoided by forming a detouring coalition to concentrate on a problematic child. If the problem is presented as being a difficult adolescent it is likely that the family are having problems renegotiating the parent–child boundary and the spouse–spouse boundary with the parents failing to accord sufficient autonomy to the young person and failing to realign their spouse spouse relationship without a child, and he or she having problems establishing peer relationships. In cases of child abuse it may be that the parents are detouring their conflict and scapegoating the child. With child sexual abuse the generation boundaries may have become blurred with the parents abdicating their protective responsibilities to meet inappropriately their own affectional and sexual needs. When the presenting problem is of psychosomatic complaints then it is likely that boundaries are enmeshed and the response to developmental life stages has become rigid.

Using the referral information to develop these fairly broad hypotheses the therapist starts the first session with a framework for collecting data. Indeed, before the first therapy session it may be possible to think about the family members' responses in relation to the hypothesis. For example, if parents of an adolescent express doubts about getting their offspring to come to the first session this is information about the way they carry out their executive functions. Frequently a mother in a family will express doubt about her partner's willingness to be involved in therapy; this is information about the organization of the hierarchy in the family. She feels able to speak on his behalf and is taking the power to decide how he is involved; if he does choose to stay away he is concurring with this arrangement. However, the power of each partner disqualifies that of the other, because by staying away he very often undermines the change activity of the other members. Madanes (1981) calls this an incongruent hierarchy. With this sort of information it would be possible to hypothesize that the executive sub-system was in disarray with an unresolved power struggle interfering with their ability to deal with life tasks.

## Joining

The therapist is able to engage the family in the change process only if attention is paid to what Minuchin has called the joining process. In all interpersonal transactions there is some process of accommodation; it has been shown that even tiny infants mirror the rhythm of adult conversation, and adults tend to respond to their conversational partners with non-verbal behaviour which mirrors that of their counterpart. Most of this behaviour is out of our awareness and all therapists will have some natural skills in relating. However, joining is a more self-conscious activity where the therapist actively mirrors the family's communication patterns, accommo-dating to their verbal and non-verbal language and style of communication. The therapist takes careful note of members' various ways of making contact and through a process of mimesis tries to make a personal connection with each person which fits his or her style. Thus, with very young children the communication will tend to include strong non-verbal elements; with de-pressed individuals the approach will be low key and slow; and with helpless, defeated parents their hopelessness will be accepted. Family members are validated by the therapist's non-judgemental response in which painful transactions are acknowledged and placed in a more positive frame. For example a mother's shielding of a child's misbehaviour can be labelled as protective. The therapist tracks the family's concerns searching for and following themes such as closeness and distance, and ways of dealing with conflict.

Hierarchical arrangements are noted but not challenged until the family is sufficiently joined. An example of this is noting when a father is clearly in charge of the family by directing all communication respectfully through him. Minuchin calls joining 'the glue which holds therapy together' (Minuchin and Fishman 1981 : 32); it is an ongoing process which needs to be given constant attention. It is often a difficult task; for example if parents are very critical of the behaviour of their adolescent child it is necessary to find a way of joining with their concern and anger without appearing to take their side against the youngster.

# Enactments

The therapist needs to gain access to the family's usual transactional patterns rather than learning secondhand information from their descriptions of their behaviour. A therapeutically potent way of doing this is to request members of the family to enact a transaction within the session. It may take the form of a discussion between two people while others observe, or an activity such as making a list, drawing a picture or making a decision. The purposes are

1 To enable the therapy team to see how the members transact rather than hearing them describe how they believe they transact.
2 To push the transactions beyond their usual thresholds in order to test the flexibility of the system.
3 To enable the participants to try out different repertoires of transacting in a safe environment.

An enactment usually has three stages. In the first stage the therapist observes the family, looking for spontaneously repeating sequences which flag structural characteristics. Then the family are requested to enact that sequence around a particular issue; at this point the therapist becomes an observer. In the final stage the therapist becomes more active and, by prolonging the time sequence, blocking parts of transactions, involving different combinations of family members or suggesting alternative transactions, enables the family to experience a new transaction.

Using enactments can be very useful in actively engaging family members in therapy, especially if there is a wide range of ages, and in improving the range and quality of the information available. They also enable the therapist who has been inducted into the family's rule system to become more disengaged.

An example may illuminate these points; suppose it has been hypothesized that in the Dalton family the mother is enmeshed with her daughter and the father is peripheral, producing an unmanageable 7-year-old. The mother could be asked to talk with her husband about how they deal with their daughter's tantrums. The therapist could then observe how involved each parent is, how knowledgeable they are about their daughter, whether they disagree about her management and so on. While they are talking it would be possible to see how the daughter becomes involved and whether she is an indispensable part of the couple's interactional pattern. Further enactments involving the mother and daughter, then the father and daughter, could be used to see if there are any differences in the way the parents relate to their daughter, especially in the dimensions of control and intimacy. If these enactments seemed to confirm the hypothesis that the father is peripheral and the mother and daughter overly enmeshed small changes could be encouraged. For example, mother could be asked to observe while father and daughter engaged in some nurturant play. In this way it would be possible to see if the father had the relevant skills to become involved with his daughter and whether the mother and daughter were able to become more disengaged.

It will be seen that these enactments relate closely to the hypothesis and are not merely random. With the focus provided by some hypothesis the therapist can organize and direct the flow of information to avoid overload. In every situation perception is circumscribed in some way. The advantage of developing hypotheses is that the theory informing action is explicit, and if a series of hypotheses are available then a sample of observations can be made.

Using enactments brings into strong relief the idea that structures are always in process of change and that data collection can become a potent force within that process. Additionally, in widening the focus of attention the family's reality or view of the problem is challenged.

## Challenging the family's reality

All families develop their own way of seeing the world, their own reality. These frames are built up over generations and are tempered by exposure to cultural influences.

Several authors have documented in some detail how these world views influence the way the families approach the world (Reiss 1981; Kantor and Lehr 1975; Olson *et al.* 1983). Minuchin proposes that one of the key tasks of the structural therapist is to challenge these realities because they constrict the repertoire of behaviours open to the family. The first challenge to the family's view of reality is when they are invited to meet the therapist as a family; already their frame, which has identified one member as having a problem, is thrown into question. This doubt is reinforced when the therapist starts to remark upon how members are linked together. This can be done in many ways but must always be done respectfully and with a non-blaming stance. This is because families who have come for help, or been sent, are hypersensitive to criticism, feeling already that they have failed in some way. Also people become addicted to their own world view, it is their explanatory scheme and everything is viewed through this frame. A challenge to this frame will have a ripple effect and may imply a radical readjustment of a comfortable and familiar world view. Consequently new frames will be resisted unless they are offered in a spirit of concern and sometimes disguised by humour or playfulness.

Minuchin has developed a rich vein of concrete metaphors which challenge in a way which disarms the family's usual objections (Minuchin and Fishman 1981). In challenging enmeshment he uses bodily images to point out how a person's autonomy is being invaded by others. For example he may ask a daughter if her hair or skin are her own, remark upon the strength of a son's hands when his father demonstrates his right to adjust his personal space, or comment upon whose voice or memory is being used. He uses images of height, weight and loudness when challenging beliefs about who holds power in the family. The use of such indirect language, often employed in a bantering tone, allows the therapist to challenge their reality while simultaneously joining with the family. Another useful way of widening the family's view of reality is to highlight complementarity. The therapist begins by remarking on the reciprocity of family members' behaviour. This can be done by describing the behaviour of one family member and assigning responsibility for that behaviour to someone else. For example the therapist could say to the parents of a difficult adolescent, 'You seem to be responsible for all your son's decisions', and to the son, 'How did you manage to get your parents to do all your work?' In this way the therapist is highlighting the interconnectedness of the behaviour, and without appearing to criticize either directly, he joins with both simultaneously. Minuchin calls this the 'kick and stroke' technique where the therapist validates a situation while also challenging it.

## Intensification and unbalancing

Minuchin remarks that an enactment is 'like a conversation' whereas intensification is 'like a shouting match between the therapist and a hard of hearing family' (Minuchin and Fishman 1981 : 141). Intensification and unbalancing can be difficult to use because they demand that both the therapist and the family break the usual rules of courtesy. Intensification can be achieved by repetition, prolonging the length of a transaction beyond the normal comfort levels, using different spatial arrangments and by refusing to be inducted into the family's well-established transactions.

Repetition can be achieved with a simple 'broken record' technique where the same question or comment is repeated by the therapist until it is heard. It can also be achieved by repeating the same message in many guises. For example in the McCowan family where it is necessary to challenge their denial of the seriousness of their son's suicide attempt they are asked to see every transaction as if he was no longer alive. Thus when the mother mentions the household chores the therapist asks who will take over the son's chores after his death; when the brother talks about his graduation he is asked how the family will celebrate the date of his brother's suicide each year after he is dead, and so on. In this way the impact his absence would have on the family is traced through the various transactions of the family.

The therapist can extend this line of questioning long after the family have signalled that they find it uncomfortable. Simple enactments can be prolonged past the family's comfort threshold to increase intensity. For example, a couple who fail to resolve their conflict because one partner psychologically leaves the field, can be encouraged to continue their interaction past several 'leave-takings' until a different way of resolving the conflict is found. Seating arrangements can be changed so that, for example, dyads who avoid close proximity are asked to sit closer together to lessen their disengagement.

Families who are organized around a sick or 'bad' member have a vested interest in maintaining their role and so attempt to enlist the therapist to rescue, treat or punish that person. Many agencies are organized to carry out these functions by for example removing problematic family members. By resisting these pressures the therapist can create intensity which forces the family to find an alternative, hopefully more constructive, solution. A common example is the helpless parents who have failed to control a misbehaving teenager and demand his or her removal from the home. The parents' helpless stance elicits controlling responses from welfare agencies which may solve the problem temporarily. But it leaves the parents in a more helpless position and as the professionals take over more decision-making, their opportunities for regaining control are further eroded. If the therapist can ignore the demands for controlling responses and insist that the teenager remain in the care of the parents while they are enabled to take charge of the situation then the intensity of the situation is not relieved and the motivation to find a solution is retained. Use of intensification in situations like this involves risk and can be used only if two principles are observed: first, that the parents receive adequate support to change their parenting approach, and second, that the legal and agency frameworks are prepared to provide an adequate backup structure. The use of intensification with the added dimension of a statutory mandate in child abuse cases is well documented by the team working at the Rochdale NSPCC unit (Dale *et al.* 1986).

Haley (1980) uses this approach with troublesome and psychotic young people to avoid imprisonment or hospitalization. In both these accounts the restructuring effect of the intensification is to restore the parents to an executive position in the hierarchy by making the boundaries clearer and where appropriate disengaging cross-generational coalitions.

As with intensification unbalancing involves an unexpected response from the therapist who appears to give up any pretence of fairness or neutrality in order to join with one part of the family. This can be done by affiliating with one person or sub-system, ignoring some members, or forming a coalition with a member against other members. The purpose is usually to change the hierarchical arrangement of the structure.

For example, in a family where the father is undermined and isolated it may be necessary for the therapist to affiliate strongly with him temporarily in order to change the power differentials within the structure. A common situation is where the parents have been rendered helpless by the symptomatic behaviour of their child and the therapist forms a coalition with the parents against the child in order to restore their executive position in the family. This can be extremely difficult to do because it is frequently the lack of parental skill which has caused the problem behaviour and they are often defeated and passive and so difficult to activate. Also, the therapist may have to join in criticism of the child which may seem quite unjustified. A type of reverse unbalancing known as runaway unbalancing can also be used to provoke change in a rigid structure. With this technique the therapist aligns strongly with the existing hierarchical arrangement in order to activate a counteracting response. For instance with an overly enmeshed dyad the care-taking activity of the dominant person can be encouraged to ridiculous extremes in order to provoke the submissive person into more assertive autonomous behaviour. It will be evident that the timing and pacing of the unbalancing intervention is very sensitive, consequently the therapist needs to be clear about the goals to be achieved, and able to work with confidence in highly charged emotional situations.

## EFFECTIVE THERAPISTS

The structural model is based upon an underlying assumption that to function well families require certain characteristics, the most salient of which are clear boundaries and an effective executive. The goals of the therapist are to help the family to achieve a structure which is congruent with these characteristics and which also fits their prevailing beliefs and cultural milieu. The therapist takes an active role in defining these goals and enabling the family to achieve them. The stance is one of challenge to the existing structure and education towards a more functional one.

Therapists use their own position in relation to the family structure as a restructuring medium. They therefore need to be able to draw upon a wide repertoire of skills at a variety of levels of emotional intensity. Within the space of one session they could move from a detached position of observer of transactions, through to one of director and choreographer of enactments, to a position of intense proximity to one person in the system while excluding another. Families inevitably include a wide range of people with varying ages, styles and modes of communication. Therefore the therapist needs to be able to use many verbal and non-verbal methods to capture and maintain therapeutic movement.

In addition to a wide repertoire of skills structural therapists need to have a clear grasp of the direction and rationale of their interventions. They need to be able to hold a clear direction while responding to new information and using whatever content is presented to pursue the process aims. While working at the surface level with the minutiae of the problem behaviour the therapist needs to be aware of the broader canvas of the repetitive sequences maintaining the structure and the multiple levels of meaning invested in them. To carry out this enterprise successfully the therapist needs to have well-developed communication skills, some of which can run on automatic pilot much of the time.

The therapist needs to be sensitive and responsive to the emotional content of transactions, and must not only tolerate high levels of emotional intensity, but also use them for therapeutic change.

Because of these multiple demands therapists usually work in teams using a live supervision model in which some of the functions can be shared. For example, the live supervisor can undertake a substantial part of the observation of process, generate more useful hypotheses and help the therapist to maintain therapeutic direction. As the therapist works in close proximity to the family it is hard not to become inducted into the family's rule system and the live supervisor helps to prevent this happening.

Practitioners have found that restructuring can be carried out in many styles; a quiet voice can sometimes command more attention than a more dramatic tone. Learning to move about during family sessions has freed up many therapists and helped them to avoid becoming frozen in an attentive, passive stance. As different aspects of systems theory have developed into distinctive schools of therapy (Fisch *et al.* 1982; Palazzoli *et al.* 1980), structural therapists have been able to integrate some additional techniques into the structural model. For example, circular questioning (Palazzoli *et al.* 1980) can be used effectively to create intensity; Fisch and Weakland's methods of eliciting information about the family's 'position' (belief system) can be useful when preparing to challenge the family's reality.

The structural model has a clearly defined set of skills which can be readily learnt. The training model is congruent with the theoretical framework in that the trainer adopts a hierarchical position in relation to the trainees challenging their preconceptions and through demonstration, coaching and supervision educating them to become structural therapists.

The main principles of the conceptual model are easy to grasp and herein lies a danger. The inexperienced therapist can use some concepts, for example the axes of enmeshment and disengagement, as shorthand to describe and analyse transactions which are complex and subtle. Because the concepts are elegantly economical teams can suffer from tunnel vision and self-fulfilling hypothesizing. When teams find that they are repeatedly seeing the same family structure, they need to examine their work carefully or seek outside consultation. If they are failing to evolve new or more complex hypotheses, their own system is in danger of stagnating or dying.

The micro-skills of the main intervention can be mastered at an early stage of training producing beginning therapists who practise them with apparent fluency but without having a secure rationale for using them with a particular family at a particular stage in therapy. Often inexperienced therapists fail to pace their interventions sensitively and do not know how to use the outcomes of their interventions therapeutically. It is the function of the trainer and/or live supervisor to recognize these phenomena and to take remedial action. Of course these pitfalls during the early stages of practice are not confined to the structural model of family therapy! As Lynn Hoffman points out, it is an easily learned theoretical framework but its application to practice is much more complex and requires 'much experience and extensive live supervision by a master' (Hoffman 1981 : 271). Because the model has been developed by charismatic, virtuoso practitioners, and mainly in the USA, it has been suggested that it may be less suited to the more reserved style of the British therapist (Burnham 1986). However, it is being used extensively by many British agencies and appears to lend itself particularly well to work with families with child-focused problems.

## A FAMILY IN THERAPY

A simultaneous request for Mrs McNulty's reception into residential care was received by a social services area team from Mrs McNulty's daughter, Mrs Wilcox, and her family doctor. The referral information stated that Mrs McNulty was suffering from senile dementia and had required virtually full-time care for the last two years. This had been given by her daughter, Mrs Wilcox who lived close by, but recently the strain was proving too much and her doctor advised that she must have some respite.

Using this information and knowledge of who is in the family the team generated the following hypotheses:

1 That Mrs McNulty's dementia had reached the stage when she could no longer be cared for at home.
2 That the family were experiencing difficulty in managing two transitional life stages and the structural arrangement had become stuck.
3 That the request for residential care was a conflict avoidance mechanism. The conflict may be, for example, between Mr and Mrs Wilcox, Mrs Wilcox and Mildred, Mr and Mrs Wilcox and Angela.
4 Mrs Wilcox and Mrs McNulty were enmeshed and the referral was an attempt by other members of the family to re-engage Mrs Wilcox with them.
5 Mrs Wilcox was an overburdened executive with Mr Wilcox and Mildred disengaged. The referral was an attempt to create a substitute executive.
6 Mrs Wilcox was triangulated between her husband and mother, or between her husband and sister.

*Figure 4.1* The McNulty/Wilcox family

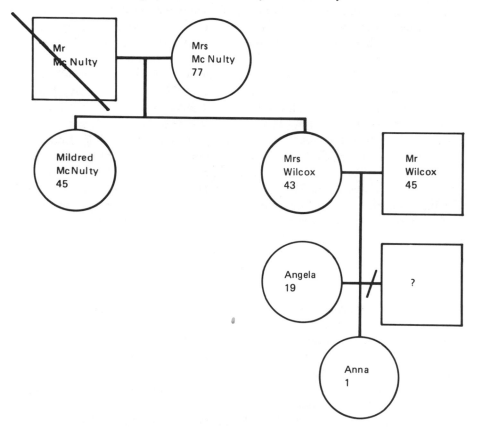

These hypotheses could be tested by:

1 Tracking Mrs McNulty's needs and how they are met.
2 Finding out how decisions are reached and carried out, especially the decision to come to the Social Services Department.
3 Exploring the boundaries between various sub-systems, to see how flexible they are; for example seeing how the two sisters co-operate in caring for their mother and how Mr Wilcox is involved.
4 Discussing how life stage transitions are usually managed, for example Angela's pregnancy and the arrival of her daughter.

The therapy which is described took place over a period of four months with five family meetings. In the first session it quickly became apparent that Mrs Wilcox and her GP were the only people who had briefly discussed the possibility of residential care for Mrs McNulty and that other family members including Mrs McNulty had not been aware of this. Mr Wilcox and

Angela forcefully expressed their shock and anger at such a thought saying they had understood that Mrs Wilcox had applied to the council for a four-bedroomed house so that Mrs McNulty could come to live with them. Mrs Wilcox responded to these criticisms in a despondent way, saying she did not want her mother to have to go to the old people's home but she couldn't go on worrying about her falling and being alone at night.

This information and transaction suggested that Mrs Wilcox was isolated and overburdened in the family and had called for support from outside professionals to reinforce the executive sub-system; it also suggested that Mr Wilcox and Angela were in a sibling-type coalition which gave them the right to criticize without any obligations to carry out executive functions. This hypothesis was tested by asking Mr Wilcox and Angela to talk together about how they thought the problem could be solved. This enactment demonstrated that Mr Wilcox and Angela co-operated well together but that their knowledge of Mrs McNulty's needs was sketchy. At this point Mrs Wilcox was drawn into the enactment with the request that she detail for her husband and daughter the tasks that she carried out for her mother each day. Mrs Wilcox did this very hesitatingly, dismissing most of the tasks as 'what any daughter would do for her mother'. As she talked her sister Mildred, her husband and daughter felt free to criticize and disqualify her. Mrs McNulty also undermined her daughter by repeatedly saying she could manage perfectly well on her own. However, a detailed tracking of how different members of the family were involved in supporting Mrs McNulty's daily living, showed that she needed almost constant supervision which was provided exclusively by Mrs Wilcox. Mr Wilcox and Angela were heavily invested in caring for Anna and were like a small new family unit. Mrs Wilcox was largely excluded from this triad as she was drawn more and more into hourly contact with her ageing mother. Mildred had very little contact with her mother and was heavily invested in her career; however, as an older sister she maintained the right to criticize Mrs Wilcox's efforts.

It was clear that the family believed that they should care for their own dependants within the family and that to consider requesting residential care Mrs Wilcox must have been feeling pretty desperate. This desperation was easy to appreciate in view of her disengagement from any executive support within her own generation. However, it seemed likely that even if the executive was strengthened by outside professional help it may be covertly eroded by the non-cooperation of either Mr Wilcox, Mildred or Mrs McNulty or any combination of the three. This seemed a clear example of an incongruent hierarchy where the care-taking competence of Mrs Wilcox was disqualified by the denial of the need for help from Mrs McNulty and by the critical non-supportive stance of Mr Wilcox (supported by Angela) and Mildred.

In view of the strong family belief that they should care for their own which Mrs Wilcox's request had violated it seemed that a more powerful family imperative to avoid conflict at all cost must also exist. By enlisting outside help Mrs Wilcox could avoid any conflict which may arise if she called for more assistance from her husband, her sister or her daughter. This hypothesis was tested through a series of enactments between Mrs Wilcox and Mr Wilcox, Mrs Wilcox and Mildred, and Mildred and Mr Wilcox in which they discussed a number of issues such as how decisions were made, whether sons and daughters should have similar or different responsibilities towards elderly parents, and how the various tasks involved in the care of Mrs McNulty could be shared out between family members. It became clear from these enactments that Mildred and Mr Wilcox had many differences of opinion and that Mrs Wilcox alternatively tried to please both. Thus she was triangulated and unable to take effective decisions without either displeasing one person or having the decision rescinded. She worked hard to avoid disagreeing with either and also to keep them from coming into close contact because 'sparks always flew' when they were together. Mr Wilcox avoided conflict by disengaging from his wife, to the extent that he was unaware of her level of stress. He spent many hours playing with his granddaughter, Anna, because he thought Angela should have 'some fun'. This self-appointed task also gave him opportunity to meet his own affectional needs. Although she resented this take-over at times, Angela was not prepared to challenge him for fear of the conflict it may provoke and to avoid any threat to her freedom. The family structure could be summarized as two enmeshed sub-systems:

1 Mrs McNulty and Mrs Wilcox
2 Mr Wilcox, Angela and Anna.

Their two sub-systems were disengaged from each other and in addition Mrs Wilcox was triangulated by Mr Wilcox and Mildred; as a consequence of this structural arrangement the executive was in disarray, hence the appeal for outside assistance from the GP and Social Services.

Before constructive decisions could be made by the family about the care of Mrs McNulty a clear executive had to be formed. This could be achieved by de-triangulating Mrs Wilcox and re-aligning at least one dyad (either Mr and Mrs Wilcox or Mrs Wilcox and Mildred) in a clear executive sub-system. This would involve a series of restructuring moves using intensification and unbalancing. They began in an unexpected place when the therapist, sensing Angela's underlying resentment of her father's central role in caring for Anna, affiliated strongly with Angela in her role as a young single mother. While being careful to define Mr Wilcox as a grandfather who played a very special role in Anna's life the therapist talked at length with Angela about the rewards and difficulties of being a single parent. During this prolonged conversation other family members were ignored. With encouragement

Angela began to talk more authoritatively about what she wanted for her daughter and how she would differ from her parents in the way she brought her up. This had two effects: it disengaged Angela from Mr Wilcox and offered a model to Mrs Wilcox of a strong young woman expressing her own views without any family calamity ensuing. Gradually the therapist began to include Mrs Wilcox in this conversation, asking her advice as a woman about the needs of daughters, thus placing her firmly in a hierarchical position in relation to Angela and Mr Wilcox. The women were framed as decision-makers while Mr Wilcox was complimented on the skills he had helped Angela achieve and on his freedom as a grandfather to spoil his granddaughter. When Angela said she wanted Anna's speech to improve Mrs Wilcox was encouraged to help her to plan how this could be achieved. Thus an alliance between Mrs Wilcox and Angela was built while Mr Wilcox's enmeshment with Angela was gently challenged. He was then consulted as a son-in-law who could be more detached about Mrs McNulty's position and encouraged to talk with his sister-in-law about how the family could ensure that Mrs McNulty could be kept safe. It became apparent that, although they disagreed on many things, they both felt excluded from contributing to Mrs McNulty's care because she openly expressed her preference for Mrs Wilcox. During a very long enactment between Mr Wilcox and Mildred, whenever they showed sign of disagreeing or becoming locked in uncomfortable silences, Mrs Wilcox's attempts to reduce the tension were blocked by the therapist. By insisting that they come up with some practical suggestions the therapist ensured that the dyad demonstrated that they could resolve conflict without triangulating Mrs Wilcox. The therapist also insisted that the suggestions were acceptable to Mrs Wilcox, as the chief care-taker to date, thus placing her on a more equal footing with her husband and sister. Thus, by first affiliating with Angela, then with Angela and Mrs Wilcox, and then with Mr Wilcox and Mildred, the therapist unbalanced the structure leaving the way clear for a rearrangement in which there were clearer executive sub-systems, less conflict avoidance and more opportunity for individuals to achieve life stage tasks. If the therapist had not included the four generations the interconnectedness of the sub-systems would not have been experienced and the possibilities for restructuring unrealized. For instance, as long as Mr Wilcox remained enmeshed with Angela, and in unresolved conflict with Mildred he would have remained unavailable to his wife. At the end of five family sessions the three adults in the second generation had agreed on a programme of care for Mrs McNulty which included contributions from themselves and the home help service, and a day centre. Mr and Mrs Wilcox were assisting Angela to parent Anna in a less intrusive way and Mildred was re-engaged with her mother in a more satisfying way for them both. Throughout the family sessions, Mrs McNulty was consulted in a respectful way about her needs and wishes and as far as she was able, given her degree of dementia, she made them known.

# REFERENCES

Burnham, J. (1986). *Family Therapy: First Steps Towards a Systemic Approach.* London, Tavistock.

Dale, P., Davies, M., Morrison, T. and Waters, J. (1986). *Dangerous Families: Assessment and Treatment of Child Abuse.* London, Tavistock.

Fisch, R., Weakland, J.H. and Segal, L. (1982). *The Tactics of Change: Doing Therapy Briefly.* San Francisco, Jossey-Bass.

Haley, J. (1976). *Problem-Solving Therapy.* San Francisco, Jossey-Bass.

—— (1980). *Leaving Home: Therapy of Disturbed Young People.* New York, McGraw-Hill.

Hoffman, L. (1981). *Foundations of Family Therapy.* New York, Basic Books.

Kantor, D. and Lehr, W. (1975). *Inside the Family.* San Francisco, Jossey-Bass.

Madanes, C. (1981). *Strategic Family Therapy.* San Francisco, Washington, London, Jossey-Bass.

Minuchin, S. (1974). *Families and Family Therapy.* London, Tavistock.

—— (1984). *Family Kaleidoscope: Images of Violence and Healing.* Cambridge, Mass., Harvard University Press.

Minuchin, S. and Fishman, H.C. (1981). *Techniques of Family Therapy.* Cambridge, Mass., Harvard University Press.

Minuchin, S., Montalvo, B., Guerney, B.G., Rosman, B.L. and Schumer, F. (1967). *Families of the Slums: An Exploration of their Structure and Treatment.* New York, Basic Books.

Minuchin, S., Rosman, B.L. and Baker, L. (1978). *Psychosomatic Families: Anorexia Nervosa in Context.* Cambridge, Mass., Harvard University Press.

Olson, D.H., McCubbin, H.I., Barnes, H., Larsen, A., Muxen, M. and Wilson, M. (1983). *Families: What Makes them Work?* Beverly Hills, Calif., Sage.

Palazzoli, M., Cecchin, G., Prata, C. and Boscolo, L. (1980). Hypothesising, circularity, neutrality: three guidelines for the conductor of the session. *Family Process*, 19, 3–12.

Reiss, D. (1981). *The Family's Construction of Reality.* Cambridge, Mass., Harvard University Press.

# CHAPTER 5

# BEHAVIOURAL FAMILY THERAPY: SYSTEMS, STRUCTURES AND STRATEGIES

## *Ian R.H. Falloon*

## INTRODUCTION

Behaviour therapists have always considered the family members a vital resource in their problem-oriented treatment approaches. However, the family system has not been considered the only system of relevance in the mental health field. In one of the earliest descriptions of a community mental health programme that was based on behaviour therapy principles Tharp and Wetzel outlined the relevance of the individual's social network:

> Reinforcers lie within the environment of the individual, and are imbedded within this social nexus: whether the reinforcer is a smile or a candy, a bicycle or a slap, reinforcement is frequently dispersed by people articulated into the individual's social environment. If the environment is the hospital, these people are the nurses, doctors or other patients: if the environment is the school, they are the principal, teachers or other pupils; if it is the family, they are siblings, the spouse or the parents. . . . the potent reinforcers for an individual ordinarily lie within his natural environment, and these reinforcers are controlled by those people to whom he is naturally related.
>
> (Tharp and Wetzel 1969 : 3)

This broad concept of 'the family', that extends beyond the nuclear family and blood relationships to all persons in the social environment who have an intimate, confiding, day-to-day relationship with an individual, is the basis for the many applications of social learning theory principles that have developed under the aegis of behaviour therapy.

*Family therapy in Britain*

# THEORETICAL ASSUMPTIONS

Behavioural family therapy tends to view the family as a major health enhancing resource rather than a 'pathogenic' factor. It is assumed that at all times every member of the family unit is doing his or her very best to maximize pleasant events in their immediate social environment and to minimize unpleasant events. All family behaviour is viewed in these terms. No matter how destructive the behaviour may appear to outside observers it is always considered to be that individual's best effort to cope with the interpersonal situation which he or she is experiencing. The constraints placed upon an individual at any particular time will determine his or her choice of responses. The choice will always be that individual's perceived 'best' option in the circumstances. Rarely will this be his or her 'only' option, and the choice will be determined by his or her problem-solving functions. The choice of a response to a situation will be affected by many factors. These include:

1  Environmental factors relating to the current situation. The precise environmental contingencies, for example time, place, activity, person, will play an important role in the selection of a response.
2  Psychological factors relating to the current situation. These will include previous experiences of responding to the specific situation or similar contexts, the person's ability to recall and replicate previous successful responses, the presence of cues that trigger cognitive or emotional responses, both pleasurable or unpleasant thoughts and feelings.
3  Physiological factors relating to the current situation. Such factors as hormonal levels, drug effects, including alcohol and illicit drugs, may affect a person's choice of responses. Physical assets or handicaps or other constraints may be important.
4  Other social factors such as availability of finances, ethnic and cultural background must be considered.

All these factors may govern whether a child responds to his mother's request that he pick up his clothes by complying immediately, giving her a cheeky answer, refusing to comply or saying he will do it later. Given the complexity of human problem-solving in most home environments, behaviour therapists have not chosen any one frame of reference, such as assuming that problem behaviours stem basically from early developmental experiences, or biological anomalies, or interpersonal contexts. Rather the behaviour therapist takes each problem at its face value. An analysis of the exact contingencies that increase the likelihood of performance of the problem behaviour is made using a combination of interview, and wherever feasible, direct observation of the problem behaviour. When a problem behaviour is manifest repeatedly, it is assumed that a small number of common factors occur either as antecedents of the behaviour or as consequences and that these factors tend to serve as prompts and reinforcements of that behaviour. These contingencies are usually not fully recognized by family members, or if recognized, they find themselves unable to modify the context in a consistent fashion. The behaviour therapist assists the family to pinpoint the contingencies and to develop strategies to modify these sequences consistently. I will provide examples of this behavioural assessment in the next section, on the therapy process.

It is assumed that optimal family functioning occurs when individual family members are all able to maximize their creative potentials within their socio-cultural environment. This is usually possible when the problem-solving functions of the family unit are highly efficient and allow rapid long-term resolution of environmental stress factors, and efficient resolution of basic living needs, such as housing, nutrition, education, intimate interpersonal contacts, and so on. Apart from major stresses related to life's hazards, for example death, accidents, illness, job losses and divorce, family problem-solving may assist individuals in their achievement of personal goals in work, relationships, aesthetic and sports pursuits. The emphasis is upon mutual, shared problem-solving to minimize the collective stresses and maximize the collective achievements of the family group as well as the social network or community in which the family lives.

Problems are defined as specific behaviours that mediate against this process of mutual family development. They usually result in long-term stress and are associated with inefficient problem-solving by the family unit. Such breakdowns in functioning may contribute to the aetiology of mental disorders where stress is considered a causal factor. To date, there is limited evidence that stress plays any *specific* role in the development of mental disorders. The best evidence supports the view that stress factors may expedite the development of major mental disorders, trigger florid episodes, and mediate against rapid remissions. For these reasons the behavioural family therapist tends to make unequivocal statements that 'There is no evidence that anything families do actually *causes* a person to develop a mental illness', but on the other hand 'There is abundant evidence that suggests that the manner in which families cope with the mental illnesses of its members has a significant influence on its outcome'. The studies of 'expressed emotion' provide the clearest evidence for these statements (Falloon and McGill 1985).

## THE THERAPY PROCESS

The behavioural approach is often equated with specific behavioural change strategies, such as contingency contracting or operant conditioning. While it is undoubtedly true that most cases treated according to this approach employ such strategies frequently, and that most published research deals almost exclusively with the effectiveness of such strategies, the clinical practice of behavioural family therapy is characterized by a willingness to experiment with an unlimited range of interventions. The key restriction placed upon the selection of a therapeutic strategy is that it can be shown to produce the specific change that is targeted as the therapist's goal for that particular family, preferably in the most efficient manner. The empirical validation of many psychological interventions that have been derived from social learning theory makes these strategies particularly attractive to the behavioural therapist, but in every case the precise way in which they may be applied will be based upon the initial and continuing behavioural assessment. The unique qualities of every family and every individual family member are emphasized in this comprehensive assessment process.

The increasing complexity of behavioural assessment is addressed in the analysis of observed family interactions. Rather than simply counting the frequency of positive and negative statements of family members a sequential analysis is conducted. Hahlweg and his colleagues (Hahlweg *et al.* 1988) have shown that arguments tend to arise, not merely from one person's ill-advised comment, but from a series of coercive statements that gradually escalate in a mutually destructive manner illustrated by Patterson and Hops (1972) earlier. By contrast, constructive problem resolution on the same topic may include many similarly negative statements, but does not allow the same escalation. Simply encouraging family members to communicate in a more positive and less negative manner may produce only limited improvement. Instead the behavioural analysis suggests that specific training in constructive problem-solving and conflict resolution strategies may be necessary.

The way in which advances in clinical practice and family assessment develop in partnership is characteristic of the behavioural approach. Theory and practice are linked inseparably. Such an intimate link between assessment and intervention has tended to favour change of readily observable, easily operationalized behaviours. It has been assumed that to induce lasting change of an overt behaviour, such as making positive statements, having sexual intercourse, or washing the dishes, underlying cognitions about family relationships must have changed as well. Behavioural family therapists were satisfied to note that the changes induced by their early intervention strategies did tend to prove stable, at least for a few months after the end of therapy. Few studies followed families for more than six months. Thus if a relatively straightforward approach could produce the lasting benefits requested by the families themselves, there appeared little reason to develop more complex strategies. However it became increasingly evident that the effectiveness of therapy was essentially short-term and the changes often fell short of the family members' expectations for change. For this reason behavioural family therapy has begun to look beyond strategies to enhance family communication to strategies to improve the efficiency of family problem-solving.

It is recognized that families who communicate with one another freely, expressing their feelings, both positive and negative, in a direct, open manner, do not necessarily solve their mutual problems. While good interpersonal communication is a prerequisite to conflict resolution and stress management, it does not achieve this end unless accompanied by effective problem-solving skills. A couple may improve their communications with one another so that major arguments and coercive nagging may be replaced by constructive criticism and pleasurable interchanges. But unless crucial problems are addressed true intimacy may not be achieved. However, at the time of the initial family assessment it may be difficult for a family to pinpoint the critical conflicts in their relationship. This may be achieved only after enhanced interpersonal communication facilitates a therapeutic milieu that promotes a greater awareness of deeper problem issues. The superficial problems of untidy bedrooms, unappreciated efforts, uninteresting sex, and inconsiderate teenagers that litter every household, give way to considerations of more crucial issues such as long-term commitment to the family unit, mutual recognition and assistance in achieving realistic life goals, caring for a disabled member, or adaptation to role changes with time.

In order for a family to develop and thrive it is considered essential that mutual problem-solving and goal achievement occur on a regular basis. Behavioural family therapy provides training in the identification and resolution of problems or goals using a highly structured approach. The behavioural approach attempts to teach families a method to apply to all problems regardless of the nature of the issues involved. The focus is on the *structure* of problem-solving discussions rather than the content of a particular problem or the strategic solutions implemented by the family. Key aspects include the process by which family members identify specific problems and goals, the manner in which alternative solutions are elicited and evaluated, and the methods employed in devising effective plans to implement the optimal solution. The family, not the therapist, decides what problems are addressed and the focus is on finding creative solutions from within the family resources, with the therapist functioning as a facilitator of this process, not as an expert problem-solver.

It should be clearly noted that behaviour therapy is founded upon scientific principles. Detailed observations lead to hypotheses about the factors associated with the occurrence of a specific behaviour which are tested by specific modification of the implicated factors with specific observations to indicate whether the hypotheses have been proven. Strict adherence to this empirical process provides the major theoretical basis for this approach. Social learning theory is the core body of knowledge from which the methods have been developed. However, systems theory, sociology, social and cognitive psychology and child development theories have all played important parts in the development of current approaches. It should be stressed that behavioural family therapy is not a unitary approach. The methods employed vary according to the nature of the presenting problem. However, in the next section I shall endeavour to describe some of the approaches that are commonly deployed irrespective of the presenting problem.

## Behavioural analysis of the family system

The baseline assessment of family functioning and the continual review throughout the course of therapy are the framework upon which behavioural family therapy is constructed. The initial behavioural analysis may involve many hours of individual and conjoint interviews as well as naturalistic observations, especially where the presenting problem is complex. During this assessment phase the therapist seeks to obtain:

1 A therapeutic alliance with all family members.
2 The presenting problem(s) is used as a starting-point for the analysis of the functioning of the family as a problem-solving unit. Each component of the system (individual, dyad, triad, and so on) is explored in order to discover its strengths and weaknesses in relationship to that specific issue. At its most straightforward level this consists of defining the specific contingencies that surround a specific problem behaviour. For example, what precedes a family row, or a child's tantrum, and what are the consequences of that behaviour. By interviewing each family member individually the therapist is likely to gain a broader picture of the setting of the presenting problem than the consensus view provided by a family group. Family mythology of the '*everytime* Mother says this, Father does that' variety is thus avoided more readily. However, reports of problem behaviour are always distorted by the search for simple causal relationships, so that at this stage the therapist can derive only a series of hypotheses to be confirmed in subsequent observations of the actual behavioural sequences.
3 Detailed information about each family member's observations, thoughts and feelings about the presenting problem.
4 Information about each family member's interaction within the family system; his or her attitudes, feelings and behaviour toward the other family members; and his or her motivation and current efforts to resolve the presenting problem.
5 Information about each family member's function in settings outside the

family unit; his or her personal assets and deficits that might be relevant to problem resolution.

Ideally, observations of family functioning are conducted in the circumstances where the presenting problems arise. Such naturalistic observations were pioneered by Gerald Patterson in Oregon, where he developed methods to code in detail the behaviour of people in their own homes during the early evenings when aggressive behaviour of young children was most frequent (Patterson *et al*. 1967). Although home-based observations of this kind are invaluable, they are too costly for routine practice. Alternatives include having the family tape-record interactions at targeted times, time sampling of recordings with automated time switches, re-enactment of problem situations by family members, or family discussions about 'hot issues'. Nevertheless, at least one home visit is an essential part of the behavioural assessment and usually provides the therapist with an abundance of valuable information seldom accessible in clinic-based assessments.

The behavioural family therapist is interested in pinpointing not only the setting in which problem behaviour is most likely to arise, but also the family's past and current efforts to cope with the behaviour. It usually emerges that any problem is present only a small proportion of the time and arises on only a small proportion of occasions when it might be expected. Looked at from another point of view, most family interaction is positive or neutral (that is non-problematic), and for the most part families have learned to prevent or cope with the problem. Thus the behavioural family therapist is just as interested in uncovering the contingencies that exist when the problem is least likely to emerge, as well as those existing when it emerges but results in minimal distress. It is assumed that the family generally has developed patterns to cope with the problem, but that these coping behaviours are only partially effective, often because family members are inconsistent in their application and do not persist enough to derive the full benefits from their efforts. Where such effective strategies can be pinpointed the therapist is left with the relatively straightforward task of assisting the family to enhance the efficacy of their pre-existing interaction patterns. Such an intervention may take a session or two, but the behavioural analysis that precedes it may be a much longer process.

## Patterns of family reinforcement

Patterns of family behaviour may appear disorganized and even chaotic to the outside observer. However, such behavioural patterns are seldom random. If we have the opportunity to observe repeatedly a family going about their everyday lives we will begin to see sequences of behaviour being repeated. Such patterns have been acquired over time and tend to be based on the fact that people tend to do habitually the things that either produce the greatest rewards or reduce pain and suffering the most.

One method of assessing the patterns of family interaction is the *reinforcement survey*. Each family member is invited to describe their most frequent activities, as well as the people, places and objects that they spend most time in contact with. In addition, family members are invited to nominate those activities, places, people and things that they would like to spend more time with, if that was possible. Discrepancies between current and desired reinforcers often help disclose areas of dissatisfaction and motivation to change. This can prove extremely helpful when attempting to define specific goals related to each person's quality of life. A comparison of the reinforcement surveys of different family members may reveal current or potential sources of conflict that may need to be considered in the treatment plan. For example, a mother might want to spend more time conversing with her teenage son, while he wishes to spend more time out of the family with his friends; or a husband may wish to spend more time at home with his wife, while she would prefer to spend more time with her women friends. Discussion about these issues enables family members to define mutually compatible goals and to clarify areas of conflict in their current and future relationships.

Attention is then directed towards aversive situations that family members tend to avoid. These unpleasant situations may vary from common phobias to a variety of family interactions, such as arguments, discussion about finances or sexual concerns or other intimate issues. Feelings of isolation, rejection, coercion, lack of support, intrusiveness and mistrust may be discussed within this context. These feelings can be linked with specific behaviours in most situations. Family members are invited to provide examples of interactions where they tend to experience these feelings. For example, a wife who felt rejected by her husband described how he had gradually spent more and more time at his work in the evenings and had joined a golf club that occupied most of his weekend time.

The reinforcement survey provides a fascinating picture of the manner in which family members' everyday activities intertwine in patterns of mutual reinforcement, positively in happy families and negatively in distressed families. Some families show clear patterns of avoidance of intimacy, confrontation, or intrusive over-involvement. More often, a mixture of positive and negative patterns is found. Because this survey is conducted through a series of interviews it is assumed that some distortions are involved in the reporting so that it is not taken to be an accurate representation of actual family behaviour, rather the family's perceptions of their behaviour. To obtain a more precise picture of actual behaviour we may wish to have family members complete daily activity schedules.

An additional use of the reinforcement survey is in selecting positive reinforcers for use in promoting targeted behaviour in the treatment programme. Specific activities, places, people and material objects that are highly desirable can be employed to mediate change in this manner. For example, a meal that a boy enjoys may be used to reward him for help with the garden, or an activity that he would like to engage in more often, such as kicking a football with his father, could be used as the basis for increasing positive interaction between them.

## The functional analysis: a behavioural system

Behavioural family therapy postulates that patterns of family behaviour are learned over repeated episodes of trial-and-error problem-solving. Vicarious experience of parental and grandparental problem-solving provides a framework for at least the initial efforts of a developing family. However, the influence of a multitude of other factors will govern the precise response of any family member to any situation at any time. These factors may include biological variables (for example premenstrual tension, hunger, illness-related behaviour), psychological variables (for example intelligence, verbal ability, memory functioning), social variables (for example financial resources, availability of job opportunities, religious views of divorce), interpersonal variables (for example assertive skills, reciprocity, concern for others), in addition to those issues concerning family rules and structure that are emphasized by systems theorists. It is assumed that whatever the pattern of family behaviour, at all times it will represent the optimal responses of every family member to resolve the problem (or achieve the goal) in the manner that is most rewarding (or least distressing) to them, given the various constraints imposed by the biopsychosocial system at that moment.

It is evident that such a formulation makes targeted intervention extremely difficult. Most therapists employ an unidimensional approach. An unhappy housewife may be given a diagnosis of depression and prescribed an antidepressant drug, or provided with financial aid, or trained to be more assertive with her husband, or encouraged to view her plight as an attempt to emulate her mother. The behavioural family therapist may consider all of these issues and many others in an attempt to understand the pattern of family behaviour.

A functional analysis is the attempt to pinpoint the key reason why a family should resort to a pattern of behaviour that persistently contributes to the distress of one or more members. The aim is not merely to achieve insight, but to pinpoint the specific issue where minimal intervention may produce maximal progress towards the goals of every family member.

During the functional analysis the therapist seeks answers to the following questions:

1 How does the presenting problem handicap this person (and his or her family) in everyday life?
2 How does the presenting problem assist this person (and his or her family) in coping with everyday life?
3 What would happen if the problem was ignored?
4 What would happen if the problem occurred less frequently?
5 What would this person (and his or her family) gain if the problem was resolved?
6 What would this person (and his or her family) lose if the problem was resolved?
7 Who reinforces the problems with attention, sympathy or support?
8 Under what circumstances is the problem reduced in intensity? Where? When? With whom?
9 Under what circumstances is the problem increased in intensity?

## THE ROLE OF THE THERAPIST

While the intervention strategies commonly used by behavioural family therapists tend to be highly specific and directed towards resolution of the target problems, they are applied within the framework of a supportive therapeutic alliance. The significance of empathy and mutual positive regard has been somewhat taken for granted in most descriptions of this approach. However, the successful application of the specific strategies of behavioural family therapy requires an excellent therapeutic alliance at all times. This is initiated during the behavioural analysis when the therapist shows willingness to understand the specific needs, goals, problems, strengths and weaknesses of every family member, and commits him or herself to assisting each person to develop his or her full creative potential. This alliance is maintained by a constant reappraisal of all these issues and the flexibility to modify therapist behaviour as a direct consequence of observed progress (or lack of progress) towards these goals the family have defined. Furthermore, the therapist encourages family members to maximize their strengths and provide positive feedback for *all* their efforts, while assisting in the constructive analysis of their failed attempts in a non-judgemental manner. At all times the therapist avoids coercion and confrontation, expresses his or her own positive or negative feelings in a direct, specific manner, and takes full responsibility for resolving all difficulties encountered during the process of therapy. In short, the therapist interacts with the family in a manner that is fully consistent with the communication and problem-solving methods that he or she is encouraging them to adopt, and represents a model of competence for all family members.

Although the strategies used in behavioural family therapy are chosen according to the precise goals of each family several interventions that have empirical evidence to support their general effectiveness deserve comment. These are strategies that are frequently deployed by behavioural family therapists in a broad range of settings. They include communication training, problem-solving training, operant-conditioning approaches, and contingency management.

## Intervention strategies

*Communication training*
The behavioural approach emphasizes the importance of clear, direct communication of each family member's thoughts and feelings in the efficient resolution of problems and the achievement of personal goals. The expression of specific positive feelings, ideas and plans is considered as crucial as the expression of negative feelings. Most behavioural family therapy intervention programmes include an initial emphasis on positive communication. Distressed families are characterized by a lack of positive communication and an excess of expression of negative feelings. Such a family atmosphere is not conducive to efficient problem-solving. The therapist seeks to increase the frequency that pleasing behaviour is noted by all family members. This mutual enhancement of positive interaction provides a milieu where problem issues can be discussed more readily.

Once this has been achieved the therapist moves on to the expression of negative feelings in a constructive manner that facilitates problem resolution. In addition families may be trained to make specific requests rather than coercive demands, and to become more empathic, active listeners when others are attempting to clarify their problems or goals. More detailed training in basic information-giving communication may be included when assisting family members to cope with mentally handicapped or disturbed children, or seriously mentally ill adults.

A skill-training model is employed. Family members are invited to re-enact their attempts to communicate their feelings and are coached by therapists and other competent family members. Instructions, feedback, modelling and positive reinforcement are used to shape communication skills until they are expressed in a clear, concise and direct style that suits the personality of each family member. Congruence of verbal and non-verbal expression, the expression of one's own feelings and the specification of the precise behaviours that have engendered those feelings are key areas of competence that are considered. Statements such as 'I really liked the apple pie you cooked for dinner tonight, Mum', are preferred to 'You're a great Mum!' or, 'I was very upset when you walked through the kitchen with your wellies covered in mud, John. I'd like you to take them off at the door in future', is preferred to 'You're an inconsiderate layabout. If you mess up the kitchen again I'll throw you into the street!' The potential for these two contrasting expressions to facilitate efficient problem-solving and goal achievement is obvious.

### Problem-solving training

As is the case with all behavioural interventions, the therapist does not seek merely to achieve competent performance during therapy sessions, but is satisfied only when clear evidence is provided that these skills have been absorbed into everyday interactions. Diary sheets on which family members make daily records of specific communication skills are employed between sessions and family members are prompted to attempt to use these skills whenever the opportunity arises. The therapist reviews the homework at the beginning of each session, invites family members to re-enact their expressions and provides feedback and further coaching where necessary. It should be stressed that it is the structure of communication that is the focus of this approach, not the specific content or the precise words employed. Family members are encouraged to adapt the structure of their own style of expression so that it feels natural to them.

Behavioural family therapists have moved recently towards training families to adopt structured problem-solving strategies which can be applied to any problem or goal that they may wish to discuss. Thus rather than having the family depend on the therapist as the source of clever ideas and skilfully devised plans, the therapist attempts to facilitate the creative problem-solving potential of the family unit. At its most basic level the therapist invites the family to arrange a regular time and place for family discussions outside therapy sessions.

In addition, the therapist may train the family to adopt a structured approach to their discussions. Currently the most favoured method involves a six-step model:

1  Agreeing on the exact nature of the problem/goal.
2  Brainstorming and listing all possible solutions (at least five alternatives).
3  Highlighting the advantages and disadvantages of each proposed solution.
4  Choosing the optimal solution.
5  Formulating a detailed plan to implement the solution.
6  Reviewing the implementation effort and continuing the problem-solving process when necessary.

Almost any problem or goal can be discussed using this approach. Family members are chosen to chair the discussion and to record notes for future reference. The approach seeks to diffuse the burden of coping with a problem or responsibility for achieving a goal and to draw on the collective resourcefulness of the entire family unit. The imposition of a high degree of structure cuts across many detrimental patterns of family interaction, for example a domineering or disruptive member. The level of family tension is reduced dramatically enabling even the hottest family issues to be addressed in a reasonably calm manner.

Once the structured approach has been outlined by the therapist, he or she tends to withdraw and to observe the family conduct their own problem-solving discussions during sessions. The therapist may provide feedback and coaching to refine their methods and prompt the continual use of effective communication skills. Occasionally, like a football referee, the therapist may need to intervene where serious infringements occur that are likely to impede further problem-solving. However, it is hoped that the family chairperson will learn to adopt a similar function so that the therapist becomes redundant at the earliest possible time. The family therapy sessions are used as workshops. At all times the emphasis is on the application of these methods in the family meetings at home. The family reports on the effectiveness of these discussions at the beginning of each session.

At times of major family crises the therapist may need to become a more active participant in the problem-solving and to chair the discussion. But at all times the therapist is expected to employ the same communication and problem-solving skills that he or she is attempting to train the family to adopt.

The therapist's problems with the process of therapy, such as poor attendance or inadequate compliance with homework assignments, are handled in the same problem-solving manner. The therapist indicates that he or she has a problem, expresses his or her negative feelings directly to the family, and engages in a six-step problem-solving discussion in an attempt to seek a plan to resolve the problem. This has proven a simple, yet highly effective method to address all forms of therapeutic resistance.

*Operant-conditioning strategies*
The principles of operant reinforcement are used widely in behavioural family therapy and have been developed into several highly effective behaviour change strategies. Among the strategies are the following.

*Successive approximation (or shaping).* A person is encouraged with prompts and praise to approximate his or her behaviour to a clearly specified goal in a series of small steps. Parents display this skill when they encourage a baby to walk. Every effort that resembles walking is warmly praised as the baby slowly increases his or her competence. Negative features are played down or ignored.

*Contingency contracting.* A contingency contract is a strategy that is widely used to decrease coercive, blaming patterns of family behaviour by replacing this aversive control by mutual exchange of desired behaviour in two or more family members. Each family member requests one or more specific behaviours he or she desires another family member to perform and offers to perform one or more specific pleasing behaviours for that person. A reciprocal contract is negotiated so that each person both gives and receives pleasing behaviours. A written agreement of this contract is usually produced. Implementation of the contract is reviewed at treatment sessions, and amended when necessary.

Example: Jane complained that her husband Bill, who had been unemployed for over a year, spent all his time lying about the house, and had lost interest in everything, including herself and their children. Bill complained that Jane nagged him every time he attempted to help her around the house and that she didn't want to do anything that interested him. The following contract was negotiated:

|  *Responsibilities* | *Privileges* |
|---|---|
| *Bill* | |
| Get out of bed before 8.30 am every morning. | Cup of coffee made by Jane and hug. |
| To do one major household chore of Jane's choice every day. | Paid £3 per hour for work. |
| Play with the children for 30 minutes after school. | 30 minutes with Jane. Bill to choose activity. |
| *Jane* | |
| To plan a pleasurable, low-cost activity outside the home every day. | Bill to drive Jane to evening class. |
| To cook an evening meal (not convenience foods). | To watch TV programme of choice. |

It is important to note that these contracted behaviours are clearly specified and that a specific reward is contingent upon completion of each agreed-upon event. Whenever possible the rewards are provided readily. The quid-pro-quo contract, whereby the desired behaviour of one person is made contingent upon the performance of the desired behaviour of the other, is considered less effective. Such arrangements are prone to arguments and power struggles, and are seldom used by behavioural family therapists.

*Token economy.* This is a variant of the contingency contract, but is usually applied to one family member. A list of desired behaviours is specified, the performance of each gains the family member a specific number of points (or tokens). The points can then be exchanged for a variety of rewards, each of which is worth a pre-arranged number of points. Undesired behaviour can be punished by deducting points in a similarly specific way.

Example: Dennis was a 22-year-old man, recovering from a schizophrenic disorder. His parents were attempting to increase his constructive behaviour and to reduce his angry outbursts. The following plan was devised:

| *Desired behaviour* | *Rewards* |
|---|---|
| Brushing hair: 2 points | 1 ice cream: 5 points |
| Shaving: 5 points | 1 cup of coffee: 2 points |
| Wearing clean clothes: 2 points | |
| Reading for 10 minutes: 5 points | 30 minutes television: 5 points |
| Gardening for 10 minutes: 5 points | 30 minutes drive: 10 points |
| Making bed: 3 points | |
| Taking rubbish out: 5 points | |
| Washing dishes: 5 points | Eating at a restaurant: 10 points |
| Helping with shopping: 5 points | 1 slice of cake: 5 points |
| Making tea/coffee for family: 3 points | 1 candy bar (Mars, etc): 5 points |

This list was enlarged as more activities and rewards were contracted. A record of points earned and points expended was kept on the household noticeboard. After a month Dennis was earning more points than could be readily exchanged. It was necessary to revise the contingencies in order to balance the economy.

*Time out.* This is an extinction strategy that is most effective when undesirable behaviour occurs in a setting where it is impossible to ignore. The family member exhibiting the unpleasant behaviour is removed from contact of others in a matter-of-fact way for a brief period. Children's temper tantrums, threats or actual violent behaviour, impending arguments may be modified by imposing this cooling-off period. A suitable unrewarding area to use for time out may be crucial. A bathroom or spare bedroom may prove adequate. The door should not be locked. Adults may find it helpful to take a walk outside to cool off, and may be trained to monitor their tension levels and to excuse themselves from stressful situations before problems arise. Parents have been trained to recognize when a discussion is escalating and to employ structured problem-solving methods to resolve the issue.

*Limit setting.* Defining clear guidelines for family behaviour is an important intervention. Although covert rules exist in most families, specific limits may not be agreed upon. As a result, individual family members may choose their own limits, in conflict with other household members. Problem-solving can be used in an attempt to reach a family consensus on important limits as well as devising strategies for dealing with non-compliance with these guidelines.

Example: Susan, aged 15, agreed that she would go out with friends on one night a week (until 10 pm), and one night at the weekend until 11.30 pm. A 30-minute violation would lead to a £1 reduction in her weekly pocket money allowance, and any longer violation would lead to an additional removal of these privileges.

*Homework tasks*

The sessions of behavioural family therapy are considered primarily as training workshops, during which family members are able to try out different response patterns and receive supportive feedback and coaching from therapists and their relatives. It is the attempts to incorporate more efficient patterns of problem resolution and goal achievement into family life outside the treatment sessions that are of vital importance. To this end specific assignments of homework tasks are a key strategy. These homework tasks always involve efforts to practise new interaction patterns that have been rehearsed in the treatment sessions.

The ultimate success of therapy is measured primarily by the observed enduring changes that have occurred in everyday family life. Providing the initial and continuing behavioural analysis has been adequate, such changes should correlate closely with perceptions of more satisfying family relationships. Where discrepancies exist between behavioural and cognitive changes they usually result from an inadequate behavioural analysis, or the imposition of the therapist's goals and values upon the family system. However, such difficulties are evident long before the completion of therapy where reports of dissatisfaction emerge from attempts to complete homework tasks. Thus the session-by-session review of homework assignments provides a crucial feedback component of the ongoing behavioural analysis.

# EFFECTIVE THERAPISTS

Training in behaviour therapy has tended to be poorly organized, and to focus on specific strategies for specific disorders, rather than an overall approach to assessment and intervention. Courses in behaviour therapy are few and far between, but brief workshops on specific techniques are readily available.

Behavioural family therapy is one aspect of behaviour therapy and should not be trained independently. In order to become highly proficient in the method a therapist will generally need to acquire an understanding of social learning theory and the various strategies that are derived from it. However, it could be argued that many behaviour therapy methods are applied in the most efficient manner in a family context. Studies of social skills training

(Falloon *et al.* 1977), agoraphobia (Mathews *et al.* 1981), obsessive-compulsive disorder (Cobb *et al.* 1980) and manic-depression (Falloon *et al.* 1988) have all demonstrated the importance of close collaboration with family members. Thus behavioural family therapy may serve as an excellent introduction to the broad scope of behaviour therapy.

To date, there is very little written about training in behavioural family therapy. There is little doubt that a therapist with a grounding in social learning theory can learn the technical skills in between ten and twenty hours of workshop training. However, the application in clinical practice may take considerably longer. There is no substitute for case supervision. As a result, the shortest time such a student is likely to achieve competence is about six months. For a person unfamiliar with behavioural theory and practice, a longer period is often necessary.

The key element of therapist training is the ability to acquire the same communication and problem-solving skills that are taught to families, and to use them throughout therapy sessions. In other words, the therapist is taught the same problem-solving methods he or she will subsequently teach families. Feedback provides an opportunity for the therapist to praise specific strengths he or she observes in each family member's performance.

Specific deficits are addressed in terms of constructive suggestions of alternative behaviours that may prove more effective. Requests for behaviour change are made in the same positive vein: 'I would like you to do (this or that)', rather than 'Now do (this or that)'. When the therapist's direct communication skills fail, he or she may resort to problem-solving using the same six-step structure he or she expects the family to use. The fidelity of therapist skills provides a powerful model for the family, and avoids the confrontation and resistance so often engendered by the kind but coercive therapist style commonly employed.

Training is most efficient when a workshop model is employed. Preparation involves reading appropriate texts that detail the theoretical rationale, provide instructions and clear examples of the methods (e.g. Patterson 1971; Jacobson and Margolin 1979; Falloon *et al.* 1984). Workshops are then focused upon modelling of the skills, either live or on edited video-tapes, with subsequent role rehearsal of the skills in mock family sessions. Each role rehearsal is brief – seldom more than ten minutes each – and is followed by brief, constructive feedback to the trainee therapist, both by the supervisor and by the peers who are role-playing the family. The focus is upon the specific skill of the therapist, not upon the responses engendered by the therapy. Each session is structured around one or more modules of the intervention.

Immediately after each workshop session trainees are encouraged to apply the skills in clinical practice with a family. Sessions are recorded for subsequent review by the trainee and supervisor. Ratings of competence are completed by the supervisor on the specific and 'non-specific' skills displayed by the trainee. Non-specific skills include rapport with the family, efficient use of time, presentation and review of homework tasks, troubleshooting and crisis intervention. The clear structure of the interventions enables the supervisors to evaluate competence with relative ease. Furthermore the continual use of a behavioural analysis enables the effectiveness of the intervention to be judged in a reliable manner.

While there is usually a high correlation between competent application of the interventions by the therapist and progress towards the family's goals, discrepancies do arise. The commonest source of lack of progress is an inadequate behavioural analysis. Key issues have not been uncovered, or inappropriate goals have been targeted. A common family complaint is, 'We do all this already'. Very often this is true. Families may know all the skills that are presented. The therapist may have failed to acknowledge their competence, and have failed to provide an adequate rationale for reviewing these skills. Such a rationale may point out the need for super-efficient everyday use of these skills so that they can be employed to minimize stress under everyday conditions as well as at times of high tension.

Research into therapist training is remarkably limited and sorely needed. Little is known about the selection of therapists for training, the specific trainer-trainee qualities that predict training success, or the relative advantages of various training strategies. Effective training is a costly venture and deserves much greater scrutiny than has been prevalent in the family therapy field.

## OTHER ISSUES

### Resistance to change or inadequate therapy?

Behavioural family therapists have begun to accept the limitations of their approach, particularly those methods that involve training family members to adopt highly structured interaction patterns. However, rather than assuming that resistance to change is a basic characteristic of human family behaviour a more empirical understanding has been sought. The potential reasons why a family are slow to change their behaviour and to adopt the patterns proposed by the therapist vary substantially. Some of the most obvious have been described by several authors (Munjack and Oziel 1978; Weiss 1979; Spinks and Birchler 1982; Patterson 1985). They include practical issues such as family members not understanding or forgetting instructions, problems in the delivery of the training, for example a confronting or coercive therapist style, as well as more complex dynamic factors associated with the family system and family members' formative experiences.

In order to counter resistance the behavioural family therapist attempts to anticipate the most likely sources of resistance during his or her extensive behavioural assessment, both before beginning the training phase of the intervention and throughout the course of training. Special care is taken to avoid resistance due to inadequacies in the presentation of the intervention. However, a comprehensive behavioural analysis is often vital to enable the skilled therapist to chart a course through the roadblocks each family may set up to slow the process of change. The challenge of any intervention is being able to meet the needs of 100 per cent of people for whom it is applied. This entails achieving success with all difficult cases, as well as avoiding drop-outs. Behavioural family therapists are continually working to achieve this ideal. They tend to eschew the routine use of gimmicky strategies, such as paradox, and favour the less dramatic approach of painstaking behavioural analysis and repeated problem-solving.

## The indications for behavioural family therapy

To date there are no contra-indications to behavioural family therapy approaches, or case descriptions that suggest that the approach, when applied competently, has produced any significant negative effects. For this reason, the indications for behavioural family therapy are difficult to specify. However, in recent years several specific approaches to specific problem areas have been derived from the basic behavioural family therapy approaches. These include methods such as parent training, behavioural marital therapy, sexual therapy, marital enrichment, spouse-assisted behaviour therapy, family management of serious mental illness, premarital counselling and divorce mediation.

Many of these approaches are applied as standardized packages, without a comprehensive behavioural analysis, or extensive therapist training. However, the broad range of client groups for whom this approach has been demonstrated as highly effective in uncontrolled studies is impressive. Relatively few studies have compared the behavioural approach to other models of family intervention, so that it is difficult to state the relative merits of this specific method. The few studies that have involved a contrasting family approach have been in the areas of marital therapy and parent training. They have tended to show advantages for the behavioural method, particularly in facilitating change in specific targeted problem areas. However, the added benefits of behavioural family therapy have not been impressive and any claims for superiority for any target population would be premature. It is hoped that the future development of behavioural family therapy will define the relative indications and contra-indications of these methods with specific disorders with respect to other effective intervention methods.

## Efficacy of behavioural family therapy

Despite claims for an empirical base, behavioural family therapy methods have not been subjected to an extensive series of clinical trials. Most of the earlier claims for the efficacy of these methods have come from uncontrolled case studies. In the past decade several controlled trials have been conducted that have compared behavioural family therapy with a variety of control conditions. The majority of these studies have involved marital therapy or parent-training derivatives of behavioural family therapy.

Comparisons between behavioural family therapy and family interventions based upon different theoretical concepts are rare. Perhaps the best examples are the marital therapy studies of Crowe (1978) and Liberman *et al*. (1976). Both these studies suggest that the behavioural approach is more effective in producing improvements in specific presenting problems. However, despite statistically significant benefits, global measures of marital satisfaction have not supported this trend (Jacobson 1984). Similar problems have muted the early claims for the benefits of parent-training programmes for disturbed children (Patterson 1985).

It is evident that these approaches have tended to neglect the all important behavioural analysis of the family system and have shown limited benefits where complex relationship issues contribute to the presenting problems. While some behaviour therapists have advocated an integration of behavioural and systemic approaches (Bennun 1987; Birchler and Spinks 1980), others have always considered that comprehensive behaviour analysis involves a systemic conceptualization (Alexander *et al*. 1976; Falloon *et al*. 1984). There is a clear need for well-controlled comparative studies to evaluate the relative strengths and weaknesses of the various schools of family therapy. The present lack of comparative outcome data allows irresponsible claims by charismatic therapists to govern the prevalence of various family therapy methods to the detriment of the advancement of the field within clinical practice. Such a state of affairs is highly unsatisfactory.

Behavioural family therapy has been applied to a wide variety of psychiatric disorders, with studies supporting its efficacy in conditions such as adolescent and childhood conduct disorders (Alexander and Parsons 1982; Patterson *et al*. 1982; Herbert and Iwaniec 1981), senile and pre-senile dementias (Zarit and Zarit 1985); mental handicap (Risley and Wolf 1967); anorexia nervosa (Fichter 1977); alcoholism (Fichter and Postpischil 1988); schizophrenia (Falloon 1985); depression (Follette and Jacobson 1988); manic episodes (Falloon *et al*. 1988); obsessive-compulsive disorders (Hand 1988) and anxiety disorders (Cobb *et al*. 1984).

There are no reports of detrimental effects of behavioural family therapy, and contra-indications would appear minimal. In order to benefit, family members must be capable of receiving and processing verbal information.

Such processing may prove difficult for psychotic, perceptually impaired or demented individuals. However, the straightforward structure provided by the method, and employed by less impaired family members, tends to assist such persons to cope with their stressors. But in such cases sessions may be shortened, assessment, training and goals simplified. Providing these modifications are made, there would appear to be no absolute contra-indications to this approach. Further research is needed to establish the cost-efficiency of family therapies and other forms of psychosocial intervention. One study that attempted such an analysis showed a 250 per cent advantage for behavioural family therapy over individual supportive therapy in the long-term community management of schizophrenia (Falloon 1985). With evidence that there is relatively little to choose between the efficacy of various family therapies, the approach of choice for any specific disorder may be determined largely by economic factors. Two methods may produce similar clinical outcome, but if one method achieves these benefits at a substantially lower cost, it should be favoured.

## A FAMILY IN THERAPY

Harry, a 32-year-old married man, had developed paranoid schizophrenia two years earlier. He presented with a problem of not having a job. The initial phase of behavioural analysis pinpointed the problem as a wish to 'engage in constructive activities for at least six hours of every weekday'.

It was evident that the main difficulties arising from this problem were that Harry had always enjoyed working hard, had few hobbies or friends outside work, a relationship with his wife, Jackie, that was cordial but not an intimate friendship, and that his self-confidence was closely linked to his work achievements and earnings. He did not fit into the everyday activity around the house and his wife found him a nuisance that got in her way.

His lack of constructive activity allowed him to spend much of his day lying in bed contemplating exciting career possibilities and day-dreaming about future enterprises. It prevented him from contact with old friends and workmates, who did not understand his illness and tended to give him unhelpful advice, for example persuading him to stop taking any medication.

When the problem was ignored, Harry remained concerned, but made no attempt to resolve it. The gains of having more constructive activity were that Harry would feel more confident, have more interesting topics to discuss with his wife and children, and, if the activity was remunerated, he would be able to supplement the family income that was severely stretched. He would cease to feel he was a burden to his wife and a household nuisance.

If the problem was resolved, Harry would lose the comfortable, low-stress life-style that he found quite enjoyable. The family would worry more about him when he was late home from a job. He would no longer be available to care for his children after school or when they were ill, or to be able to drive his wife to her work. But above all, he would lose his sickness benefit payments, and would need to earn a substantial salary to improve the family's finances significantly.

Jackie tended to sympathize with him and provide suggestions about constructive activities Harry could pursue, but these discussions were brief and did not lead to any active planning. She seemed very tolerant of his invalid behaviour and tended to encourage him to stay in bed where he was 'out of the way'. She found his presence in the living-room an embarrassment whenever her friends or her children's friends visited.

The problem was made worse when Jackie nagged him to help about the house, when she complained about their financial difficulties, when relatives told him to 'pull his socks up', when he drank alcohol, and when he brooded about it. On the other hand, he felt more motivated to make an effort to increase his constructive activity at times when he was asked to do specific tasks in which he had expertise. He was more likely to tackle these jobs when encouraged by Jackie and prompted to get started in a non-coercive manner.

Harry had previously enjoyed working alone, setting his own pace. He was sensitive to criticism. He was shy and had difficulty making conversation about everyday topics. Jackie used to help him by role-playing interpersonal situations he had difficulty dealing with, particularly those concerning work activity.

Mark, their 14-year-old son, was reported as fighting with his peers at school and performing below his abilities in the classroom. He was non-compliant in his conduct in the family, frequently calling his father 'lazy' and a 'nutter'. Jackie tended to discipline him, and was critical of Harry for not being firm with him. Helen, aged 8, was well adjusted and helped her mother with the household chores from time to time.

The treatment programme was constructed to take account of the strengths and weaknesses of this family. Initially the entire family received three sessions of education about the nature of schizophrenia and its treatment. Harry was encouraged to describe his paranoid experiences and the manner in which his thinking was derailed. He described how he had continuing difficulties getting his thoughts 'into gear' and how that impaired his everyday activities.

A lack of acknowledgement of any constructive behaviour among family members was remedied by teaching each person to express positive feelings whenever they detected another person doing something that they felt a little pleased about. Jackie noted that she hardly ever missed an opportunity to pick up anything that displeased her, and found that focusing on Mark's pleasing behaviour seemed to reduce his level of non-compliance. She also noted that Harry seemed more responsive to her encouragement and withdrew more when she nagged him. The family members were taught to express negative feelings directly and in a more targeted fashion, so that significant sources of dysfunction and distress could be identified and worked on in a systematic fashion.

Once the family were beginning to communicate their feelings in a direct, specific manner they were taught to set up weekly problem-solving discussions. The six-step problem-solving approach was introduced and they were encouraged to address all important problems in this format. Although they were able to engage in excellent discussions during therapy sessions, Jackie found it very difficult to gain the co-operation of Harry and Mark outside the sessions. The therapist employed the problem-solving approach to address this resistance, with partial success.

However, despite use of the structured method and satisfactory interpersonal communication, Harry's difficulties getting involved in constructive activities remained. Further behavioural analysis revealed that Harry had little interest in household chores, but was keen to explore activities outside the home, particularly those that might improve his long-term career prospects. He began to search the papers and employment bureaux for courses that appeared of interest. After some time he enrolled in a specialist landscape gardening course.

Mark's conduct improved substantially in response to improved communication of his needs and feelings, as well as greater family attention for his good behaviour. His parents involved his class teacher in two problem-solving discussions that resulted in considerable improvement in his difficulties at school.

Over a two-year period Harry's schizophrenia remained in stable remission on a low dose of neuroleptic drugs. On several occasions he and Jackie became very despondent at their lack of finances and overall difficulties. On these occasions they were assisted by the therapist to pinpoint a specific goal that they felt able to tackle and worked out a plan of action. This tended to resolve their feelings of despair and assisted them to keep going despite the enduring stress that they suffered. The family had improved the efficiency of their problem-solving functions substantially, their interpersonal communication was more supportive and constructive and they had learned several useful behavioural strategies. However, vulnerability to schizophrenia is a lifelong problem and follow-up is provided indefinitely for such families. The therapist continued to make three-monthly visits to the family and to remain available for telephone consultations whenever a crisis occurred.

# CONCLUSION

Behavioural family therapy is an approach to family intervention that is derived from social learning theory principles. Its most characteristic feature is the structure that is imposed by extensive, continuous assessment of clearly specified family problems and goals. This behavioural analysis aims to pinpoint those key deficits that limit the capacity of the family unit to resolve the continuing problems that handicap each family member in their efforts to maximize their creative potentials.

The goal of intervention strategies is to build upon the current strengths of family problem-solving functions in order to overcome the specific weaknesses that have been observed. Assumptions about the nature of the goals of family members or about the dynamics of family interaction patterns are minimized. Family members are invited to attempt alternative methods of interpersonal communication and problem-solving, and are taught strategies for addressing specific issues. However, at all times the therapist attempts to harness the creative problem-solving potential of the family unit so that family members adopt problem-solving strategies that suit their unique needs.

Despite two decades of development, few behavioural family therapists are satisfied with these approaches. Refinement to facilitate cost-efficiency is sought constantly. As a result, the utilization of behavioural family therapy in all branches of the mental health field has become standard practice. In some instances these methods have contributed to major advances in the management of mental disorders. However, further substantial work is required in the development of therapist training courses and in controlled research studies before the value of these methods can be fully recognized.

# REFERENCES

Alexander, J. and Parsons, B.V. (1982). *Functional Family Therapy*. Monterey, Calif., Brooks/Cole.

Alexander, J.F., Barton, C., Schiavo, R.S. and Parsons, B.V. (1976). Systems-behavior intervention with families of delinquents: therapist characteristics, family behavior and outcome. *Journal of Consulting and Clinical Psychology*, 44, 656–64.

Bennun, I. (1987). Behavioural marital therapy: a critique and appraisal of integrated models. *Behavioural Psychotherapy*, 15, 1–15.

Birchler, G.R. and Spinks, S. (1980). Behavioral-systems marital and family therapy: integration and clinical application. *American Journal of Family Therapy*, 8, 6–28.

Cobb, J.P., McDonald, R., Marks, I.M. and Stern, R. (1980). Marital versus exposure therapy: psychological treatments of co-existing marital and phobic-obsessive problems. *European Journal of Behavioural Analysis and Modification*, 4, 3–17.

Cobb, J.P., Mathews, A.M., Childs-Clarke, A. and Blowers, C.M. (1984). The spouse as co-therapist in the treatment of agoraphobia. *British Journal of Psychiatry*, 144, 282–7.

Crowe, M.J. (1978). Conjoint marital therapy: a controlled outcome study. *Psychological Medicine*, 8, 623–36.

Falloon, I.R.H. (1985). *Family Management of Schizophrenia: A Study of the Clinical, Social, Family and Economic Benefits*. Baltimore, Md, Johns Hopkins University Press.

Falloon, I.R.H. and McGill, C.W. (1985). Family stress and the course of schizophrenia: a review. In I.R.H. Falloon (ed.) *Family Management of Schizophrenia*. Baltimore, Md, Johns Hopkins University Press.

Falloon, I.R.H., Boyd, J.L. and McGill, C.W. (1984). *Family Care of Schizophrenia*. New York, Guilford.

Falloon, I.R.H., Hole, V., Pembleton, T. and Norris, L. (1988). Behavioral family interventions in the management of manic-depressive disorders. In J.F. Clarkin, G. Haas, and I.D. Glick (eds) *Family Intervention in Affective Illness*. New York, Guilford.

Falloon, I.R.H., Lindley, P., McDonald, R. and Marks, I.M. (1977). Social skills training of outpatient groups: a controlled study of rehearsal and homework. *British Journal of Psychiatry*, 131, 599–609.

Fichter, M.M. (1977). An integrated hospital-community program for severe psychosomatic disease. Paper presented at the IVth World Congress of Psychiatry, Honolulu, Hawaii.

Fichter, M.M. and Postpischil, F. (1988). Behavioral family therapy in alcoholism. In I.R.H. Falloon (ed.) *Handbook of Behavioral Family Therapy*. New York, Guilford.

Follette, W.C. and Jacobson, N.S. (1988). Behavioral marital therapy in the treatment of depressive disorders. In I.R.H. Falloon (ed.) *Handbook of Behavioral Family Therapy*. New York, Guilford.

Hahlweg, K., Baucom, D.H. and Markman, H. (1988). Recent advances in behavioral marital therapy and in preventing marital distress. In I.R.H. Falloon (ed.) *Handbook of Behavioral Family Therapy*. New York, Guilford.

Hand, I. (1988). Systemic-strategic behavior therapy for obsessive-compulsive patients and their families. In I.R.H. Falloon (ed.) *Handbook of Behavioral Family Therapy*. New York, Guilford.

Herbert, M. and Iwaniec, D. (1981). Behavioral psychotherapy in natural home settings: an empirical study applied to conduct disordered and incontinent children. *Behavioural Psychotherapy*, 9, 55–76.

Jacobson, N.S. (1984). The modification of cognitive processes in behavioral marital therapy: integrating cognitive and behavioral intervention strategies. In K. Hahlweg and N. Jacobson (eds) *Marital Interaction: Analysis and Modification*. New York, Guilford.

Jacobson, N.S. and Margolin, G. (1979). *Marital Therapy: Strategies based on Social Learning and Behavior Exchanges Principles*. New York, Brunner/Mazel.

Liberman, R.P., Levine, J., Wheeler, E. *et al.* (1976). Marital therapy in groups: a comparative evaluation of behavioural and interactional formats. *Acta Psychiatrica Scandinavica Supplementum*, 266.

Mathews, A.M., Gelder, M.G. and Johnston, D.W. (1981). *Agoraphobia: Nature and Treatment*. London, Tavistock

Munjack, D.J. and Oziel, L.J. (1978). Resistance in the behavioral treatment of sexual dysfunction. *Journal of Sex and Marital Therapy*, 4, 122–38.

Patterson, G.R. (1971). *Families: Applications of Social Learning to Family Life*. Champaign, Ill., Research Press.

—— (1985). Beyond technology: the next stage in developing an empirical base for parent training. In L. L'Abate (ed.) *Handbook of Family Psychology and Therapy*, vol. 2. Homewood, Ill., Dorsey Press.

Patterson, G.R. and Hops, H. (1972). Coercion, a game for two: intervention techniques for marital conflict. In R.E. Ulrich and P. Mountjoy (eds) *The Experimental Analysis of Social Behavior*. New York, Appleton-Century-Crofts.

Patterson, G.R., Chamberlain, P. and Reid, J.B. (1982). A comparative evaluation of a parent-training program. *Behavior Therapy*, 13, 638–50.

Patterson, G.R., McNeal, S., Hawkins, N. and Phelps, R. (1967). Reprogramming the social environment. *Journal of Child Psychology and Psychiatry*, 8, 181–95.

Risley, T.R. and Wolf, M.M. (1967). Experimental manipulation of autistic behaviors and generalization into the home. In S.W. Bijou and D.M. Baer (eds) *Child Development: Readings in Experimental Analysis*. New York, Appleton-Century-Crofts.

Spinks, S.H. and Birchler, G.R. (1982). Behavioral-systems marital therapy: dealing with resistance. *Family Process*, 21, 169–85.

Tharp, R.G. and Wetzel, R.J. (1969). *Behavior Modification in the Natural Environment*. New York, Academic Press.

Weiss, R.L. (1979). Resistance in behavioral marriage therapy. *American Journal of Family Therapy*, 7, 3–6.

Zarit, S.H. and Zarit, J.M. (1985). Families under stress: interventions for caregivers of senile dementia patients. *Psychotherapy: Theory, Research and Practice*. 10, 284–95.

# CHAPTER 6

# BRIEF THERAPY

## Harry Procter and George Walker

## INTRODUCTION

The first use of the term 'Brief Therapy' in its present sense known to the authors was in the conversations between Erickson, Haley, Weakland and Bateson in the 1950s (Haley 1963; 1985). Both Haley and Weakland went on to develop interactional therapies, the latter founding the Brief Therapy Centre at the Mental Research Institute, Palo Alto, with Fisch, Watzlawick, Jackson and others (Watzlawick *et al.* 1967; 1974; Weakland *et al.* 1974; Watzlawick 1978; Herr and Weakland 1979; Bodin 1981; Fisch *et al.* 1982). We have used and developed this tradition within the British context. The present chapter summarizes the basic principles of this approach. However, the cases presented are our own.

## THEORETICAL ASSUMPTIONS

Brief Therapy is of narrower compass than some of the approaches described in this volume. It is not grounded in a theory of healthy mental functioning, either of individuals or of family systems. Its focus is the communication between people and how this creates and maintains problems. It is a theory about the nature of human problems and the process of their resolution. It is not concerned with explaining the genesis of problems in terms either of psychopathology or failures in adequate learning and its perspective is contemporary rather than historical.

Interpersonal problems are seen as a direct function of how the

individuals concerned understand the problem and the social context or circumstances within which it occurs. It is assumed that, faced with a problem,
people will act in what they take to be sensible ways in attempting its
resolution. These *attempted solutions* together with the frame of reference,
the way of looking at things within which the attempts seem sensible, are the
primary focus of Brief Therapy.

The essential tenet of this approach is that sufferers' very attempts to solve
their problems actually maintain them. Therapy consists of helping people
to stop or modify their attempted solutions, thereby interrupting the process
maintaining the problem. Most often this is achieved by persuading people
to undertake some action which itself excludes the possibility of their
persisting in their existing attempted solution.

Since, confronted by a problem, people will do what seems sensible to
them, therapy often involves persuading people to try things they would
never have contemplated. Accordingly a secondary focus of Brief Therapy
concerns how a therapist ought to communicate so as to be influential. Brief
Therapy combines a precision of work together with a fundamental respect
for the individual's or family's views and values. Their views and the
resulting efforts to solve their problems are *accepted* and *utilized* in the
business of problem resolution.

This respect is first shown in the care taken to learn how the individuals
understand their circumstances and subsequently in the therapist's efforts to
stay within this frame of reference. Rather than presuming that these beliefs
will need discussion or change, the therapist, by a kind of literal-mindedness,
learns to speak the family's language of causal attributions, working within
rather than challenging their version of reality.

For example, with a child-centred presentation, rather than taking issue
with parents complaining endlessly about apparently ordinary childhood
behaviour the therapist might rather use that frame of reference offered by
the family, saying, 'Since yours is such a difficult child then unusual steps,
such as those I propose, are necessary'.

The background to this approach is the notion of an unfolding family life
cycle (Haley 1973) whereby, emancipating from their families, young
people court, form couples, and then have children who need to be cared for.
These children when grown leave the family, repeating the process while
parents become aged and may need to be cared for.

Given the challenges inherent in this process, to say nothing of the
interpersonal complexity occasioned by the construction of stepfamilies, it is
presumed that most people will inevitably encounter some difficulties in life,
that there will be some bad patches in marital relationships. Young children
will be exhausting, and older children exasperating. Disappointments will
triger transient discouragement and depression. People will manage stress
by over-indulging their appetites for food and drink, or occasionally have

difficulty in sleeping. Ordinarily, given average resourcefulness and flexibility, these difficulties can be lastingly resolved, there being no requirement of elegant solutions. People then get on with their lives.

Problems are envisaged as being created when, in the face of initial failure to resolve a difficulty, rather than trying something different, more and more energy is devoted to persisting with the non-effective way of dealing with the difficulty. As individuals understand themselves to be failing in resolving the difficulty, it tends to be perceived as more serious, and consequently alarming. Accordingly more and more effort is indicated. Given the apparent gravity of the situation, a narrowing tends to occur in that range of actions people will consider as potentially applicable solutions. This reduction in resourcefulness, which may be accompanied by the recruitment of other family members (or outsiders) to help may render the problem ever more central in life, interrupting the natural unfolding of the individual and family life cycle. This has been likened to becoming 'stuck' and has been described by Watzlawick *et al.* (1974) as 'more of the same'.

An important feature of this model is that the duration of a problem's existence is not of itself taken as an index of its severity. Viewed in this way, chronicity becomes a measure of how long people have been stuck with a problem. Thus a problem is seen to consist of a circular, repeating pattern of behaviour (see Figure 6.1) either within an individual, marriage or family or, indeed, in any group of people. This world view is exemplified by a remark attributed by Weakland to one of his patients. 'Whereas life is just one damn thing after another, a problem is the same damn thing over and over again' (Weakland 1984).

Once the self-maintaining pattern is interrupted and bypassed, life can move on again with people negotiating new issues and difficulties. A new problem may occur, of course, but the model assumes optimistically that people are robust and have the resources and abilities to live their lives but that these become temporarily suspended whilst all their energy is devoted to attempts to resolve the problem.

*Figure 6.1* Problem

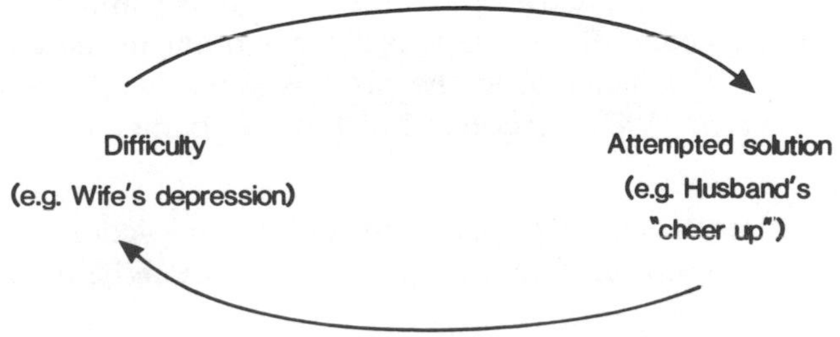

Difficulty
(e.g. Wife's depression)

Attempted solution
(e.g. Husband's
"cheer up")

*Figure 6.2*   Change

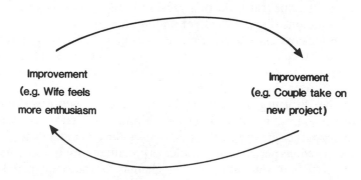

Improvement                                Improvement
(e.g. Wife feels                           (e.g. Couple take on
more enthusiasm                            new project )

Brief Therapy aims to be neither curative nor educational, but only to understand something of the mechanism whereby people become stuck with problems and how to go about getting them unstuck. Once rolling, the process of positive change is seen as a progressive snowballing process following the same logic as the stuckness of problems (see Figure 6.2).

This account covers most of the theoretical aspects of the model. The Mental Research Institute (MRI) group have been concerned to refine and clarify their model as much as possible. Its original, more elaborated framework can be found in *Pragmatics of Human Communication* (Watzlawick *et al.* 1967). Although the model is apparently simple, it is rather deceptively so. A study of the group's work reveals a subtlety and creativity in the face of the variety of cases presented to them. The model is far simpler to conceptualize than to apply.

## THE THERAPY PROCESS

### Setting up the therapy

In order to achieve the rapid resolution of a problem, Brief Therapy focuses all the therapist's efforts in making a single intervention in a carefully planned fashion. Much consideration is given to case planning between therapeutic sessions. Progress is by a series of carefully planned steps. Up to the point of intervention these steps ordinarily occur in the context of a polite interview. Fundamental to the process is the identification of the problem. Fisch *et al.* (1982) describe a Martian viewpoint on the nature of a problem:

1 The client expresses concern about some behaviour – actions, thoughts or feelings – of himself or of another person with whom he is significantly involved.

2 This behaviour is described as (a) deviant – unusual or inappropriate to the point of abnormality – and (b) distressing or harmful, immediately or potentially, either to the behaver (the client) or to others.

3 It is reported that efforts have been made by the client or others to stop or alter this behaviour, but they have been unsuccessful.

4 Therefore, either the client or others concerned are seeking the therapist's help in changing the situation, which they have not been able to change on their own.

(Fisch *et al*. 1982 : 11)

Initially a problem is defined by whoever first seeks help. The complainant first considers matters serious enough to merit outside assistance. In our National Health Service (NHS) context, self-referral is rare, ordinarily the complainant has spoken first with his or her GP, social worker or health visitor who has subsequently made the referral. We have found it beneficial to research the referral usually by phoning the referrer. This enquiry focuses on issues of how the referral was explained to the family members and what views they then expressed were received. In practical terms, the referrer is politely asked, 'What did you say?' and 'Who said what then?' From the information gained it is often possible to tailor the initial contact with the family to match more accurately the complainant's perception of the family problem. In particular, consideration is given to whom to invite to the first session. When possible only those family members who, from the available information, seem motivated to attend, are invited. Similarly if opposed coalitions are known to exist amongst family members, the different factions can be separately invited to consecutive therapy sessions. Having given careful thought to such matters, our practice is to phone the family to explain that the referral has been made and to enquire if the family consider the referral to be sensible. If they do, an appointment is arranged and who is to attend this appointment is carefully negotiated. In making this initial contact with the family great care is taken to match the pace with which the encounter develops. Each of the issues listed above constitutes a step which must logically be taken before the next is attempted. A careful step-by-step approach, timing each new step in accordance with the family's acceptance of the last, is characteristic of Brief Therapy.

Having negotiated a first session, the therapist then seeks to identify those family members who take the problem seriously enough to follow counsel. This willingness to go along with therapeutic suggestions when they are finally offered has been termed 'customership' (Segal 1980). Although somewhat unfortunate in its associations, this term is valuable as it emphasizes that co-operation with the therapist is entirely optional even for those family members motivated to achieve change. Similarly this motivation to co-operate with the therapist cannot be assumed to be a static quality.

Rather it may be thought of as fluctuating with the degree to which the therapist demonstrates a sensible comprehension of the individual's viewpoint and beliefs.

In the NHS context, it can quite often be the case that the initial customer is some third party (GP, social worker, psychiatrist) who initiated the referral. Experience has taught us the necessity of carefully negotiating a version of the problem that permits family members to become customers. To begin this process our practice is often to read from the referral letter such extracts that seem appropriate, taking the attitude, 'This is what I've been told, to what extent does it need correction?' The corrections suggested are usually those of emphasis rather than fact. Involving the family in this way makes it clear that it is *their* understanding of the problem that is sought and does so indirectly. This makes sure that those family members present see a problem and want help with it. This is necessary to convert a referral by a third party to a condition of self-referral required by the method. If this is neglected, there is a danger of the family members taking a passive stance of: 'We came along out of politeness to the referrer'.

One feature of this approach which is relatively uncommon in family therapy is a bias towards seeing in therapy sessions only those family members who are actively motivated to seek change. This shows itself most clearly in those cases where the identified patient does not attend therapeutic sessions, the most frequent examples of this being those cases where childhood or teenage misbehaviour is dealt with by seeing only the parents or parent.

Occasionally the therapist will never meet the problem-bearer as in the case of a schizophrenic problem one of us (Procter) worked on entirely through the parents or the compulsively gambling husband helped through interviewing his wife (Walker 1985). This capability to intervene in a whole social system by working through part of it is a significant extension of therapeutic influence that springs from the theoretical position. The therapy is not 'done to' people during sessions by changing their minds through argument or education. Rather change is understood to result from the acquisition of new information which, changing the individual's understanding of his or her context, initiates changed behaviour appropriate to this new understanding. Accordingly, how the absent identified patient is handled by those family members who will attend is understood as a proper focus for therapeutic attention. This feature of Brief Therapy can be misunderstood as being more akin to individual therapy. However it is a deliberate tactic to define the optimum treatment unit and it largely circumvents the difficulty of accommodating simultaneously two conflicting versions of reality held by different factions within a family. Where possible, individuals known to have radically conflicting views will not to be seen together but, if necessary, would attend subsequent sessions. In simple terms, this means fewer people to contend with in sessions, although there is an absolute necessity to keep firmly in mind those family members who are not in the therapy room. Family therapy in Brief Therapy terms has much more to do with how the therapist thinks about the problem than it does with how many individuals attend the therapy sessions.

Similarly because of the planned step-by-step nature of this approach, there is little to be gained from the practice of cotherapy. Far more valuable is the assistance of colleagues in supervising the therapist as he or she enacts a planned course of therapy. Ideally such assistance is provided by live supervision, using a one-way screen, earphone and the like. In many agencies, this ideal is unattainable. In such cases a regular case-planning seminar is probably essential. Although it is possible to practise Brief Therapy unaided, it is certainly easier for a team to sustain the particular frame of reference necessary.

With the proviso of others helping in case-planning, this approach lends itself to many contexts. It is as applicable in dealing with difficulties between residents of a long-stay hospital ward or residential home as it is in resolving conflicts of interest amongst members of clinical teams. With particular reasons for doing so, families may be seen in their homes, although other things being equal, the therapist is likely to prefer to meet the family on his or her territory rather than on their own, as his or her control of the session is thereby enhanced.

The Brief Therapy method is designed to facilitate the rapid resolution of problems; thinking about clinical matters in this way permits the brevity of treatment. It was initially our practice to make it clear to our patients at the outset of therapy that we would see them for ten sessions. In this we were following early MRI practice (Bodin 1981). However, with knowledge that an average family receives six or seven sessions, we no longer make any explicit mention of this. Rather the expectation of brevity is communicated throughout the therapy, largely by the way in which the therapist gains information and the nature of the information he or she requires. Although MRI practice is largely that of weekly sessions, our appointments are often of necessity three or four weeks apart. These longer inter-session intervals do not seem overly disruptive to this approach and may enhance the degree to which individuals hold themselves responsible for any changes which have occurred since they were last seen.

## The nature of change

Change in therapy is not different in any way from that which occurs in ordinary everyday life when problems are resolved. We assume with Kelly (1955) that the person is a 'form of motion'. No external forces or bribes are needed to explain humanity's continual search for new ways of seeing things, negotiating life in new and creative ways. Action or behaviour is governed by the evolving frames of reference which the individual and family use to make sense of their lives.

Behaviour also provides *evidence* for people which leads them to make judgements, comparisons and distinctions. Cognition and behaviour are in a sytemic relationship with each other. A change in behaviour or circumstances can lead to new thinking about the problem. New thinking, a new perspective or metaphor leads to new action and interaction (Procter 1981; 1985; 1987).

Watzlawick *et al.* (1974) distinguish between 'first order change' and 'second order change'. The former is change among a set of alternatives (see Figure 6.3); for example in dealing with his 'lazy' child a father might use certain approaches: scolding, pleading, threatening, ignoring. Second order change occurs when the set of alternatives itself alters, when for example he comes to see the problem in a different light, or shifts his attention to another area of concern, with a new set of alternatives. The relationship is formally exemplified in a car where each gear (second order) has a certain range of speeds controllable by the accelerator (first order).

The mechanism of change in Brief Therapy (as in any successful problem resolution) is of a second order type. The family members start behaving and understanding in a different way, entering a new configuration of the cognitive/interactional system. Such change does not require conscious analysis or even awareness on the part of the people concerned. Insight is not a necessary condition for change. It may occur at the point of intervention, concurrently with the change, later, upon reflection, or not at all. We assume that all the time in our lives, much psychological change and learning is occurring without our conscious knowledge. We learn a great deal from our cases without always recognizing what we have learned.

In reporting changes and improvements the family member may attribute them to a particular cause or may simply be unaware of how the change was achieved. It tends to have an 'effortless' quality about it, the 'forcing' of

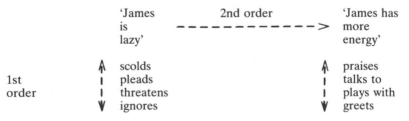

*Figure 6.3* First and second order change

oneself or 'trying harder' being a phenomenon associated with first order changes. How to respond to this in therapy will be discussed in the next section.

## THE ROLE OF THE THERAPIST

It is not possible to do justice to all the creative methods that have been devised within the tradition in a chapter of this length, especially to the many types of interventions used. We can only refer the reader to the various sources in the references for a more elaborate consideration. We will now consider in more detail some of the basic procedures used in the course of conducting Brief Therapy. Procedures can be divided up into (1) information gathering, (2) case planning, (3) interventions, and (4) dealing with improvements.

### Information gathering

The information sought is the definition of the problem, the attempted solutions, the goal, discovering the family's position on the problem and their position on treatment.

The problem (or if there are several, the one focused upon, that is the 'chief problem') must be ongoing, occurring in the present, either continuously or from time to time. For example a husband presents his wife's affair of five years ago as a problem, as evidence of her untrustworthiness. She insists that this is the long dead past. In this situation the therapist will want to know, 'How is this a problem to you now?' Recurrent rows about the issue would be acceptable as a problem to work on in therapy.

The problem is defined in specific, behavioural terms as much as is possible, where and when it occurs, its frequency and duration, who is involved and the sequences of behaviour occurring in the social context. Specific examples are examined. When interviewing several members of a family this emphasis on the concrete is very valuable for teasing out and clarifying the differences in their views of the problem. Typical therapist questions might be, 'What actually happened on that Tuesday night? Let's go over it in detail. Who said what when? What happened after that?' The process is somewhat akin to the work of a detective investigating an event, but obviously conducted in a sympathetic rather than an accusatory way.

Having negotiated a problem, the attempted solutions applied by the symptom bearer or identified patient him or herself as well as those closely involved are investigated in detail. Thus the therapist may enquire; 'When this problem occurs, what do you *do* in order to try and stop it? How do you try to help your son?' This gives us an understanding of the way the problem is maintained systemically in the interaction. It also has the effect of 'clearing the decks' of unsuccessful approaches to the problem, reducing the chance of the therapist repeating previous errors.

Next the goal or change that the family members would like to see achieved as a result of the therapy is defined. This should be achievable, specific and defined positively. Usually the family will start with a vague and Utopian goal, for example, 'We just want to be happy all the time' or with a negative goal 'Just to stop these panic attacks', 'Not to feel so depressed'. Considerable care is taken to negotiate a clear behavioural goal. Ordinarily people are asked to consider what smallest change would convince them that a glimmer of light was present at the end of the tunnel. Often then, further work is necessary in reducing the magnitude of the goal first offered. For example a mother who complained of shouting continually and ineffectually at her idle and difficult teenagers produced an impressive list of their shortcomings. Asked to select the least serious item as an initial goal she chose their failure to keep their rooms tidy. It was suggested from what she had already said that this would represent too complete a change of heart on her children's part. She was asked to choose just one aspect of the state of their rooms on which to focus. She chose their failure to make their beds.

From knowledge of her usual approach to her children it proved possible to suggest how to handle the issue of bed-making in such a way that the beds got made. So impressed was this woman at the success of this intervention that she generalized the same principle to her other dealings with her children to great effect.

It is important that the problem, attempted solutions and goal are all defined in the correct order since together they can be thought of as forming a template which can be fitted over the complex situations that are presented in therapy. This in itself has a clarifying effect for both therapist and family which allows new thinking and planning to occur. Sometimes a careful investigation of this type is sufficient in itself to effect significant change.

This template can be fitted over a situation in differing ways until a workable contract is negotiated. For example one might start therapy with a woman's depression as the main complaint. Attempted solutions to this complaint by the woman herself, her husband, her mother, her doctor are investigated. A goal is defined. The woman then begins to mention that her husband behaves in a way she finds intolerable: he talks and acts in an unacceptably coarse way. The therapist finds her motivation in this area to be much keener than the original problem which was emphasized by the mother and by the doctor who referred the case on this basis. The therapist therefore proceeds in investigating attempted solutions and goals in the new area: what has she done to try and get husband to behave better, how does she *want* him to behave? This is now made the basis of the therapeutic contract rather than the depression. This kind of shift will sometimes be made several times over the course of therapy as in a case where first the husband's depression was addressed. With improvement in this area, the family said that the wife was depressed and had been so all along. Later, problems she was experiencing with her daughter were focused upon. Resolution of these enabled the therapy to be completed in a way very satisfactory to all the family members.

In practice positive change in any area begins to effect beneficial change in other areas of the clients' lives. Which aspect to negotiate as the problem therefore becomes a strategic matter, based on factors of motivation, and whether the therapist can foresee a workable therapeutic strategy.

The therapist is careful to ascertain the clients' understanding of or *position* on their problem and what they see as an appropriate treatment. This can be done explicitly thus: 'What do you make of this problem? Why do you think it is occurring? What do you think I should be recommending in the way of advice?' It also will be gained implicitly by listening to them and observing their behaviour, noting the kind of value system they use in their discussion. For example parents may have a medical, a psychodynamic or a moral position about their son's addiction which could be seen as an illness, or the result of unhappiness when younger or as simple laziness. These positions lead the parents into applying particular attempted solutions (respectively pills, long talks or admonishment) and the position will be most readily ascertained from the attempted solutions. Since such positions are intimately involved in problem maintenance, great care is taken to avoid any premature challenge of them lest stimulating family members to defend their beliefs inadvertently enhances their commitment to them.

Before proceeding with therapy, the individual or family's willingness and motivation should be checked by asking, 'Would you like to do some work with me to help sort the problems out?' A brief explanation of therapy can be given at this point: that meetings usually take place every two or three weeks and that the therapist will give them things to do or think about between the sessions. In asking, 'Do you *want* to work with me?', the therapist will require an affirmative answer before proceeding. If there is any resistance or doubt, this will be apparent from facial expression or voice tone. Doubt can often be usefully met by suggesting that they 'go away and think about it for a few days and let me know if you want to proceed'. The important thing is that the therapist does not get into the position of being more motivated to achieve change than the client, however much the former may see that beneficial change can be effected.

## Case planning

The two kinds of information thus gathered, the specific events and the families' understanding of them, are the raw materials of case planning. Various attempted solutions generally spring from a particular way of understanding the problem. Like musical variations on a theme they differ in superficial detail, but are identical in spirit. It is this essential but unstated premise which underlies the attempted solution (and hence the maintenance of the problem) which we have called the 'nub' of the problem. It can be hard to extract this necessary general principle from a mass of specific detail. A useful check at this stage is to state this central idea as a simple slogan. If this cannot be done, more information or planning is required. Thus in the case of an agoraphobic daughter, both parents and her previous therapists had practised many variations on the theme of 'You can beat it if you try'. This 26-year-old woman had left home but had returned following a divorce.

Once the nub of the problem has been identified, some equally general but mutually exclusive alternative is constructed. For most practical purposes this may be thought of as its opposite. In this case it was reasoned that the opposite of the parents encouraging their daughter to confront her agoraphobia was to restrain her from doing so. Clearly an adequate intervention must embody this general principle and apply it to some specific aspect of the problem. However, since this ran precisely counter to the parents' thinking, plausible reasons were needed to restrain her from going out.

It is to provide such plausible reasons that the second type of information is collected. Information about *their* position or understanding is used in order to create a frame of reference within which the intervention seems credible. This is accomplished by endorsing and rearranging those positions expressed by the family to create another way of understanding the problem. This is called reframing.

> To reframe means to change the conceptual and/or the emotional setting or viewpoint in relation to which a situation is experienced and place it in another frame which fits the 'facts' of the same concrete situation equally well or even better and thereby changes its entire meaning.
>
> (Watzlawick *et al.* 1974 : 95)

In this case the therapist reframed while under considerable pressure from the family to do something. She volunteered that she was fully in agreement with the family and their previous theapists that the daughter should, by gradual steps, regain her independence, saying 'However, this is a serious case, and clearly the steps attempted have not been small enough and everyone has been trying to go too quickly in her treatment. It hadn't been working because she was being rushed.' Once a reframe is accepted, the therapist will ordinarily present an intervention as a specific application of that general principle, so that what is asked of the patient is seen to be consistent with the reframe.

It was known that this agoraphobic woman was idle all day whereas in her years away from home she had been a housewife. Accordingly it was suggested that domestic rehabilitation should precede efforts to get her out and about. She was encouraged to stay at home and to take on gradually more and more domestic responsibility. This was done gradually over several months. Although initially co-operative, the patient soon tired of the domestic round, her agoraphobia faded away and she resumed normal mobility.

## Interventions

The general rationale for intervention is to provide the family with strategies which will modify or interrupt the existing attempted solutions. Since it is these that are maintaining the problem, a successful intervention leads to a significant improvement. This is often experienced as a spontaneous change and is not necessarily attributed to the therapy.

A skilled Brief Therapist will already begin to intervene quite early in the therapy with shifts in meaning, subtle reinterpretations, and so on. However more commonly a particular strategy is worked out and applied only after thorough investigation of the problem with its associated attempted solutions, goals and positions. Careful case planning outside the therapy hour is essential, followed by systematic laying of foundations and testing of the ideas before giving the intervention proper. This is a planned process that builds up to one intervention, which is directed at the nub of the problem.

Since the problem itself stimulates the family's attempted solutions, one way of proceeding consists of *restraining the family from trying to make changes*. This may be done in various ways, asking the family 'not to try and make changes for the time being', to 'proceed slowly' or to point out certain dangers that would occur if the change was made. Thus it may be pointed out to the obese patient that if he or she were to reduce his or her eating at this point it might lead to increased marital conflict or to a sense of loneliness and isolation. A very useful strategy which can be used almost routinely early in therapy is to get the family to monitor the problem, noting down the date and time of its occurrence so that a proper study can be made before attempts are made to deal with it. In our experience this alone may lead to significant improvement.

Symptom prescription, asking that someone deliberately produce his or her symptom, is an indirect way of interrupting attempted solutions and is very useful for example with panic attacks, obsessional thinking and child behaviour problems. It may be presented as a way of attaining 'control' over the problem. Learning to produce the behaviour at will teaches one a lot about how to prevent it at will. Reframing the problem, for example saying that marital conflicts are ways that people use to try and get closer to one another also works by undermining the previous attempted solutions. In our experience it is rarely necessary to be 'dishonest'. Successful Brief Therapy interventions usually turn out to correspond with a deeper 'truth' about the family's situation.

In one case, that of a wife's depression and agoraphobia, the couple were seen separately because of their widely differing positions. The wife, a Christian, was encouraged to pray regularly. The husband, a scientifically minded and very competent man who had recently retired (this coinciding with the onset of the problems), was given an elaborate explanation of the psychodynamics of depression and how low self-esteem is maintained through the person continually comparing herself unfavourably to other more competent role-models. He was asked to show his wife some small sign of weakness each day. For example to come in from the garden complaining of a headache saying, 'I don't know, I don't seem to feel myself today', and to sit on the sofa and do nothing for half-an-hour. The couple returned a month later, she having completely recovered. The husband reported that he had not even used the strategy but had thought a great deal about it. A subtle change in his behaviour towards his wife, replacing his previous over-helpful and frustrated admonishments, released the couple from their entrenched positions.

It cannot be overemphasized that the intervention must be worked out anew with each case taking full cognizance of the unique situation. Standardized prescriptions from other cases and from the literature may sometimes be used as a basis but must be fully reconstructed and modified to fit the circumstance of the case.

## Dealing with improvements

The way improvements are dealt with in this approach is one of the most useful aspects of the model. How one deals with a reported change, even a minimal one, can make a very significant difference to the outcome of the therapy. The idea of improvement work is to consolidate the change and to reinforce the locus of responsibility for it in the client, not in the therapy. Careful definition of the problem has the additional advantage of allowing even small changes for the better to be detected. Sometimes, improvement is reported at the first interview, in which case the following procedures may be applied immediately instead of going into the problem.

The improvement is defined carefully. Thus the therapist might say, 'What makes you say that he is better? Can you give me an example of how things are better?' This is done at some length and has the effect of consolidating the change and of indirectly encouraging a more optimistic frame of reference in the family. Next, the family is asked to account for how they achieved the change. Thus 'How did you manage it? How do you think your wife managed it?' It may be useful then at this point to comment that the improvement indicates that change is possible. Thus 'It seems that you have it in you to make changes. You have the ability to be more relaxed and cheerful.'

After this one might ask for possible ways in which each of the family members could deliberately create a relapse. This often leads to the family themselves seeing how their attempted solutions were problematic. Thus 'I know you wouldn't want to, but what would you have to do to go back to how things were before you made this improvement?' Each family member can be asked to consider this at some length, but no particular use is made of the material other than a summary. Thus 'I see, if you were to nag and get at your daughter a lot, *that* could lead to her slipping back.' This again helps to consolidate the change and make it less likely that they will revert to the old patterns. It also helps to prevent spontaneous recurrences of the problem from escalating.

Finally, if the improvement still seems rather tenuous, a stronger version of the above can be offered in the form of a relapse prescription. It is suggested that they deliberately produce the problem again, usually at a definite time in the coming weeks, in order to learn some more useful things about the problem and how to 'nip it in the bud' should it recur spontaneously.

In terminating therapy we nearly always say to people that, should a setback occur which they are unable to resolve, they should contact the therapist for an appointment. This rarely leads to dependency and may consolidate improvement further by connecting relapse with the inconvenience of arranging further therapy. If people do need to come back it allows the therapeutic work to be resumed with the minimum disruption, often allowing quite minimal intervention to deal with the problem.

## EFFECTIVE THERAPISTS

It has been argued that people become 'stuck' with their problem as a consequence of the narrowing that occurs in their perspective as they fail in initial attempts at its solution. The therapist's main value to individuals in this position is that of not being personally involved, and therefore being able to take a wider view of the social context within which the problem occurs; colloquially, being able to see the wood for the trees.

The therapist strives to be *modest* in regard to his or her ability to influence people. In particular he or she does not expect anyone to be influenced before the therapist appears to them to be credible as a source of help. To seem credible the therapist demonstrates an intelligent comprehension of their reality, largely by endorsing it.

The process of Brief Therapy involves patient gathering of information during therapy sessions and careful case-planning between them. It is a methodical, step-by-step approach, each new step being timed in accordance with the family's acceptance of the last and great care being taken to match the pace offered by the family. The qualities the therapist would seek to exemplify are those of a patient and thorough interviewer. The techniques through which these qualities are manifest are largely interviewing skills. Since the therapist would not seek to change anyone's mind either through explanation or argument, Brief Therapy is devoid of therapeutic techniques of confrontation or the fostering of insight.

On initial meeting, the therapist's attitude should be that of an interested but uninformed outsider seeking to understand the problem and taking at face value the explanations given by those involved. Respecting the family members' understanding of their circumstances in this way necessitates matching the degree of concern shown by family members in regard to the problem. The therapist will take matters no less seriously than the most concerned family member.

The therapist's concern at the opening of therapy is to gain information while remaining credible to the family members as a potential source of help. As described in the previous section, behavioural descriptions of the problem, attempted solutions and a goal are the therapist's first priority. In attaining this, care is taken to respect the pace at which the family can proceed, each new item of information being carefully clarified and checked before proceeding to the next. The therapeutic skills used are of two types: those associated with obtaining the necessary information and those associated with maintaining credibility.

In gathering information, the therapist typically follows the client, asking questions to clarify whatever he or she has just been told. Reflective listening is of great value in such clarification. 'Let me check that I am understanding you correctly. What you are saying is . . .' 'So, am I right in saying that on Monday Charles and his father were at home having an argument and you . . .' Asking for behaviourally specific information tends to encourage the person to attend to images and memories of the events. This can be seen from eye movements. Generally the therapist learns not to interrupt clients when their attention is directed internally. It is also important to be able to interrupt gracefully if the interview is getting sidetracked into too much detail.

In addition to taking the family's lead as to the pace and seriousness of the therapeutic encounter, the therapist attempts to learn and subsequently speak the language used by the family in describing the problem. Often this involves a willingness to use descriptive terms before their referents are clear. For example, hearing a wife's outbursts of temper described by her husband as 'head fits' and observing the wife to acquiesce with this description, the therapist's next question might well be of the form, 'When you have a head fit, how then does your husband react?'

A more difficult aspect of information gathering is that of persisting with each stage of the enquiry until the necessary information is obtained. This consists of a skilled process of getting people to be specific in their descriptions of the problem and of their efforts to resolve it. Thus 'What did you actually do at that point?' 'What were his actual words?'

Segal (1980) has described Brief Therapy as 'a body of ideas about how to influence people'. To be influential means gaining credibility in the family's eyes as one whose counsel they would wish to follow. This credibility is assumed to be in direct proportion to the degree of comprehension shown by the therapist of the family's view of the problem. The challenge to the therapist is to show sufficient agreement with their construction of reality as to be credible, while leaving sufficient leeway to negotiate a solvable problem.

The essential skills in this regard are those of manoeuvrability (Fisch *et al.* 1982). These are used to avoid any premature confrontation of the family's version of reality. These skills are primarily linguistic in nature. Accordingly saying the therapist is very careful in what he or she has to say to preserve sufficient leeway to permit subsequent revision. Often this is a matter of qualifying any assertions made in order to be sufficiently vague as to avoid committing oneself absolutely. Interestingly this is the direct opposite of the communicational style fostered in the family members by the therapist's polite persistence in pursuit of behavioural descriptions.

Given sufficient qualification it is possible to pull back from any statement as soon as the slightest degree of resistance is encountered, for example the response of 'yes, but' or the absence of a confirmatory head-nod. So vital is this aspect of technique that Herr and Weakland (1979) give a full chapter to a discussion of how to recognize a potential argument and how to extricate oneself from it. When a disagreement is manifest within a family, the therapist will seek to remain neutral while indicating his or her comprehension of each opposing view without adopting any particular one. In the face of a continuing dispute, the therapist may well try to get the parties to agree to differ in order to continue in a more orderly fashion.

The therapist shows a disinclination to any use of expert status or presumed therapeutic ability. Even when specifically asked for comments and advice, he or she is unlikely to be drawn. For example in response to such an enquiry, the therapist might well say, 'I appreciate the urgency of your plight but I wouldn't be treating it with the seriousness it merits if I replied without giving the matter careful thought. I may need more information.' In particular the therapist will not assume any responsibility for defining the nature of the problem or determining what the goals of treatment should be.

Once sufficient information has been gained for case planning to suggest a possible intervention, consideration must be given to how to get the family members to do what is envisaged. Care having been taken to note and to accommodate to the understandings that family members have in relation to

their problem, these positions may now be rearranged by reframing to generate a perspective within which going along with the suggested intervention
seems logical. The therapist's ability to influence people is now tested
directly and so particular care is given to sustain manoeuvrability. In particular, the therapist will wish to be unhurried in laying the groundwork for
intervention, mentioning ideas and checking their acceptability before committing him or herself to them. The ability apparently to hesitate to offer
guidance may at this stage often motivate family members to request instruc-
tion. Such hesitancy requires no particular technique but is often useful in
helping others to feel the urgency of the situation. A simple and often
effective way of maximizing motivation at this stage consists of alluding to an
idea that might prove beneficial but suspecting that it will be unfortunately
unacceptable in some way to the family members. And then allowing them
to prove the therapist wrong in this assumption.

Another component of manoeuvrability at this stage is a willingness to
take up a clear position in opposition to that taken by family members. This
affords them an opportunity to defend those views thereby enhancing their
commitment to them. Thus having secured an individual's compliance with a
particular therapeutic suggestion, discussion will be offered about the
potential difficulties that may arise in its performance. In this discussion
much will be made of these difficulties to afford a genuine opportunity for
the individual to argue, 'Well it won't be as bad as that'. For similar reasons,
after successful intervention, the first news of improvement is often handled
by suggesting a slowing of the pace of improvement.

Training in these qualities and their component skills is ordinarily by
apprenticeship within a small clinic team working together for half a day a
week. Full use is made of live supervision of trainees and video facilities
(Walker and Procter 1981; Procter and Stephens 1984).

Most of the skills described herein are verbal interview skills and are not
difficult to learn. The respectful qualities of Brief Therapy make it essentially non-confrontative, so a trainee is less likely to feel uncomfortable during
sessions and thus can think more clearly. The skills of respectfulness and
manoeuvrability are somewhat easier to acquire than the dogged but polite
persistence necessary in acquiring behavioural descriptions. Brief Therapy
may be thought of as an interrogative method and much practice in such
questioning is necessary.

While beginning therapists enjoy the clarity and apparent simplicity of the
Brief Therapy method, those trainees with experience in other approaches
to family therapy may have real difficulty in suppressing the urge either to
confront or explain the family system, since throughout interviews opportunities for such attempts at direct influence will continually present themselves.

While the method of Brief Therapy can be clearly stated, it is difficult to practise well. This difficulty is principally one of case planning, that of attaining the clarity of thinking necessary to organize complex clinical data in relation to ideas as simple as that of a problem's being maintained by the efforts to solve it. This difficulty is largely a psychological one of sustaining a sufficiently wide or general viewpoint in the face of a welter of very specific details, each of which implies the way of looking at the social context that is maintaining the problem.

In case planning, the value of team work cannot be overemphasized. Once a case is planned it may well seem very simple, as though it ought to have been obvious all along how to proceed. Ordinarily a good deal of careful and sometimes frustrating discussion will be necessary before a suitable intervention emerges.

A final quality seems impossible to train. This is the deftness, the economy with time and words shown by the seasoned practitioner. In Oxford in 1984, John Weakland did a live consultation as part of a conference. The precision with which he obtained only the information he required, the sureness with which the focus of enquiry was shifted, all looked very simple, quite easy to do and obviously right. Bateson called this quality 'grace'. It is not yet apparent in our work.


# A FAMILY IN THERAPY

Charles, aged 25, was referred by his GP. Some years previously he had been given the diagnosis of schizophrenia and received various forms of treatment, including group therapy, at a University Clinic after he had experienced difficulties during the first year of his course. Subsequently he had left his course and had lived at home with his parents and sister Ann. The family again asked for help, having found his behaviour intolerable.

Charles was seen alone for two sessions and proved very difficult to interview since he interrupted with questions, disqualifications and mischievous personal remarks about the therapist (Procter). He said that he had a split personality and had been told that he was a schizophrenic. He wanted to know immediately, 'Am I a schizophrenic?' He feared that he was a homosexual and had been thrown out of the local cricket club for 'looking at people'. 'Are they allowed to throw me out of the cricket club?', he enquired.

The therapist seized on his notion of split personality and asked him to describe the two parts in detail. The therapist was told that one part was homosexual but had no capacity for sexual arousal and had 'bad thoughts'. The other part enjoyed looking at pretty girls and got sexually aroused.

Occasions when one or the other part was predominant were ascertained from recent examples. He said that, as a Catholic, he had had suicidal thoughts as 'homosexuality is a mortal sin'. Details of his experiences at convent school and at university, including his activities in a Maoist group, were obtained. It was discovered that his parents were extremely critical of his behaviour and that they had initiated the referral to the GP.

The second session was concluded with a long explanation of Fairbairn's theory of personality, that each of us has three parts called the central ego, the libidinal ego and an anti-libidinal ego. A contract for therapy of ten sessions was made and the therapist stated that he also wanted to work with the rest of the family on some occasions so that he could understand the situation as thoroughly as possible before making any recommendations.

In the next session Charles was seen with his mother and father. Mother, of German origin, having married and settled in England in the 1950s, was the chief spokesperson. She dominated the session with a list of complaints about Charles and said she was nearly at the end of her tether. Her attempted solutions consisted of demanding explanations from Charles of his behaviour, instructing him to wash more often and to tidy his room; she had also hit him on one occasion. She complained that he would not change his underwear and asked him on most days if he had put on clean underpants. She became most incensed at continual arguments between Charles and his father and broke down in tears in response to these.

Father, a mild man who had recently retired from a responsible job in the Civil Service, was most worried at Charles's lack of socializing. He urged Charles to get out more instead of spending so much of his time in his room. They usually had lunch together in various pubs selected by Charles as being acceptable to him.

Charles's mention of homosexuality was like a red rag to a bull to his parents and immediately stimulated a shower of indignant anger from the mother. Father met it with reassurance that it was not true. Mother responded to this by criticizing her husband for being too soft on Charles. He should be, she said, stricter with him and had he been so in the past Charles would not be in the state that he was in now.

The family were seen in various combinations over the next eight sessions. It was learned that Charles's sister, Ann, was engaged to be married and the wedding occurred towards the end of this series of sessions. Charles had always been closer to his mother, and Ann to her father, when they were younger. Therapeutic interventions consisted mainly of attempting to modify the patterns of the family's behaviour through prescribing it. These were given under the general rationale that the family were at a point of transition in the life cycle when the children were becoming independent. Ann's relationship with her fiancé had left her father isolated and lonely. Charles was reframed as having developed a 'heterophobia' in order to slow down his own developing independence in order to provide his father with companionship.

This work met with mixed results. Improvements were reported in Charles's behaviour but were followed by setbacks largely undoing the changes. The family went through a number of crises, with desperate telephone calls to the therapist between sessions. Charles was briefly admitted to the psychiatric ward on one occasion.

The breakthrough occurred after mother was seen alone on the eleventh session. She spoke at great length about her own family, most of whom had died. She expressed great regret at having married her husband. However it would be impossible to break up her marriage and return to Germany now. All her roots were here now and of course there was Charles. A recent occurrence was for her simply the last straw. A parcel had arrived for her at work. She was a secretary at a very respectable private school. She opened the parcel in front of her colleagues only to find a pair of Charles's soiled underpants.

The session was concluded with a 'pact'. The therapist said that he could think of a method that the mother could use to sort out Charles's behaviour, but that it was essential that she commit herself to using it before knowing what it was. This was necessary because it would only work if she persevered with it over a number of occasions. During these occasions she might be tempted to give it up before it had a chance to take effect. If she gave it up sooner, it would not work and could even lead to a deterioration in the situation. This was done in the context of good rapport in which the therapist had told her of his own German mother, with discussions of the German way of life and the difficulties of leaving one's country of origin.

She returned to the next session determined to carry out anything that might help with the situation. Accordingly she was given an intervention modified from one used in the Brief Therapy literature (Fisch *et al.* 1982).

When Charles played her up in his various ways, she was to say to him, 'Look Charles, I know I can't stop you but I do wish that you would stop doing that.' She was asked to repeat back what she was to say. In her thick accent she said what she thought approximated the message. She came up with something entirely different, changing it to a much more demanding directive, of the type she had already been using with so little success. The wording was repeated with an explanation of the difference. Over the next few minutes she seemed to begin to understand what was required.

She was then asked to translate the words into German. Again she changed the meaning into a more hierarchically 'one-up' command, but with a little discussion was able to find a German sentence which when translated resulted in the intended meaning: 'Ich weiss dass ich dich nicht davon abhalten kann, aber ich würde mich wirklich freuen wenn du das nicht tun würdest . . .'

She left the session in a rather excited frame of mind. She returned having been most pleasantly surprised about the effect. Charles had responded in a co-operative way on several occasions. Charles began to improve his behaviour and it was possible to terminate the therapy a short time later. A chance meeting with Charles two years later confirmed a picture of no further problems with his having successfully held down a job for several months.

With hindsight it can be seen how work with the mother alone could have produced results much more quickly. Mother had been the chief 'customer' in the situation. Since that time (1980) the therapist has been able to use the principle of working with the most motivated individual in the family in many cases with most pleasing results.

# REFERENCES

Bodin, A. (1981). The interactional view: family therapy approaches of the Mental Research Institute. In A.S. Gurman and D.P. Kniskern (eds) *Handbook of Family Therapy*, New York, Brunner/Mazel.

Fisch, R., Weakland, J. and Segal, L. (1982). *The Tactics of Change: Doing Therapy Briefly*, San Francisco, Jossey-Bass.

Haley, J. (1963). *Strategies of Psychotherapy*. New York, Grune & Stratton.

—— (1973). *Uncommon Therapy: The Psychiatric Techniques of Milton H. Erickson*. New York, Norton.

—— (1985). *Conversations with Milton H. Erickson, MD. 1. Changing Individuals*. New York, Triangle Press.

Herr, J. and Weakland, J. (1979). *Counseling Elders and their Families*. New York, Springer.

Kelly, G.A. (1955). *The Psychology of Personal Constructs*. vols 1 and 2. New York, Norton.

Procter, H.G. (1981). Family construct psychology: an approach to understanding and treating families. In S. Walrond-Skinner (ed.) *Developments in Family Therapy*. London, Routledge & Kegan Paul.

—— (1985). A construct approach to family therapy and systems intervention. In E. Button (ed.) *Personal Construct Theory and Mental Health*. Beckenham, Kent, Croom Helm.

—— (1987). Change in the family construct system: the therapy of a mute and withdrawn schizophrenic patient. In R. Neimeyer and G. Neimeyer (eds) *A Casebook of Personal Construct Therapy*. New York, Springer.

Procter, H.G. and Stephens, P.K.E. (1984). Developing family therapy in the day hospital. In A. Treacher and J. Carpenter (eds) *Using Family Therapy*. Oxford, Blackwell.

Segal, L. (1980). Conference given on Brief Therapy at Bristol University.

Walker, G. (1985). The Brief Therapy of a compulsive gambler. *Journal of Family Therapy*, 7, 1–8.

Walker, G. and Procter, H.G. (1981). Brief Therapeutic approaches: their value in contemporary day care. In *New Directions for Psychiatric Day Care*. London, NAMH.

Watzlawick, P. (1978). *The Language of Change: Elements of Therapeutic Communication*. New York, Basic Books.

Watzlawick, P., Beavin, J. and Jackson, D.D. (1967). *Pragmatics of Human Communication*. New York, Norton.

Watzlawick, P., Weakland, J. and Fisch, R. (1974). *Change: Principles of Problem Formation and Problem Resolution*. New York, Norton.

Weakland, J. (1984). Conference given on Brief Therapy at Oxford.

Weakland, J., Fisch, R., Watzlawick, P. and Bodin, A. (1974). Brief Therapy: focused problem resolution. *Family Process*, 13, 141–68.

# CHAPTER 7

# EXPERIENCING THE PAST IN THE PRESENT: A HISTORICAL APPROACH TO FAMILY THERAPY

## Paul O'Reilly and Eddy Street

## INTRODUCTION

This chapter presents an approach to family therapy that is based on an understanding of how the past influences and directs present-day behaviour. As with any approach to therapy many variants could be described. There are those family therapists who stress the explication of historical issues through the educative role of therapy (Lieberman 1979; Paul 1976). Bowen (1978) and Framo (1976) suggest that clients need to work through historical issues with their parents and other family members. This may take place in the session or as a result of exercises and tasks given to any individual by the therapist. Byng-Hall (1978) underlines the importance of working with the 'historical' myths and rituals which the family bring to therapy. Whitaker (1975; Whitaker and Keith 1981) considers that problematic past events are replayed symbolically through the family's interaction with the therapist, and he suggests that the therapist uses his or her own presence to provide an experience that is reparative. Our own therapeutic styles are more towards the use of the experiential aspects of the past in the present and this aspect will be stressed in this chapter. The approach emphasizes the experience of the therapist as much as that of family members. Readers will use their own experience and knowledge of their own history and their own family to add the emotional dimension we are unable to present fully in words alone. We hope that you will be affected by our writing. We all carry our history with us. As family members we influence and are influenced by others; as therapists we are not neutral, we interfere in other people's lives.

We therefore need to develop theories and guiding principles which enable us to 'interfere' positively and which are based on our experiences as well as those of the families we see. These are central issues in the way we construct our therapeutic practice.

# THEORETICAL ASSUMPTIONS

## Major theoretical concepts

Central to our method of therapy is an understanding of the family life cycle (Carter and McGoldrick 1982; Street 1985). Families change and develop. There are a number of stages in the life cycle as the individuals in a family grow and hence demand change, such as courtship and marriage; children being born, going to school, becoming adolescent and leaving home. Different individuals and the different generations are all engaged in a struggle with different issues at the same time. But always those issues follow the same pattern which extends from birth until death. The cyclical nature is such that we can enter the process at any point yet return to the same life cycle point within another generation. Any position on the life cycle is in itself embedded in a context which is ever changing, expanding, or contracting, though not always in helpful ways.

All family members are potentially able to experience the roles of every generation; a woman in her later years may have the experience of being a grandmother, a mother and a daughter. Even though we assume that these roles change over time, there is a part of the self that is forever a daughter, and forever a mother. Try as we may we are unable to lose the experience of childhood; the experience of being cared for in a certain way, of having certain behaviours expected of us, of being given certain knowledge of ourselves and others. Naturally if this is our experience, when we were children our parents were not only experiencing being parents but were also reliving aspects of their childhood while they cared for us. It is these issues that both link and separate the generations; these are the issues that are truly transgenerational (Boszormenyi-Nagy and Sparks 1973).

Each family member struggles with closeness and with distance: with *intimacy* and *autonomy* (Winnicott 1965). This is a central paradox in growth and development: growth is promoted at the same time as dependency is necessary. The same paradox occurs for the therapist, in that people are helped to help themselves but therapeutic involvement may promote dependency and possibly helplessness. A dance develops (Brody 1977) full of intricate weaving patterns as people move close and are then repelled by intimacy, move apart and are then frightened of aloneness. In many respects we can regard the emotional aspect of family life as the continual relearning of how to deal with intimacy. These two forces, of the fear of abandonment and the fear of engulfment, are developed in infanthood such that they remain central issues for all throughout life. Our solutions to the balance of these forces will be echoed in the generations succeeding us. The task for every person is to develop a sense of self, to individuate, to differentiate from others enough to be able to maintain a balance of mature dependency coupled with a personal responsibility in having needs met. The way in which we learn this will depend, to a considerable extent, on how our parents learnt it and how their parents learnt it. Each individual will be shown certain ways of reacting to stress, be encouraged to relate to certain types of people and have clear instructions on how to produce and react to emotions. Each individual will be presented, through his or her family history, with a blueprint of how a male or female life should unfold. This 'script' will suggest or even demand that particular life-styles are followed; that certain types of individuals are chosen as marital partners and that roles such as 'black sheep', 'clever person', 'prodigal son' and 'caring daughter' are followed. The script will provide the framework on which a person will construct a self-image. To ensure that all scripts are interlocking the family will have a series of 'myths' in the form of stories of past family members; these stories develop so as to inform the family now as to how the roles are to be played *vis-à-vis* each other and hence organize the 'family' sense of identity. For example, in telling a story of how a grandmother dealt with a serious illness, the family was given the message that women should act stoically when faced with ill-health. This myth informed both the men and women in the family as to what they should expect and how they should behave should illness strike a woman in the family. Myths and scripts, even though they change throughout each lifetime, are continually present to remind individuals of the origins of their identity. It is possible to look back through families' histories and note the repeating occurrence of similar events and situations, as each generation faces similar tasks in similar ways or follows the paths that have been agreed in the family myths and scripts as the proper ones to follow.

Myths and scripts provide the 'rules' that individuals are taught to follow in their relationships. Hence the nature of intimacy and autonomy will be the same through successive generations. Each person will have needs to be intimate with other individuals, and so the desire for dyadic interaction will be paramount. However, particular aspects of this way of relating will be problematic for particular families. Some will be unable to cope with conflict, some will have difficulties dealing with emotions such as sadness or confusion, and others will be unable to tolerate the expression of personal needs that dyadic relating can allow. In order to deal with stress in a dyad, the pair attempt to include a third person to lessen the intensity of the feeling produced between the two. This process of triangulation is present in all families, and within any family there are a number of individuals with whom to relate dyadically and who can be triangulated (that is become inappropriately involved in what should be a dyadic interaction). Thus each individual is a member of many dyads and only a few less triads.

Bowen (1976) writes of the *family ego mass* to describe the central overlapping dynamic that occurs as a result of each member's input into the family system. This represents the extent to which individuals are involved with each other; in families where autonomy has been neglected and identity depends on an over-closeness to other family members, the ego mass is then undifferentiated. Under these circumstances, family members acquire their 'strength' in the world only by submerging their identity and rigidly following the agreed family patterns. Even when children grow and leave families, the links with the original 'ego mass' remain very strong and triangulation is dominant. Boszormenyi-Nagy and Ulrich (1981) describe the *loyalty* that individuals unconsciously feel to parents, and grandparents and previous generations, through the 'family transmission process' that occurs as individuals leave families and find partners. Some strive to recreate the family they left or, in just as determined a manner, some strive to make sure that this family will not be like the previous family. These are covert, invisible, intangible forces surrounding individuals and families. We can sample them as therapists in the mutual transference and countertransference that occurs in sessions as we respond intuitively to the feelings family members bring with them. They can be made explicit for us by families as we observe the rituals they enact, listen to the myths that determine their lives, discover the secrets that everybody knows, and track the scripts that have been written way back over the generations.

## The nature of healthy family functioning

For all families, the way each organizes itself so as to carry out its tasks is covert rather than overt; it is not a matter for conscious discussion but is demonstrated in action and reaction. The family that is functioning successfully provides a place of nurturance and relative safety for its members, at the same time as allowing each to explore, to grow and develop. It has a feeling of history and belonging, and it can locate itself both now and in the past. The members can give an account of how things are now, and how they have come to be like that. Stories, myths, rituals and humour have developed in a flexible and creative manner. These can be employed to solve problems as they arise. Byng-Hall (1978) has commented on the force that is held in families by the myths that generations manufacture about each other. Bowen (1978) has cast a view of maturity as being the extent to which an individual is bound by these myths and messages. Individuals naturally vary in the extent to which they have differentiated, that is the extent to which they have been able to put aside the scripts, myths and messages and live their life just as themselves. In healthy functioning differentness is tolerated, discipline and authority clearly used and acknowledged. Authority and responsibility for the family are vested in the parents, though this may vary from time to time as occasions demand that the responsible group consists of different members. Discipline is a public matter and covert punishment is used minimally. Conversations can occur between and amongst all members about rule-infringement and the consequences of such infringement. The generations within the families know their place and have acknowledged responsibilities to each other. There are clear boundaries within and around the family. The family knows who belongs and who doesn't, and knows too the extent of the belonging. Family members have some sense of positively carrying on a tradition, that has served previous generations well, while at the same time each individual has the potential to use the strengths of his or her own history in order to change history for him or herself. Roles within the family are freely movable – occasionally parents may behave as if they were children, and children may behave in a parental manner, to their own parents. Children learn by practising for the future, and for this to be possible parents need to have been able to integrate enough parts of their past positively into their current lives. Opportunities are made available for practice to occur and thus family members can behave freely in a manner 'as if' they were playing another role. This is a central hallmark of a well-functioning family – that it has a richness of metaphorical communication and behaviour such that dangerousness is maintained at a tolerable level. There is anxiety, fearfulness, love and hate; and anger and fury are possible. Parental rage can be expressed and forgiveness can follow this. Members are allowed to apologize and it becomes easy to make amends. Intense emotions affect the whole family and the family affects all the parts. Members share their own internal worlds in a variety of ways and this aids the process of each 'healing' the other. Individuals move in and out of the family's emotional space as relationships with others outside the family are tolerated.

A family that functions well will naturally contain conflictual elements. It is not full of conflict but disagreement and difference can be labelled and tolerated. Fighting leading to resolution can and does occur and this resolution may be verbalized or may occur through action. At times of conflict, especially between two members, the others can remain outside the arena, so triangulation does not occur but if it does it is a momentary phenomenon. Conflict from one issue can be acted out on an unrelated issue but this detouring of conflict is not permanent (though some detouring can be a helpful matter) and disqualification of members is minimal. Deviance is shared; at any one time, there will always be a 'deviant' member, who confirms the others by the fact of his or her deviance. But this role of the deviant as that of the scapegoat is rotated amongst all the members. At times of stress the family members unite, becoming increasingly strong as a group of people. At these moments, the family can reaffirm its sense of belonging and of identity, as well as engage in acts of transmission of family myths and history which help overcome the stress. Crises help members to develop a sense of adventure and of containment, for within a well-functioning family change is always possible within the security of stability.

## The nature of family disturbance

Lack of healthy functioning does not, of course, imply ill-health. All families do not function well enough from time to time. Unforeseen events occur, unemployment, serious illness, death and the usual other catastrophes of living. Healthy functioning is not an absolute. There are an infinite number of ways in which families may approach the daily tasks of living. The crucial issue is that no one is being abused, seriously injured – physically, sexually or emotionally – and that the way in which the family is choosing to behave is working out well enough for all to grow and develop.

The problems that families face will certainly present many features that will be historically determined. Either someone will not have been taught how to deal with one of the usual tasks of family life, or someone will be rigidly following a family path loyally even though that way of being is not currently appropriate. Whatever the actual nature of the historical link, it more often than not involves a parent of the family not being adequately differentiated from his or her family of origin. The marital partner unconsciously colludes with this lack of differentiation. The ambivalence between the couple about the issues of differentiation and separation naturally have considerable repercussions on how the couple will manage the parenting of their children.

As issues in their dyadic relationship are felt to be unsolvable, the parents will need one of their children to be triangulated. This lessens the emotional intensity and maintains some distance between the parents on that particular issue (Byng-Hall 1980). Children therefore become triangulated on various marital themes (anger, closeness, criticism) and adopt particular roles (helper, carer, distractor) in order to allow the parents to maintain some 'stand-off' in their relationship. Children rapidly acquire their triangulated roles for reducing parental emotional intensity and distance, and if the child develops in an undifferentiated way, these roles will be carried forward into his or her own marital relationship. The triangulation will be passed on to the next generation. As triangulation becomes a dominant way of dealing with each other families find difficulty in allowing the person some separateness while at the same time providing some closeness, therefore the natural growth towards individuation is hampered.

When this happens differences become intolerable for as members strive to individuate, the striving becomes very threatening to others. Confusion and chaos ensue; with boundaries disappearing and executive functioning becoming minimal. Covert criticism grows; anxiety levels highlighted and there may be no permission for anyone to experience strong emotions. The pressures can grow as members of the family develop physiologically and as the outside world imposes requirements on them all. Generally the more a family cannot deal with anxiety and tension the more difficulties will occur over a long period of time and hence the greater the level of chronicity when the family finally seeks help, or is sent for help. As each crisis point is reached, and each attempted solution does not work, then the degree of family disturbance escalates. The family becomes frozen in a particular mode of dealing with each other and with the world. The family, in fact, remains stuck in a developmental phase that is appropriate for an earlier time in family life; consequently the ways in which they interact are not appropriate to the tasks they need to solve in the here and now. Typically it is found that the 'frozen' phase of the developmental cycle is one in which the parents themselves encountered difficulties as children.

A constant tension exists between the demands of development and the preferred mode of interaction of family members. When this tension occurs one member, usually a child, will exhibit symptomatology resulting from the strains of triangulations. Sometimes, however, the couple will 'elect' one of themselves to be symptomatic to skew their relationship. Bowen (1976) has seen this process as the couple agreeing unconsciously that between them they only have enough ego resources for one of them to function in the world and the one who 'lends' some ego strength to the other becomes depleted and symptomatic, not meeting tasks of living. The family organizes itself around the symptomatic person in such a way that other difficulties need not be addressed. There is disease in all family members and this can be managed only by more and more inflexibility and rigidity. Options become more and more limited even though change becomes more and more necessary. The delicate balance between growth and stability is lost.

# THE THERAPY PROCESS

## The nature of change

The essence of the therapeutic experience when a distressed family meets a therapist is that somehow the family come to be able to deal with the future by reaching an understanding of the past. The central techniques involve evoking memories of past experiences but the nature of setting allows family members to experience those feelings in an appropriate interpersonal context. It is assumed that such contexts have not been available to family members in the past and the therapist must therefore prepare experiences where the full range of a family's or an individual's emotional response is allowable and where it is contained and accepted. The family's appreciation of the transgenerational transmission process is not gained by 'insight', it is gained through the experience of confronting and challenging the problems they face daily.

Family members are perceived as being in distress because of the nature of the triangulated processes in the family, or they may be emotionally cut-off from various parts of their family and their history and may be struggling in an uncomfortable way with the process of differentiation. To assist people to make those changes they wish to make, the therapist will be aiming to:

1  Detriangulate, by attempting to construct dyadic relationships between family members both in the past and in the present.
2  Reverse the process of 'emotional cut-off'. This requires family members to recontact some part of their past family so they can check against reality the myths they follow about themselves. This also allows for the beginning of the construction of dyadic relationships in the family of origin.
3  Increase the differentiation of the self. Each individual is encouraged to take responsibility for themselves in an age-appropriate manner. In this way, new dyadic relationships are established in the present family.

The therapist assists the change process by encouraging the family to establish a more healthy balance between intimacy and distance and to allow them to re-evaluate the experiences that therapy symbolically creates. The essence of this is achieved experientially by the therapist offering an intimate relationship. At the core of the therapy process is the therapist, subtly demanding that the family move to a different way of relating through the means of relating with him or her. The therapist is therefore a central feature of the change process and, although seemingly dealing with the practical problems of the family, is constantly saying, 'But can you deal with me as another human being with good and bad points?' By insisting on an intimacy while problems, worries, fears and threatening fantasies are dealt with, the therapist holds out hope for the future.

However, one of the uncertainties with which therapists have to contend is the uncertainty of what it is they have done that has made the difference. Hoffman (1981) writes of the 'Thing in the Bushes' when she describes what it is that therapists want to change, for as therapists, we do not really know what it is we quite want to change and, generally, we cannot predict what will happen as change occurs. Indeed, as changes occur because of the natural process of growth that exists within every family, the therapists will and should query whether they made any contribution at all. It is this paradox of being and not being important that provides the most important experience that therapists themselves encounter as they engage in the process of change.

## The setting of therapy

To undertake work of this nature the therapist must begin by feeling comfortable in the setting in which the family is seen. For many therapists this means that they see families only in the 'clinic' but there are others who feel able to work in family homes, school, residential establishments, indeed anywhere a family can be brought together. Typically all family members are seen together on the first few occasions (all the family equals all the household). If a member does not come our practice is to send the rest away or spend time with them about the impossibility of progress in the absence of the non-attending member. An absent member is considered to be an issue of control. It is understandable that people in distress, frozen in a limited option position and fearful of change, wish to be in control of the therapy, for it is a very dangerous, risky business for them. We do not wish to battle with them but we wish to let them know that we appreciate their difficulties. We wish to begin as we mean to go on by making offers of expansions of possibilities rather than demanding and insisting that they behave differently.

The intense emotional nature of therapy means that there are powerful arguments that we should work with co-therapists. A variety of ways are possible, as equal partners, as a silent and active couple, or as part of a team. There are advantages and disadvantages to each method. However, we tend to vary the way we work, believing it is disrespectful, oppressive and probably incompetent to use the same method with every family seen. Families are seen in appointment patterns that depend on their particular needs: sometimes weekly, sometimes fortnightly, occasionally three-weekly or monthly; infrequently, less often than that. Occasionally too, families are seen (for a period at least) two or even three times weekly. There will be a period of 'assessment', and then a period of working towards agreed objectives. Objectives are often stated in the public form of goals to be achieved. We help families to clarify goals that involve all the members and we are quite willing to change goals as the therapy develops. We frequently engage in contract-making exercises with families. Following this will be a period of ending which includes a review (two to three months after termination session) and a follow-up (six months after the review). The period of therapy can last between one session and more than twenty over several years.

# THE ROLE OF THE THERAPIST

## Therapeutic conditions created by the therapist

In order to deal with the past we must be able to accept the present; hence the starting-point for the therapist is always the 'here and now'. Unless current emotions are accepted and contained, the family will be unable to move back through past experiences and towards dealing with the possibilities of future time.

Family members with limited options and feelings of distress, or even refusal to feel distress, arrive at sessions with very mixed feelings. Initially there is an experience of embarrassment and shame, a feeling of failure, because of the necessity to come to see a therapist. In addition, there may be feelings of lack of self-worth expressed as not being worth anyone's attention. There will be anger and disappointment too and there will be anxiety and fear of the unknown; of what will happen as a result of meeting the therapist. Similar feelings will be shared by the therapist as well.

Circumstances need to be created where there is confidence, a feeling of mutual struggle, where anxiety is possible and able to be utilized creatively and where desperation is energizing. The therapist needs to demonstrate acceptance, not only to the family but also of him or herself. The family need to be allowed the experience that the feelings they bring along are permissible. There are to be no secrets though the therapist is not necessarily going to share all his or her thoughts all at once with family members. In demonstrating acceptance the therapist will, at the same time, be establishing that he or she too has boundaries and limits. The family need to feel both the therapist's containment and personal rules about offering that containment. Family members need to know that the therapist is concerned about interactions; that the therapist notices how things happen and wants to hear from everyone regardless of how each chooses to communicate in the session.

The therapist therefore makes use of the material that children provide and from this base allows the child in all adults to be expressed. Demonstrating an ability to do 'childish' things and to be 'silly' is an essential element of the therapeutic conditions. The parents will be encouraged to allow their 'child' expression; as this occurs, the therapist may find him or herself moving from a 'child' to a 'parent' to a 'grandparent' as differing roles are necessary in order to contain what is expressed. All the while, the therapist is insisting on 'being me', a 'me' which the family hopefully see as containing a whole variety of behaviours from absurdity to seriousness but all of which come from a secure core of identity.

This approach does involve ways of relating not typical in Britain. Direct talking about intense emotions is not a strong point of the British life-style but we are impressed by how adventurous families are, about how they will go along with us into some ludicrous situations, about how they will enter the world of the absurd, of craziness, so as to develop strengths and investigate weaknesses. Everyone has an awareness of changing over time, as well as the experience of being a consistent being, the same person, and it is in the experience of this paradox that the seeds of growth are found, when the past can be brought into the present.

## Principal methods of therapist intervention

The essential foundation to this approach is the construction of knowledge of the family's history; knowledge that is recognized by the family members among themselves and is shared with the therapist. Some experienced therapists are able to collect the information in a piecemeal fashion and demonstrate awareness of it to the family. Others utilize specific tasks set both in and out of family sessions for the material to be collected and presented to the therapist. The beginning therapist, however, will need much experience of collecting this information by the relatively formal means of a genogram. A genogram is a pictorial representation of the family's history through the generations with the dates of important events included. As such, it is a family tree, but much more emotional material is invested in a genogram. To construct a genogram the therapist will need to begin with the family that has presented and then work back through history. All births, deaths and miscarriages need to be recorded together with the dates of divorces, leaving home, marriages, separations, and so on (see Figure 7.1, p. 166). While this information is being collected, the therapist will be noting patterns, and perhaps pointing out how an event in one generation was followed within a short space of time by an event in another generation. For example, deaths are sometimes shortly followed by births or marriages; divorces are sometimes linked to major illnesses elsewhere in the family. There is little doubt of the impact on the family of seeing in graphical form their family history; it is an experience in which clients feel embedded in the influences that have formed them. It is the process of confronting these influences that allows for the development of choice.

As the genogram is being constructed family members become aware of some aspect of their history of which they are uncertain or even ignorant. They become aware of being distant, cut off from aspects of their emotional heritage. This lack of knowledge can be utilized to assist family members to establish helpful relationships with their extended family as well as motivating them to seek information useful to the reconstruction of their image of their history and hence themselves. It is notable that one of the easiest ways to make a personal contact with someone is to ask them about their early life and family history. This act itself begins a process of relationship negotiation and allows for the development of new meaning. For example, someone may be requested to visit an uncle to enquire about his view of the parents' divorce, or information about infancy years may be sought from an older sibling who has not been seen for a long time. Bowen (1974), Lieberman

(1979) and Framo (1968) have described their own personal work on this type of task. The easiest way to begin is for the adult to ask his or her parents about their knowledge of family history. This information allows for a reappraisal of the parent–child relationship which hopefully results in an enhancement of individual self-esteem for the adult. This will have far-reaching influences in the family created by the marriage of the adult.

The elaboration of historical links introduces another essential method, namely the use of metaphor. There is a sense in which all interaction in families is metaphorical: nothing is quite as it seems; other meanings can always be implied or inferred. This is particularly the case when transgenerational issues are being dealt with. Should a therapist, for example, refer to a father wishing to be a 'sort of boyfriend' to his daughter, not only is attention being drawn to the nature of the father–daughter relationship but also it allows the mother to think about her relationship with her father. The discussion of one can be the metaphor for the other. It is the case that nearly all families have some implicit understanding of particular metaphors that apply to the entire family. The therapist needs to seek such metaphors particularly as they relate to family myths. Metaphors can range from the links of chains, trees in a forest to ships' crews, hospital staff, and so on. The therapeutic task is to use 'evidence' from the family history to show that variation is more permissible than anyone has believed. In this sense, the therapist helps the family adapt and extend their myths by using new metaphors for themselves.

Since a major aim is to make past events available for present experiencing, some therapists make use of specific experiential techniques. Family sculpting is a favoured technique for some therapists (Duhl *et al.* 1973; Walrond-Skinner 1976); here family members are encouraged to place themselves in spatial relationships symbolic of how they perceive their emotional relationships. The role-playing of family events is also often used (Byng-Hall 1980) where family members may play different family roles from their own and where the therapist takes on a specific role. Paul and Paul (1975) have used photographs of past family members as well as the use of video-taping for feedback to the family. Williamson (1978) has devised a set of experiential techniques for helping adults differentiate from dead parents. Whatever the method the therapist will be demonstrating an ability to react to and contain the emotions experienced in the 'here and now' so that, from this basis of security, past experiences and perceptions can be re-evaluated.

## Family responses to the change process

All families have in some sense prepared themselves to meet the therapist long before the referral is even made. Each family will have worked out a position within the family group that they wish the therapist to fill. As change is threatening, the family need to feel that they can place the therapist into some role in their interactional system that does not demand that they have to make any major alteration. The position offered is always a triangulated one which would prevent the therapist being effective. For example, some families offer the position of 'judge' requiring the therapist to decide whether it is mother or father who is 'wrong'. Other families want the therapist to be a magician who will cure a child's behaviour while yet others require an omnipotent expert, a 'friend for father' or an 'ally for mother'. Street (1985) has outlined the typical triangulated positions offered to therapists when the problem is child-focused. As therapy progresses and the change process occurs, the family reacts by changing the nature of the triangulation that is offered to the therapist and this can be a very rapid event as the family try to find a position that removes the force of the therapeutic effort because of their fears of change. Throughout therapy the therapist is therefore engaged in a struggle with the family not to enter any of these roles. The style of the therapist will determine whether one directly confronts the historical symbolism of these roles or whether one deals with it tangentially by metaphor and other techniques.

## Assessment of change

In common with all the other schools of family therapy, we have very little 'objective' evidence for the efficacy of the approach (Gurman and Kniskern 1981). Many families who attend would probably benefit from any model of family therapy, depending on the competence of the therapist and team. Inherent in our model though is a continual process of assessing, hypothesizing, intervening and assessing, both at a micro-level (within session) and at a more macro-level (between sessions, after therapy stops). We like to review progress with families and to follow up after an appropriate interval.

We see evidence of change as children are relieved of inappropriate responsibility and are allowed just to continue developing. As growth occurs parents enjoy being parents as well as finding it easy to be a couple and individuals at the same time.

Those families that come to articulate a different view of their history also show evidence of change but the assessment of change involves the intertwining of the therapists' role with the families' history, for effective therapy always seems to have occurred when we, as therapists, feel that we have personally benefited from the encounter. Somewhere in effective therapy there is change and development for us too.

## EFFECTIVE THERAPISTS

### Qualities of effective therapists

We have written elsewhere of some of the personal qualities that effective family therapists of this persuasion should possess (O'Reilly 1983). They need to be the kind of individuals who are attracted to this way of working and who find it personally rewarding; they also need a high level of personal awareness. Having a strong sense of personal boundary is important; to be able to know what is I and what is Not-Me is necessary in a field of people where intense emotions are being experienced by all. Therapists require an intimate knowledge of their own internal world. They should have good knowledge of as many aspects of self as possible and be able to see how they are not so very different from those people who come along to the consulting room because of distress or disintegration. An ability to tolerate uncertainty and insecurity is further required. There will be many times when a therapist using this method *will not know*, will not have a clear idea of what is happening, or even how it has come to happen. The capacity not to know is a most useful one – it is a good point from which intuition can flow.

Therapists need an awareness of their limitations – of what cannot be done, what cannot be handled emotionally at any point. Therapists can be distressed too but they then need to embark on an exercise of limited endeavour, so that they do not take on too much. Finally, they should have done as much work as possible on their own families and current relationships. Therapists must ask themselves many questions. What were our roles in our families of origin? What myths and secrets existed? What was it like for our parents in their growing-up and how did they meet? What happened around us as we were growing – locally, nationally and internationally? How did we leave home? How did we or do we form relationships? How are we intimate? How do we know about our erotic parts? In what ways do we like to be powerful and influential? What are our strengths as males and females? Why am I a therapist?

As therapists we need to be aware of the struggle that we have undertaken in order to differentiate ourselves from our family of origin. We should question the nature of our intimate relationships with our mother and our father. We need to question constantly the 'natural' way in which we become triangulated in relationships and the way we triangulate others. The sex-role system in which we grew, and in which we are currently embedded is continually to be analysed. The questions that we pose about ourselves are endless, but perhaps it is only necessary that we ask them, and that we seek answers. Therapists need to be individuals who see life as an exploration that will bring both joy and pain.

The final quality of therapists of this persuasion is that they need to know how to allow themselves to be taken care of. They need to appreciate and enjoy the roles of client, sick person, worn-out person, and needy person. They need to know where and how to find succour for themselves and know how this is beneficial to them. They need to know how to share all bits of themselves with others. The personal support systems of therapists are therefore crucial. Our partners, lovers, families, friends and colleagues must comprehend how we are affected by our work, how making use of 'self' in engaging with and struggling with families in a passionate way can be temporarily a depleting experience even if the rewards are sometimes immense.

## Skills required by therapists

Therapists who adopt this approach should have a clear background knowledge in the way a person's history affects him or her. They should have the ability to collect historical and current information from any type of source and file this away until an appropriate moment. To make use of information and to make use of self, therapists should have the skill of forming whole pictures from only a little evidence; they should be able to form larger gestalts from small amounts of information gestalts and then be able to communicate this constructed wholeness to the family. It is necessary to have the skills of receiving feedback in such a way as to be able to use it, and of being able to monitor self. Therapists should seek to have an internal supervisor in their head (Casement 1986). Another important skill to develop is the ability to make use of other people's ideas and skills, to use techniques and thoughts developed by other therapists in other schools of therapy; for example using structural techniques or behavioural tasks. Perhaps the most important and most useful skill of all is being able to work with children in some depth and intensity; such a skill is crucial in working with family systems. All too often, therapists conduct adult, individual or couple therapy in the presence of young children, or move quickly to marital work without the children attending sessions. The presence of children is of great benefit to all. We need to be able to imagine what life is like for them, and to recall how life as a child was for us. This is a difficult process as most of us have tried so very hard to put away the bad parts, the parts that we thought were unacceptable in our childhood.

Although it is straightforward to list skills that therapists require, there is one activity that is not a skill but needs to be an essential part of a therapist's behaviour. Therapists need to develop their own creativity (Pascoe 1980). This can be achieved only by therapists' developing their own style so that their own personality is an integral part of everything they do. This is the only route to becoming creative as a therapist.

## Training model for therapists

Trainees need some life experience, especially painful experience of loss and/or separation. They need to have struggled and to have experienced passion. They should have trained professionally first and have worked for some time in other models of therapy and hence have acquired a professional approach to helping others in distress. They should have had many hours of clinical experience of sitting in rooms over long periods of time with distressed and pained people. They need to have achieved some notion of what 'therapy' means. They should have undertaken a journey of personal enlightenment/awareness. They will have worked strenuously on their own differentiation from their own family of origin. This might be done formally by seeing a therapist, or informally through supervision and consultation and group work.

They then need to learn about being family therapists. There are a number of stages: formal teaching about theory, long-term experience of practice, involving a good deal of live supervision and consultation, as well as co-therapy and team-work. Finally after a long period of immersion in the method, the family therapist can let go of techniques, become him or herself and allow all that has been learnt, all that is known to flow from the self as a natural interaction with those individuals labelled as 'clients'. This latter aspect of training will always require the continual examination of issues deriving from relationships in, and with our families of origin, as well as exploration of personal matters in ongoing intimate relationships

## A FAMILY IN THERAPY

Clare, aged 14, was referred to the child guidance clinic by the local paediatric department. She had a long history of abdominal pain resulting in sporadic school attendance. Treatment by the GP and the paediatrician had produced no change. The clinic requested that all the family attend the first appointment but it was Mrs Davies who arrived with Clare and her other child Kay, aged 16. She expressed surprise that the family were referred to the clinic as there was nothing 'mentally wrong' with anyone. She resented the implication that the family had a 'bad home'. The therapist had a strong sense that Mrs Davies was keeping the appointment to appease the authority figures of the school, the GP and the paediatrician. The therapist chose to deal with this and the convening issue of father's absence by agreeing with the mother as a 'joining' measure. He stated that he felt she was correct about her daughter and herself (which she was), and that he wished they did not have to attend (which they didn't), but that the authority figures would complain about him if he did not make some effort (which they would). To

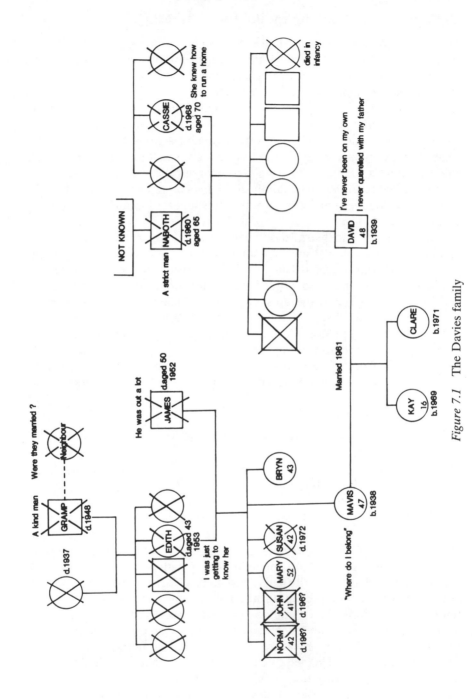

*Figure 7.1* The Davies family

prevent the therapist from incurring the wrath of others he asked Mrs Davies to do him a favour by attending with everyone. The therapist had been offered the triangulated position of incompetent authority figure and he had been able to remove himself from this as Mrs Davies and the girls agreed to the request.

At the next session when all the family attended, some time was spent on understanding what exactly happened when Clare had a stomach ache and then refused to go to school. The therapist was keen to have the parents see him as attempting to understand exactly what they perceived as being a problem. It was soon apparent that Mr Davies was somewhat distant from other family members, that his contact with family activity was through Kay. Mrs Davies presented as unsupported and as a weak person, and Clare behaved similarly. Mr Davies, when asked, would say that people should stand on their own two feet and that his wife and daughter should not be so ineffectual in the way they dealt with the world! Both daughters were triangulated with the parents, Kay as a 'healthy helper' and Clare as a 'sick child'. The therapist hypothesized that the family were stuck at a stage of development more appropriate for the caring for very young children and not adolescents preparing to individuate. The session ended with the therapist setting the task for Mr and Mrs Davies to ensure that each knew what happened to both girls each day; this was designed to give the couple some joint activity, without being too threatening to the triangulated process in the family.

On the next session the genogram was constructed (see Figure 7.1). On the mother's side of the family there was a clear repetitive history of family illness and death. There was also uncertainty about how it happened that Mrs Davies had been placed in another home when a young child. Mrs Davies had a role in her family as 'uncared-for-person'. Mr Davies' history was rather sketchy and apart from his remembrance of his father as a distant biblical type of figure, he was unable to reveal much; the therapist had the feeling that Mr Davies had not been, and was not, close to anyone in his family. His family script told him to be 'distant' from those close to him. As the family history unravelled, it was clear that the girls were fascinated by their parents' history; it was as if they were discovering for the first time where they came from.

Over the next couple of sessions the problem behaviour was discussed. The therapist was able to link metaphorically the theme of Clare's leaving home for school with mother's uncertainty of how she had left home. Was she indeed sent away, and for what reason? As these themes developed Mrs Davies would become very tearful but nobody except Clare would begin to make an effort to comfort her. The theme of not being cared for was therefore constantly present and it was possible to relate this to Mrs Davies' early history. The myth of how the parents met emerged and Mrs Davies recalled how she had formed a relationship with Mr Davies and how she felt cared for by joining his family, because there were a lot of people around. She remembered how she became a lodger in the family's household, and how kind Mr Davies' mother had been to her. This produced memories for Mr Davies and he recalled his fondness for his mother. The therapist was able to link how inadequate Mr Davies felt in caring for his mother with his undeclared feelings of inadequacy in caring for his wife. This session ended with the therapist and family joking with each other about leaving the therapy room, for the therapist would be left behind and how would he know they would come back.

The theme of the parents' attempting to support each other also dominated the next session, during which Mrs Davies was requested to visit a family member to find out why she had left her family at such an early age. This was done to reverse her unconnectedness from members of her past family. As this was being discussed the therapist had the feeling that the therapy had been about the child-like fears of the parents and the adolescent girls had been left out. He was aware that he had not dealt directly with the issue of triangulation in the current family. He simply expressed this thought and Clare immediately began to talk of her fears of being left alone. She became verbal for the first time and she reported how Kay often did things that did not help her and how her sister made her mother more anxious. The way in which they maintained the family interaction had previously not been apparent. The theme of parental discipline then arose with father being given the job of monitoring the situation closely and telling Kay off when she had not helped.

At the following session no further progress was reported and the family obviously felt ill at ease when the therapist asked about the last task set. Mrs Davies had prevented her husband from telling Kay off on several occasions by finding excuses for the girl. This was a return of the 'uncared-for' theme, for Mrs Davies did not feel that a person could be angry toward someone and still care for them. Mr Davies became somewhat angry with his wife and she immediately became tearful. Even though she was clearly very vulnerable the therapist felt it right to push Mrs Davies and as he did so she began to talk about her own death. She described her feelings of being 'beyond her time' and that her death was imminent as well as that of her sibling. She revealed her fear of dying when her daughters were angry with her for being a 'bad mother'. This was linked to her feelings that she had no chance to 'make her peace' with her mother when she died. (At this point the therapist could have role-played that scene using one of the girls as her own grandmother.) As everyone was upset the therapist supported Mr Davies in looking after his wife and gave comfort to the girls who were also distressed. Mr Davies was able to tell his wife that he wanted to be firm to help the girls and that he wanted to go to the doctor's with her to find out exactly whether or not she would die. The family left the session in a sad but determined mood. The therapist by pushing Mrs Davies had clearly touched on some central issues for her own differentiation from her family of origin. It also allowed Mr Davies to explore similar themes from his past. This approach was therefore continued.

After a total of seven sessions over a period of six months Clare was attending school regularly and it was decided to terminate treatment. The family rang up for another appointment some nine months later. Kay had just left home to work in a nearby town, and the parents were afraid of Clare's becoming frightened of going out again. It was clear that the family was checking on the availability of the therapist. They had his 'ghost' almost living with them and they needed it confirmed in reality. The therapist reinforced the ways in which the parents were dealing with Clare and the family left happy.

Throughout the therapy contract with this family the therapist related to each member in a highly symbolic fashion – as child in need, as surrogate husband and wife, as caring parent, as cruel (not available enough!) parent, and eventually as helpful professional. The history of Mr and Mrs Davies was such that it required these symbolic relationships, and as therapy drew to a close the symbolic parting was underlined by the fear of personal mortality of one of the family members; the unspeakable could be said.

Each member had many strengths, many resources, so that the family could be left with all of the pain therein – as a beginning, the key relationship between the parents was strengthened in such a way that Kay would leave home, and Clare could leave to go to school. The development of the family was allowed to continue in its natural way.

# REFERENCES

Boszormenyi-Nagy, I. and Sparks, G. (1973). *Invisible Loyalties*. New York, Harper & Row.

Boszormenyi-Nagy, I. and Ulrich, D.N. (1981). Contextual family therapy. In A.S. Gurman and D.P. Kniskern (eds) *Handbook of Family Therapy*. New York, Brunner/Mazel.

Bowen, M. (1974). Towards the differentiation of a self in one's own family. In F. Andrew and J. Lorio (eds) *Georgetown Family Symposium Papers*. Georgetown, Georgetown University Press.

—— (1976). Theory in the practice of psychotherapy. In P.J. Guerin (ed.) *Family Therapy*. New York, Gardner.

—— (1978). *Family Therapy in Clinical Practice*. New York, Jason Aronson.

Brody, W. (1977). *Family Dance*. New York, Anchor.

Byng-Hall, J. (1978). Family myths used as defence in conjoint family therapy. *British Journal of Medical Psychology*, 46, 239–50.

—— (1980). Symptom-bearer as marital distance regulator: clinical implications. *Family Process*, 19, 355–65.

—— (1985). The family script: a useful bridge between theory and practice. *Journal of Family Therapy*, 7, 301–5.

Carter, E. and McGoldrick, M. (1982). *The Family Life Cycle: A Framework for Family Therapy*. New York, Gardner.

Casement, P. (1986). *On Learning from the Patient*. London, Tavistock.

Duhl, F., Kantor, D. and Duhl, B. (1973). Learning space and actions in family therapy: a primer in sculpture. In D. Bloch (ed.) *Techniques of Family Therapy*. New York, Grune & Stratton.

Framo, J.L. (1968). My families, my family. *Voices*, 4, 18–27.

—— (1976). Family of origin as a therapeutic resource for adults in marital and family therapy: you can and should go home again. *Family Process*, 15, 193–210.

Gurman, A.S. and Kniskern, D.P. (eds) (1981). *Handbook of Family Therapy*. New York, Brunner/Mazel.

Hoffman, L. (1981). *Foundations of Family Therapy*. New York, Basic Books.

Lieberman, S. (1979). *Transgenerational Family Therapy*. London, Croom Helm.

O'Reilly, P.V.J. (1983). Personal psychology and the therapy of families. In D. Pilgrim (ed.) *Psychology and Psychotherapy: Current Trends and Issues*. London, Routledge & Kegan Paul.

Pascoe, W. (1980). Overcoming blocks to creativity in family treatment. *Journal of Family Therapy*, 2, 211–24.

Paul, N. (1976). Cross-confrontation. In P.J. Guerin (ed.) *Family Therapy*. New York, Gardner.

Paul, N. and Paul, B. (1975). *A Marital Puzzle*. New York, Norton.

Street, E. (1985). From child-focused problems to marital issues. In W. Dryden (ed.) *Marital Therapy in Britain. 2. Special Areas*. London, Harper & Row.

Walrond-Skinner, S. (1976). *Family Therapy: The Treatment of Natural Systems*. London, Routledge & Kegan Paul.

Whitaker, C. (1975). Psychotherapy of the absurd. *Family Process*, 14, 1–16.

Whitaker, C. and Keith, O.V. (1981). Symbolic-experiential family therapy. In A.S. Gurman and D.P. Kniskern (eds) *Handbook of Family Therapy*. New York, Brunner/Mazel.

Williamson, D.S. (1978). New life at the graveyard: a method of therapy for individuation from a dead former parent. *Journal of Marriage and Family Counseling*, 1, 93–101.

Winnicott, D.W. (1965). *The Family and Individual Development*. London, Tavistock.

# CHAPTER 8

# FAMILY THERAPY: AN INTEGRATED APPROACH

## Andy Treacher

## THEORETICAL ASSUMPTIONS

Gurman and Kniskern's (1981) monumental tome *Handbook of Family Therapy* is generally accepted as the most comprehensive family therapy book yet published. In many ways the book's title is a misnomer since the more comprehensive title of *Handbook of Family and Marital Therapies* would do more justice to its contents. The development of marital therapy and family therapy, at least in the hands of some theorists, has often been very symbiotic so it is not possible to talk about the development of family therapy in isolation, but it is also true that the family therapy movement has always had distinctive strands within it so it is not possible to talk about family therapy as a single entity. Over the years these strands have crystallized into different schools whose practitioners have tended to adhere to one model while eschewing the ideas of practitioners whose ideas are derived from other models. No doubt such factionalism has contributed to the development of new ideas and new techniques but there is a darker side to this process.

In a recent paper which attempts to provide a conceptual framework for reconciling some of the differences between models, Sluzki (1983) has contributed some insightful ideas about the process of differentiation that has taken place.

> As any sample of family therapy literature can easily demonstrate, each of these [family therapy] models tends to be presented by their proponents as *the*, and not *a*, translation of the systemic paradigm, as *the* privileged set of observables and hypotheses. Perhaps this is the undesirable effect of an unavoidable [situation]

... the student of a given model or 'school' may need to retain – for a while, at least – a compartmentalized view in order to explore the confines of the model in question and acquire a sense of mastery. Perhaps there are also reasons of marketing on the part of the teachers – each of us may wish to feel and convince others that our model washes whiter, so to speak, in order to sell it more.

(Sluzki 1983 : 470)

Wittingly or unwittingly, Sluzki's use of such a commercial style of language seems to me to be very appropriate. Family therapy is an almost exclusively American invention and its leading practitioners tend to market themselves and their therapies with gusto. Good marketing hinges around the huckster's ability to prove the superiority of his product over his rivals so we should not be surprised to find that American family therapists have not paid much attention to developing integrated models of family therapy which draw upon ideas gleaned from different models.

It is also true that the development of schools of family therapy has been heavily influenced by the context in which pioneering family therapists worked. Nichols (1984) has explored this issue in depth and has recently summarized his position by pointing out that

*the predominant influence of social context, emphasised in family therapy, also applies to family therapists themselves and to the systems of treatment they develop.* The pioneers of family therapy worked in different settings and with different patient populations. They did not set out to invent family therapy. They were working on other problems – analysing communications, discovering the etiology of schizophrenia, treating delinquent children – and family therapy turned out to be part of the solution. . . . the variations in setting, population and intent of the developers combined to influence the nature of the various family therapies and also help to determine the type of patients that each method is most suited to.

(Nichols 1984 : 562–3, emphasis added)

Nichols' points are important – they help to explain the peculiar and uneven development of family therapy but they can be used as a springboard for criticizing family therapy. The development of schools has been haphazard and uncoordinated but I do not think it is defensible for family therapists to continue to accept the status quo so passively. Typically (because of the lack of proper training in this country) a therapist gets some training in a particular model because a trainer has put on a course locally. That model then becomes accepted as the only method for undertaking family therapy. Other methods of working are largely ignored and the 'scholastic' divisions within family therapy are preserved. To be strictly fair there are a number of integrated models to be found in the literature. Some therapists have reacted to the factionalism of the American scene by attempting to develop models which draw upon the strengths of other models. Turning once again to Gurman and Kniskern's *Handbook*, it is, I think, significant that two of the thirteen or so chapters devoted to major schools of family therapy embody the notion of 'integration' in their titles. Framo's (1981) chapter

(The integration of marital therapy with sessions with family of origin) and Duhl and Duhl's (1981) chapter (Integrative family therapy) are clearly specifically written in order to provide an integrative approach but it is easy to overlook the fact that both Skynner's (1981) chapter (An open-systems, group-analytic approach to family therapy) and Boszormenyi-Nagy and Ulrich's (1981) chapter (Contextual family therapy) are equally integrative since both are prepared to draw upon concepts and techniques originating within other schools of therapy. It is also important to add that Bentovim and Kingston (1981) have pioneered an elegant integrated model in this country.

It would be interesting to know what factors influenced these particular therapists in developing their integrative approaches. Perhaps some dialectical process has been at work so that the process of differentiation has at the same time produced its antithesis, a process of integration. At a more personal level, perhaps therapists just differ in terms of whether they are 'synthesizers' who wish to exploit ideas derived from many different frameworks or 'thesizers' who prefer to exploit ideas derived from a single framework.

My own interest in developing an integrative approach has developed over a number of years. I originally trained with Brian Cade at the Family Institute in Cardiff and like many beginning therapists, I somewhat uncritically adopted the style of my first family therapy mentor. So for about two years my style was fairly similar to Brian Cade's and was based mostly on the work of Haley (1976). At that time I was a fairly rigid 'thesizer' who naively thought that the strategic framework was rich enough to provide all the conceptual tools and techniques required by a family therapist. (The term strategic therapy is a generic one, and within this volume is discussed under the title 'Brief Therapy' in Chapter 6.) I gradually accumulated a number of very disappointing treatment failures (alongside a fair number of successful cases) but it was the failures that gave me most food for thought. I was also exposed to the work of Minuchin for the first time and spent a fascinating month undertaking a practicum at the Philadelphia Child Guidance Clinic. Emotionally I felt much more at home using a structural framework (see Chapter 4) but I was still sympathetic to many facets of the strategic approach. Under these twin influences I eventually evolved a do-it-yourself structural-strategic approach. The main thrust of my therapeutic work was structural (with a strong emphasis on joining and using overt, contractually derived methods of intervention) but I was still prepared to interleave techniques which were derived mostly from Haley's work. I was also strongly influenced by the work of the Mental Research Institute group based at Palo Alto (Fisch *et al.* 1982 – see Chapter 6).

As I became more experienced as a therapist, I gained in confidence but periodically I became uneasy about the universality of the model I was using because I still had some disconcerting failures, even with well-motivated families who seemed ready to change. One family in particular (which I will call the 'X' family) caused me particular angst. After successfully completing a series of family and marital sessions, the family was discharged with an agreement that there should be a follow-up six months later; the follow-up was duly undertaken and revealed that the apparently significant structural changes that had occurred during therapy were being maintained. The family was then finally discharged. Eighteen months later (and much to my surprise) the family was re-referred by their general practitioner because the original presenting problem (acute depression being suffered by Mrs X) had recurred.

It's always fairly unnerving for me to experience such a situation. Cases with which I've obviously failed are worrying but I usually have a reasonable idea of why the therapy has failed; often I can make an appropriate referral to another therapist, but when a successful case turns into a failure, then I'm forced back to the drawing board in quite a different way. In this particular case the failure was complex but it seemed to depend on two factors. First, because the therapy had been almost exclusively conceived within the here and now, I had failed to touch some important unfinished business issues which were so powerful that they continued to permeate the life of the family despite changes that had occurred in other facets of family life. A second dimension concerned the specific factors that contributed to the causation of Mrs X's depressed behaviour. While Mr X had undoubtedly triggered depressed behaviour in his wife prior to therapy, his behaviour had shifted and yet Mrs X was still prone to depression. Her fifteen-year history of bouts of depression had, not unexpectedly, left her with a well-developed capacity to turn comparatively trivial events into major self-downing episodes and the therapy had not really succeeded in eradicating this relentless process.

The lessons from this case were hard won but I now set different goals when undertaking the therapy of depression. My current practice not only attempts to untangle the deeper family of origin issues that are usually involved in depression, but also incorporates Beck's cognitive therapy approach which is, I believe, ultimately the best way of ensuring that a client is not subject to a recurrence of depression (Beck *et al.* 1979). Beck's self-help technique may appear (to the systemic therapist) to be hopelessly linear (and intrapsychic) but I would argue that the approach can be successfully integrated within a systemic framework. For example, Beck's notion of silent assumptions can be translated into interactional language. I believe that they are essentially family or relationship scripts which have become part and parcel of a client's cognitive world. Because a given client has been involved in a day-to-day learning process with a range of significant others (whose positions in his or her psychological space enable them to be powerfully influential) it is not surprising that he or she internalizes their thoughts as being his or her own. The voice of the significant other who originated the thought becomes silent so the client loses his or her capacity to debate and disagree. He or she therefore becomes self-programmed to be unfree and not to exert adult choices about how to behave (see Treacher 1985 for a more detailed discussion of these points).

More and more my experience leads me to believe that successful family therapy must include methods for directly confronting these levels within the overall system. In the hands of Beck, and other workers of a similar stance, behaviour therapy has developed in a cognitive direction, recognizing that human beings are not rats or robots but complex self-conscious organisms who possess a crucial ability to be reflective about their own behaviour (Murray and Jacobson 1978; Mahoney 1978). I believe that family therapy also needs to move in this direction.

So to pull the threads of my argument together – the structural-strategic model that I originally evolved has been more recently expanded to absorb techniques derived both from transgenerational frameworks (see Chapter 7) and from cognitive behaviour therapy. In effect the model is four tiered: the structural-strategic facets of the model are mainly concerned with generating interventions that are aimed at the current interactional process which maintains the symptom. The transgenerational facets of the model are, unsurprisingly, used to provide interventions that are designed to attack the unfinished business that helps maintain the symptom in the here and now. The cognitive facets of the model are mobilized in order to confront the highly entrenched cognitive distortions that distressed clients tend to use. Such interventions encourage clients to take a direct responsibility for the fact that they themselves make a unique contribution to the problems in which they are embroiled. This fourth strand in the model is influenced not only by Beck's work but also by the work of Kelly (1955). Personal construct theory (PCT) has made an invaluable contribution to psychotherapy since it enables a therapist to understand the phenomenonological world of his or her client in very precise ways. By extension, the phenomenonological world of a family can also be understood using a PCT approach (Procter 1984).

The four-tiered model I propose may seem idiosyncratic at first sight but as I have already pointed out many other therapists have also become increasingly uncomfortable with work within the confines of one school. Stanton (1981) has fortunately provided an elegant rationale for a structural-strategic approach but I had begun working in a similar way before I came across his work. As yet I know of no research that supports this approach apart from one study by Stanton himself (Stanton 1981); this is unfortunate but therapies do not evolve on a rational scientific basis as psychotherapy researchers would no doubt desire. New therapies emerge; they then survive and flourish through their conceptual appeal to practitioners, not because they have proven efficacy but because they offer new solutions to the problems that practitioners face. Later on research may well be undertaken that provides some justification for adopting the approach but usually the research is by no means definitive. (See Treacher 1983 for an extended discussion of this point.) Within family therapy it is interesting to note, for example, that the current popularity of the Milan approach (see Chapter 3) is certainly not derived from its proven efficacy – it must be other features of the approach including its intellectual coherence, its elegance and perhaps the charisma of some of its leading exponents that create its popularity.

So my justification for adopting an integrative approach is decidedly personal. In order to deal with treatment failures (and families with which I become stuck) I was prepared to broaden my approach. At a theoretical level I think this is eminently plausible. Scheflen has made much the same point:

> The contemporary psychotherapist is exposed to a variety of conceptual models and paradigms. These are usually presented as opposing truths in different doctrinal schools but actually they are all valid from one point of view or another and accordingly they are all tactically useful at some point or another.
> (Scheflen 1978 : 59, cited by Grunebaum and Chasin 1982)

Such statements are fine in theory but at a practical level – at the level of actually helping a particular family at a specific time in its life cycle – severe difficulties can arise because the therapist has to face the daunting task of finding a way of undertaking therapy that is fitted to the family in therapy. Some schools of family therapy – notably the Milan School – seem to ignore this issue since they monolithically adopt the same approach irrespective of the type of family they have in therapy. Unfortunately, there is no convincing empirical evidence that demonstrates that such approaches are less effective than a more multifaceted approach but I nevertheless suspect they are indeed less effective, particularly if initial and overall drop-out rates are taken seriously.

## THE THERAPY PROCESS – EXPLORING THE STRUCTURAL-STRATEGIC CORE OF THE INTEGRATED MODEL

Fortunately Stanton (1980a) has provided some interesting rules for applying a structural-strategic approach. He argues convincingly that structural and strategic approaches are in agreement about many theoretical and technical issues. He lists no fewer than seventeen issues about which they are broadly in agreement but at the same time he is aware of their differences.

The main difference between the approaches can be summarized as follows: in structural family therapy the focus is primarily on a therapy family's structure and not on a theory of change. In strategic family therapy the stress is upon a theory and means for ensuring change and not upon a family theory. This theoretical difference between the two approaches obviously has practical implications but in my view the structural model is both more basic and in one sense more theoretically rich since its prime concern is with understanding the relationship between particular family structure and particular patterns of symptoms. The strategic approach is essentially more pragmatic since it is concerned with producing sufficient change to remove the presenting symptom. In particular, strategies are devised which disrupt the attempted solution to the problem which the family habitually uses. Since Chapters 4 and 6 of this book have been devoted to structural family therapy and strategic family therapy, it is not necessary for me to explore these approaches in depth. However, it is useful to demonstrate that the two models have developed complementary techniques. Stanton provides useful inventories of these techniques.

## Structural techniques

1 The basic goal is to induce a 'more adequate family organisation' of the sort that will maximise growth and potential in each of its members.
2 The thrust of the therapy is toward 'restructuring' of the system, such as establishing or loosening boundaries, differentiating enmeshed members and increasing the involvement of disengaged members.
3 The therapeutic plan is gauged against knowledge of what is 'normal' for a family at a given stage in its development, with due consideration of its cultural and socio-economic context.
4 The derived interactional change must take place within the actual session (enactment).
5 Techniques such as unbalancing . . . and intensifying . . . are part of the therapy.
6 The therapist 'joins' and accommodates to the system in a sort of blending experience but retains enough independence both to resist the family's pull and to challenge (restructure) it at various points. He thus actively uses himself as a boundary marker, intensifier and general change agent in the session.
7 Treatment is usually limited to include those members of a family who live within a household or have regular contact with the immediate family. However, this might involve grandparents living nearby, or even an employer, if the problem is work-related.
8 The practice is to bring a family to a level of 'health' or 'complexity' and then stand ready to be called in the future, if necessary. Such a model is seen to combine the advantages of short and longer term therapy.

(Stanton 1980a : 429–30)

Stanton's summary is very valuable but his point about the importance of enactment is overstated. While a structural family therapist may well prefer to produce change through enactment and re-enactment in the actual session, it is often just not feasible to do so. A homework task may well be utilized to produce change when this is so. If team supervision is being undertaken then team members can be called into the session to play the roles of absent grandfathers, grandmothers or any other figures who have not been convened but, in practice, few therapists experience the luxury of being able to do this.

Turning next to the strategic approach, Stanton lists the following six major dimensions as being the most important.

## Strategic techniques

1  The utilisation of tasks and directives.
2  The problem must be put in solvable form. It should be something that can be objectively agreed upon, e.g. counted, observed or measured so that one can assess if it has actually been influenced.
3  Considerable emphasis is placed upon extra-session change.
4  Power struggles with the family are generally avoided, the tendency being to take the path of least resistance and use implicit or indirect ways of turning the family investment for positive use.
5  'Positive interpretation' . . . to the family of its symptom(s), motives, and homeostatic tendencies is readily employed.
6  'Paradoxical' interventions are common and may be directed toward the whole family or to certain members.

(Stanton 1980a : 431)

Placing these two lists side by side is an interesting exercise because, at least in my eyes, it reveals (as I have already suggested) that the lists do not in fact clash at a fundamental level. For example, I find it perfectly feasible to run a session mainly along structural lines with a firm emphasis on enactment and re-enactment (Street and Treacher 1980). But at the same time I can utilize strategic directives and messages devised by the back-up team behind the screen *and* set homework tasks which are planned in the time-out session which is usually taken near the end of the session.

Stanton has attempted to devise some general rules for adopting a structural-strategic approach. These rules have been well thought out and clearly reflect the complex and demanding work that Stanton has undertaken, particularly with alcoholic and drug-abusing families. The three rules that Stanton has suggested are as follows,

1  Initially deal with a family through a structural approach – joining, accommodating, testing boundaries, and restructuring, that is, assume a direct posture toward the family.
2  Switch to a predominantly strategic approach when structural techniques are not succeeding or are unlikely to succeed.

3 Following success with strategic methods it may be advisable to revert once again to a structural approach if therapy is to continue.

(Stanton 1980a : 434)

## Evaluating Stanton's rules for undertaking structural-strategic family therapy

The bland stating of these rules does not give any insight into the many theoretical and even ethical issues that have prompted Stanton to advocate their use. Stanton's arguments are important but many of the structural-strategic elements of my model have been developed for different reasons. In order to elucidate these differences I will therefore explore Stanton's arguments but at the same time I will discuss where I part company from his position.

Stanton's first rule is really an answer to the question, 'Why should a therapist adopt a structural model in the first place?' Stanton's answer (with which I strongly agree) is very robust: why overcomplicate therapy by adopting an indirect approach when a direct approach will do? I would personally add an ethical footnote to this. A direct approach allows the therapist to be contractual and open with the family. As I have explored at greater depth in two previous papers (Treacher 1986; 1987), there are crucial difficulties involved in using certain aspects of the strategic model which have almost entirely escaped discussion in the family therapy literature. I have little space to explore this point in detail but I am personally very unhappy about using covert intervention methods to produce change within families. If I do use covert methods then I always 'debrief' the family at subsequent sessions so that I do not have to carry the burden of using secretive methods with the family and the family can have a chance to explore the full implications of the intervention I used and to take me to task if they feel upset by it.

Stanton's second reason for starting 'structurally' is also concerned with simplicity; he argues that it is, in fact, easier for the therapist to intervene structurally. Strategic work is, according to Stanton, often more sophisticated because it requires more complex skills or, to quote him specifically on this point,

> [Structural work] is more comprehensible, especially for the less experienced therapist, because the reactions of the family to interventions are immediate and easy to observe, not requiring guesswork as to what will happen outside and after the sessions. Intervention directed toward extra-session behaviour often demands a good deal of therapeutic experience and without this the therapist is 'flying blind'.

(Stanton 1980a : 435)

Stanton also claims that structural work is easier to grasp at a theoretical level than strategic work, particularly if paradoxical techniques are being used.

I'm not at all sure whether these last two reasons stand up to close scrutiny. Possibly structural work (as a theory of therapy) is theoretically less sophisticated than strategic work but my own experience of training structurally oriented family therapists has led me to conclude that, on balance, an effective structural worker needs to have a broader armament of skills than a strategic worker. This I believe is derived from the fact that so much of strategic work is concerned with data-collecting, brainstorming and the devising of directives and tasks. A fully fledged structural worker would need all these skills but must at the same time be able to direct the session in a far more dynamic way (often using skills which are very similar to some forms of psychodrama). For example, to persuade clients to undertake an enactment in a session requires more skills than asking them a set of circular questions.

Stanton's fourth point is also fairly weak; he merely states that structural work has demonstrated its utility with many different kinds of symptoms and problem groups (Gurman and Kniskern 1978; Olson *et al*. 1980; Stanton 1980a) and is therefore to be commended as a reasonably well-validated approach. Sadly this is not strictly true since in another paper Stanton (1981) himself has commended strategic work as being better researched than other schools of family therapy. He argues that strategically oriented family therapy researchers have used better research designs than researchers from other schools of family therapy. Aponte and Van Deusen (1981) in their comparable review of structural work can find only two controlled studies. (Ironically one of these studies – by Stanton *et al*. 1979 – is also included in Stanton's strategic list.) There are a number of uncontrolled studies quoted by Aponte and Van Deusen but they obviously do not carry the same weight as properly controlled studies.

Obviously these research findings are embarrassing to my position (and Stanton's for that matter); it would perhaps be more justifiable to argue in favour of a model with a much stronger strategic bias. But for me to do so would be to negate the evolution of my way of undertaking therapy which I have already explored in this chapter. So, to justify my position, I have to invoke yet another dimension of the argument. One prime reason for commencing structurally hinges around the twin issue of joining and accommodation and the impact it has upon retaining families in therapy. Because the structural model strongly emphasizes the necessity for joining every family member and yet accommodating to the family's overall style, I believe that it is likely that experienced structural workers are much more skilful at keeping families in therapy. But this strength may also create a weakness because it may well be possible that structural workers risk experiencing 'stuckness' with families (Treacher and

Carpenter 1982) more often than strategic workers.

Stanton's second rule invites a therapist to switch to strategic work when structural work has become stuck or is unlikely to succeed. His rationale for this rule is intriguing since he argues that many strategic techniques were developed in order to treat excessively homeostatic families (e.g. those of schizophrenia) and are therefore likely to be more effective in dealing with extreme forms of stuckness or resistance (to use his term). It is therefore logical to mobilize strategic techniques when stuckness has occurred. According to Stanton there are three situations in which switching is necessary.

1 When either resistance (stuckness) mounts as structural therapy continues or no change occurs.
2 When prior knowledge of the family indicates that structural work is likely to fail.
3 When confusion and loss of understanding by the therapist has occurred.

(Stanton 1980a : 435)

I personally find Stanton's argument somewhat confusing at this point. It seems to me that it is inappropriate to talk about 'switching' tactics in relation to the second situation. In a strict sense, to use strategic tactics from the beginning is to use a *strategic*-structural model (cf Andolfi *et al.* 1980). I would also dispute whether it is appropriate to switch to strategic techniques when the therapist is confused. A tactic that is more likely to succeed is to invite a consultant to undertake an interview involving both the therapist and the family. This enables the stuckness to be properly evaluated before deciding how to deal with it.

Given my objections to two out of three of Stanton's categories, I would choose to simplify his model by arguing that the switch from structural to strategic work should take place when the therapist and the family are clearly stuck *and* yet the therapist has a good understanding of why he or she is stuck. If stuckness is occurring and the therapist is confused then an alternative approach involving consultancy should be adopted. (This point will be discussed in greater detail below.)

There is also another situation when resorting to strategic techniques may be indicated. I do not agree with Stanton's rather doctrinaire approach which says that it is only when therapy is failing that strategic techniques should be used; I prefer to give myself more options. It may be that the use of a strategic intervention is the best way forward irrespective of whether the therapy is stuck or not. For instance, I often use a no-change prescription at the end of a first interview in order to create a feeling of safety for the family I have in therapy. Usually this no-change prescription takes the form of requesting the family to remain as they are because it is most helpful for me, in seeking to help them, to have a static situation in which the problem

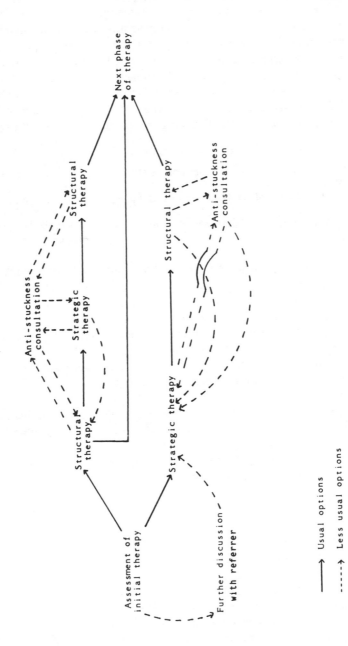

*Figure 8.1* Options available during the structural-strategic phases of family therapy

remains as it was before they entered therapy. This approach can have the effect of preventing the family from making premature and ill-grounded attempts to change which, if unsuccessful, can undermine their confidence about continuing in therapy.

Stanton's third rule advises a switch to structural methods when the period of strategic work has produced results. The justification for this tactic is very clear. Stanton assumes that strategic techniques will have begun to induce systemic changes which will have liberated the identified patient from his or her central role so that family members are beginning to behave more independently, rather than as a system which can respond only reflexly to changes that it encounters. Structural techniques with their potential for enhancing individuation therefore become appropriate. I readily agree with Stanton's argument at this point but my integrated approach allows me to choose a wider range of alternatives. For example if one member of the family is persistently depressed or anxious, there would be scope for introducing cognitive techniques to deal with his or her problems. If a member was persistently unable to individuate because of recurring problems caused by unfinished business, transgenerational techniques would be mobilized to deal specifically with these unique problems which are not shared by other family members.

Since my presentation of Stanton's position has been fairly lengthy, it is probably best for me to summarize what I take from his work. The best way of doing this is by means of a flow diagram (Figure 8.1) which demonstrates the phases of therapy that a worker using a structural-strategic model can utilize while completing a contract with a family.

The simplest pathway using the model would be

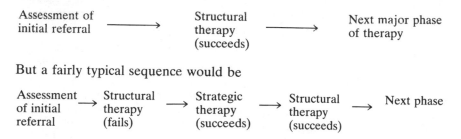

But a fairly typical sequence would be

A switch in the type of therapy only occurs when the therapy is failing or else, in other words, success breeds success, so there is a rapid movement from left to right without having to loop back to previous stages or having to revert to other tactics, such as the anti-stuckness consultation. This consultation is carried out by a colleague who interviews both myself and the family in order to clarify the nature of the stuckness. (See Treacher and Carpenter 1982 for a further discussion of stuckness.)

The switching between structural and strategic approaches is somewhat similar to Stanton's but I do not utilize his category three ('therapist confused') to decide the switch. Instead I would tend to use an 'anti-stuckness' consultation instead. This process enables me not just to opt mechanically for a strategic intervention. I find that structural work can fail at many different levels. For example there may be a crucial failure at a contractual level, the family (or more usually, certain family members) and I may not agree about the goals of therapy *or* the means to achieve those goals or both. Another common problem hinges around failure to create sufficient intensity during the sessions. Often a therapist can be on the right track but because family members are reluctant to accept the full implications of the changes that face them they use a variety of tactics to block the therapy. Some therapists resort to strategic tactics at this point but in my opinion this switch may be premature. I prefer to use the structural technique of intensification (Minuchin and Fishman 1981) before considering a switch to strategic work. Minuchin's famous aphorism, 'Families are often deaf, they may need to hear it ten times before they can listen', is worth bearing in mind at this point. The therapist can increase the intensity of his or her interventions by, for example, creating a crisis in therapy by suggesting that perhaps therapy should stop because the family is not ready to change. Some families (particularly if they are well joined) will respond to such a challenge by sharing their fears about the future; the therapist can then respond appropriately and the therapy can move forward. Obviously intensification techniques need to be custom-built to suit each individual family since the clumsy use of intensity may cause more problems than it solves.

One final addendum to my argument needs to be made at this point. Because I have also been influenced by the work of the Mental Research Institute at Palo Alto (as I noted earlier in this chapter), I am also prepared, when faced with stuck therapy, to opt for working with individuals rather than the whole family system. Not unexpectedly, I find it is perfectly possible to unbalance a very sclerosed system by resorting to this tactic. Coaching an enmeshed adolescent to be more independent is a good example of this but it is also possible in couple work to create motivation in an apparently unmotivated partner by insisting on temporarily *not* working with him or her but with the partner.

I have chosen not to include this type of option in my flow chart because it would make it very complex but this option is available as another way of overcoming stuckness. This means that a stuckness interview may result, in a small number of cases, in opting for individual work. A wide range of techniques (including cognitive techniques derived from the work of Beck) may be mobilized during this phase of treatment before returning to family or couple work.

# INTEGRATING MARITAL AND FAMILY THERAPY

I've chosen to use the somewhat nebulous term 'the next phase of therapy' in Figure 8.1 because this point in therapy can be straightforward but it can also be complex. In many cases it seems appropriate to move towards termination but in other cases it seems more appropriate to undertake further therapy in order to consolidate the gains that have been made. My own practice primarily involves child-focused problems since I work in a child guidance setting. The initial phases of therapy are usually very much concerned with such problems because they are the ticket of entry used by the parents or parent to engage in therapy. Over the years my approach has evolved so that the final stages of therapy are more and more preoccupied with both marital and political issues. Many child guidance workers are wary about undertaking marital work but I have a different view. Since I believe that marriage is an institution that oppresses women and that child-rearing can be one of the most soul-destroying tasks that anybody can be asked to face, I am concerned as a therapist to get such issues placed on the agenda for therapy. Family therapy (a mainly male-invented form of therapy) has been notoriously blind to such issues (Goldner 1985; Osborne 1983; Simon 1984) but in being blind, family therapy has obviously left itself open to the criticism that it is reactionary (see Chapter 13). I now therefore always attempt to undertake couple therapy in such a way that the gender issues can be openly faced.

The exact details of the marital therapy I undertake differ markedly from couple to couple (see Treacher 1985 for an extended discussion of the techniques of marital therapy), but the flow chart in Figure 8.2 provides a useful overview of my approach. The chart was partly inspired by Crowe (1985). Crowe's model is an integrated one which seeks to combine at least four different techniques: behavioural, structural and strategic techniques are used but he also seeks to include specialized techniques derived from the work of Falloon and Liberman (1983), who have carefully researched methods for working with couples whose problems include schizophrenic symptoms (see Chapter 5). In order to provide an overview of the phases of couple therapy that I undertake, I have produced this flow chart which summarizes some of the typical 'pathways' that I adopt.

The core of the approach is contained in steps 1 to 5. I would normally expect to undertake work with a couple under all five of these headings before terminating but the actual sequence involved can be complicated. For the sake of clarity I have left out some possible steps in the sequence; for example, with a given couple it would be perfectly possible to move through stages 1 and 2 in the usual sequence but then move directly to stage 5. This recently occurred with a couple whose marital difficulties were partly

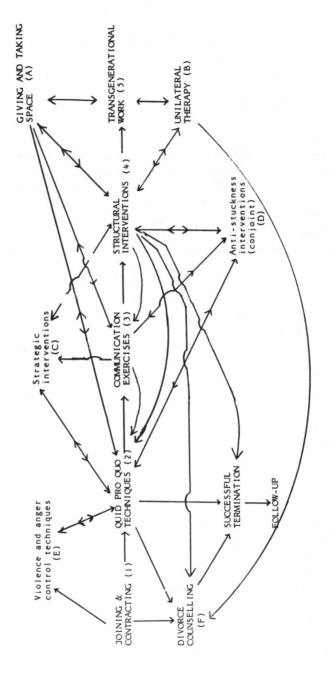

*Figure 8.2*  Some typical pathways involved in couple therapy

dependent upon an over-close relationship between the wife and her mother. It proved very difficult to create any movement using quid-pro-quo techniques (Lederer and Jackson 1968). At this point of failure, the wife openly and spontaneously acknowledged that she felt unable to co-operate because she was so dominated by her mother's continual intrusions into her life. After due discussion, we agreed that she should work individually with me in order to begin to form a better boundary between herself and her mother. It proved unnecessary to convene her mother in order to undertake this work which fortunately proved very easy to complete since the woman was utterly fed up with her inability to say no to her mother. Once this work had been completed we returned to phase 2 and then moved through phases 3 and 4 before successfully terminating.

It should also be stressed that the model is by no means undirectional. It is perfectly possible, for instance, to move through stages 1 and 4 getting very little therapeutic gain, only to find that stage 5 proves very fruitful. This success would then enable the therapy to loop back to any of the previous stages. This approach may seem complex but it does ensure that the therapist struggles to custom-build the therapy to suit the couple and the problems they bring to therapy.

I have little space to explore fully all the possibilities of the model but you will notice that the flow diagram contains two categories (strategic interventions 'C' and anti-stuckness interventions 'D') which I have already introduced in relation to the 'family therapy' phase of treatment. The use of these alternatives is essentially similar so I will not explore them further. Alternative 'A' ('Giving and taking space') is a recent innovation in my approach. I rarely work with very disturbed adult clients but when I do so I seriously debate whether traditional forms of couple therapy would help. For instance, a couple I worked with were very devoted to each other but the husband was an extreme workaholic whose ability to be close to his wife was very limited. Any attempt to use quid-pro-quo techniques or communication exercises to increase closeness produced panic in the husband. Transgenerational work was then attempted with the husband but he was not a customer for such an approach. My co-therapist and I then decided to see the couple separately, with my co-therapist helping the wife to be more independent of her husband. In my individual sessions with the husband I helped him establish clearer rules about how much contact he could tolerate and helped him overcome his guilt about not being closer to his wife. In essence, the 'therapy' hinged around 'managing' the problem rather than intending to change it. The parallel with the work of Falloon and Liberman (1983) is quite strong; as a therapist I find such work goes against the grain but if one partner in a couple relationship feels unable to change and yet his or her partner is not prepared to divorce him or her, then such a way of working is undoubtedly worthwhile.

The alternative 'B' (unilateral therapy) encompasses many ways of working. Often I use cognitive behaviour therapy techniques (Beck *et al*. 1985; Burns 1980) during this phase of therapy. This usually occurs in close conjunction with transgenerational work because I usually find that the basic assumptions that often lie at the root of the client's difficulties are family scripts passed down from one generation to another. (See Treacher 1985 : 277–81 for a case illustration which demonstrates this way of working.) In fact this rubric of 'unilateral therapy' draws attention to the fact that I often find it useful to work for a short period with one well-motivated partner than to struggle on in conjoint therapy with one partner who wants change and one partner who is indifferent. Unsurprisingly, divorce counselling may well ensue but it is certainly misleading to assume that this is always the outcome. Brief Therapists often produce very interesting results working with single clients (Szapocznik *et al*. 1984; Fisch *et al*. 1982) so I am increasingly prepared to opt for this way of working rather than keeping to the rule that couple therapy is ineffective if it is not conjoint (see Wells and Gianetti 1986 for a controversial discussion of whether this rule stands up to close examination).

Finally, a brief mention needs to be made of the remaining two alternatives in my overall scheme. Violence and anger control techniques (Deschner 1984) are very important in my approach; I attempt to establish whether violence is occurring in the relationship very early on. Too often I've failed to pick up the essential clues so that much of my initial work with a couple has been decidedly unproductive. If I do discover violence, then I immediately establish a contract to work on the violence because I believe it is an issue that cannot be under-focused: to do so is to place oneself in a very invidious position.

Divorce counselling (Kaslow 1981) (the remaining alternative in my scheme) is, at least as I view it, an essential part of couple therapy. There is nothing more liberating than helping a couple to get out of a destructive relationship. Because I've been married for twenty-two years and see marriage as a positive institution, at least for many people, I tend to start with couples optimistically, assuming that it's best to have a go at improving their relationship, but I have no qualms about turning in the opposite direction if the therapy is proving pointless.

Termination is a neglected topic in family therapy and I am afraid I am going to continue the tradition by not spending enough time discussing it. I attempt to achieve termination successfully by getting the couple (or individual) to review what they have gained from therapy. I then explore what solutions they will mobilize if similar problems occur. Finally, I negotiate a highly variable follow-up session. These follow-up sessions can be very powerful in leaving the ghost of the therapist (the phrase is Minuchin's) with the couple so that the therapy does not in fact terminate at the final session but is taken back home.

# A FAMILY IN THERAPY

The Smith family referred themselves to me because of bitter conflicts within the family. The family consisted of Lesley (35), John (36) and four children, Peter (12) (John's son by a previous marriage), Alice (10) and Timothy (8) (children of Lesley's previous marriage) and Andy (3) (a child of the current marriage). The ostensible reason for the referral was extreme conflict between Lesley and Peter. An initial contract was negotiated to work on this issue as a result of the first session. My initial approach was purely structural; during the second session I completed a brief genogram in order to clarify the complex history of the family and to establish whether there were any significant unresolved issues involving the ex-spouses. Fortunately careful tracking did not reveal any major conflicts so therapy focused primarily on the relationships within the nuclear family.

By the end of the third session I had clarified that there was a major hierarchical problem which helped to explain the acute conflict between Lesley and Peter. John, despite his warm feelings towards Lesley, treated her as an inferior – he saw himself as the burdened 'captain' of the ship who needed to take responsibility for everything, and hence treated Lesley rather like a midshipman. She was labelled as 'illogical' and 'spendthrift' by him but at the same time she received no support in standing up to Peter, who had readily absorbed John's chauvinism and treated her with total disrespect. Lesley seemed very anxious in the sessions so I began to suspect that the conflict between Lesley and Peter (which was often physically violent) might conceal undisclosed violence between John and Lesley.

Given the very wide rift between John and Lesley (which was revealed very poignantly during a sculpting session with the family), I wanted to move rapidly to the next phase of therapy: working on the couple relationship, but given the severity of the conflict surrounding Peter, I felt I needed to gain some credibility with John and Lesley through making some impact on the presenting problem. My joining of both the parents and the family had by this time deepened and I had been able to communicate successfully my liking and respect for them. The family, despite its manifest structural weakness, was lively and caring and very humorous. Peter was genuinely very worried by his violence and was struggling to relate better to Lesley. The violence between Peter and Lesley was worrying but Lesley had not been injured by Peter, who took ineffectual swipes at her and then wrestled with her as she attempted to send him to his room. The violence was, if anything, more worrying at a verbal level because Peter swore like a trooper, modelling himself on his father (consciously or unconsciously).

The strategic task I devised for the family was as follows: Peter was to continue as normal, not attempting to change his behaviour in relation to Lesley because it was clearly not possible at the moment to change his behaviour, despite his wish to do so. Lesley was to handle him in her usual way, not attempting to make any changes, but was to keep careful notes of what happened. John was to go over Lesley's notes with her at a set time every evening but was to refrain from giving her any advice about how to change things because it was essential to have good baseline data before thinking about an intervention.

John and Lesley returned two weeks later for the next session but, apart from one minor incident, they had nothing to report. I cautioned them to be alert and not expect this premature change to be long lasting; I then switched my attention away from Peter and focused on John's violence towards Lesley. The violence was infrequent but had been very severe with Lesley being knocked unconscious on at least one occasion. I made my own ethical stance clear on the issue – that physical violence between partners is totally unacceptable and grounds for divorce if it persists. I then negotiated to see John separately in order to teach him some anger control techniques recommended by Deschner (1984) and Burns (1980). Before closing the session I introduced John to the 'T' for time-out technique so that he could find a way out of potentially violent situations. This very simple technique of training a violent partner to signal (by making a 'T' with his hands) to his partner can be remarkably effective, particularly if the partner is co-operative and makes no attempt to prevent her partner from taking space away from him directly he has signalled.

Fortunately John and Lesley were able to use this technique so the level of violence dropped from this session onwards but the violence was not totally inhibited; John did lose his temper with Lesley about two weeks later – he threw a bottle of milk over her – but he was very disturbed by his failure to use the time-out technique. There then followed a further incident about a month later, during which John physically shook Lesley very hard, bruising her upper arms. Sensing a slide back into the old pattern of behaviour, I decided to increase the intensity of my approach to this issue by negotiating with John that if he committed another act of violence then I would reserve the right to report the incident to the police. He readily agreed to this contract which was fully endorsed by Lesley. Since negotiating this contract, no further violence has occurred, although there are times when John feels he needs to use his time-out technique.

It was necessary to focus periodically on the issue of violence in the therapy but the main thrust of the therapy was concerned with tackling the hierarchical issues which bedevilled the marital relationship. I utilized some quid-pro-quo techniques to open up these issues but John strongly resisted renegotiating salient aspects of their marital contract. For example he had absolute control of the money and allowed Lesley only very limited 'pocket money' (his term). In practice, this meant that she had no budget to buy clothes and had to stretch her housekeeping in order to buy essential items of clothing for herself. John resisted any movements on this front so vehemently that I suspected that his position was being determined by a whole range of previous experiences to do with his previous marriage and his family of origin. Lesley's passivity and lack of assertiveness were also very marked so I decided to switch my approach in order to explore the unfinished business which maintained the circularity between them. I therefore undertook an extensive joint genogram, focusing on issues of dominance and violence on the one hand and passivity and acceptance on the other. John came from a very violent family: his maternal grandfather was very violent, his own mother and father fought violently and used quite violent methods to control their children. John's father was an aggressive businessman, a paterfamilias of the old school who sat his sons each side of him at the dinner table and boxed their ears if their behaviour offended him. His parents had eventually divorced very bitterly with his mother adopting a peculiar almost itinerant life-style – she would settle into a new home for six months, only to sell up and move on.

Lesley was an adopted child with miserable, bickering parents, who undermined her sense of worth and self-esteem. They were critical and dismissive of her throughout her childhood. This left her prone to bouts of depression, which were often brought on by incidents during which she felt criticized. Since John was highly critical of her at times, his behaviour resonated with the previous behaviour of her father so she experienced him as a 'double dose'!

The genogram was successful in enabling me to reframe their problems and to relieve their sense of guilt about their ability to relate to each other better. John began gradually to shift his position; Lesley began to take risks as she began to believe in herself more. I used unbalancing tactics siding with Lesley against John during the course of negotiations over reorganizing financial affairs and achieving team-work in relation to the children. Lesley accepted an invitation to join a women's group and was able to use the support she gained in the group to clarify what she wanted from her life. Her self-assertion blossomed and she was able to gain more from the marital work that was undertaken concurrently. John relaxed his dominant position and came to respect his wife's abilities and resourcefulness. Lesley was introduced to Burns's self-help approach to depression (Burns 1980) and opted for a contract for four sessions with me in order to master the technique fully. Her mastery of triple columning techniques marked yet another turning-point in the therapy since she no longer experienced periods of depression. John was able to cope with her markedly increased self-assertiveness and did not revert to his 'captain of the ship' role.

The final phase of therapy involved two family sessions during which I evaluated the structural changes that had occurred during the course of therapy. The couple were now partners (rather than captain and midshipman) and Peter no longer fought with his stepmother. Andy had begun regular nursery school, enabling Lesley to begin retraining, Alice had made the transition to secondary school without a hitch, while Timothy, who had been excessively shy at the time of the first interview, had become much more outward going. The final session of therapy was concerned with exploring the issue of family violence and making sure Peter could control his violence using the time-out technique.

## Commentary

This case history illustrates my integrated approach reasonably well. No one example could possibly illustrate all the facets of the approach but this case history does contain many of them. The main thrust of the work was structural, and a strategic intervention was interleaved with this work in order to gain therapeutic leverage for the marital phase of therapy which involved the use of a combination of quid-pro-quo, structural and transgenerational techniques. The final phase of the therapy involved the whole family and was concerned with consolidating the gains that had been made. Peter became the focus of my attention, since I felt there was a risk that he would carry the tradition of family violence with him and hence inadvertently help create yet another generation of violent men.

## CONCLUSION

This integrated approach model, is designed to be servant and not mistress. It enables me to make my therapeutic work more coherent but at the same time it frees me up so that I can shift focus and not persist in working at one 'level' of therapy when another may be far more productive in creating the next step towards change.

## REFERENCES

Andolfi, M., Menghi, P., Nicolo, A. and Saccu, C. (1980). Interaction in rigid systems: a model of intervention in families with a schizophrenic member. In M. Andolfi and I. Zwerling (eds) *Dimensions of Family Therapy*. New York, Guilford.

Aponte, H.J. and Van Deusen, J.M. (1981). Structural family therapy. In A.S.Gurman and D.P. Kniskern (eds) *Handbook of Family Therapy*. New York, Brunner/Mazel.

Beck, A.T., Rush, A.J., Shaw, B. and Emery, G. (1979). *Cognitive Therapy of Depression*. New York, Guilford.

Beck, A., Emery, G. and Greenberg, A.T. (1985). *Anxiety Disorders and Phobias: A Cognitive Perspective*. New York, Basic Books.

Bentovim, A. and Kingston, W. (1981). Brief focal marital and family therapy. In S. Budman (ed.) *Forms of Brief Therapy*. New York, Guilford.

Boszormenyi-Nagy, I. and Ulrich, D.N. (1981). Contextual family therapy. In A.S. Gurman and D.P. Kniskern (eds) *Handbook of Family Therapy*. New York, Brunner/Mazel.

Burns, D. (1980). *Feeling Good: The New Mood Therapy*. New York, New American Library.

Crowe, M. (1985). Marital therapy: a behavioural systems approach – indications for different types of intervention. In W. Dryden (ed.) *Marital Therapy in Britain. 1. Context and Therapeutic Approaches*. London, Harper & Row.

Deschner, J.P. (1984). *The Hitting Habit: Anger Control for Battering Couples*. New York, Free Press.

Duhl, B.S. and Duhl, F.J. (1981). Integrative family therapy. In A.S. Gurman and D.P. Kniskern (eds) *Handbook of Family Therapy*. New York, Brunner/Mazel.

Falloon, I.R.H. and Liberman, R.P. (1983). Behavioral family interventions in the management of chronic schizophrenia. In W.R. McFarlane (ed.) *Family Therapy in Schizophrenia*. New York, Guilford.

Fisch, R., Weakland, J.H. and Segal, L. (1982). *The Tactics of Change: Doing Therapy Briefly*. San Francisco, Jossey-Bass.

Framo, J.L. (1981). The integration of marital therapy with sessions with family of origin. In A.S. Gurman and D.P. Kniskern (eds) *Handbook of Family Therapy*. New York, Brunner Mazel.

Goldner, V. (1985). Feminism and family therapy. *Family Process*, 24, 31–47.

Grunebaum, H. and Chasin, R. (1982). Thinking like a family therapist: a model for integrating the theories and methods of family therapy. *Journal of Marital and Family Therapy*, 8, 403–16.

Gurman A.S. and Kniskern D.P. (1978) Research on marital and family therapy: progress, perspective and prospect. In S.L. Garfield and A.E. Bergin (eds) *Handbook of Psychotherapy and Behavior Change*, 2nd edn. New York, Wiley.

—— (eds) (1981). *Handbook of Family Therapy*. New York, Brunner/Mazel.

Haley, J. (1976). *Problem-Solving Therapy*. San Francisco, Jossey-Bass.

Kaslow, F. (1981). Divorce and divorce therapy. In A.S. Gurman and D.P. Kniskern (eds) *Handbook of Family Therapy*. New York, Brunner/Mazel.

Kelly, G. (1955). *The Psychology of Personal Constructs*. New York, Norton.

Lederer, W.J. and Jackson, D.D. (1968). *The Mirages of Marriage*. New York, Norton.

Mahoney, M.J. (1978). Cognitive and self-control therapies. In S.L. Garfield and A.E. Bergin (eds) *Handbook of Psychotherapy and Behavior Change*, 2nd edn. New York, Wiley.

Minuchin, S. and Fishman, C. (1981). *Family Therapy Techniques*. Cambridge, Mass., Harvard University Press.

Murray, E.J. and Jacobson, L.I. (1978). Cognition and learning in traditional and behavioral psychotherapy. In S.L. Garfield and A.E. Bergin (eds) *Handbook of Psychotherapy and Behavior Change*, 2nd edn. New York, Wiley.

Nichols, M.P. (1984). *Family Therapy: Concepts and Methods*. New York, Gardner.

Olson, D.H., Russell, C.S. and Sprenkle, D. (1980). Marital and family therapy: a decade review. *Journal of Marriage and the Family*. 42, 76–92.

Osborne, K. (1983). Women in families: feminist therapy and family systems. *Journal of Family Therapy*, 5, 1–10.

Procter, H.G. (1984). A construct approach to family therapy and systems intervention. In E. Button (ed.) *Personal Construct Theory and Mental Health*. Beckenham, Kent, Croom Helm.

Scheflen, A.E. (1978). Susan smiled: an explanation in family therapy. *Family Process*, 17, 59–68.

Simon, R. (1984). From ideology to practice: the women's project in family therapy. *Family Therapy Networker*, 8, 28–40.

Skynner, R. (1981). An open-systems, group-analytic approach to family therapy. In A.S. Gurman and D.P. Kniskern (eds) *Handbook of Family Therapy*. New York, Brunner/Mazel.

Sluzki, C.E. (1983). Process, structure and world views: toward an integrated view of systemic models in family therapy. *Family Process*, 22, 469–76.

Stanton, M.D. (1980a). An integrated structural/strategic approach to family therapy. *Journal of Marriage and Family Therapy*, 7, 427–39.

—— (1980b). Family therapy: systems approaches. In G.P. Sholevar, R.M. Benson and B.J. Blinder (eds) *Emotional Disorders in Children and Adolescents: Medical and Psychological Approaches to Treatment*. Jamaica/New York, SP Medical and Scientific Books (Spectrum Pubs).

—— (1981). Strategic approaches to family therapy. In A.S. Gurman and D.P. Kniskern (eds) *Handbook of Family Therapy*. New York, Brunner/Mazel.

Stanton, M.D., Todd, T.C., Steier, F., Van Deusen, J.M., Marder, L.R., Rosoff, R.J., Seaman, S.F. and Skibinski, E. (1979). Family characteristics and family therapy of heroin addicts; Final Report 1974–1978. Submitted to the National Institute of Drug Abuse (Grant no. RO1 DA 01119).

Street, E. and Treacher, A. (1980). Microtraining and family therapy skills: towards a possible synthesis. *Journal of Family Therapy*, 2, 243–57.

Szapocznik, J. *et al.* (1984). One-person family therapy. In B. Lubin and W.A. Connors (eds) *Ecological Models: Applications in Clinical and Community Health*. New York, Wiley.

Treacher, A. (1983). On the utility or otherwise of psychotherapy research. In D. Pilgrim (ed.) *Psychology and Psychotherapy: Current Trends and Issues*. London, Routledge & Kegan Paul.

—— (1985). Working with marital partners: systems approaches. In W. Dryden (ed.) *Marital Therapy in Britain. 1. Context and Therapeutic Approaches*. London, Harper & Row.

—— (1986). Invisible patients, invisible families: a critical exploration of some technocratic trends in family therapy. *Journal of Family Therapy*, 8, 267–306.

—— (1987). Family therapists are potentially damaging to families and their wider networks. Discuss. In D. Watson and S. Walrond-Skinner (eds) *Ethical Issues in Family Therapy*. London, Routledge & Kegan Paul.

Treacher, A. and Carpenter, J. (1982). 'Oh no! Not the Smiths again!' – An exploration of how to identify and overcome 'stuckness' in family therapy. *Journal of Family Therapy*, 4, 285–305.

Wells, R. and Gianetti, V. (1986). Individual marital therapy: a critical reappraisal. *Family Process*, 25, 43–51.

# PART 2
# SPECIAL ISSUES

# CHAPTER 9

# CONTEXT AND THE CONSTRUCTION OF FAMILY THERAPY PRACTICE

## Dave Dungworth

## CLINICAL THERAPY AND A SYSTEMS ORIENTATION

An essential theoretical feature of family therapy is claimed to be its adherence to systems theory. If this is the case, it should be possible to apply many of the principles that have been derived from the application of systems thinking to human situations other than the family. The questions posed are whether family therapy is merely a clinical technique or whether its principles allow interventionists to be involved in other systems. This chapter attempts to address these problems to the particular issue of how family therapists themselves can construct their practice of therapy in specific agencies and contexts.

As far as I am aware, very few authorities or agencies in Britain are specifically employing family therapists; most are content to mention family therapy skills as an option. There are very few work settings where the worker is not faced with the dynamic tensions created by using a particular therapeutic approach within the confines of an existing service provision. Compromise seems inevitable when faced with the agency structure, its existing staff ideology and values and its avowed aims or statutory obligations. Resources may also play a part, but too often this is used as a justification for failure. Our ability, therefore, to help those who are deemed to be either patients or clients will not simply rest on the assimilation of appropriate skills. We need the ability to deploy them in relation to the 'family' and to include others who have a powerful influence directly and indirectly on the family. I intend not only to illustrate how family therapy offers not just another set of skills, but also to suggest principles that can guide and direct the practice of those skills.

All workers need to create order and place boundaries around their work, and often this can lead to taking easy options in relation to practice which denies the wider context in which problems arise. Minuchin (1970) offers the following appreciation of a child's behaviour and its relationship to treatment.

> A child's behaviour is caused by many factors, some are inside the child like neurons, brains and glands as well as memories, motivations, introjects and drives. 'Outside' the child are factors like his parents, his siblings, his family's socioeconomic status, his house, his school (teachers, peers and curriculum), his neighbourhood, his neighbourhood peer group, the hue of his skin, television and many others. Problems, formation and maintenance should take account of these, but the major theoretical systems in child psychiatry have always been concerned with the influence of both internal and external factors on the development of the child. . . . But techniques of intervention which have been developed by child psychiatry have been aimed almost entirely at the child as a separate organism.
>
> (Minuchin 1970 : 41)

He goes on to argue that while subscribing to theories which stress the importance of external factors, actual techniques of intervention have not reflected this. Similarly other theories have accepted the role of outside influences. Family therapy, however, marked a step forward in recognizing two important factors beyond this acceptance of 'outside' influences. First, that the therapist and family members are involved in creating a new set of transactions; the therapist is not simply an observer but actively participates in the newly created system of family plus therapist. Second, both worker and family bring to this new grouping 'outside' influence that will have a marked effect on how the problem is maintained and how the process of helping proceeds. In broad terms we are faced with two potential problem areas. First, how do we select the most appropriate grouping around the present problem that is helpful? Is it the dyad, the nuclear family, the family plus wider kin, or a social network (and does it include professionals)? Second, how does our position within a work setting affect our ability to reach the most advantageous decision regarding the most appropriate grouping?

While family therapy has recognized the need to take account of the interaction across the boundaries between individual family members, family sub-systems and between family and significant 'outside' systems, it, like psychiatry, has been hemmed in by clinical ideology. There are notable exceptions (Minuchin being one of them) but in general the clinical ambience of family therapy has simply moved pathology from the individual to the family unit. This may, in some part, be a reflection of wider political processes that seek to redefine the 'family' as a problem. In this process, both political theories of the left and right identify the family as a major reason for the 'ills' of modern society.

Family therapy practice underpinned by systems theory should lead adherents to more flexible thinking and approaches in their work setting. However, as Hoffman and Long (1969) illustrate, helping agencies can undermine the functioning of a family, and hence be detrimental to therapeutic needs. Unfortunately it is common to find that the clinical experience of the USA has been simply transported into Britain. For example, dogmatic attempts to bring together whole families where one child has been labelled by the courts as the problem, often lead to failure and frustration for the would-be family therapist. This unfortunately, reinforces the notion that family therapy is best practised within and on those families who are willing to attend.

A further problem arises from the concept of therapy or treatment. It is easy to conceive of treating an individual or even a family but how does one act as a therapist for a social network or for the family plus other agencies? This needs a much broader interpretation and application of family therapy concepts. For example, a mother from a single parent household refers herself to a social services department because she is concerned by the behaviour of her 9-year-old daughter. The girl is stealing from her mother and is abusive and uncooperative. The mother works part-time to supplement the family income and the girl is cared for by the maternal grandmother who lives nearby. One likely hypothesis would be that the maternal grandmother is undermining the mother's abilities and powers as a parent. Treatment could focus on mother and grandmother with the possible inclusion of the girl. Yet the mother cannot afford to offend her mother whose support she needs if she is to continue working. The mortgage is in arrears and she cannot pay a child-minder as a substitute for the grandmother. As a single parent she feels isolated, unsupported and ill-equipped to act as two parents. In this case the worker may need to negotiate with the building society (and other agencies or companies), to help the mother develop a supportive social network and address the relationship between herself and her own mother. Such problems are often far more complicated than this, however.

Pincus and Minahan (1979) have devised a useful model for separating the various system groupings that impinge on the worker and the family. They suggest four major systems.

1 *The Change Agent System*, which would include the worker and his or her agency. The operation of this system would be influenced by the legal and organizational structures that form its boundaries. The agency structure defines which difficulties can be addressed.
2 *The Client System* is the person, group, organization or community that employs or empowers the worker in his or her capacity as a change agent.

This can be the individual client or customer or a larger system such as the judiciary.

3 *The Target System* refers to those people, groups, and so on that the Change Agent needs to influence to bring about change. It is worth emphasizing that the Client System and the Target System do not always coincide, a point to which I will return to later.

4 *The Action System* includes the worker and those individuals and groups he or she selects to work with to bring about change. Selection is inevitable and important when faced with a large number of potential members of this system.

Strategic issues of power, influence and availability will inevitably influence the composition of the action group. This model helps the worker when faced with a referral to consider the influence of his or her work context on the help offered. The worker can determine who is empowering him or her to act and their expectations of his or her action. The worker can evaluate the individuals and systems he or she needs to involve in attempting to bring about change, and finally, can select the larger target system through which he or she will make interventions.

This simple systems model therefore allows the worker to begin to develop an understanding of the context in which he or she operates.

## The influence of context

Clearly the nature of the particular context in which one works will have strong influences that will shape and mould the opportunities to practise family therapy and will affect the form that the 'therapy' actually takes. Client expectations, colleague ideology, administrative procedures, statutory obligations and the role expectations on workers will play their respective parts and each will be considered in turn.

### Client expectations
Within the definition that Pincus and Minahan have provided, 'client' can become a problematic term. Client or patient is the term commonly used to identify those individuals who are receiving treatment, therapy, advice or practical help. Unfortunately, particularly in statutory situations, these 'clients' do not necessarily see themselves as clients. Where a juvenile court has made a child the subject of a care order, who is the client? The court makes the local authority responsible for the child but the child and his or her family may actively resent this act. Palazzoli *et al.* (1980) rightly point out that most individuals and families are referred through third parties and this process can positively hinder or obstruct our attempts at offering help. Family therapists have used the term 'customer' to describe the individual or group that is wanting change. A client may not, necessarily, be a customer

for change, particularly when the relationship between worker and client is legally defined.

Referrers can often have 'hidden agendas' and the form the referral takes can restrict opportunities to form a workable contract with the family. A GP with a troublesome and time-consuming patient may make a referral to the social services department stating 'concerns' about the patient's abilities as a mother, hoping to involve a social worker with the patient and, therefore, ease his own situation. The patient may have a totally different perception of her problem. A paediatrician or GP who refers patients with psychosomatic symptoms, while continuing active tests or prescribing drugs, places the worker in a very difficult situation. By maintaining the person in a 'sick role' a double message is being given which will affect the expectations brought to the helping process.

Some client expectations are more clear cut: 'This is the problem child, you cure him/her'. As Viaro (1980) states:

> It is never the patient asking for help for himself; the decision is made by the family (often particularly by one of the parents). Yet, as a rule, the family is physically absent at the moment of first contact with the therapist who usually meets the identified patient accompanied by the mother only. . . . Almost without exception, the application is motivated by the wish to know what is the matter with the child and what must be done in order to solve the problem.
>
> (Viaro 1980 : 36)

Viaro does not construct a therapeutic contract by setting the number of meetings or stating who should attend, as a 'formal' offer of family therapy would directly confront the family's expectations. Viaro works on the idea of 'smuggling family therapy through'. The family is invited to a 'preliminary' meeting and subsequent family meetings are given other context-related titles. The workers do not call themselves family therapists, but consultants in child pathology, this being congruent within the context of the agency. Viaro claims that using this approach 'a high level' of attendance by families is achieved. Clients who receive or seek help often have clear ideas of the roles of different professional groups. These may be misguided, but they have a marked influence on the outcome of work. For example, social workers have struggled against being seen as simply the 'welfare'. Again, as Viaro's example illustrates, staying within role can minimize conflict between worker and family and any significant others. Strategies can be devised to 'widen' or renegotiate these expectations, examples of which will be discussed later in the chapter.

*Colleague ideology*
Colleague reaction can vary enormously, from the fervour that arises from 'conversion', to obstruction that stems from a rejection of the efficacy and appropriateness of family therapy within an agency. Both extremes can be equally disabling and unhelpful. Over-enthusiasm can lead to inappropriate

and ill-considered referrals. Equally it can create in other colleagues not practising family therapy a good deal of resentment. This can be heightened if family therapy as an approach is perceived as threatening the professional value systems of the others. All agencies and their workers have both explicit and implicit rules on how 'help' should be provided. A worker who goes against the accepted orthodoxy is in danger of being isolated and subverted. In working with colleagues, the family therapist must adopt an approach similar to working with families, that is begin where they are, recognizing their strengths, finding areas of commonality, sharing with them your ideas and seeking their advice. Any other path will lead to an island of family therapy surrounded by a vast ocean of distrust and resentment as the accepted orthodoxy is challenged head on.

*Needs of the agency*

Very few, if any, agencies simply exist to promote therapy. Most, according to practitioners, take on a life of their own that is self-maintaining and owing little to the aims of the agency. This life is expressed through the administrative and procedural rules and tasks that workers have to comply with. Many of these procedures run counter to systemic thinking, such as identifying individuals as the statistical base for calculations about worker time and caseload and how material and financial help can be offered. The need to fill in standardized forms and records can be time-consuming. It can also be unhelpful in the sense that the kind of records that are needed when practising family therapy can be different from that demanded by the agency.

Against this, the worker needs to remember that the agency is not employing a family therapist, it is employing a social worker, psychologist, and so on, who may have different tasks and roles to perform. The message is again the same to the would-be family therapist: accommodate to and exploit the system in which you work. Lauffer *et al*. (1977) have produced an excellent concise guide to understanding and exploring agencies. In this book several perspectives are considered which form part of a larger systems approach to organization. The reader explores his or her own agency by completing exercises suggested by the authors, and a step-by-step approach to organizational problem-solving is suggested. Arming oneself with a clear understanding of how the agency works is essential if you wish to expand your manoeuvrability as a worker; Dimmock and Dungworth (1983) have provided some examples of this manoeuvrability where the structure and hierarchy of the agency are used by the worker in the therapeutic process. In one example, to prevent a precipitate action being taken the worker emphasized his need to consult with his superior before a decision can be made. This practice was congruent with the formal structure of the agency, while provoking a breathing space in which to plan a more considered intervention.

*Statutory powers*

Many agencies have statutory powers such as care orders in respect of juveniles or powers under the Mental Health Act. Workers can view these as a mixed blessing. Some of the reasons for this have been already discussed. But although the statutory order can identify an individual as client, it does not ensure co-operation of either the named individual or the family. For example Ainley (1984) has illustrated in relation to the probation service, how it is possible to use statutory powers in a positive way. Two approaches seem particularly useful.

First, agreeing a clear contract with the family on how the probation service will help the individual or how the family themselves will be aided to regain control of their own situation. Ainley as a probation officer shares control with the parents of difficult and delinquent adolescents. She takes responsibility for certain parts of the adolescent's life while helping the young person and the parents reach a more helpful and appropriate relationship. In this way the statutory order does not further undermine the problem-solving abilities of the family. A second, more interventionist approach (Dimmock and Dungworth 1985) uses the statutory order to create intensity and a crisis within the system. The worker needs to be able to manage and capitalize on the opportunities that a crisis brings to create change. For example, the process by which a social services department decides about the long-term future of a child who is in its care can be harnessed in this way.

*Worker roles*

The question of roles has already been touched upon but it is an especially important issue when workers occupy many roles as this can lead to confusion in the worker, the family, and other agencies. Most helping professionals find themselves operating within a number of roles. They have a professional title – clinical psychologist, social worker, psychiatric nurse – but these are general labels. Workers can find themselves monitoring and policing a family, or alternatively holding parental rights over a child, acting as counsellor or therapist, or being gatekeeper to material or financial resources. All these roles may be in relation to one family. Confusion is then easily fostered amongst family and worker.

Clearly the worker must understand and negotiate his or her roles in relation to the family. If the worker is to move between roles, clear means of punctuating those changes must be employed. This can sometimes be achieved by bringing in an additional worker who helps create a new system around a particular role and, therefore, a new focus for work. Written contracts between client and worker can also be useful, but whichever strategy is employed, making clear the role can dispel doubt, distrust or even hostility from families. It also helps workers to make more appropriate context-based interventions within the family.

# PRACTISING FAMILY THERAPY WITHIN AN AGENCY

In this section I intend to demonstrate how the contextual issues discussed in the previous section of the chapter manifest themselves within psychiatric, child guidance and social service settings. I hope to highlight these issues further by illustrating some strategies for overcoming these difficulties. Finally, I intend to provide practical, general guidelines for establishing a family therapy practice.

## Psychiatric hospitals

There are a number of possible approaches to introducing family-centred treatment to adult psychiatric care. Treacher (1984); Scott and Ashworth (1967); Scott (1973); Scott and Starr (1981) and Haley (1975; 1980) offer differing but related perspectives and strategies. Haley and later Treacher concentrate on some of the difficulties that can be encountered within the hospital, while Scott and Starr show the value of a family therapy approach that reaches out beyond the hospital. Both Treacher (1984) and Haley (1975) have considered the impact of family therapy on the values that underpin psychiatric hospitals. Haley, tongue-in-cheek, suggests that family therapy is too dangerous to be introduced, a statement with a strong paradoxical intention of challenging the psychiatric profession to try to stay the same while using a family therapy approach. Lieberman and Cooklin (1982) suggest that a family therapy approach unsettles the existing hierarchy because it opposes the prevailing orthodoxy. Family therapy models suggest very different explanations of the causation of psychiatric behaviour as it sees it rooted in relationships and not simply within the psyche of the individual. It deals with observable and concrete interactions between people. It does not speculate on the working of an inner world of fantasy nor on the possibility of ameliorating the effects of fixed biological characteristics. The ruling psychiatric orthodoxy within the institution can perceive the introduction of family therapy as a major threat or challenge to the existing order. The result can be that family therapy is strongly opposed or excluded. What is required is an approach that introduces family therapy without provoking hostile reactions. Treacher (1984) summarizes the challenge facing British family therapists in the following way:

1 Family therapists need to understand that the present organisation of the adult psychiatric services is unlikely to change radically in the foreseeable future.
2 Since these services are largely unchanging, family therapists need to develop approaches which enable them to work within the services that have been designed with a different model in mind.

3 If family therapy is to be successful, then family therapists need to be able to integrate their work with that of their colleagues within the hospital. At all cost they must avoid taking up adverse positions which undermine the work of their colleagues.

(Treacher 1984 : 168)

Psychiatric hospitals are hierarchically structured but this should not mislead us into believing that we can, or should, ignore nursing staff and others in favour of the professions with more prestige. Forming an alliance with a 'friendly' psychiatrist can lead to resentment and resistance amongst other staff groups.

Careful preparation is required. Opportunities for all staff groups to discuss and learn about family therapy are an important step. It should be remembered that nursing staff have more contact with the patient and many also see the family more regularly than the family therapist. Their active co-operation is, therefore, extremely important.

We should also consider the effect on the family of being offered a family therapy approach. The 'patient' has been labelled as mentally ill, a label which is extremely powerful in our society. It requires psychiatric staff to 'help' or 'cure' that individual. Therefore, being offered family therapy can seem irrelevant or a move to blame the family for the problem. Scott (1973) describes this process as part of the 'treatment barrier' which needs to be penetrated if work, that takes account of relationships, is to begin. Treacher (1984) agrees that, ideally, a family interview should take place prior to the admission and that on admission a well-organized reception procedure be implemented that involves the family in touring the wards to familiarize and involve them in the hospital. A family interview should take place as soon as possible after the admission. Bruggen *et al.* (1973), Bruggen and O'Brien (1982) and Jenkins (1984), in relation to adolescent admissions, have recommended similar strategies aimed at countering the process of separation, blaming and finally closure of relationships in which the individual and his or her family readily accept the new social reality of separation, leaving little opportunity for the worker to offer other possibilities. Individuals who go through such powerful labelling process commonly accept their 'sick' role, sinking into patterns of dependency and guilt. It is, therefore, doubly important to begin within the right framework.

In some situations, the patient may also be receiving treatment from another worker. This can be a further complication, particularly if the family sessions are raising painful issues. The individual's psychiatric symptoms may increase and the family therapist may find him or herself under pressure from the other worker to stop or suspend family work. Haley (1980) argues strongly that the therapist should have control over admission and discharge and that if there is any risk that he or she may be overruled or opposed by another worker, then the start of therapy should be delayed. Unfortunately this is not a position that most workers can adopt. Ideally the family therapist should undertake and have control of both areas of work, family and individual. Often this is not possible but the problem can largely be overcome by regular meetings between the workers or by the individual or group therapist observing the family sessions. Issues of confidentiality involved in the different types of meetings should be dealt with at the outset, the family and patient being made aware that the most helpful approach is a sharing of information between the workers. In situations where family therapy does take root, it is possible to take a more radical approach. Scott and Starr (1981) describe a twenty-four-hour crisis service that is available to patients and their families. This has the advantage of initiating family meetings at a very early stage, meeting the family within their social setting and, possibly, avoiding admission. Scott claims that this approach has reduced admissions and the number of patients who stay in hospital for more than one year. This kind of approach would be favoured by Haley (1980), who argues strongly for avoiding admission wherever possible, but the approach of not seeing admissions as failure (Treacher 1984), seems more realistic within the present context of British psychiatric treatment.

## Child guidance

Child guidance clinics exhibit areas of overlap with psychiatric hospitals and social services departments. All three are empowered to act by statute, although their powers vary widely. Child guidance clinics, like psychiatric hospitals, are committed to multidisciplinary co-operation. Many clinic teams would claim to be based on equality between the professions, but this is difficult to support when there are such large differences in status and power between the professions. As the focus for a number of professions, the clinics have the potential for making interventions into a number of systems and they are often seen as more acceptable to the family. The term 'child guidance' can however cause undue focus on the child and act as a barrier to treatment. In introducing family therapy, we are faced with similar problems to the psychiatric hospital. I favour the approach which closely parallels that suggested by Carpenter (1984) in writing on his experience of working within child guidance clinics. Carpenter rightly argues that Haley's position is too rigid in suggesting that family therapy will create substantial conflicts with the existing order. First, conflict and rivalry often already exist between professional groups prior to the introduction of family therapy. Family therapy may increase this, particularly if it is introduced in an unhelpful way. A rigid adherence to conjoint family therapy as the only effective method of helping families guarantees opposition and distrust. Carpenter sets a realistic target for those wishing to introduce and practise family therapy in this setting.

If family therapy brings with it an appreciation of the part that both individuals and wider systems play in the agencies and resolution of children's problems, then much will have been achieved.

(Carpenter 1984 : 15)

The first step in any attempt to practise family therapy must be a clear understanding of the structure of the clinic. Again the approach should be open and respectful of other professionals' expertise and knowledge. Fortunately child guidance has a tradition of fostering co-work that can be exploited in forming working partnerships. As in all these settings, it is best to begin work on cases that at least offer the opportunity of some degree of success. We all need to build up experience in a new method and setting before tackling the very difficult cases. It is important to beware of being led into taking on cases that are impossible! This tactic is commonly used in an attempt to prove that family therapy has little new to offer.

Child guidance clinics receive referrals through many different routes. The coming of the Education Act, 1981, has forged even closer links with schools which give rise to a significant number of referrals. In some cases referrals relate directly to that Act and do not necessarily invite a 'therapeutic' interaction within the family, nor is this appropriate in many cases. However, assessments, if handled appropriately, can become the basis for continued work with the family, for they can provide the 'excuse' for involving wider family members, friends and other professionals. This approach parallels that of Viaro (1980) as a formal contract for family therapy need not follow. Most referrals specifically name an individual and implicitly suggest that the child needs changing in some way. This is occasionally broadened to suggest that the family also needs to alter its functioning. A careful consideration of the exact 'location' of the problem is needed if we are to avoid becoming simply locked into conjoint family work. A wider systems view would suggest that the difficulties could be maintained between two or more systems, for example between family and school or family, social services department and the courts. Aponte (1976) offers an approach that deals with some of these difficulties. He suggests attempting to gain the maximum amount of information from the referring agency by involving them, at least initially, in the first meeting with the family. He uses the example of a school referral to illustrate his idea of defining the customer as the referrer.

The family/school interview, as a first session, tends to serve as an instrument to learn about the presenting problem, the relationships among the people who contribute to the problem, and the ways in which these people can help bring about change. The interview is used principally as a way to find solutions, rather than to dig for causes of trouble. The therapist attempts to make the interview a practical experience in which the family and school staff well recognise the relevance of their roles as agents of positive change.

(Aponte 1976 : 304)

This approach can be used in other settings and it provides the opportunity for a wider view of the problem, releasing the 'client' from being the sole object of change. This method, called the ecosystems approach, allows for further meetings and interventions involving selected parts of the system. The worker must be careful to respect the knowledge held by the other parties to the meeting and not to act as if he or she has a contract to treat them all. Initially this approach can be time-consuming but it provides a framework in which change is more likely to occur. There are two major pitfalls that need to be avoided however. First, it cannot be assumed that families are coming to be treated; the reality is that often they have been told to come by a powerful third party. Therefore their agenda will be very different from the workers' and Aponte's approach will uncover these difficulties. Second, within the clinic setting it is easy to slip into the conjoint family mode that by implication locates every problem with the family structure. This constrains the number of options open in seeking solutions and neglects the wider processes in problem formation. The challenge for child guidance workers is to seek ways to expand their interventions so as to include groups related to but outside the immediate family.

## Social services departments

Social services workers face exactly the opposite problem to child guidance workers: they are confronted by numerous possible roles. Additionally social services departments are not seen by clients or other professionals as centres of therapy. They employ social workers, not family therapists; indeed the social work role involves an amalgamation of tasks that at times appear to be in conflict with any notion of therapy. Social services departments, in response to their statutory duties, contain a strong bureaucratic hierarchy which can be seen as an insurmountable barrier. However, all these 'problems' can be exploited by a worker wishing to undertake family therapy (see Dimmock and Dungworth 1983).

Social worker time is split between face-to-face contact with clients (Hallet and Stevenson 1980 suggest less than 40 per cent), administrative tasks, telephone calls and attending various kinds of meetings. Client contact is usually viewed as the 'real' work but the other tasks are equally important if the family therapist is to operate successfully within the department. Social expectations cannot be ignored; social services departments are obliged to discharge welfare duties in relation to the elderly, disabled and sick. Such individuals are also part of families and are equally deserving of help. Social services departments also have a powerful role in child-care matters: they are charged with protecting children even if this appears to conflict with wider 'therapeutic' interventions. The major challenge is to combine these roles in ways that enhance the possibilities of change. In statutory situations where a child is made the subject of a care order, giving the local authority parental rights, the social worker's prime task will be to promote the 'welfare' of the child. If he or she is working towards eventual rehabilitation, then he or she will occupy other roles in relation to the family. Ensuring access, monitoring progress, guidance, help and advice, dealing with housing or benefit difficulties, for example, will form some part of a larger therapeutic plan. Social workers can use these opportunities as part of their interventions within the family. Task setting can be used with these situations to create new experiences for family members. The making of a statutory order can result in the worker's feeling inadequate as the transfer of some power from family to agency is often viewed as a 'failure'. Orders can be a mixed blessing for the family involved as they can provide appropriate custody and control while at the same time labelling a family scapegoat by making one individual the focus of the order. As Janzen and Harris (1980) argue, the situation can become so problematic that an agency can actually contribute to increasing the family's difficulties.

> Agencies which require the family to conform to agency policy operate as though the family is an extension of the agency, subject to its bidding, instead of providing support to the family's own problem-solving efforts; the policies of the agency and the action of the workers often serve to inhibit the capacity for independent thought and action. In conceptual terms, the family loses its boundaries as a separate system and becomes incorporated as part of the agency system, this increases rather than decreases its dependence.
>
> (Janzen and Harris 1980 : 81)

This is a trap into which any powerful agency can fall. It is usually the result of the exercise of power or influence within a narrow perspective that ignores the wider repercussions for the family. Again, Ainley's (1984) account of work in the probation service provides a part solution to these difficulties. She argues that the worker should take responsibility for those aspects of the juvenile's life that relate to the supervision order while working with the parents to enable them to regain control of the situation. In this way the initial loss of self-esteem and control is minimized, creating a very different climate from that described by Janzen and Harris. Social workers can use court reports and so on as an opportunity to gain access to families with a view to continuing work. Assessments are not neutral processes and where appropriate, the need for future work and its possible agenda can be written into the report. The way we set about these tasks can start the process of change, for the involvement of all the family and other relevant agencies may break long-standing patterns of interaction.

Social workers within social services departments have opportunities to intervene in wider systems around the family. Case conferences should be used to involve other important agencies in realistic plans to help the family. Work with the family can be made more difficult if other involved agencies are ignored. Competition between agencies and open conflict between the family and particular agencies can occur if all interested parties are not dealt with as a complete system within itself. Involving the family in case conferences is also to be recommended as it provides an opportunity to form contracts on the areas for future work. Case conferences can be further expanded into network meetings aimed specifically at particular problems (see Pottle 1984; Dimmock and Dungworth 1985). The network meeting can involve immediate family, wider relatives, friends, neighbours and other agencies and it can be used with a variety of client groups. The techniques required and the theoretical understandings are available within the family therapy literature. All that is required is for workers to desire a broadening of the approach to the process of problem-solving for important changes in practice to become permanent. Specific areas of social service work that benefit from a clear systems approach are fostering, hospitalization and residential care.

Eastman (1979) has contrasted the foster family with the biologically related family, stressing how the foster family must cope with issues of system integration and exit. The difficulties of penetration by outside agencies can also cause major problems for the newly formed foster family. Parry and Young (1978) have suggested ways of countering the process of family disintegration that hospitalization of a family member often brings. Street (1984) examines using family therapy in child care residential establishments, clearly pointing to the need for well-defined agreements between workers, both within and outside the establishment. Failure to reach such a position is likely to create conflict and confusion between individuals with different roles. Street (1981) has also suggested how a family therapy technique can be used in staff-group consultation. This application of family therapy principles to systems very different from the family provides a strong argument for the general applicability of a systems approach.

## Therapist support

Regardless of the actual location where he or she operates, the family therapist will need to consider carefully the type of support he or she will require. The major source of support is the family therapy support group. If structured properly, support groups provide an invaluable source of support, advice, new ideas as well as the opportunity for constructive discussion. My preference is for support groups that have an agreed membership for a stated period of time in which the members have a stated commitment to using family therapy skills and ideas. Membership is renegotiated at the end of that period, allowing new faces to join the group. However, there are dangers to this approach, as one can be accused of being 'precious' or aloof. Being open about the membership policy can disarm many of the critics.

Support groups tend to have a limited useful life and this should be recognized. Equally over a certain size, they become too unwieldy and reforming into smaller groups may become desirable. In some cases it is useful to have an agency representative (usually a manager) as part of the group. This is particularly helpful if the group is undertaking work together.

My major reservation concerning the usefulness of support groups however, lies in the tendency for some to become the only focus in an agency for the practice of family therapy. This can be avoided if there are clearly stated goals which relate directly to the actual work undertaken by members.

A family systems approach challenges the worker to consider his or her present family or family of origin. This can provide the basis for a new family game of mapping the structure, building a family-tree or sculpting the various life cycle developmental stages. This can be both amusing and revealing. As most of us have experience of family life, I believe it is legitimate to exploit this knowledge in our professional development. The danger lies in attempting some form of self-therapy on unprepared and unsuspecting family members; this can set one's own family against one's work. It is important to remember that one is just a family member at home and a therapist at work.

## Guidelines for practice

Whatever the context for the work it is possible to list a set of guidelines for introducing the practice of family therapy into any agency.

1  Spend time learning about the agency or agencies: consider the hierarchy and value system.
2  Do not get involved in time-wasting power struggles.
3  Be interested and active in the wider issues that affect the agency.
4  Avoid being too critical of the existing values and structure of the agency.
5  At all cost avoid being an evangelist.
6  Using family therapy jargon is extremely unhelpful.
7  Find at least one 'friend' for support and discussion.
8  Be ready to work with any colleague who shows an interest.
9  Use every opportunity to discuss the influence of family and wider systems on the work of the agency.
10  Present case material.
11  Respect and use the skills that your colleagues have gained through their practice.
12  Be clear about your role or roles within the agency; stepping too far outside them can create major difficulties.
13  Use co-work wherever possible.

14 Gain agreement to a parallel means of recording that helps you understand the process of your work.

15 If at all possible, use audio or video-recording of your work. This can be extended beyond recording family sessions to case conferences, network meetings, and so on.

16 Either join a local family therapy support group or create one with the help of colleagues and appropriate management backing.

17 Seek training but not only in 'narrow' family therapy issues.

18 Do not lose support at home by analysing your own family at great length!


# FAMILY THERAPY AND MANAGING SERVICES

It seems logical to suppose that family therapists will increasingly find themselves as managers and administrators. For some workers this will seem a natural progression to shape an agency's delivery of services. The problem presented will be very similar to those problems facing the individual practitioner but other issues will also need to be addressed. The manager will be concerned with referral or intake policies, the organization of staff time, workloads, statistics, training, and so on. The manager will, because of his or her position in the hierarchy, be able to gain a more comprehensive picture of the processes involved in the delivery of the service, and will act as a buffer between colleagues and wider management issues, and other agencies.

If the manager is in the fortunate position of leading a service offering family therapy, there will still need to be consideration of appropriate strategies in relation to other agencies or service groups. If the family therapy 'team' is small and part of a larger service, accommodating to the wider agency should be tackled in ways suggested earlier in this chapter; a desire to be open, to inform and 'join' with other groups will ease working relationships. The manager must observe the exchanges that take place between his or her service of the wider professional system, intervening where necessary. This may mean preventing colleagues from being too inward-looking and insisting that they join with workers outside the team. To be successful, the service offered will need to build up credibility, not only in terms of its practice but also in its dealing with other groups.

The manager or team leader will need to help shape and implement responses to referrals in a way that is congruent with the agency's policies and maximizes opportunities for constructive work. Intake policy needs to be understood by other agencies and referrers. Some intake policies can create resentment, for example, by insisting that all the family attends the interview (a desirable aim) but this usually leads to high percentages of failed appointments if it is enforced too rigidly. As a result of this, other agencies may decline to make further referrals.

Services will also need to develop in a sufficiently flexible way to deal with the real problem of gathering families together. Responding to crisis equally demands a broad and flexible response. The twenty-four-hour crisis service organized by Scott and his colleagues (Scott and Starr 1981) is an example of an appropriate and flexible response to mental health crisis. In such situations, staff time will need to be structured in a way to meet these demands. Failure to do this leads to difficulties. First, many families or significant others cannot or will not attend meetings in the normal office hours. They either become drop-outs or the process of help will take very much longer Second, an agency system can become an instrument that processes clients into 'digestible' pieces, shaping the client to fit the needs of the agency. In this way the service can develop an in-built resistance to meeting client needs.

Family therapists will also have to be clear about responsibilities for case-management. If the service is within an existing agency, it will need to be compatible with that agency's stated policies and procedures. All workers require good supervision and, I believe, need to be accountable to someone for their work. Coupled with these issues the manager should ensure that workers receive sufficient training to enhance their job satisfaction and the quality of the service provided.

If the service has out-patient and in-patient (or fieldwork and residential) components, they must act in concert. The same values and aims should suffuse both parts. Residential provision can lack the glamour given to those who are doing preventive work in the community, but in reality it is equally as important. It must share the same goal of community survival if the service is to be successful. Interchanging workers between the two parts can be useful in breaking down any division that exists. Todd (1984) correctly argues that an administrator or manager

> who remains ignorant of the details such as billing systems, work-load measures and indicators of program effectiveness will almost always find that these systems work to the disadvantage of family-oriented programs.
>
> (Todd 1984 : 329)

There are a number of reasons for this: family therapy will never be a cheap option in the short term as it requires a huge input of staff time. Many agencies believe in the principle of one worker, one client. In this environment the manager will need to be able to argue and produce evidence of the effectiveness of family therapy approaches. In the long term different approaches to statistical measures that take into account the wider number of people involved in being helped will need to be developed.

Todd (1984) has provided a useful list of guidelines for managers of family therapy services:

1 Make a clear distinction (at least in your mind) between family therapy as an orientation to all of your work and family therapy as a treatment modality to be used with particular problems or families.
2 Do not expect to establish family therapy as the exclusive modality of treatment. Make a particular effort to understand the potential contributions of other approaches and practitioners.
3 Take a careful look at the overall context of the programme and agency. Carefully examine agency structures that will hinder the implementation of family therapy such as an expectation that workers act independently of each other.
4 Try to identify factors in the context that would support family therapy.
5 Any process that encourages exchanges between workers should be considered a hopeful sign. The commitment to peer group case studies can lead to joint work, and so on.
6 Do not expect that family therapy will prevail simply because it is more effective.
7 Keep working to change policies and procedures, funding mechanisms, and other factors that emphasize individual therapy and the medical model to the detriment of family therapy.
8 Work to make outcome the measure of success rather than rewarding short sessions, regular appointments, and so forth.
9 Attempt to build on the strengths of the other professionals and model for staff members how to deal with these other professionals.
10 Train intake workers to encourage family attendance. All agency staff, including secretaries, have an important role to play.
11 Do not insist rigidly on family attendance unless it is obvious that the agency will support this stance and referral sources have been well briefed.
12 'Give away' family therapy training to other agencies and work to change those agencies, rather than trying to take on all family cases.
13 Do not mistake the enthusiasm of students and junior staff members for genuine acceptance by the hierarchy of the agency.
14 Do not expect to achieve permanent success (and keep watching for important changes in the context).

## CONCLUSION

This chapter has attempted to use a general systems approach to look at the practice of family therapy within British contexts. It will be seen that the skills of meeting with and assisting a family are essentially the same skills that one seeks to introduce a family therapy practice into any agency. I hope that readers will take away some practical ideas to employ within their own agency, and further, that they will view family therapy in broader terms, expanding and innovating as their practice develops.

# REFERENCES

Ainley, M. (1984). Family therapy in probation practice. In A. Treacher and J. Carpenter (eds) *Using Family Therapy*. Oxford, Blackwell.

Aponte, H. (1976). The family–school interview: an eco-structural approach. *Family Process*, 15, 303–31.

Bruggen, P., Byng-Hall, J. and Atkins, P. (1973). The reason for admissions as a focus of work for an adolescent unit. *British Journal of Psychiatry*, 122, 319–29.

Bruggen, P. and O'Brien, C. (1982). An adolescent unit's focus on family decisions. In H.T. Harbin (ed.) *The Psychiatric Hospital and the Family*. Lancaster, MIP Press.

Carpenter, J. (1984). Child guidance and family therapy. In A. Treacher and J. Carpenter (eds) *Using Family Therapy*. Oxford, Blackwell.

Dimmock, B. and Dungworth D. (1983). Creating manoeuvrability for family systems therapists in social services departments. *Journal of Family Therapy*, 5, 53–69.

—— (1985) Beyond the family: using network meetings with statutory child care cases. *Journal of Family Therapy*, 7, 45–68.

Eastman, K. (1979). The foster family in a system therapy perspective. *Child Welfare*, 58, 564–70.

Haley, J. (1975). Why a mental clinic should avoid family therapy. *Journal of Marriage and Family Counseling*, 1, 3–13.

—— (1980). *Leaving Home: The Therapy of Disturbed Young People*. New York McGraw-Hill.

Hallet, C. and Stevenson, O. (1980). *Child Abuse: Aspects of Interprofessional Co-operation*. London, Allen & Unwin.

Hoffman, L. and Long, L. (1969). A systems dilemma. *Family Process*, 8, 211–34.

Janzen, C. and Harris, O. (1980). *Family Treatment in Social Work Practice*. Illinois, Peacock.

Jenkins, H. (1984). Adolescent in in-patient psychiatric units. In A. Treacher and J. Carpenter (eds) *Using Family Therapy*. Oxford, Blackwell.

Lauffer, A., Nybell, L., Overberger, C., Reed, B. and Zeff, L. (1977). *Understanding your Social Agency*. London, Sage.

Lieberman, S. and Cooklin, A. (1982). Family therapy and general psychiatry: some issues. In A. Bentovim, G. Gorell Barnes and A. Cooklin (eds) *Family Therapy: Complementary Frameworks of Theory and Practice*. Volume 2. London, Academic Press.

Minuchin, S. (1970). The use of an ecological framework in the treatment of a child. In E.J. Anthony and C. Koupernir (eds) *The Child in his Family*. New York, Wiley.

Palazzoli, M.S., Boscola, L., Cecchin, G. and Prata, G. (1980). The problem of the referring person. *Journal of Marriage and Family Therapy*, 6, 3–9.

Parry, J.K. and Young, A.K. (1978). The family as a system in hospital-based social worker. *Health and Social Work*, 3, 55–70.

Pincus, A. and Minahan, A. (1979). Model for social work practice. In H. Specht and A. Vickery (eds) *Integrating Social Work Methods*. London, Allen & Unwin.

Pottle, S. (1984). Developing a network-oriented service for elderly people and their carers. In A. Treacher and J. Carpenter (eds). *Using Family Therapy*. Oxford, Blackwell.

Scott, R.D. (1973). The treatment barrier, *British Journal of Medical Psychology*, 46, 45–55.

Scott, R.D. and Ashworth, P.L. (1967). Closure at the first schizophrenic breakdown: a family study. *British Journal of Medical Psychology*, 40, 109–45.

Scott, R.D. and Starr, I. (1981). A 24-hour family orientated psychiatric and crisis service. *Journal of Family Therapy*, 3, 177–86.

Street, E. (1981). The family therapist and staff-group consultancy. *Journal of Family Therapy*, 3, 187–99.

—— (1984). Family therapy in residential homes for children. In A. Treacher and J. Carpenter (eds) *Using Family Therapy*. Oxford, Blackwell.

Todd, T.C. (1984). Family therapist as administrator: roles and responsibilities. In M. Berger and G. Jurkovic (eds) *Practising Family Therapy in Diverse Settings*. San Francisco, Jossey-Bass.

Treacher, A. (1984). Family therapy in mental hospitals. In A. Treacher and J. Carpenter (eds) *Using Family Therapy*. Oxford, Blackwell.

Viaro, M. (1980). Case report: smuggling family therapy through. *Family Process*, 19, 35–44.

CHAPTER 10

# CHILDREN'S NEEDS AND FAMILY THERAPY: THE CASE OF ABUSE

*Arnon Bentovim and Brian Jacobs*

## INTRODUCTION

Dell (1986) has recently indicated that one of the major challenges for the family therapy field is to be able to offer a view within an accepted family therapy framework of such major concerns as violence to children in the family, physical abuse and sexual abuse. The development of a systems model which focuses on circular causality and attempts to move away from linear thinking by its very nature, sees events as interconnected and self-reinforcing. A violent act which could potentially cause severe injury may indeed be activated by the provocative behaviour of the other, and so reinforce a violent circular interactional pattern. Once this causes severe damage or death, no reinforcement is possible and a linear act is completed.

In attempting to deal with these situations, Dell has shown that clinicians through their experiences find themselves of necessity using linear explanations as cause and effect. On the other hand epistemologists, that is those concerned with the development of ways of thinking, have the possibility of being able to stand outside the clinical domain and therefore can use and apply circular models of thinking. Hence the consequences of a violent act can be seen as taking the individual into the societal context of the law, with its own circularities which feed back and create new patterns.

In attempting to resolve this dilemma of a dichotomy between linear cause and effect processes, and circular reinforcing processes, Kinston and Bentovim (1978; 1980; 1987) in a series of publications have attempted to show that it is possible to describe and understand both family functioning and clinical therapeutic processes by using both circular and linear conceptual models. They have termed this as focal family therapy; the approach is developmentally oriented, and concerned with the health and well-being of the family in the context of its life cycle.

Traumatic events are regarded as the prime origins of disturbances which lead to families seeking professional help. Traumatic events occur at individual, family or social levels, and are events which may have occurred in the family of origin of the parents of the family, in the current family, or to individuals in the family. Such events cannot be talked about in the family because of their traumatic nature. Such events are dealt with by repetitive circular self-reinforcing patterns of actions and meanings which at first reduce the perceived pain of traumatic events. Later they become dysfunctional as they constrict the family's ability to respond to life events and the development of individuals in the family.

The family in crisis is thus seen as a social system with a specific set of actions and meanings which arise from traumatic events. Therapeutically it is essential to pay attention to both the repetitive patterns of action which lead for instance to abuse to a child, as well as the meanings and capacities of the family to understand what has happened to it. Therapeutic work has to change patterns of action as well as the meanings inherent in the family structure.

## WHAT IS IT THAT MAKES THE FAMILY A VIOLENCE-PRONE INSTITUTION?

There are a number of theoretical frameworks which have been put forward to account for the occurrence of violence in families. These include:

1 Psycho-pathological models, which focus on the abusers' personality, mental illness, personality disorders, alcohol, drug misuse or other intra-individual abnormalities (e.g. Smith *et al.* 1973).
2 Socio-situational frameworks which link violence to social antecedents, particularly to social structural stress, for example low income, inadequate financial resources, unemployment (Gil 1970).
3 Social learning theories which emphasize the importance of being exposed to violence and learning the social and moral justification for the behaviour (Bandura 1973).
4 Ecological perspectives (Garbarino 1978) which have attempted to place child maltreatment into a social context by focusing on the progressive, mutual adaptation of the family to the social systems in its environment.
5 Exchange social control theory (Cornell and Gelles 1982) which focuses on human interaction being guided by the pursuit of rewards and avoidance of punishments and costs. Here the emphasis is on the structural properties of families which make them violence prone, and specific

family and individual traits which make certain families more at risk from violence than other families. They focus on the absence of effective social controls and implicit social approval of violence to maintain violent interaction.

## A FAMILY SOCIAL SYSTEMS VIEW

It can be seen from the complexity of these models that child abuse is not a simple phenomenon but has to be seen in the context of the individual, the family and society. Figure 10.1 (after Kinston 1987; Bentovim and Kinston 1987) describes the relationship between the individual, family and cultural setting which initiates and maintains violent interactions. Violence itself is placed at the centre of the figure since it can be seen as a property of society, the family and the individual.

Society contains a set of attitudes, norms, rights and values about the appropriate degree of violence, discipline and punishment, which is right for children. The family contains violence as it is the setting for the violent act. The individual contains violence as the actor. Society legitimizes violence, in its approval for physical discipline in its 'proper' place, and also sets the limits for what is acceptable and when parental rights should be removed because of having gone 'too far'. The family operates with its own interactions and meanings and is the agent which reproduces society. It depends on society for its sense of values, and the values and responsibilities given for the nurturance and control of individuals – adults and children. Thus violent interaction and violent roles at various levels are inherent in the relationship between families and individuals.

Society in turn comes to be made up of individuals who confirm or react to its attitudes norms, rights and values concerning violence and violent behaviour. Extensive epidemiological research on the incidence of violent acts towards children in families (Strauss and Gelles 1979) concludes that:

1 Ordinary physical punishment is widespread in society.
2 The more parents are violent to children, the more violent those children are to siblings.
3 The more violent husbands are to wives, the more violent the wife is towards her children.
4 Violence experienced as a child repeats a generation later through elevated rates of spouse and child abuse. The degree of subsequent violence depends on intensity and length of victimization during childhood.
5 Many other variables account for individual differences in violence and for the overall incidence rate of different forms of violence.
6 There are a variety of different forms of abuse, for example expressive or

**Relationships between the individual, family and society and violence**

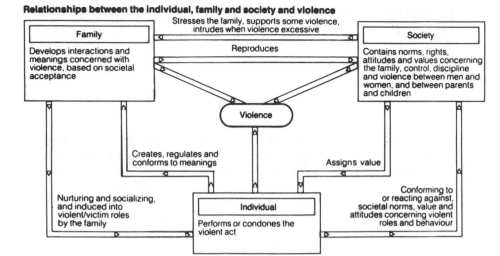

*Figure 10.1*

hostile aggression, versus instrumental aggression, for example physical punishment, i.e. hurting for an end rather than as an expression of anger and frustration, but they are not pure and both create modelling effects for family members.

7 Other forms of violence, for example sexual abuse and neglect, have similar repetitional patterns and results as does physical abuse, that is they become institutionalized in family patterns in a cross-generational fashion.

Many family interactions are inherently conflict structured, for example which television show to watch or which car to buy. Belonging to a family carries an implicit right to influence the values, attitudes and behaviours of other family members. The family is also unique in that it is made up of different ages and sexes with a potential for battle between generations and sexes. The family is a social institution which defines roles, responsibilities and authority based on age and sex rather than interest or competence. The family is a private institution insulated from the eyes, ears and often the rules of the wider society. It has its own culture and organization and where privacy is high, the degree of social control will be low. Families are exclusive organizations, where birth relationships are involuntary and cannot be terminated. There is a degree of personal, social, material, legal commitment and entrapment, so that when conflict arises it is difficult to flee the scene or resign from the group. Families are prone to stresses, transitions and the events of the life cycle, and disruptions such as unemployment and illness can be traumatic.

All such factors in the social organization of families can ensure development, affection, care and socialization but can also lead to violence and damage.

## Abuse and the professional

Bentovim and Miller (1984) have attempted to think of abuse to children in the context of family breakdown, defining abuse to a child as including a professional who has to act to terminate the abusive pattern. A great deal of concern in professional practice is focused on ways of recognizing abused children, implying that very often the family through the processes described above do not spontaneously and directly draw the attention of social agencies to the abuse within its context. When violence reaches such a level that an individual's development is being impaired, and if professional notice is drawn to it, the professional's role and task may be to have to provide alternative parenting for that individual child. Family breakdown is then described as a family context in which violent interactions and failures of care lead to the patterns of abuse and neglect, which in turn leads the professional to initiate a process by which alternative parenting is provided either temporarily or permanently for that child.

There is inevitably a contradiction between the rights of the family to be allowed to develop its own organization and to live within conditions of privacy, and the necessity to abide by societal rules. The right to be able to bring up children in a family context also gives responsibility to those parents to ensure that the basic needs of the child for care and protection are met. A failure of care and protection inevitably triggers and activates professional involvement. The duties and responsibilities of, for instance, agencies such as social services departments are to provide for the immediate care and protection of children who are abused, neglected or abandoned. The community lays responsibilities on social service agencies to provide alternative parenting for a child whose impairment can be reversed, but where the family cannot achieve or maintain protection or satisfactory care.

## DILEMMAS IN A FAMILY THERAPY APPROACH IN WORKING WITH CHILD ABUSE

In this chapter so far it has been argued that family systems ideas are extremely helpful in being able to conceptualize the ways that families operate both over time and in the here and now, to create a context where violent interactions can occur towards a particular child in the family. Indeed it could be argued that such notions are essential in being able to think about and understand child abuse as an issue. We will examine some of these issues further in the following pages.

However, if we turn to the practice of family therapy as such, are there dilemmas? Jacobs (1986) has examined some of the ethical issues for the family therapist in dealing with incest. A review of the literature on family therapy ethics (Wendorf and Wendorf 1985) examines the limited writings to date of the ethics of practising family therapy. They also decided that a systemic analysis is needed which would include the levels of the therapist and society as well as the family. O'Shea and Jesse (1982), for instance, discussed the issue of the family therapist's maintaining confidentiality with the family. They outline the ethical problems arising from a clash between systems thinking with its 'reciprocal determinism', compared with the individually oriented theories of pathology and therapy. This must be seen against the background of the social institutions and the cultural standards which aspire to meet the needs and rights of individuals. This contrast touches on the issues already mentioned of theories of circular causality and linear theories which look at cause and effect and, therefore, issues of individual responsibility and rights, compared to dysfunction of the whole – the battering parent and abused child versus the abusing family.

Grosser and Paul (1964) mention the possibility that as parental failures are brought out there may be an undermining of the parent and therefore of the control system of the family. Margolin (1982) writes about the two issues: therapist responsibility and confidentiality. She argues that the therapist's primary responsibilities to protect the rights and promote the welfare of his or her clients. The dilemma with multiple clients is that in some situations an intervention that serves one person's best interests may be counter-therapeutic to another. If the family is the client, a family therapist with his or her particular notion of responsibility might find him or herself having to promote the welfare of one or other of his or her clients. For instance a child in the family as against a parent, and the action may prove to be to the detriment of the family, particularly if, for instance, action needs to be taken to protect the child. It may be that in the family the removed child may have the important role of maintaining the togetherness of the marriage.

Margolin's view is that if there is evidence of physical abuse 'It is the therapist's ethical responsibility to abdicate the role of relationship adviser and help the threatened person to find protection' (Margolin 1982). With regard to confidentiality her view is that it is the therapist's responsibility to safeguard information obtained in the therapy session. Exceptions are 'to avoid clear or imminent danger to the client or others, or when a specific requisite of the law takes precedence' (Margolin 1982).

Boszormenyi-Nagy (1985) has put forward a useful conceptual framework to think about these issues. He describes a 'Relationship Ethical' model which includes the principle of interpersonal consequence, an important aspect of close relating.

1 Individuals are ethically and legally responsible for their actions.
2 Responsibility for consequences rests most heavily with respect to the interests of future generations. He states, 'The future life prospects for the young and even for, as yet, unborn children represent the highest ethical priority for their parents' (Boszormenyi-Nagy 1985).
3 The chain of consequences points towards the interests of posterity. Consider the case of the incestuous father's family. Besides being a part of the system of recursive current transactions, the incestuous parent's act reflects consequences resulting from his formative past. In contrast the abused child lives in a formative present which may have lasting consequences for her future survival. Moreover, if she is lastingly affected, she may have a corresponding impact on her children.

With these considerations it may be possible to deal with some of the dilemmas facing family therapists. It is clear that the therapist's primary responsibility must be to the person or people most at risk in the family. This will be the child and sometimes other siblings. This means that confidentiality between parts of the family and between the family and the outside world will be particular issues. Second, it means that the therapist may have to contravene the usual practice of protecting the privacy of the couple's relationship as this is so bound with the cross-generational or abusive activities. These positions undermine parental authority, at least temporarily. They also guide the legal and ethical framework within which a therapist tries to help a family change its customary pattern of interactions. This implies that it will be important for the therapist to be very clear with the family that his or her relationship with them will have different constraints from those they may be expecting. These constraints will be determined by the limits of confidentiality and the protection of the child.

## The limits of confidentiality

Very often a family who approaches any professional wants absolute confidentiality. They may well hope that if they are referred, for instance, to a child guidance clinic, or to a professional practising as a family therapist, or to a non-statutory family therapy agency, that in some way the abuse whether physical or sexual will be suppressed, that children will not be removed, that criminal action will not occur. Alternatively, when a family is referred for therapy there is a hope that now at last statutory agencies will not have to be informed about what is happening in the family, the family can 'tell all' or may even reveal other abusive elements in their relating, and would hope that the agency or practitioner will maintain confidentiality. This inevitably interlocks with the second issue, namely protection of the child.

## Protection of the child

When there is a child under the age of 16 involved, there is a responsibility to protect the young person from exploitation and abuse. Parental rights to make decisions about children persuade some parents that they have a right to punish or use them sexually as they were perhaps used themselves. But children through legislation have been seen less and less as their parents' property with few independent rights, to now having increasing rights to be protected from abuse, and to be nurtured in an appropriate way. This means that if a parent is not protecting and nurturing the child, society has a right to intervene and ensure that this does occur.

The implication is that the therapist as a member of society also has to support such societal views. It may be argued that to place the issue of protection of the child above that of confidentiality for the parents is to lose the freedom for manoeuvre during the therapy. It could be argued that it makes it impossible to put these parents in charge of their family in a healthy way and break cross-generational alliances. This is a trap, since it is the very inability of the parents to provide appropriate care and control that has meant that these children have been subjected to abuse which may be life threatening, or certainly emotional-health threatening. Therefore to be invited by a family to place the issue of confidentiality before that of protection is to be invited to repeat the abuse in relation to the family, and to fail to provide them with an appropriate model of care and control.

Thus for instance, in the Great Ormond Street Sexual Abuse Project (Bentovim *et al*. 1987b) which offers treatment to families, it is a working rule that families must be referred by statutory agencies and not through self-referral or medical referral only. The argument is that an agency providing therapy cannot by its very nature be a protective agency as well as therapeutic agency; so that the family is met with together with the agency that has a statutory responsibility for care. The family is offered a limited degree of confidentiality through, for instance, parents' and children's groups, where what occurs within the group is confidential to the group. However, it is stated clearly that if issues arise in groups, or in meetings, which clearly have an implication for the care of children and for the future of the family care, these issues need to be brought out into the family/ professional context. In addition, the therapist offers to help the child or parents' discuss or explore these issues with the care professionals. The whole aim of the treatment is thus to take a view that if family breakdown has occurred, a statutory agency has had to take on the parenting of the child, because temporarily that parent has failed to carry out his or her responsibilities. The aim of the work would then be to help the family make whatever changes are necessary to be able to show statutory authorities and through them, the courts, that they can indeed provide protection and deal with problems, for instance in the marriage, or major personal issues which have played an important role in triggering and maintaining abusive patterns of behaviour.

Where breakdown has occurred the family is no longer the patient but the situation becomes a mixture of individual, family and societal needs, and different agencies are assigned responsibility for different needs. The therapeutic role is a more complex one when the agency provides the therapy and attempts to meet the statutory task, but the work of the Rochdale NSPCC group (Dale *et al.* 1983) has indicated that by use of a team and a therapeutic context with a mandate to work, therapeutic work towards more effective parenting are possible.

Therapeutic work is thus lodged at the interface between the individual, the family and the agencies of society whose task it is to protect children whose development is being impaired.

## The therapeutic function and the needs of society

This leads to another issue for family therapists; any society demands of its members certain standards of conduct. If these are not met it reserves the right to punish that person – the offender – provided it can be shown that the person carried out the act and is capable of being responsible for his or her actions. It is very easy for a child or parent to be 'blamed' as responsible and therefore deserving of exclusion, or rejection. It is clearly not the therapist's role once he or she has entered a therapeutic contract with the family to be involved either in the notion of seeking punishment, nor in confirming blame.

This problem arises, however, when professionals with a family therapy orientation are involved in the initial exploration of possible abuse, or when suspicion or evidence of abuse occurs within the course of therapeutic work for what appears to be other purposes. We have already argued that it is difficult for a therapist to protect a child without linking to an agency whose task it is to do so, and it is essential to know whether there is a safe mandate for therapeutic work. The Department of Health and Social Security has issued draft guidelines (DHSS 1986) indicating that in the initial exploration of, for instance, sexual abuse there is a necessity for medical and social workers and the police to work closely together to make a proper diagnosis. In physical abuse the diagnosis is established more often through medical criteria rather than through the statements of children. In these cases the full arena of professionals do not begin to work together until a case conference stage, that is after the initial diagnostic and protective action.

There is an argument that states that unless a man who abuses sexually is prosecuted and has to attend treatment as part of a probation order for instance, successful work cannot take place with the family. Others would argue that a good deal of helpful work occurs within the context of a care order, with the family working to achieve change to show the care authority that protection is a possibility. It is thus inevitable that until these issues become clearer, reporting of an abuse case may mean that a family who have entered a therapeutic contract may find themselves reported to a statutory agency because of the issue of care and the police may be brought in as a joint exercise to maintain protection and to examine the criminal issue. The only way it is possible to work in a collaborative way is for professionals to develop a therapeutic aim to their work, for example in the spirit of the DHSS/Home Office directive (1976) which enabled police and health and social services agencies to attend case conferences about abused children and arrive at a consensus on the needs of a child and implicitly the family.

## A FAMILY SYSTEMS APPROACH TO THE ASSESSMENT OF ABUSIVE FAMILIES

Factors that correlate with child abuse can be arranged in a developmental fashion (Bentovim 1977a). Stressful events in the parents when they were children affect marital choice and interactions, which in turn affect the way the family constitutes itself when children are born; the way those children are perceived and dealt with will both precipitate and maintain violent interactions with the child.

Although one can see the 'historical' repeating pattern, our own attempts at evaluating actual work with families (Kinston and Bentovim 1978) led us to realize that we lacked a truly coherent system to describe and therefore to assess the families we were seeing in clinical practice. Bentovim and Kinston (1987) have now attempted to describe families by conceptualizing their functioning on seven levels.

### First level – conceptual notions

These include the descriptive terms applying to family therapy thinking, for example, boundaries, alliances and symmetrical and complementary communication.

### Second level – elements of interaction

Elements of interaction do not describe micro-levels of action, for example an eye-blink or a sentence, but describe interactions themselves. These encompass the interactions observed or described in family violence, for example disagreements, hit, shove and violent sexual actions.

### Third level – cycles of interaction

Elements become coherent when combined into episodes or cycles of interaction. In violent families typical cycles may take the form of a father talking to a mother who withdraws into silence, the father then criticizing and smacking the child for an innocent act. Combining such events and episodes together creates the various violent patterns and abusive syndromes, but in clinical practice it is essential to put the violent episodes into a context, of what they mean for this particular family.

## Fourth level – active meaning systems

Active meanings describe the 'context' of the events, which may be recent or longstanding in origin. In the instances cited above, the mother who withdrew into silence may have been abused as a child so activating the father to criticize the child.

Individual meanings to events gather together to form a pattern of common and intersubjective active meanings. Many active meanings in an individual are private and not directly relevant to the concerns of family members. There are, however 'common' meanings, which draw a couple together, for example their privation as children, or high levels of punishment.

Families can develop meanings unique to that particular family, which arise out of specific events and create a reality, a myth and a set of views about a particular family or family member which are outside realistic appraisal but which guide the family pattern of life and behaviour. These are 'intersubjective' meanings for the members of the family group.

Kinston and Bentovim (1982) describe the way such meaning systems come to shape and underlie the pathological interaction patterns which precipitate and maintain symptomatic behaviours.

## Fifth level (a) – the dimensions of family life

These dimensions require observations at an individual level physically, cognitively, emotionally and developmentally and in various contexts (Bentovim and Miller 1984). There are a number of schemata, for example Fahlberg (1981) and Cooper (1984), to assist in this process.

There are also a number of ways of eliciting family interaction and ways of living, to organize family observations at this level. These include the standardized Family Interview (Kinston and Loader 1984), the Family Task Interview (Kinston *et al.* 1987), the Level of Family Living Scale (Polansky *et al.* 1981), the Family Interaction Format (Loader *et al.* 1981), and the Family Health Scales (Kinston *et al.* 1987). Such scales and observations of family life rely on the fact that dysfunctional families, for example violent families, have well-defined characteristics when observed together. Bentovim and Gilmour (1981), Bentovim and Tranter (1984) and Bentovim *et al.* (1978b) have described the advantages of interviewing families together, as well as separate interviews with individuals where relevant.

In violent families we see failures in seven dimensions of family functioning which hence become dysfunctional.

### 1. Affective status
This is the emotional life of the family including family atmosphere, and the nature and quality of the relationships within the family. In violent families, the atmosphere may be dead, panicky or chaotic, and relationships may have a perverse, attacking, devaluing or grossly overdependent character.

### 2. Communication
This is the verbal and non-verbal interchange between family members, including the expression and reception of messages. Communication in violent and abusive families can affect functioning if family members have chaotic, fragmented, disruptive, violent or sexualized patterns of communicating with one another.

### 3. Boundaries
In abusive families there is often impairment of individual autonomy and development due to gross overinvolvement or isolation. Excessively rigid or blurred boundaries between parents and children make it difficult for a family to carry out primary responsibilities without abusing or neglecting children.

### 4. Alliances
Patterns of alliances in a family may contain serious deficiencies, for example *triangling*, the 'scapegoating' of a child member by an inappropriate 'secret', and a positive alliance between a parent and child which increases the force of the negative alliance with the other parent. Thus conflict between parents is 'detoured' through the child.

### 5. Stability
This refers to the sense of continuity of the family unit, while *adaptability* is linked to the family's ability to respond to changing demands and circumstances. In violent/abusive families a precarious stability is maintained at the cost of severe and pervasive pathological family interaction. Roles and relationships may be chaotic or rigid and make it impossible to adapt to changing needs or circumstances during development.

### 6. Family competence
Operations such as conflict resolution, decision-making, problem-solving and management of children's behaviour are crucial in the resolving of family difficulties and life cycle stages. Ignoring conflicts, displacing and blaming others outside mean that responsibilities are not recognized or undertaken.

## 7. Relationship to the environment

This dimension looks at the family's capacity to make links with the outside world. This may also extend to professional networks who may be aware of high levels of abuse and neglect and yet are 'extruded' by the *rigid* family boundary. In some abusing families professionals are sometimes induced to take family roles as parental figures.

# Fifth level (b) – the holistic formulations of the family

Having looked at the elements, cycles, active meanings and dimensions of violent families, clinicians need an approach to 'pull together' their observation so as to make sense of the situation. Kinston *et al.* (1987), Kinston and Bentovim (1980), Furness *et al.* (1984) and Glaser *et al.* (1984) have described a clinical method of relating the salient features of a case into a 'Focal Formulation'. This links the current complaint of 'family violence' to salient stressful and traumatic events in the family of origin of the parents as children and the current family created by those parents. It looks at the active meanings which have resulted from those events and the dimensions of family life which result in abuse and violent interaction.

## Making a focal hypothesis

Bentovim and Kinston (1987) described the process of extracting the essence of the case to form a 'Focal Hypothesis' by asking the following questions:

1 *How can violent acts be restated in an interactional form*, that is the way violence is linked to the family function, and vice versa, and how do professionals respond?
2 *What is the function of the current interaction?* The fact of abuse of a particular family member, or the recognition by professionals of abuse, i.e. how would the family interact if there were no child or parent to abuse, or if the professionals failed to intervene?
3 *What is the feared disaster and anxiety?* This refers to the 'traumatic' nature of salient stressful events in the family's life which leads to 'action' to avoid feared repetitions and re-enactments. It asks 'What would the family members worry about if they were not involved in abusive inter-action with an individual in the family?'
4 *What is the link to original stressful experiences?* Which past experience(s) are judged to be linked to the present family abusive interaction patterns?

# Sixth level – family type

At this level the overall family type is described, for example 'the sexually abusive family' – conflict avoiding or conflict regulating (Furness 1985);

severely neglectful (Polansky *et al*. 1981); physically abusive (Kempe *et al*. 1962) which subsumes other levels.

## Seventh level – changes achievable with therapeutic work

Having made a formulation and created a hypothesis to describe the case clinically it is necessary in an assessment to think about what changes would be necessary for the family to make to reduce violent effects on individuals, what changes could be achieved given the therapeutic potential available in the community, and what is the likely prognosis for this work.

Bentovim *et al*. (1987a) have found it helpful to distinguish three types of families.

1 Those for whom it is likely that rehabilitational work might succeed.
2 Families where there is doubt about the success of rehabilitational work, but where there are either some real grounds for optimism or perhaps insufficiently strong grounds to justify a category of hopelessness.
3 Families for whom there can be no hope for rehabilitation.

The areas to be explored in making this assessment (Bentovim *et al*. 1987a) are:

1 *The acceptance of responsibility for abuse and neglect*. The individual responsible for the active abuse or failure of care should take responsibility for the state of the abused family member adult or child.
2 *The degree to which responsibility is showed by parents*. For successful rehabilitation it is essential for both parents in a child abuse case to acknowledge that at some level they both have to take a share in the responsibility for the abusive pattern, even though only one partner has to take prime responsibility.
3 *Acknowledgement of the abused family members*. Do parents acknowledge not only in word but also in deed, that for instance children's needs come first when they have been abused? Is the abused child or adult blamed or scapegoated as being the cause, branded as a liar, bad, evil in some ways? Is there an extended family view about the victim which will reinforce family patterns?
4 *Acknowledgement of long-standing family problems*. The attitude towards factors of childhood and current states needs to be ascertained.
5 *The nature and rigidity of family patterns*. It is essential to speculate on the changes necessary to make the family safe.
6 *The relationship with care professionals*. This item looks at present and past relationships with care professionals. It is important to distinguish between superficial co-operation and that with depth and potential for change.

# THE FAMILY SYSTEMS VIEW OF MANAGEMENT

## Recognition/disclosure stage

During this period the essential tasks are to do with breaking the taboo of secrecy around the facts of family violence. Families may be aware of their own destructive processes or may give direct or indirect signs and signals to professional attention. It has already been stressed that the initial stages of management are to do with a complex of inter-professional work where there are various roles depending on whether this is physical abuse, neglect or sexual abuse. It is essential to establish whether there is a safe setting within the family, whether an alternative provision needs to be provided and whether some of the issues outlined previously, for example, taking responsibility for abuse, provision of absolute protection and looking at family issues are occurring. The use of case conference systems, legal processes to protect and give a mandate for work have to be considered during the crisis period of establishing a diagnosis and beginning to work with the family context.

## Work during separation

In most forms of severe violence there needs to be a period of separation and one of the issues that needs establishing is what context is necessary to test whether the family can achieve the aims outlined as being necessary for the protection of the children? A variety of settings, day and residential have been described where parents and children can come together for limited or extended periods of time to complete assessments and to test the possibilities of therapeutic change (Bentovim 1977b; Cooklin 1985). Contracts for such work where tasks for the family and the professionals are clearly specified can create a helpful focus (White 1984). Wolkind (1984) has assessed contributions from child psychology and development which describe the capacity of younger children under the age of 6 months to be placed in new families without detriment, and the sensitive period between 6 months and 3 years of age when disruptions of attachment can lead to long-term detrimental effects. It is necessary to consider the child's needs, in the context of what changes need to occur for the whole family.

During the phase of separation, work is possible to develop parenting skills, for example in sexual abuse work with parents together and with mothers and children improve the relationship between them, improving communication and building up trust. Resentment and rivalry can be dealt with in this context or in the context of the whole family. A variety of other approaches often need to feed into this; Bentovim *et al.* (1987b) have described a method in which an integrated treatment approach links the growth of individual assertiveness in groups to family therapy and professional meetings.

## Towards rehabilitation

The rehabilitation phase of work has to represent the peak period for family work in family therapy in whatever context it is best achieved. For rehabilitation to occur:

1 Lasting changes need to be achieved in the family structure and relationship and dimensions of family life.
2 Whatever individual treatments are necessary must be satisfactorily in train and changes demonstrated.
3 Victims need to feel confidence in themselves and in their available protectors without feeling inappropriately in control of the whole family.
4 Families need considerable help in thinking about future crisis and risk points.

## Working towards a new family

In those families of doubtful prognosis where contract aims have not been met, placement may be necessary either through fostering or adoption. Work needs to be carried out with the old family in terms of mourning and loss, and with the new family in terms of ensuring that the expectations of children, and the common meanings they carry do not reactivate abusive patterns in the new family.

To illustrate the process of work a case referred to a non-statutory family therapy agency will be described.

## A FAMILY IN THERAPY

The N family was referred by a voluntary agency because of Mr N's preoccupation and sexual interference with his stepdaughter. At the first meeting, Mr and Mrs N attended. Mrs N told the therapist that her daughter Brenda, aged 15, was staying over the road with the maternal grandparents for a few days because of 'family difficulties'. The grandparents were not told the real reason. Social services or the police were not involved. The couple were told that the agency could not guarantee confidentiality from the social services department; a decision would be made at the end of the session, as to the best course of action.

During this meeting, the following information emerged. Mr and Mrs N had known each other for five years. They lived together for eighteen months before marrying. Mrs N already had a daughter, Brenda, who initially rejected Mr N, and who used to try to keep the couple apart by going to her mother's bed. However, she later grew very fond of Mr N. There had been several incidents of sexual abuse by Mr N. The final one had involved hitting Brenda around the head to coerce her. Finally he had told his wife that he was frightened by being strongly sexually attracted to Brenda.

Mr N was the youngest of three children. Mr N's father had been an alcoholic and violent to his wife. They separated when Mr N was young and his mother remarried when he was aged 6 years. The natural father left Britain and Mr N did not see him again. His father had died several years previously. Mr N said his stepfather was a stable man, good to his wife, but 'dull'. Mr N's mother was described as a forceful woman, close to Mr N in his childhood, but she had several episodes of psychiatric illness since Mr N's sister died during their early childhood and Mr N's brother used to beat him up regularly. He also recalled allowing himself to be attacked at school, because he felt powerless. In adolescence Mr N described himself as a loner who was unable to establish relationships with girls. He had a poor view of himself and 'never cared for anyone'. He dealt with his sexual frustration by watching sexually explicit films and by 'compulsive masturbation'.

Later, at the age of 24, he had an intense affair with a 15-year-old girl. This was broken off by her and he took a large overdose. He met his wife a short time later and married at 26. He said that 'relationships are intense or destructive'. He is described by Mrs N as still being close to his mother. He said he has a better relationship with his brother as an adult.

Mrs N said she came from a stable family. She experienced her own mother as an ogre during childhood. She became pregnant at 17 years and Brenda was born. Brenda's father left her when Brenda was 10 months old and she returned to live with her parents. After this there was a brief passionate affair with a married man who was able to excite Mrs N sexually very easily, but he then abandoned her. To her surprise she said that she became very close to her own mother during this period. She described her mother as forceful, 'a lady who demands dependency'. Mr and Mrs N then lived across the road from Mrs N's parents.

The couple described their relationship as tense. They said that their sex life was poor. In particular, Mr N stated that his wife had never really satisfied his sexual needs. At a later stage in therapy, Mrs N said, 'Nothing affects the way we feel about each other'. They explained that though the sexual relationship was unsatisfactory, each defined the relationship as being stable and strongly affectionate.

## The formulation

*Step 1*

How did the symptom make the family interact amongst themselves and with professionals including the therapist?

*The sexual approaches of the stepfather bound Brenda and him in fear of discovery*. He was afraid that his wife would find out and reject him. Brenda was afraid that her mother would find out because she thought that Mrs N could not cope with another failed relationship. *Brenda's mother was solicitous of her husband, because she was guilty about being unable to satisfy his sexuality.* He cared for and protected his wife because he felt guilty for abusing her daughter and preferring Brenda to his wife. *The symptom of child sexual abuse held the family together.* After discovery, the therapeutic agency is asked to take on the same task.

### Step 2

How might the family have interacted if the particular presenting problem were not there?

If the incest had not occurred, *Mr N's frustration would have reached a level at which he would have had an affair outside the family or would have left*, possibly after violence between him and his wife. *Each adult would have felt guilty* towards the other and the *daughter would have felt very responsible for her mother.*

### Step 3

What was the feared disaster for this family and why was the interaction in Step 2 avoided?

*Each of the adults was very afraid of the effects that dissolution of their marriage* would have on themselves and others. Mrs N's self-esteem would fall to new depths and Mr N might have committed suicide. Brenda might have re-experienced the loss of her mother through her being emotionally unavailable. A sexually active relationship might lead to a pregnancy and a dependent child and this was a fear for both adults. This fear had become associated for each of them as being incompatible with *safe sexual affection.*

### Step 4

What were the important original experiences in this family and the families of origin that linked to the presenting dysfunction?

Mr N had seen the devastating effect of a violent alcoholic father on his mother and her mental health. He had experienced the further effect of a death in the family during his childhood. *He became very close to his mother because of these shared experiences. This interfered with his own ability to individuate in adolescence and take risks over sexuality safely.* It was reinforced when he was abandoned by his younger girlfriend in early adulthood.

*Mrs N was required by her mother to be in a dependent position.* She knew her father also had a potential for violence. She attempted to free herself from that family by becoming pregnant but was abandoned by her boyfriend, placing her again in a dependent position to her mother. *This couple's joint wish not to have children is a crystallization both of their fears of dependency and of fears of abuse towards their joint child. In short, only asexual marriages are safe, since passionate sexuality leads to loss, abandonment and destruction.*

*Step 5*

What were the requisite changes during therapy in interpersonal behaviour that would indicate that the recursive pattern has been overcome by the family members?

*Brenda must be protected by her mother from Mr N's passion. Mr and Mrs N might improve their sexual relationship* so that it was safe to have caring and excitement without feeling that being abandoned was an inevitable consequence. *Mr N should find ways to desensitize himself to Brenda.* This process should ideally involve his wife. Brenda should grow more confident about establishing friends and boyfriends outside the family.

## The ethical issues

This family presented voluntarily through another non-statutory agency before guide-lines about referral of all cases to statutory agencies were formulated. They did not want social services to be involved because it would in their view mean the inevitable destruction of their family. The couple had already made moves to provide some *protection* to the daughter by placing her with the maternal grandparents. However, this was only over the road and at that stage nobody but Mr and Mrs N and Brenda knew the real reason for this.

Mr N seemed willing to accept *responsibility* for his actions. He seemed to have a strong desire to change. Mrs N behaved very loyally to him and said she was willing to help. The therapeutic team were concerned because Mrs N initially appeared quite unworried about the effects of the sexual abuse on her daughter. We were not sure that Mrs N would be able to protect Brenda if she was living at home with Mr N. However, on balance, we agreed that confidentiality could be preserved *for the present* because the daughter was protected by staying with her grandparents, and the adults appeared to accept responsibility. The danger was that we could not know that the child was really protected, for example because the adults caring for her did not know the real reason. Mr N talked strongly of moving to a bedsitter if the situation did not improve. The therapeutic team were drawn into the family fears of breakdown and accepted a contract of work.

## Therapeutic process

The therapist tried to build up Mrs N's determination to protect her daughter and to be suspicious of her husband's promises. This was coupled to his accepting responsibility for the abuse. The purpose of this move was to try to prevent a continuation of the behaviour and to release the daughter from her role of conflict-diffuser in the marriage. Mr N still found himself attracted to the daughter and so moved into a bedsit. The therapist then attempted to tackle the couple's relationship and their sexual dysfunction. The impetus for this was avoided by the difficulty in their continuing a relationship with him in a bedsit and by the pressure on Mrs N from her own parents for the daughter to return home.

However, progress on their sexual relationship was blocked by Mr N's inability to tackle his cravings for his stepdaughter. Mrs N colluded with this. It seemed to represent a terror that if sexuality were really established between them, it would mean their affection would be lost or they would be saddled with enhanced and mutual dependency/vulnerability and the possibility of their own child.

Mr N then decided that he wanted individual help with his psychosexual difficulties. However, this was a very ambivalent decision. He cancelled several appointments before attending for assessment.

The therapy regularly became stuck and the mother remained apparently blind to the continuing need to protect her daughter from Mr N's cravings. The daughter's position was very difficult in view of the neediness of this couple. She found herself arranging to meet the stepfather alone accidentally on more than one occasion in her effort to 'look after' the couple. Despite major efforts by the therapist, it was not possible to help this couple resolve their sexual difficulties during eighteen months of the family therapy supervision team's work. The team was placed in the difficult position that it felt uncertain of the mother's ability to continue to protect her daughter without continued surveillance and support; it was unclear what, if anything, social services would be able to do if they were informed at this late stage. In these circumstances, continuation of contact and support was offered while Brenda matured, provided Mr N continued with his individual treatment.

## Interaction of ethical/therapeutic issues

This case is an example of one where recent sexual abuse in a young teenager had occurred and where there was continuing risk. It illustrated the difficulty that a therapist in a non-statutory agency faces in assessing the ability of the system to provide coherent and sufficient protection at any one point and the will to sustain this. It further illustrates the problems that arise when there is insufficient leverage to enable the couple to overcome the feared disaster of any change in their relationship.

The attempt to accommodate to the wishes of people struggling to provide good enough protection (in a hostile family environment) led to a half-way house with the treatment becoming stuck. The mother too was torn in her loyalty to her daughter and her husband. During an ensuing period of one year's follow-up the situation remained stable: a false but 'valuable' solution. The girl was protected and was individuating from the family, the couple remained affectionate, but their sexual life remained static. Not surprisingly there was a reverse when Brenda had her first boyfriend and Mr N left the family once more.

## Assessment of therapy

The goals to be achieved under Step 5 of the formulation of the N family were not achieved wholly here. A therapeutic approach which focused on improving the mother–daughter relationship, ensuring protection and attempting to shift the marital relationship so that affection and sensuality could co-exist, succeeded only in the former and not the latter. A professional will need to be 'part' of the family system until Brenda is adult. Would there have been a different result if the protective and therapeutic roles had been split between a statutory and therapeutic agency? Would the family have used the therapeutic agency to make the changes to 'prove' to the statutory agency that they could be trusted to live together? Would the agencies have been caught in conflict with each other, mirroring the family's own difficulties. It is hard to know, but it must be emphasized that the parents in this family had major traumatic experiences in their own lives. Working with trauma is the essence of working with abusive families, and the limited change achieved here is common in this most painful of working contexts. The fact that Brenda was maturing into a confident and sociable adolescent may mean that her formative present, future survival and impact on her children (Boszormenyi-Nagy 1985) have been assured, even if the consequences of the parent's formative past have not been fully worked through.

# CONCLUDING COMMENT

In this chapter we take the view that children and their needs be seen as part of an interacting family context. Family breakdown in functioning leads to abuse and creates a situation where professionals may need to intervene to provide alternative parenting. The family therapist is part of the professional network concerned with child abuse and they have the role of working with such dysfunctional relationships, recognizing the societal and ethical need to give primacy to the needs of the children in terms of their present well-being and future survival. To work in the field of abuse it is essential to have a model which helps the therapist to make sense of the phenomena, helps describe the families seen and helps define the aims of the work, paying particular attention to the notion of 'treatability'.

We present a focal model which links traumatic events in the lives of family members, to the creation and maintenance of dysfunctional interactional patterns which emerge. Such patterns constrict the families' abilities to deal with tasks in the family life cycle, particularly those to do with the care of children and thus abusive patterns are recreated. Only within a secure conceptual framework can the powerful and effective techniques developed by family therapists be used to assist families in demonstrating to child care agencies that they can protect their children in the future, or indicate that a new family is required.

# REFERENCES

Bandura, A. (1973). *Aggression: A Social Learning Analysis*. Englewood Cliffs, NJ, Prentice-Hall.

Bentovim, A. (1977a). First steps towards a systems analysis of severe physical abuse to children in the family. In *First Report from Select Committee on Violence in the Family*. 3, Appendices, 659–69.

—— (1977b). Therapeutic systems and settings in the treatment of child abuse. In A.W. Franklin (ed.) *The Challenge of Child Abuse*. London, Academic Press.

Bentovim, A. and Gilmour, L. (1981). A family therapy interactional approach to decision-making in child care, access and custody cases. *Journal of Family Therapy*, 3, 65–78.

Bentovim, A. and Kinston, W. (1987). Focal family therapy. In A Gurman and D.P. Kniskern (eds) *Handbook of Family Therapy*. New York, Brunner/Mazel.

Bentovim, A. and Miller, L. (1984). Family assessment in family breakdown. In M. Adcock and R. White (eds) *Good Enough Parenting*. London, British Agencies for Adoption and Fostering.

Bentovim, A. and Tranter, M. (1984). A family therapy approach to decision-making. *Adoption and Fostering,* 8, 25–32.

Bentovim, A., Elton, A. and Tranter, M. (1987a). Prognosis for rehabilitation after abuse. *Adoption and Fostering*, 11, 26–31.

Bentovim, A., Elton., A, Hildebrand, J., Tranter, M. and Vizard, E. (1987b). *Sexual Abuse in The Family*. Bristol, John Wright.

Boszormenyi-Nagy, I. (1985). Commentary: transgenerational solidarity – therapists' mandate and ethics. *Family Process*, 24, 454–6.

Cooklin, A. (1985). The family day unit. In C. Fishman and B. Rosman (eds) *Festschrift for Salvador Minuchin*. Boston, Mass., Harvard University Press.

Cooper, C. (1984). 'Good enough' borderline and 'bad enough' parenting. In M. Adcock and R. White (eds) *Good Enough Parenting*. London, British Agencies for Adoption and Fostering.

Cornell, C.P. and Gelles, R.J. (1982). Adolescent to parent violence. *Urban Social Change Review*, 15, Winter, 8–14.

Dale, P., Davies, M., Morrison, T., Moyes, P. and Roberts, W. (1983). A family therapy approach to child abuse countering resistance. *Journal of Family Therapy*, 5, 117–45.

Dell, P. (1986). In defence of linearity. *Family Process*, 25, 513–21.

DHSS/Home Office (1976). *Non-Accidental Injury to Children: The Police and Case Conferences*. LASSL (76) 2 CMO (76) 2 p (iv), 25.

DHSS (1986). Child abuse – working together for the protection of children (draft).

Fahlberg, V. (1981). *Attachment and Separation*. London, British Agencies for Adoption and Fostering.

Furness, T. (1985). Conflict-avoiding and conflict regulating patterns in incest and child sexual abuse. *Acta. Paedopsychiatrica*, 50, 6–15.

Furness, T., Bentovim, A. and Kinston, W. (1984). Clinical process recording in focal family therapy. *Journal of Marital and Family Therapy*, 9, 147–76.

Garbarino, D. (1978). The elusive 'crime' of emotional abuse. *Child Abuse and Neglect*, 2, 89–99.

Gil, D. (1970). *Violence against Children: Physical Child Abuse in the United States*. Cambridge, Mass., Harvard University Press.

Glaser, D., Furness, T. and Bingley, L. (1984). Focal family therapy – the assessment stage. *Journal of Family Therapy*, 6, 265–74.

Grosser, G.H. and Paul, N.L. (1964). Ethical issues in family group therapy. *American Journal of Orthopsychiatry*, 34, 875–84.

Jacobs, B. (1986). Incest: the relationship between ethics and family therapy in a non-statutory agency. Dissertation. London, Institute of Family Therapy.

Kempe, C.H., Silverman, F.N., Steele, B.F., Droegemueller, W. and Silver, H.K. (1962). The battered child syndrome. *Journal of American Medical Association*, 181, 17–24.

Kinston, W. (1987). A general theory of symptom formation (discussion paper).

Kinston, W. and Bentovim, A. (1978). Brief focal family therapy where the child is the referred patient. 2. Methodology and results. *Journal of Child Psychology, Psychiatry and Allied Disciplines*, 19, 119–43.

—— (1980). Creating a focus for brief marital and family therapy. In S.H. Budman (ed.) *Forms of Brief Therapy*. New York, Guilford.

—— (1982). Constructing a focal formulation and hypothesis in family therapy. *Australian Journal of Family Therapy*, 4, 37–50.

—— (1987). Description of the family at seven levels (discussion paper).

Kinston, W. and Loader, P. (1984). Eliciting whole family interaction with a standardised clinical interview. *Journal of Family Therapy*, 6, 347–63.

—— (1988). The family task interview: a tool for clinical research in family interaction. *Journal of Marital and Family Therapy* (in press).

Kinston, W., Loader, P. and Miller, L. (1987). Quantifying the clinical assessment of family health. *Journal of Marital and Family Therapy*, 13, 49–67.

Loader, P., Burck, C., Kinston, W. and Bentovim, A. (1981). Method for organising the clinical description of family interaction format. *Australian Journal of Family Therapy*, 2, (3), 131–41.

Margolin, G. (1982). Ethical and legal considerations in marital and family therapy. *American Psychologist*, 37, 788–801.

O'Shea, M. and Jesse, E. (1982). Ethical values and professional conflicts. In L. L'Abate (ed.) *Values, Ethics, Legalities and the Family Therapist*. Rockville, Md, Aspen.

Polansky, N.A., Chalmers, M.A., Buttenwieser, E. and William, D.P. (1981). *Damaged Parents: An Anatomy of Neglect*. Chicago, Ill., University of Chicago.

Smith, S., Hanson, R. and Noble, S. (1973). Parents of battered babies: a controlled study. *British Medical Journal*, 5, 5889, 388–91.

Strauss, M. and Gelles, R. (1979). *Behind Closed Doors: Violence in the American Family*. Garden City, NY, Anchor.

Wendorf, O.J. and Wendorf, R.J. (1985). A systemic view of family therapy ethics. *Family Process*, 24, 443–53.

White, R. (1984). Written agreements with families. In R. Adcock and R. White (eds) *Good Enough Parenting*. London, British Agencies for Adoption and Fostering.

Wolkind, S. (1984). A child psychiatrist in court using the contributions of developmental psychology. In *Taking a Stand*. Discussion series 5. London, British Agencies for Adoption and Fostering.

CHAPTER 11

# DIVORCE AND CONCILIATION: A FAMILY THERAPY PERSPECTIVE

## *Janet Walker*

Divorce can be viewed in the context of the evolution of the family. . . . family therapy has only recently addressed in a practical way the problems encountered in families of divorce . . . yet a number of family therapy concepts and practices lend themselves particularly well to the understanding and management of the complex, multiphasic, transgenerational phenomena of divorce.

(Berenson and White 1981 : 356, 357)

## DIVORCE CONCILIATION IN CONTEXT

### Current divorce trends

In 1956 the Morton Committee reported that divorce involved about 20,000 children under 16 each year. By 1984 there were 148,600 children under 16 involved in 144,507 divorces in England and Wales (OPCS 1985). During the 1970s Britain experienced a dramatic increase in the number of divorces and the rate of marriage breakdown. Haskey (1982; 1983) has forecast that at present rates of divorce and fertility one in twenty-two children will experience their parents' divorce by the age of 5, and one in five children will have the same experience by the age of 16, based on one in every three marriages eventually ending in divorce. Not surprisingly such trends and predictions have produced growing alarm and concern, particularly about the fate of the children of these 'broken homes'.

Despite the increase in divorce, marriage is as popular as ever, even for those who are divorced. In 1981 over 33 per cent of all marriages involved at least one remarried partner (*Social Trends* 1983). As the merry-go-round gains momentum re-divorces are also increasing; in 1982 18 per cent of divorces were 'second time around' for at least one partner (*Social Trends* 1983). Although the total number of divorces seems to have levelled off during the 1980s, the proportion of re-divorces continues to rise. Marriage breakdown is now recognized as a public issue and no longer simply a private family matter.

## From rich to poor

Until the mid-nineteenth century the ecclesiastical courts held a monopoly on the dissolution of marriage, on the strictly limited grounds of nullity. Divorce on any other grounds could be obtained only at the High Court by Private Act of Parliament – an expensive procedure available only to the rich. For the poor, legal separation and divorce were impossible, although it is perhaps important to remember that in the early nineteenth century many marriages were ended earlier by death. There is now evidence of a clear social class gradient which finds couples in social class V more likely to divorce than couples in social class I (Haskey 1984). As Burgoyne *et al.* (1987 : 35) have pointed out, 'If we are to understand the relationship between divorce and social class [in the 1980s] more clearly, we must first consider how belonging to a particular social class exposes or insulates partners from the stresses which might lead to marriage breakdown'. They suggest that material deprivation may be particularly significant both as a predisposing and as a precipitating factor for lower socio-economic groups, whereas conversely, the professional groups are more protected from hardship-related stress during marriage, and have far more to lose when they consider divorce. Economic factors may be even more pressing in second marriages, particularly in lower socio-economic groups, and hence in second divorces.

## The law

'The history of divorce law in England, like so much legal history, is the story of gradual social change punctuated at intervals, in this case very long intervals, by reforming legislation when social pressures reached a critical level' (Burgoyne *et al.* 1987 : 42). The present divorce law aims to perform two major functions: '(a) the support of marriages which have a chance of survival, and (b) the decent burial with the minimum of embarrassment, humiliation and bitterness of those that are indubitably dead' (Law Commission 1966 : 10–11). Although largely inquisitorial in practice, the current process is based on an adversarial model of justice which is expected to balance a firmly held value that 'marriage matters' and is worthy of state protection, with the growing awareness that 'divorce matters', so requiring the state to take seriously the needs of divided families. This has led to a number of confusions and ambiguities in current legislation (Maidment 1984; Walker 1986a). For example, to obtain a divorce there must still be *evidence* of breakdown, and unless couples are prepared to wait for two years' agreed separation one partner is obliged to find fault with the other. In 1984 41 per cent of all divorces were based on the specified fact of unreasonable behaviour and a further 28 per cent on adultery. This hardly squares with the notion of 'minimum embarrassment, humiliation and bitterness' (Law Commission 1966). Furthermore, state legal aid is no longer available to contest divorce – a measure introduced in 1977 to reduce the number of bitterly contested divorces and to save public money – and yet paradoxically legal aid *is* available to contest such ancillary matters as money, property and children. There is good evidence to suggest that unresolved tensions about the grounds for divorce may be transferred to bitter fights about children and money (Davis 1981; Eekelaar and Clive 1977; Gibson 1980). A study of divorce by Kressel and Deutsch (1977) found that the single most frequently cited predictor of a difficult divorce was one partner's eager desire to end the marriage coupled with the other partner's reluctance to do so. At a time when there is a widespread belief that divorce can have damaging consequences for the children of the marriage, particularly when bitter or prolonged conflict exists between the parents, this seems rather worrying, given that the welfare of children is the overriding principle which governs matrimonial proceedings. This view has been echoed recently by the Law Commission (1986a) stating that the law relating to the upbringing of children 'is bedevilled by the complication and duplication of remedies and procedures which have developed according to no clear principle, (para. 1.2). They refer to 'ad hoc legislation designed for particular situations without full regard to how they fit into the wider picture' (para. 1.4).

The legal system in Scotland differs from that in England and Wales, although the divorce laws are broadly similar. However, divorcing parents rarely attend court, not even in connection with arrangements for children, which are provided in writing by means of sworn affidavits and are rarely investigated by the court (Eekelaar and Clive 1977; Seale 1984).

## Private ordering

British research demonstrates that about 94 per cent of divorcing parents agree between themselves the future arrangements for children and the court acts as a rubber-stamp to such agreements, rarely disturbing the residential status quo of a child (Eekelaar and Clive 1977; Maidment 1976). Private ordering, as such negotiations are called, is thought to be a better, more civilized way of making settlements, yet the appropriateness of judicial procedures for overseeing such a process remains confused (Elston *et al.*

1975; Mnookin 1983). It is in this arena that divorce as a public issue and as a private experience meet head on. If the welfare of children is to be a dominant public concern, the law has to maintain its investigative protective role. At the present time a judge must declare satisfaction about the arrangements for children before a divorce is made absolute. Encouraging private ordering and minimizing conflict raise difficult issues for the legal process as principles of family autonomy are clumsily balanced with the need for state approval.

# DIVORCE – A SERIES OF TRANSITIONS

## Adults

Marriage is an arrangement by which two people start by getting the best out of each other and often end by getting the worst.

(Brenan 1978 : 63)

Marriage is a relationship entered into by most individuals at some time during their lives.

Each individual brings to marriage his/her unique set of needs, expectations, goals and capacities, . . . which are multidetermined and deep-seated. . . . During the course of the marriage, people continue to develop and change and may grow in ways that are no longer complementary or parallel.

(Kaslow 1981 : 667)

The solution to disenchantment, conflict and marital unhappiness may be to dissolve the union. It is now well documented, however, that ending a marriage may not end the unhappiness and conflict but that it involves such a range and intensity of emotions that misery may in fact be increased, at least in the short term. Separation and divorce are stressful; they can bring about the complete disintegration of an individual's life. Divorce may offer opportunities for personal growth and longed-for liberation and it would be unhelpful to categorize it as totally negative, but while not all separations are overburdened with conflict, few are completely painless and intense emotional responses are largely universal.

Divorce must be viewed as a process and not as a discrete event. Several models of stages in the divorce process have been delineated (Kessler 1975; Salts 1979; Weiss 1975). One of the most detailed is that put forward by Bohannan (1973) who talks of six 'stations' in divorce which capture both the traumatic personal experience and the social and legal process. These 'stations' occur in varying sequences and at different intensities, but Bohannan believes that each individual experiences them at some stage before, during, or maybe long after the actual physical separation. These models are well documented elsewhere (Burgoyne *et al.* 1987; Cherlin 1981;

Kaslow 1981; Weiss 1975). It is sufficient here to be aware of the essential elements which have major implications for the kind of professional intervention which may be appropriate.

*Emotional divorce*
Separating from an individual with whom one has shared a deep intimacy can be painful in the extreme and even the most unhappy marital partners experience some mourning for the lost relationship. The emotional responses may occur in different combinations and with varying intensity, but the grieving process normally involves feelings of denial, anger, bargaining, depression, fear, hostility, bitterness, blame and, eventually, acceptance (Froiland and Hozman 1977; Kübler-Ross 1969; Weisman 1975).

*Legal divorce*
Although divorce is virtually available by post and may often take only a few months to finalize, if there are conflicts between the partners, particularly about children, the legal process may become complex with the potential for increased conflict.

*Economic divorce*
Financial assets, including property, usually have to be divided. Money is often a very emotive subject, particularly in marriages where one partner has taken on the major role as 'homemaker'. It is not uncommon for decisions about money to be closely linked to those about custody of and access to children, despite the law's attempt to separate the issues. Each partner is likely to be financially worse off following divorce and this may well be exacerbated if remarriage puts the needs of first and second families in direct competition. It is often the *results* of economic difficulties which draw attention to divided families.

*Parental divorce*
When parents separate it is inevitable that parenting patterns and responsibilities, and relationships between parents and children, will change. Non-custodial parents (usually fathers) cannot execute their parental responsibilities as before, and often find it difficult to maintain a central role in their children's lives (Inglis 1982; Rowlands 1980; Wallerstein and Kelly 1981). They may feel that they are 'losing' their children as regular contact is forfeited.

*Social divorce*
A rising divorce rate has not necessarily meant that divorce is more socially acceptable, and many would argue that stigma is still prevalent (Hart 1976; Itzin 1980). Social networks are often severed and this may increase feelings

of isolation and loneliness during the process of 'status passage' (Hart 1976) from 'married' to 'divorced' and a shift in the source of personal identity. Such discomfort may precipitate the leap into second marriages.

*Psychic divorce*

Bohannan talks of 'the separation of self from personality and influence of the ex-spouse' (Kaslow 1981 : 488) and considers it to be the most difficult transition to accomplish. Inner turmoil may lead to the quest for understanding of how the marriage went wrong, and feelings of personal failure are common. Psychic divorce is not complete until self-worth and hope for the future are established. This commonly takes up to two years to accomplish (Johnson and Alevizos 1978).

Divorce and separation are a 'becoming' experience. Each transition involves a set of emotional responses and presents a number of tasks which have to be accomplished.

> Marriage failure plus grief, minus social approval multiplied by emotional stress and divided by low self-esteem, equals depression, anxiety, perhaps panic and the behaviour these emotions elicit.
>
> (Roman and Haddad 1978 : 75)

## Children

> It's weird, funny, nothing seems to make sense, and there's no escape.
> (Johnny aged 13, five years after his parents' separation)

Children find out in a variety of ways that their parents are separating. Some parents tell their children calmly and carefully, offering reassurance; others are less protective and involve the children in their own bitterness. Many say nothing at all, leaving children to make sense of a bewildering jigsaw (Mitchell 1981; 1985; Murch 1980). While children may have been aware of quarrels and difficulties between their parents, few are prepared for separation, and shock and disbelief are common reactions. How children cope varies according to age, temperament, and the behaviour of their parents. Most parents do worry about the long-term effects of divorce but may be unable to deal with the immediate impact because of their own overwhelming worries, fears and feelings.

Children of any age are nearly always distressed and anxious and desire to see their parents reunite. Indeed this hope for 'normality' in family life may continue long after the divorce and, for some, long after the subsequent remarriage of one or both parents. Children experience the same range of emotional responses as their parents and also have to negotiate a similar process of transitions and readjustment. Differences in reaction according to age are now well documented (Inglis 1982; Kaslow 1981; Mitchell 1985; Wallerstein and Kelly 1981; Weiss 1975). What is evident is that children feel immense pain, guilt and fear. Children may feel responsible for the separation, and they feel confused. Intense distress may last for only a short time, but the quality of the subsequent relationship between the child and his or her parent, and the quality of the relationship *between* the parents, is a key to understanding the longer-term effects. There is good research evidence to confirm that the better and less conflictual these relationships are, the quicker the child readjusts to the new situation. The poor, conflict-ridden relationships are likely to cause prolonged emotional disturbance which may result in poor school attainment and behaviour problems (Dunlop and Burns 1984; Leupnitz 1983; Wallerstein and Kelly 1981). The crucial factor seems to be what happens to children *after* separation, and here the importance of continued parenting from both mother and father cannot be over-emphasized. Parenting patterns must change, they might even improve, but research shows that, sadly, they invariably worsen and many children lose meaningful contact with the non-custodial parent quite quickly (Wallerstein and Kelly 1981).

Little (1982) suggests that the roles children adopt during and after divorce are shaped by parents' demands and expectations. She delineates five roles: stabilizer, competitor, hostage, obstacle or care-taker, all of which are rooted in past family history and the way the parents exercise power. Children with the stabilizer role are the least disturbed by divorce, whereas the hostage and care-taker children find themselves in the centre of a battlefield between their parents.

## A FAMILY MATTER

> Divorce implies a rearrangement of family bonds and raises questions not only of how emotional bonds can be maintained but also of actual physical location of family members. Divorce thus challenges the meaning of family ties and forces family members to appraise their relationships.
>
> (Little 1982 : 1)

Divorce is not simply about two adults splitting up. It is an experience which touches whole families. Even if there are no children of a marriage relationships with wider kin are inevitably changed, redefined and often broken altogether. The experience of divorce and its impact on individuals can be fully understood only in a family context, and interventions which focus only on the marital couple may well fail to offer appropriate help to other family members, and may underestimate the importance of the family system. It is vital to assume a systemic orientation and to view the family as an interactive unit within which changes must be negotiated. New family units are formed which may threaten existing relationships and require the inclusion of new 'family' members, especially new partners and step-parents. If we use 'family' in a broad sense to include people who provide each other with emotional and economic support (Lemmon 1985), the fact that all family members are involved in and changed by the divorce process has not been centrally recognized until the emergence of a family systems perspective in social work and mental health practice. Previously the needs of children and adults were viewed separately. Focusing on children's needs may not help parents who are struggling to be competent during an emotional crisis, while responding only to the adult needs may ignore the 'best interests' of children (Robinson and Parkinson 1985).

Families are constantly undergoing change and adjustment while striving to maintain an equilibrium during a number of transitional periods: for example, the birth of a child, school age years, adolescence and leaving home (for a fuller description see Street 1985). Divorce can occur in any one of these periods in the family life cycle and will cause a distinct disruption of that phase. Families are forever solving internal and external problems, but what is special about divorce is its magnitude in requiring a high degree of change and adaptation in all aspects of day-to-day living and coping. This is not to say that divorce is pathological but rather that it is a crisis in which massive restructuring must take place. Life events may themselves be the trigger for separation; some couples stay together 'for the sake of the children' and separate as children leave home. Brannen and Collard (1982) have adapted the Brown and Harris (1978) 'life events schedule' to try and identify critical life events and their impact on the present situation. They found that marriages in trouble were frequently linked to a major critical event which had depleted the emotional resources of the individuals concerned, thus reducing coping behaviour. Bain (1978) has argued that the 'meaning' of these critical life events for the individuals is extremely important.

Children and parents tend to express distress during times of natural developmental family crisis, and Saposnek (1983) has pointed out that each family member responds to the others in a circular rather than a linear fashion. If communication is already distorted, as is common during separation and divorce, the stresses escalate the family conflict, which in turn increases the stress. Children's normal coping mechanisms are insufficient, and age-specific behaviour problems frequently result. It is not unusual for a child's behavioural difficulties to be the trigger for seeking outside help and to be the presenting problem. Looking at this from a family perspective the professional can understand not only the impact of change on family relationships in a way that places the family in its 'historical' context, but also the impact on individual well-being in a way that places the individual in the context of his or her experience and feelings which are often confused and confusing.

Furthermore, within the family individual experiences may not be simultaneous or congruent. Adults have to cope with the loss of an intimate partner and often with strong feelings of anger, hate and hostility, while children want to love and have easy access to both parents and need information and reassurance about the future and relationships which are conflict free. How decisions are handled at this time can be extremely important either in helping families through the transition or in causing severe interference in relationships which can never be adequately repaired.

So what do divorcing families need? It is helpful to distinguish the tasks which have to be accomplished: individuals have to pass through a number of phases and cope with a variety of emotions; families need to restructure and renegotiate relationships; decisions have to be taken about a number of issues such as children, money and living arrangements. Such different tasks require different types of help.

## THE PROFESSIONAL RESPONSE

There has not been any one agency, statutory or voluntary, in Britain whose sole task has been to offer help to separating and divorcing families. Rather, a number of agencies have become involved in various aspects of work with this group.

The investigation of matrimonial disputes and arrangements for children has rested with the probation service in England and Wales since 1937. The traditional task has been to prepare reports for the court in which judgments are made about the children's best interests. In 1971 courts were encouraged to refer some couples to the Divorce Court Welfare Officer who was charged with the duty of meeting with the parties to 'decide whether there is any reasonable prospect of reconciliation . . . or that conciliation might assist the parties to resolve their disputes or any part of them by agreement' (Practice Direction on Matrimonial Conciliation 1971 : 1). Thus, the probation officer's professional task incorporates three rather different duties – reconciliation, investigation and conciliation – the (con)fusion of which is the subject of recent statements by the President of the Family Division and other senior members of the judiciary (Re H. (a minor) (1986) 130 *Solicitor's Journal* 128). The probation service still operates with the authority of the court and has severe resource limitations imposed on its civil work (about 8 per cent of its annual budget), its major work being with criminals.

Marriage guidance, now known as Relate although it has widened its boundaries in recent years, is still associated with marriage-mending. Local authority social services departments are more likely to become involved with separating families because of practical difficulties arising before, or because of, marital breakdown, drawing their clients largely from the lower socio-economic groups, and have the ultimate power to remove children from their parents (14,877 children were under local authority supervision in England and Wales in 1983 following an order made in divorce proceedings – Law Commission 1986b: para. 7.16). Relatively few families therefore receive specialist help during separation and divorce. Family conciliation services have mushroomed since the early 1980s in order to fill this role. The concept of conciliation gained popularity following the *Report of the Committee on One-Parent Families* (Finer Report 1974). The committee's definition of conciliation has been widely adopted:

> assisting the parties to deal with the consequences of the established breakdown of their marriage . . . by reaching agreements or giving consents or reducing the area of conflict upon custody, support, access to and education of the children, financial provision, the disposition of the matrimonial home, lawyers' fees and every other matter arising from the breakdown which calls for a decision on future arrangements.

> (Finer Report 1974 : 176)

It is seen as a new 'process of engendering common sense, reasonableness and agreement in dealing with the consequences of estrangement . . . having substantial success in civilising the consequences of the breakdown' (Finer Report 1974: 183, 185). Finer's recommendations were not accepted by the government and civil service so that the innovations in divorce process, and in particular in conciliation, have come from the spontaneous enthusiasm of legal and social welfare practitioners, reflecting their own particular professional interests and leading to the present patchwork of services and procedures (Walker 1986a). The emphasis is on assisting couples to make decisions consequent on the marriage breakdown while reducing bitterness and conflict. In practice the focus is on child-related issues, mostly custody and access. It is seen as an adjunct to legal advice and not a substitute for it, and the process is considered to be confidential and legally privileged.

Conciliation is not available in all areas of Britain and where it does exist it may be offered by the probation service either within the court setting or in the community, by an independent service (most of which have strong links with statutory and voluntary welfare agencies), or by both, but with no agreed consensus as to what its aims are or should be and even less agreement on how it should be practised. Conciliation in the court setting is associated with the authority of the law and is often a quite different experience from conciliation offered by an agency with no formal connection to the legal process. Although the dichotomy between court-based and independent schemes is grossly over-simplistic (Walker 1986a) it does highlight an important distinction between the services as they currently exist, particularly in relation to the content and process of conciliation. (There are no court-based schemes in Scotland.)

The use of the term 'conciliation' to describe these new services is itself troublesome. It is strikingly similar to 'reconciliation', causing considerable confusion for clients and professionals alike, particularly as many con*cilia*-tion services are proud of their *recon*ciliation rate! The term 'mediation' is more widely used in North America, although there it embraces wider aims than conciliation in Britain. Nevertheless the terms tend to be used inter-changeably, and for the purposes of this discussion I shall use the term conciliation in relation to Britain and mediation in relation to North America. The term conciliation *counselling* is commonly used in Australia and New Zealand when describing a similar process.

While the need for a separate service to help families during divorce would seem unquestionable, it is curious that conciliation services have not been overwhelmed with referrals; indeed the vast majority see fewer than a hundred families a year. Patterns of help-seeking by separating and divorc-ing couples must be to some extent determined by the help offered. As long ago as 1960 Gurin and his colleagues in the USA found that 22 per cent of separated and divorced men and 40 per cent of separated and divorced women had sought professional help for personal problems, often of a medical nature (Gurin *et al.* 1960). In Britain the stiff-upper-lip approach to personal problems renders it less likely that divorcing families will seek help directly with the consequences of divorce. Weiss (1975) has suggested that many individuals require help in managing the transition from marriage through divorce but only a few receive this help. It is more likely that doctors will see patients suffering from stress but may not relate this to marital breakdown (Hunt 1985). If it is the case that doctors are most commonly consulted by the divorcing population, this may be a powerful argument for providing conciliation, counselling and therapy facilities in surgeries or health centres. 'Clients often categorise in their own minds what help is appropriate from where' (Hunt 1985 : 37), signifying the importance of agencies making it clear what help they offer for which problems. In my view conciliation services have failed to give clear unambiguous messages to the population as a whole and to their clients in particular. The very name of the agency is crucial to this understanding. The context in which conciliation is offered must influence the service offered and, therefore, the types of clients referred.

## FROM FAMILY THERAPY TO FAMILY CONCILIATION

Kaslow commented that 'every known therapeutic approach has been adapted to working with individuals and couples in every stage of the divorce process' (Kaslow 1981 : 682) but until recently no treatment technique was specific to working with separating families. Family conciliation in attempting to fill that gap has been heavily dependent on other strategies, notably family therapy.

> Most therapists see their role as a supportive one and use their professional skills in assisting families to solve their problems and stay together. However, there are times when no amount of intervention can hold a marriage together. In this context the family therapist has a special responsibility to develop mediation skills. . . . Once divorce is inevitable the professional's role changes to one of attempting to make the separation as painless as possible, to help the couple maintain their individual dignity, and to assist the children to make the transition by reducing the conflict inherent in the process of divorce.
>
> (Haynes 1981 : 4)

Haynes clearly views conciliation as an extension of therapy, while others have defined the conciliation task more narrowly as a 'process in which the parties negotiate with each other in the presence of one or more facilitators' (Gaddis 1978 : 43). 'Although this process may be therapeutic for the couple, the chief objective of the professional is not to apply therapy but to help the couple negotiate a fair, workable plan' (Little 1982 : 197).

'It is wise for the mediator to heed the warning: mediation is not therapy or counselling' (Little 1982 : 48). Parkinson (1985a : 1986) has attempted to distinguish between these three methods. Divorce counselling often involves only one partner, and may focus on personal adjustment with no formal links with the legal process. Tyler (1961) defines counselling as a helping process, the aim of which is not to change the person but to enable him or her to utilize his or her own resources for coping with stresses and changes. On the other hand, 'The goal of family therapy is to help the members of the system change their patterns of interaction from dysfunctional to functional – to help them operate in an optimal fashion' (Grebe 1986 : 55). Conciliation is about encouraging parents to reach agreements which have legal, social and emotional implications for the family as a whole. Put simply the three methods seem to fit neatly with the tasks delineated earlier. The overlap, however, is considerable and has promoted a debate about 'boundaries' which are often more theoretical than practical. 'Maintaining the distinctions, given the range of commonality, poses continual problems of restraint, definition, and value clarification' (Gold 1985 : 16). So what is conciliation, and what skills are utilized?

It is difficult to find a definition of conciliation which is universally acceptable, but the simplest refers to conciliation as a method of 'resolving disputes with the aid of an impartial third person' (Lemmon 1985 : 6). The cornerstone of conciliation is decision-making based on a number of basic principles:

1 Involvement in the process is voluntary.
2 The parties should be empowered to make their own decisions.
3 The conciliator is non-judgemental and cannot enforce agreements.

4 Conciliation is confidential and legally privileged.

(Robinson and Parkinson 1985)

There is a clear focus on change in the 'here' and 'now' directed towards improved family functioning for the future.

Systems theory provides conciliation with its theoretical model for understanding the family: family therapy allows us to understand communication patterns and provides a body of interventive skills for helping parents to reduce the conflict and come to agreement. It also takes into account the children and other 'family' members, all of whom must adapt to a changing situation. Both structural and strategic family therapy (see Chapters 4 and 6) place emphasis on the notion of hierarchy, where parents are expected to be clearly in charge of their children, and on changing structure. As one of the tasks of conciliation may be to differentiate the parental sub-system from the old marital sub-system, enabling parents to make decisions about their children while changing the old family structure, these models of family therapy are particularly helpful. It is possible to delineate different structural maps (Minuchin and Fishman 1981) which aid understanding of different types of families, providing clues for intervention to change sequences of action and patterns of relationships. 'Families come with different shapes and structures, and since form will affect function, families will respond to stresses in certain ways that are necessitated by their shape' (Minuchin and Fishman 1981 : 50). The therapist must 'use the facts that the family recognise as true, but out of these facts she will build a new arrangement' (Minuchin and Fishman 1981 : 207). Restructuring utilizes a wide variety of techniques such as reframing, challenging dysfunctional communication, questioning unhelpful 'myths', task setting, articulating hidden agendas, testing assumptions and encouraging the expression of feelings, many of which are used by other therapeutic orientations. All of these are complex skills, but are well known in family therapy practice (Haley 1976; Haynes 1981; Lemmon 1985; Minuchin and Fishman 1981; Saposnek 1983).

'One of the unique contributions of structuralists . . . stems from how they address triadic social relations' (Keeney and Ross 1985 : 174). Triadic patterns frequently emerge when the issues for conciliation concern relationships between parents and children. These include

(1) triangulation, where each parent demands that the child sides with him against the other parent [the child agrees with both parents' point of view as necessary, keeping each side 'happy', but escalating conflict] (2) detouring, where the negotiation of spouse stresses through the child serves to maintain the spouse sub-system in an illusory harmony [both parents 'agree' on access but the child supposedly sabotages the arrangements]; and (3) stable coalition, where one of the parents joins the child in a rigidly bounded cross generational coalition against the other parent [frequently the custodial parent and child against the non-custodial parent].

(Minuchin 1974 : 102 quoted in Keeney and Ross 1985 : 175)

# CONCILIATION – THE PROCESS

Conciliation normally proceeds through a number of steps: empathic listening; problem identification; problem-solving; problem-coping; termination. Engagement is the process of beginning work and requires the conciliator to meet both parents. Unlike family therapy, the children and other family members are not normally invited to the first session, but are sometimes brought along by parents. It is essential that the conciliator establishes him or herself in charge of the process, particularly as conciliation is often surrounded by hostility and anger with emotions running high. Containing and managing this conflict is an essential task for the conciliator if the parties are to feel safe and able to work. This is quite consistent with allowing the parents to be responsible for their own decision-making.

## The first interview

The first session is a difficult one, because the mediator must attempt to achieve a number of goals. He/she must establish the mediator's credibility and set the tone for the subsequent relationship, while explaining the process, clarifying the clients' expectations, and establishing empathy with them. At the same time he/she must determine whether they are really ready for mediation.

(Haynes 1981 : 56)

Several writers have documented the conciliation process (Haynes 1981; Irving 1981: Lemmon 1985; Saposnek 1983) and all put emphasis on the importance of the first interview. A useful structure has been provided by Haley (1976) whose four-stage family therapy session fits well with the conciliation task.

1 Social stage – joining with the clients; explaining the aim of the process of conciliation; establishing the present situation in the family, that is who lives where, with whom, and so on; establishing ground-rules for conciliation (see Haynes 1981). All are crucial activities at the beginning of conciliation.
2 Problem stage – each partner is asked to state his or her own perception of the difficulties and the issues in dispute. Just as each partner experiences his or her own marriage differently, so each partner will have a different version of the present problems. An important part of this stage is to clarify what changes each partner desires, since this allows the conciliator to begin to evaluate the bargaining positions.
3 Interaction stage – if the emphasis is on enabling and empowering the partners to solve their own disputes, encouraging them to talk together about the issues from their respective positions is an important step towards improving the communication between them and beginning negotiation.

4 Goal-setting stage – the issues are defined, prioritized and agreed on, the desired changes are clarified and possible bargaining positions opened up. It is helpful to get agreement to work on the issues without implying blame and escalating hostility. This is an important first step towards problem-solving.

This structured process offers a way of making sense of what is often 'chaos' in the lives of family members attending a conciliation interview. It establishes a clear pattern for any future sessions and can provide hope for both partners at a time of emotional and physical turmoil. While establishing an atmosphere of trust, confidentiality and openness, it provides the conciliator with much-needed information about the family and the issues in dispute. Maybe clients would be less critical of and disappointed with conciliation if a clearer negotiating structure existed which allowed the conciliator to assess adequately the problems to be worked on and to determine the most appropriate method of intervention. I have argued elsewhere that an essential prerequisite of any work with couples and families during separation and divorce is accurate assessment of the issues for conciliation and a consideration of the appropriate timing and pacing of intervention (Walker 1986b). From the information provided in this first session the conciliator can not only understand both the family's old and emerging structure and who may be important to the conciliation task, but also learn about family communication patterns, roles, affect, power, meaning and the family's developmental stage. This allows the conciliator to develop some hypotheses about the family, the presenting issues, and the ways in which *this* family might be facilitated to find solutions and reach agreements. Haynes (1981 : 69) develops a family profile before beginning negotiation in conciliation. Although families need to move to a new structure during separation, in order to assist this transition the conciliator needs knowledge of the old family structure which has been 'discarded' by divorce and yet is maintained through communication patterns. The presenting problem (commonly disagreements about the non-custodial partner's access to the children) can be understood *only* within the family context. Only then can the conciliator move on to intervene as a catalyst of family change.

## THE GREEN FAMILY IN CONCILIATION

Mrs Green's solicitor referred her for conciliation because she was unhappy about her husband's access to their two sons Darren, aged 12, and Stephen, aged 7. The conciliator was warned that recently Mr Green had been violent towards Mrs Green, who was terrified of face-to-face contact with him. This highlights the special difficulties of convening separating couples. It may seem paradoxical that when a family is struggling to separate, it is often possible only if a war-like situation is created; the conciliator must put considerable effort into re-joining the family and indeed into reducing the conflict. Couples may be forgiven for misunderstanding this manoeuvre, believing that the conciliator is trying to save the marriage. Yet to help the family to restructure and to maintain healthy relationships between each parent and the children it is essential that parents and often other family members do come together to create the desired changes. Engaging both parents is therefore a delicate task for the conciliator.

In this case the conciliator wrote separately to Mr and Mrs Green explaining the purpose of conciliation, inviting them to attend a joint interview and saying why this was important, acknowledging that feelings between them may be running high but reassuring them of the conciliator's ability to help them to manage these feelings.

Mr and Mrs Green came to conciliation and were brought into the interview room immediately. Mrs Green promptly hit her husband with her very large handbag and had to be physically restrained by the conciliator. Instant information was provided about how this couple communicated when together! The conciliator placed two chairs back to back, about four feet apart, for Mr and Mrs Green and then sat so that both could see her but not each other. During the social stage of the interview they were instructed not to look at each other nor to talk directly to each other 'so that everyone can feel safer since there are obviously strong feelings between you'. Thus the dysfunctional communication was effectively challenged and controlled by the conciliator and ground-rules were established. The conciliation task and process were explained. The initial interaction between Mr and Mrs Green was reframed positively as their obvious desire to show each other and the conciliator how it felt for each of them, and provided the basis for the problem stage of the interview.

Mr and Mrs Green were each asked to explain their own views of the present difficulties and solutions which might be considered, while the other partner was instructed to listen carefully. Mr Green listened to his wife's story with growing non-verbal agitation, while Mrs Green constantly interrupted her husband, 'speaking for' everyone in the family. The conciliator reframed Mrs Green's constant bid for control as her desire to help the conciliator by explaining everything, but urged her firmly to let her husband have his say as the conciliator could understand the problems only if they allowed her to hear from them one at a time.

Mr and Mrs Green gave similar accounts of a stormy marriage punctuated by Mr Green's discovery of his wife's adultery. He described how he felt angry, hurt and 'made a fool of' by her behaviour. Mrs Green described her struggle to bring up two demanding sons while her husband was 'too drunk to notice' that she felt neglected and unhappy. She now wanted peace and quiet and to be able to 'get on with' her life without her husband's violent temper. A violent scene had led to Mrs Green taking the boys to her sister's home, refusing all contact with her husband and insisting that the boys had no wish to see him again as 'he's never bothered with them before'. Mr Green spoke of his 'rights as a father' to see the boys, accusing his wife of 'twisting their minds' against him. He threatened to apply for custody if access was refused and 'wouldn't be held responsible' for the consequences! Darren and Stephen served as 'hostages' in this family which was characterized by open and sometimes violent hostility. By the time of separation neither parent was able to protect the boys from his or her own anger (Little 1982).

Throughout their accounts the couple were each reminded to talk only to the conciliator, about themselves and not about the other partner. This controlled the tendency warring partners have to accuse, insult and blame each other, and detoured and diffused the conflict through the conciliator, who thereby adopted a triangulated position (Burnham 1986).

The emerging issues were:

1 Mrs Green's determination to prevent access.
2 Mrs Green's claim that Darren and Stephen did not wish to see their father.
3 Mr Green's desire for access which if thwarted would lead to an application for custody.
4 The anger felt by both parents which frequently resulted in violent behaviour.

The conciliator wrote these up on a large sheet of paper and Mr and Mrs Green agreed that these were the main problems which had to be solved. This was an important opportunity to recognize that Mr and Mrs Green, by agreeing on the issues in dispute, could begin to work on them and so they were congratulated and given the confidence to continue.

It became obvious that neither parent had given much overt consideration to the feelings of the boys and their perceptions of the present issues and future arrangements. They had been used as the 'football' for Mr and Mrs Green to kick around in order to justify their own feelings and needs. Moving to the interaction stage of the interview the conciliator asked Mrs Green to tell her husband about the demands two lively sons made on her, and for them both to consider as *parents* how they would be able to cope with these demands in the future. This was prefaced by the conciliator acknowledging that they had both demonstrated that they were caring parents by coming along to talk about the problems.

By focusing on the children the parents moved easily into the interactive stage without provoking further hostility. This part of the session was abruptly interrupted when Mr Green exclaimed angrily at the conciliator: 'This is — ridiculous; how can she and I talk sensibly about this if we're not allowed to see each other?!', turned his chair round, helped his wife to do the same and proceeded to ask his wife how she was coping with the 'little buggers'. She admitted to finding them a handful 'just like I always did', especially at weekends. He suggested taking them off her hands on a Saturday as he had done in the past and she began to see some advantage in this.

It would have been tempting for the conciliator to seize on this, congratulate them on making an agreement, write it down and send them on their way. Another successful conciliation! However, what had been negotiated was access 'in principle', but without any thought to the practicalities and the best arrangements for parents and children. Although a previously functional sharing of parental tasks could be continued this now had to be negotiated within a changing family structure. Furthermore, Mrs Green's assertion that the boys did not wish to see their father needed to be examined. The limited goal was to introduce access arrangements the following weekend and to reconsider the issues between Mr and Mrs Green in a week's time. Tasks were agreed with Mr and Mrs Green which ensured that the arrangements for access were clear and would test how a changing family system could incorporate a process and experience which was new to everyone.

Mrs Green was to

1 Talk with Darren and Stephen about seeing their father.
2 Have them ready to be collected at 10 am on Saturday.
3 Meet them at 5 pm at the bus station to take them home.

Mr Green was to

1 Collect the boys at 10 am from his sister-in-law's house.
2 Take them to the bus station for 5 pm to meet their mother.

The next week Mrs Green, looking flustered and angry, arrived at the conciliation service with Darren and Stephen and insisted that they should be involved in the session. Inviting them into the room with their parents, the conciliator asked Mrs Green to introduce the boys and requested the parents to 'sit quietly and relax for a few mintues while I talk to Darren and Stephen'. The conciliator sat with the boys a little away from the parents who were glowering hostilely at each other. The conciliator explained why Mr and Mrs Green had come to talk the previous week, positively connoting this as showing how much they both cared about Darren and Stephen and wanted to sort out the problems that had meant that Mr Green had not seen them for a while. Although Mrs Green made several attempts to interrupt, the conciliator unbalanced the accepted pattern of communication in which mother always spoke for the children by insisting that she wanted to talk with the boys first. This increased the status of the child sub-system and ignored the family switchboard, that is mother. 'Therapeutic joining is, in essence, a technique of affiliation. . . . The focus on one family member changes the position of all family members' (Minuchin and Fishman 1981 : 161–2). Part of the joining with the boys focused on a discussion of football, mentioned as their overriding interest by Mr Green the previous week. They were asked to write down the names and positions of the players in the previous Saturday's cup match and they engaged in this eagerly.

Each parent was then asked about the access task. Mrs Green's version was that she got the boys ready for 10 o'clock. By 11 o'clock Mr Green had not arrived so, angrily, she took them to town before marching them to the father's home. Mr Green was not in, 'proving he did not care about the boys'. Mrs Green was told by a neighbour that her husband had gone to the pub, and she told the boys to 'forget your "drunkard" father' forthwith; 'They'll tell you themselves'. This offer was not taken up by the conciliator, and to Mrs Green's annoyance the boys got on with their task despite her 'meaningful' glances at them. Mr Green's version was that he had left home at 9.45 am, missed the bus to his sister-in-law's home and waited for the next one. He had arrived at 11.15 am to be told that Mrs Green had taken the boys out and that he was not going to see them again! Mr Green returned home, miserable, met a neighbour and decided to drown his sorrows at the local pub. Darren and Stephen had clearly heard these stories; they nudged each other now and again and commented, rather rudely, that their parents were 'mad'. The conciliator asked them to say how they felt about Saturday and they described the event as 'typical': 'Mum was impatient and lost her temper', and 'Dad felt sorry for himself and went to the pub'. The interaction patterns familiar to the marriage were being re-enacted. Direct parental communication was present only in the form of verbal and physical abuse with which the boys were clearly familiar. Darren and Stephen were 'fed up' because they guessed that their father would have tickets for the football match, and instead they 'dragged round town all day'.

The conciliator commented how everyone had been upset by the failure of Saturday's arrangements. Mrs Green's behaviour was reframed as 'the natural response to being let down' (Mr Green had not collected the boys as planned, thus spoiling her shopping trip with a girlfriend) and Mr Green's behaviour as 'the natural response to being disappointed' (he had looked forward to seeing Darren and Stephen and taking them to the match). Establishing from each family member that it would be good to 'get things to work' the discussion focused on how this might be achieved. Interestingly the boys had ideas about 'letting people know if things go wrong' and Darren suggested that his father could telephone as their aunt was 'on the phone' and his mother could leave a message with Dad's next-door neighbour. With the help of the boys as therapeutic allies a plan for 'communication first-aid' was drawn up which was to be deliberately tested the following Saturday. Mr and Mrs Green left the session much less angry and the children had not been drawn in as weapons against their father, which had clearly been Mrs Green's reason for bringing them along – a hidden agenda which the conciliator recognized and controlled by maintaining therapeutic responsibility. The children were able to witness their parents co-operating, as well as being heard themselves. Contrary to their mother's claims they were wanting to see their father.

Mr and Mrs Green and the boys returned the following week having agreed on the telephone beforehand to tell the conciliator that it would be easy to arrange access from now on as Mr Green had decided to have a telephone of his own – 'so that we can all talk to each other'. Mr Green said that he felt happier now that contact with the boys was re-established and they would be able to talk to him whenever they wished. Mrs Green said she enjoyed 'getting rid of the boys occasionally' and was quite happy for them to spend time with their father. No further allegations were made about violence or drunkenness. When asked about custody they agreed that 'it won't be a problem now' as Mr Green had withdrawn his application.

By this third session Mrs Green was visibly calmer and beginning to sort her life out, talking about looking for somewhere to live fairly near to the boys' father to avoid the transport problem between the two homes. Mr Green was much less hostile towards his wife and was convinced that he would help his wife by looking after the boys now and again. At no time had the marriage, the reason for its ending, nor the allegations of violence been subjects for discussion. Conciliation had been clearly focused on the issues in dispute, but the interventions of the conciliator had diffused the anger, put the parents in charge of their own decision-making, taken account of the parents' interests while being centrally aware of the children's needs, and allowed everyone to move on into the future with more functional patterns of interaction.

Although the inclusion of children is well accepted in family therapy, there are some conciliators who view the conciliation task as an adult one, and as an inappropriate forum for children. Clearly 'children must not feel that they have adult powers of decision-making' (Bentovim and Gilmour 1981) but there are a number of situations in which the direct involvement of children may be helpful (Saposnek 1983):

1 When a parent indicates that a child has clear views about how he or she would like the relationship with the parents to function, it can be helpful to elicit the child's own views.
2 When a child indicates that he or she would like an opportunity to talk with the conciliator.
3 When arrangements are made for adolescent children, their own feelings about those arrangements may need to be sought. The needs of teenage children may not be sufficiently understood by either parent. Children can

help parents to realize that arrangements have to take into account the natural process in this phase of the family life cycle of 'letting go' of children reaching adulthood. This can be a painful, difficult process in intact families, but can be exacerbated by divorce, and the need of one or both parents to cling on to the children as the marriage crumbles. 'Children who adjusted best and were happiest were those whose access arrangements met their needs – in younger children for regularity, in older ones for flexibility' (Walczac with Burns 1984 : 120).

4 To explain to a child what arrangements have been made and to help parents to talk honestly and simply with their children. Studies of children's reactions to divorce (Lund 1984; Mitchell 1985; Walczak with Burns 1984) show how children need to be kept informed about what is happening and need to be heard and understood.

From a systemic viewpoint it is impossible to believe that the children are not centrally affected by what their parents do and say. In all communications with children establishing trust is essential, as is offering support when painful and difficult issues are at stake (Saposnek 1983). 'One of the most helpful features of conciliation, for families, may be the opportunity it offers to draw on each family member's perceptions and proposals' (Parkinson 1985b : 256). Research indicates how parents' assessments of children's feelings and needs differ markedly from those of the children (Mitchell 1985).

## THE HARDING FAMILY IN CONCILIATION

Changes in one part of a system inevitably involve adaptation in other parts. If parents have new partners, the new relationships contribute to and are affected by the decisions taken about future arrangements for the children. It may be necessary to include new partners at some stage in the conciliation process. Sometimes it is obvious that new partners are instrumental in creating and maintaining conflict between original spouses, and are therefore well able to sabotage conciliation if excluded.

Mr Harding left his wife and 5-year-old daughter, Anne, to live with Jane (previously his wife's best friend). Mrs Harding had turned to John Robson, a colleague at Mr Harding's work, for emotional support and he subsequently left his wife and family to live with Mrs Harding. The divorce process was complete for Mr and Mrs Harding, and Mr Harding and Jane were married. Mr Robson's wife refused to divorce him and hoped for a reconciliation. Mr Harding contacted the conciliation service when access to Anne had become an upsetting experience for all concerned. The conciliator wrote to each parent explaining the purpose of conciliation and stating that as the problem seemed to centre around access visits it would be helpful if they as parents could meet together initially to explore the issue with the conciliator, recognizing that other members of the family may be included later if appropriate. Anne's parents attended for the first session, during which it became clear that Mrs Harding had not forgiven her friend Jane for 'stealing my husband', and Mr Harding was hurt by Mr Robson taking over his paternal role with Anne. Access was typically a very distressing experience whenever Mr Harding and Jane arrived to collect Anne from the former matrimonial home. Mr Robson refused to let Mr Harding speak to his first wife, Jane screamed instructions and abuse from the passenger seat of the car, and Anne sobbed uncontrollably upstairs, clinging to her mother. Mr Harding blamed Mr Robson; Mrs Harding blamed Jane.

It was possible for Anne's parents to agree during the first session that both knew that access was important for Anne, that Anne should not be upset by the experience, and for each parent to admit that the other was an important part of Anne's life. The problem seemed to be the relationship each parent had with the other's new partner, and the unresolved feelings of bitterness from Mrs Harding towards her ex-husband and his sense of guilt in 'running off with Jane'. During the interactive stage each parent was able to talk about these feelings with expressed emotion on both sides. This was possible because the conciliator stressed how important it was for them to continue to be good parents to Anne and how their feelings were getting in the way of this. This was the first occasion that they had talked alone together since Mr Harding left fifteen months earlier. Previously either one or both of the new partners had been present and had done most of the talking. Anne's parents had abandoned the original family structure without being able to maintain a boundary around the parental sub-system. The conciliation session redrew this boundary, having allowed both parents to express their feelings about the divorce which had clearly obstructed the attempts at access. The conciliator recognized that the end of the marriage had coincided with Anne beginning school so that her mother was having to cope with the 'loss' of her marriage and a major transition point in the life cycle where her role as a 'full-time' mother was undergoing change. Her relationship with Mr Robson was tenuous, her ex-husband had remarried, and Anne had become the one stable relationship she had. Mr Harding had found himself 'between the devil and the deep blue sea' not wanting to hurt his former wife further, under pressure from his new wife to 'insist on seeing Anne', and upset by Anne's obvious distress when he called.

With these feelings shared the parents were able to agree to organize access differently. This was to be attempted the following Sunday when Mr Harding would call for Anne on his own at lunch-time, while Jane prepared lunch and Mr Robson was visiting his own children.

In the second session both parents agreed that access had been much less stressful. Although Anne had been reluctant to see her father at first, after he had spent half an hour in the former matrimonial home she willingly agreed to go back to his home for lunch. The destructive pattern of interaction had been broken, but Mr Harding reported that Jane felt 'left out' and Mrs Harding said that Mr Robson had accused her of pandering to her ex-husband, thus causing a row between them. It seemed essential to include them in conciliation and Anne's parents welcomed this suggestion, although feeling rather apprehensive about 'coming face to face' with the respective new partners. The conciliator wrote to Mr Robson and to Jane inviting them to attend as important people in Anne's life, who could help her parents to ensure that access could be beneficial for everyone.

The following week Anne's parents were helped to explain to their respective new partners how they all wanted what was best for Anne. Jane admitted that she was scared that if access did not take place Mr Harding might return to his wife because of his affection and concern for Anne. Mr Robson said that he felt vulnerable when Anne went to her father's because he was not free to marry Mrs Harding, and was not able to offer her constant support when she was upset.

The four adults in this case were struggling to adjust to new relationships while carrying feelings and hostilities from the past. Because they had not resolved personal issues Anne had become the focus for their emotions and fears. Neither of Anne's parents had successfully negotiated new relationships within changed family structures and sub-system boundaries had become blurred as Jane and Mr Robson became involved in parental arrangements. Maintaining a parental relationship while discarding a marital relationship is often difficult, especially when new structures are emerging. The new partners' intrusion into the parental sub-system was positively connoted as protecting Anne's parents, but their roles were redefined as the 'supporters' of Anne's parents who were empowered to talk directly to each other about Anne, but not to 'take-over' from her parents. Enabling them to talk openly, using their mutual concern for Anne and their own need for stability in the future, made it possible for access arrangements to be agreed, ensuring that neither Jane nor Mr Robson would continue to escalate conflict. Anne was not involved in conciliation, but the whole process revolved around her needs.

> The goal in mediation is to help the parents separate the ending of their relationship through the divorce from the rearrangement of the family that the divorce will require.
>
> (Woolley 1979 : 149)

## IS CONCILIATION THERAPY?

Haynes believes that it is the therapist who offers a divorcing couple the best set of specialist skills. In the interest of achieving a settlement on any issue 'therapeutic or counselling training teaches him/her to be self-aware, empathic to clients, and understanding of past issues that may never be resolved' (Haynes 1981 : 11). When the issues for settlement involve parties who will continue some form of relationship subsequent to the separation then the decisions to be made must in part relate to the terms of the future relationship. Divorce does not bring family relationships to an end, especially if there are children of the marriage. 'Hence it is important that any dispute settlement system helps to facilitate constructive relations in the future, rather than leading to the exacerbation of existing relations' (Sander 1984 : xii). Negotiating agreements must, therefore, imply some restructuring of the family. The mere fact that conciliation is necessary suggests that there are blocks within the family system preventing agreement. Because adjustment is necessary on a number of dimensions – cognitive, affective and behavioural – change in any one or all of these can facilitate settlement. Change is central to restructuring and to negotiation. Both might involve conflict, and conciliation is uniquely placed to be able to control and work through the conflict as the cognitive, affective and behavioural dimensions interact during the process.

Restructuring family relationships and negotiating difficult issues are inextricably related. Therapy may focus primarily on the restructuring, however, while conciliation focuses primarily on the negotiation and settlement of issues in dispute. Girdner (1986) demonstrates this difference of emphasis in her conceptual framework of conciliation practice. She suggests that family conciliation operates within a continuum, at one end of which is a welfare orientation represented by therapy, and at the other a legal orientation represented by law. Therapists working within a family systems paradigm are oriented towards restructuring relationships, emphasizing the needs of family members, especially children, with the premise that changes within the family structure will facilitate settlement. Lawyers, at the other extreme and operating from a bargaining model, are oriented towards making settlements and de-emphasizing the affective dimensions in favour of those which take account of legal rights and norms – truly 'bargaining in the shadow of the law'. The emphasis on restructuring diminishes and that of negotiating agreements increases as the legal orientation is reached.

On this continuum the middle ground between therapy and legal bargaining is that belonging to the emerging practice of conciliation. Here therapy and legal considerations are synthesized and balanced so that the conciliator assists disputing parties to arrive at 'mutually agreeable, fair, workable settlements which attempt to be responsive to individual and joint needs of all family members and are made with recognition of their rights and of potential other outcomes' (Girdner 1986: 26). This provides an appropriate framework for integrating the theory and practice of family therapy within a legal paradigm. Family therapy and conciliation are clearly different. The skills used may be very similar but the aims and goals have a different focus Conciliators do not need to be family therapists, but they do need to understand family systems and to develop skills which are currently used in family therapy practice. The background, training and practice orientation of the conciliator will determine where he or she operates on the continuum.

This raises the vexed question: 'Who should conciliate?' There is evidence in Britain and North America of struggles for ownership of conciliation as a new profession. Sadly such struggles have encouraged argument about what conciliation is not – 'mediators are cautioned not to "do" therapy and not to "do" law' (Fargo 1986 : 3), thus creating boundaries around conciliation which are unhelpful and unrealistic. Divorce occurs within the family system and within the legal system. If conciliation is not to do with therapy or law, one wonders what it can possibly be about! Conciliation is task-oriented, and the skills of both therapy and legal practice need to be blended. As Folberg has pointed out, therapists are well qualified to move families through psychological and emotional barriers which inhibit openness and communication, whereas lawyers are 'problem-solvers who deal daily . . . with the creative exploration of compromise alternatives' (Folberg 1984 : 207). They are skilled at balancing power by equalizing bargaining positions – a principal role for any conciliator. This may suggest that interdisciplinary conciliation teams can present the most flexible approach to divorce conciliation. The lawyer can then concentrate on the legal aspects while the therapist focuses on the interpersonal and emotional aspects. At the present time most couples who receive conciliation are also each represented separately by a lawyer who is unlikely to be centrally involved in conciliation. Communication between the professionals is often clumsy, and in some areas almost non-existent. Relatively few divorcing families use conciliation services in Britain and the 'boundary' issues may well contribute to this poor take-up of services. If the emphasis in conciliation is improved co-operation between the parties, the professionals involved would do well to increase their own co-operation in providing a service which is more truly an alternative to the adversarial system, rather than just a separate experience grafted on to it.

## FUTURE DEVELOPMENTS AND DILEMMAS

The discussion of the boundary between conciliation, family therapy, and the legal process poses fundamental questions of definition and has important implications for the future development of conciliation and the training of conciliators. The legal system aims to provide just and fair settlements based on evidence and facts while having as its paramount concern the best interests of the children. The law and the courts do not necessarily seek to resolve conflict or improve communication, although such benefits are seen as worthy. Lawyers seek to safeguard individual rights and to provide the most advantageous settlement for their clients. Conciliation, on the other hand, aims to give the parties the power to negotiate their own settlements, which may not be in one or the other's best interests, nor necessarily as advantageous a settlement as a court might have determined for them. In addition, conciliation offers other 'quality of life' benefits, highlighting the distinction between the philosophy of law and the philosophy of social welfare. The values and institutional bases render the processes significantly and fundamentally different.

Enabling parties to retain power over their decision-making may rest uneasily with a legal process which is expected to approve settlements in divorce especially in relation to children. If 'reaching agreements' is the focus for conciliation, then there is a potential problem if couples reach socially unacceptable solutions, for example a decision for one parent to cease all contact with a child (Walker 1986c). Little (1982) has suggested that it might be more important to consider what is 'feasible' and to allow families to define fairness in their own way. But how does this sit within a legal framework which endorses the welfare principle of 'best interests'? Conciliators may then explicitly or implicitly guide parents towards socially acceptable solutions. Is Bienenfeld (1985 : 47) correct when she states that 'creating a better outcome for the children is the whole purpose of mediation'? If she is, then does the conciliator determine the 'best interests' of the children and, if so, on what criteria? Should conciliators act as advocates for children, guarding their interests and protecting them from socially unacceptable parental decisions? If families are helped to reach their own agreements whose rights should be considered? What are the limits of family autonomy? Do conciliators start with assumptions about access and about custody? (The legal system operates a presumption in favour of mothers having care and control of children, especially young children.)

If conciliation services advertise themselves as helping *families*, should children and other family members be included? Conciliators will need skills in working with family groups of different shapes and sizes.

> If the concern of the legal system is to minimise the known potential risks of divorce, then this . . . ought to be embodied in the provision of facilities for advice and counselling. . . . This is a task going well beyond present proposals for conciliation services.
>
> (Maidment 1984 : 176)

> In matrimonial cases . . . there is no limit to the hurt people will inflict on one another. . . . There are few conditions of stress so protracted and so personal and

incapable of being shared with other people. . . . Friends are ripped apart, the whole fabric of life is torn. It is unlike any other stress situation.

(Felder 1971 quoted in Saposnek 1983 : 23)

Divorce is a family crisis, a personal trauma and a legal issue of public concern. 'It is a matter of the heart and of the law' (Folberg 1984 : 195). Conciliation has developed as a new service, crossing the boundaries of social welfare and law in an attempt to bridge the gap between family matters and legal process. 'A goal in mediation is to facilitate communication between the separating pair so that they will come to an agreement that will structure their future' (Maida 1986 : 55). Conciliation is not divorce counselling nor family therapy, but rather a unique blend of both, operating in a traditional legal framework. The identity of conciliation has been obscured by its uniqueness and like many emerging interventions it has had to struggle for recognition and acceptance.

Family systems theory and the interventive techniques of family therapy contribute substantially to an understanding of the needs and tasks of families in transition and to ways of resolving difficulties in terms of interactions between family members. 'It is only by adhering to the systems point of view, in which there is typically neither individual truth nor objective reality . . . that the mediator can succeed in resolving the dispute' (Saposnek 1983 : 26). The present range of practices in family conciliation offers the opportunity to fit conciliation to the needs of families, but the struggle for supremacy between professionals is in danger of forcing families to fit the needs of conciliators. We have yet to develop a coherent, unambiguous mode of conciliation practice.

> Developing an understanding of the similarities and differences among current modes of practice can lead to a clearer articulation of the processes and their synthesis, which in turn can improve practice and contribute to theory development in the dispute resolution field.

(Girdner 1986 : 28)

Conciliation does not set out to offer therapy, but by its nature it is often therapeutic. 'A realistic approach of how best to aid the client through the divorce process is needed during this time of expansion of both the fields of therapy and mediation' (Weaver 1986 : 86).

# REFERENCES

Bain, A. (1978). The capacity of families to cope with transitions: a theoretical essay. *Human Relations*, 51, 675–88.
Bentovim, A. and Gilmour, L. (1981). A family therapy interactional approach to decision-making in child care, access and custody cases. *Journal of Family Therapy*, 3, 65–77.

Berenson, G. and White, H. (eds) (1981). *Annual Review of Family Therapy*. New York, Human Sciences Press.

Bienenfeld, F. (1985). The power of child custody mediation. *Mediation Quarterly*, 9, 35–49.

Bohannan, P. (1973). The six stations of divorce. In M.E. Lasswell and T.E. Lasswell (eds) *Love, Marriage and Family: A Developmental Approach*. Illinois, Scott, Foresman.

Brannan, J. and Collard, J. (1982). *Marriages in Trouble*. London, Tavistock.

Brenan, G. (1978) Thoughts in a dry season. In J. Green (1982) *A Dictionary of Contemporary Quotations*. London, Pan.

Brown, G.W. and Harris, T. (1978). *Social Origins of Depression*. London, Tavistock.

Burgoyne, J., Ormrod, R. and Richards, M. (1987). *Divorce Matters*. Harmondsworth, Penguin.

Burnham, J. (1986). *Family Therapy*. London, Tavistock.

Cherlin, A.J. (1981). *Marriage, Divorce, and Remarriage*. Cambridge, Mass., Harvard University Press.

Davis, G. (1981). *A Study of Conciliation: Its Impact on Legal Aid Costs in the Resolution of Disputes Arising out of Divorce*. Bristol, University of Bristol.

Dunlop, R. and Burns, A. (1984). *Adolescents and Divorce: The Experience of Family Break-up*. Unpublished draft report. Australia: Macquerie University, NSW.

Eekelaar, J. and Clive, E. (1977). *Custody After Divorce*. Oxford, ESRC Centre for Socio-Legal Studies.

Elston, E., Fuller, J. and Murch, M. (1975). Judicial hearings of undefended divorce petitions. *Modern Law Review*, 38–609.

Fargo, J. (1986). Academic programs in family mediation: some thoughts from a family life educator. *Mediation Quarterly*, 13, 3–20.

Felder, R.L. (1971). *Divorce: The Way Things Are, Not the Way Things Should Be*. New York, World.

Finer Report (1974). *Report of the Committee on One-Parent Families*. London, HMSO.

Folberg, H.J. (1984). Divorce mediation: the emerging American model. In J. Eekelaar and S.N. Katz (eds) *The Resolution of Family Conflict: Comparative Legal Perspectives*. Toronto, Butterworths.

Froiland, D.J. and Hozman, T.L. (1977). Counseling for constructive divorce. *Personnel and Guidance Journal*, 55, 525–9.

Gaddis, S.M. (1978). Divorce decision-making: alternatives to litigation. *Conciliation Courts Review*, 16, 43–5.

Gibson, C. (1980). Divorce and the recourse to legal aid. *Modern Law Review*, 43.

Girdner, L.K. (1986). Family mediation: toward a synthesis. *Mediation Quarterly*, 13, 21–31.

Gold, L. (1985). Reflections on the transition from therapist to mediator. *Mediation Quarterly*, 9, 15–26.

Grebe, S.C. (1986). A comparison of the tasks and definitions of family mediation and those of strategic family therapy. *Mediation Quarterly*, 13, 53–61.

Gurin, G., Veroff, J. and Field, S. (1960). *America Looks at its Mental Health*. New York, Basic Books.

Haley, J. (1976). *Problem-Solving Therapy*. San Francisco, Jossey-Bass.

Hart, N. (1976). *When Marriage Ends*. London, Tavistock.

Haskey, J. (1982). The proportion of marriages ending in divorce. *Population Trends*, 27. London, HMSO.

—— (1983). Children of divorcing couples. *Population Trends*, 31, 20 and 25.

—— (1984). Social class and socio-economic differentials in divorce in England and Wales. *Population Studies*, 38, Table 7.

Haynes, J. (1981). *Divorce Mediation*. New York, Springer.

Hunt, P.A. (1985). *Clients' Responses to Marriage Counselling*. Rugby, National Marriage Guidance Council.

Inglis, R. (1982). *Must Divorce Hurt the Children?* London, Maurice Temple Smith.

Irving, H. (1981). *Divorce Mediation: A Rational Alternative to the Adversary System*. New York, Universe Books.

Itzin, C. (1980). *Splitting Up: Single Parent Liberation*. London, Virago.

Johnson, S.M. and Alevizos, P.N. (1978). *Divorce Adjustment: Clinical and Survey Research (Preliminary Report)*. Oregon, University of Oregon.

Kaslow, F.W. (1981). Divorce and divorce therapy. In A.S. Gurman and D.P. Kniskern (eds) *Handbook of Family Therapy*. New York, Brunner/Mazel.

Keeney, B.P. and Ross, J.M. (1985). *Mind in Therapy: Constructing Systemic Family Therapies*. New York, Basic Books.

Kessler, S. (1975). *The American Way of Divorce: Prescription for Change*. Chicago, Ill., Nelson-Hall.

Kressel, K. and Deutsch, M. (1977). Divorce therapy: an in-depth survey of therapists' views. *Family Process*, 16, 413–33.

Kübler-Ross, E. (1969). *On Death and Dying*. New York, Macmillan.

Law Commission (1966). *Reform of the Grounds of Divorce: The Field of Choice*. Cmnd 3123. London, HMSO.

—— (1986a). *Family Law: Review of Child Law: Custody*. Working Paper 96. London, HMSO.

—— (1986b). *Family Law: Review of Child Law: Custody: Custody Law in Practice in the Divorce and Domestic Courts*. J.A. Priest and J.C. Whybrow, supplement to Working Paper 96. London, HMSO.

Lemmon, J.A. (1985). *Family Mediation Practice*. New York, Free Press.

Leupnitz, D.A. (1983). *Child Custody: A Study of Families after Divorce*. Lexington, Mass., Lexington Books.

Little, M. (1982). *Family Breakup*. San Francisco, Jossey-Bass.

Lund, M. (1984). Research on divorce and children. *Family Law*, 14, 198–201.

Maida, P.R. (1986). Components of Bowen's family theory and divorce mediation. *Mediation Quarterly*, 12, 51–63.

Maidment, S. (1976). A study in child custody. *Family Law*, 6, 200.

—— (1984). *Child Custody and Divorce*. Beckenham, Kent, Croom Helm.

Minuchin, S. and Fishman, H.C. (1981). *Family Therapy Techniques*. Cambridge, Mass., Harvard University Press.

Mitchell, A. (1981). *Someone to Turn to: Experiences of Help before Divorce*. Aberdeen, Aberdeen University Press.

—— (1985). *Children in the Middle: Living Through Divorce*. London, Tavistock.

Mnookin, R. (1983). Divorce bargaining: the limits on private ordering. In J. Eekelaar and S.N. Katz (eds) *The Resolution of Family Conflict: Comparative Legal Perspectives*. Toronto, Butterworths.

Murch, M. (1980). *Justice and Welfare in Divorce*. London, Sweet & Maxwell.

OPCS (1985). *Population Monitor*, FM2 1985/1, Tables 1, 56 and 7 (includes 755 annulments of marriage). London, HMSO.

Parkinson, L. (1985a). Divorce counselling. In W. Dryden (ed.) *Marital Therapy in Britain. 2. Special Areas*. London, Harper & Row.

—— (1985b). Conciliation in separation and divorce. In W. Dryden (ed.) *Marital Therapy in Britain. 2. Special Areas*. London, Harper & Row.

—— (1986). *Conciliation in Separation and Divorce: Finding Common Ground.* Beckenham, Kent, Croom Helm.

Practice Direction on Matrimonial Conciliation (1971). 27 January. All ER 894 (1971) 14 WLR 223.

Robinson, M. and Parkinson, L. (1985). A family systems approach to conciliation in separation and divorce. *Journal of Family Therapy*, 7, 357–77.

Roman, M. and Haddad, W. (1978). *The Disposable Parent: The Case for Joint Custody.* New York, Holt, Rinehart & Winston.

Rowlands, P. (1980). *Saturday Parent.* London, Allen & Unwin.

Salts, C.J. (1979). Divorce process: integration of theory. *Journal of Divorce*, 2, 233–40.

Sander, F.E. (1984). Introduction. Towards a functional analysis of family process. In J. Eekelaar and S.N. Katz (eds). *The Resolution of Family Conflict: Comparative Legal Perspectives.* Toronto, Butterworths.

Saposnek, D.T. (1983). *Mediating Child Custody Disputes. A Systematic Guide for Family Therapists, Court Counselors, Attorneys, and Judges.* San Francisco, Jossey-Bass.

Scale, S. (1984). *Children in Divorce: A Study of Information Available to the Scottish Court on Children Involved in Divorce.* Edinburgh, Scottish Office Central Research Unit.

*Social Trends* (1983). Central Statistical Office. London, HMSO.

Street, E. (1985). From child-focused problems to marital issues. In W. Dryden (ed.) *Marital Therapy in Britain. 2. Special Areas.* London, Harper & Row.

Tyler, L. (1961). *The Work of the Counselor.* New York, Appleton-Century-Crofts.

Walczac, Y. with Burns, S. (1984). *Divorce: The Child's Point of View.* London, Harper & Row.

Walker, J. (1986a) Divorce mediation: an overview from three countries – Great Britain. In J.P. McCrory (1987). *The Role of Mediation in Divorce Proceedings: A Comparative Perspective – United States, Canada and Great Britain.* Vermont, Canada, Vermont Law School.

—— (1986b). Assessment in divorce conciliation: issues and practice. *Mediation Quarterly*, 11, 43–57.

—— (1986c). Divorce mediation: is it a better way? In J.P. McCrory (1987). *The Role of Mediation in Divorce Proceedings: A Comparative Perspective – United States, Canada and Great Britain.* Vermont, Canada, Vermont Law School.

Wallerstein, J. and Kelly, J. (1981). *Surviving the Breakup: How Children and Parents Cope with Divorce.* London, Grant McIntyre.

Weaver, J. (1986). Therapeutic implications of divorce mediation. *Mediation Quarterly*, 12, 75–90.

Weisman, R.S. (1975). Crisis theory and the process of divorce. *Social Casework*, 56, 205–12.

Weiss, R.S. (1975). *Marital Separation.* New York, Basic Books.

Woolley, P. (1979). *The Custody Handbook.* New York, Summit Books.

CHAPTER 12

# FAMILY THERAPY AND ETHNIC MINORITIES

## *Annie Lau*

## INTRODUCTION – THE TASK FACING FAMILY THERAPISTS

This chapter explores the tensions in the interface between British family therapists and their client families from an ethnic minority group. It is suggested that an attitudinal shift is necessary on the part of family therapists in order to mobilize strengths in family systems rooted in value orientations different from therapists' own backgrounds. Theoretical assumptions about the nature of dysfunctional families may need to be modified.

British therapists working with ethnic minority families may be handicapped by a number of factors. They will not possess the same world view as their client families; they will not be aware of how normality and pathology are culturally defined; how the prevailing belief system organizes the perceptions and behaviour of the group; what is idiosyncratic, and would be accepted by the group as being deviant, and what is culturally sanctioned behaviour. They will not be familiar with culturally prescribed rules for sex roles and family roles, and how they are different from rules deriving from a Western European cultural context. Furthermore, they may be hampered by difficulties in communicating with the family if they are not fluent in English. Should they use an interpreter or rely on a relative to translate? What is the relevant family network and who should be invited to an initial meeting?

Here are a few case examples.

## Example 1

A social worker is faced with a Black male adolescent from a single-parent family, who is 'out of control'. He is delinquent and does not go to school. This generates considerable anxiety in the professional network. The social worker takes on the role of rescuer and relieves his anxiety about the case by quickly removing the boy from home on a place of safety order. There was no attempt to help the mother mobilize her social network supports, or even to check out the nature of these supports. For the social worker, the fact that the biological father did not live at home meant an absence of male authority in the family. A confrontative situation is set up; the mother becomes defensive and angry, and becomes labelled as paranoid and unworkable. She relinquishes responsibility for her son. Examples like these are reflected in the disproportionate high rate of admissions into care of young Black people.

## Example 2

A Muslim girl is told by her family that for her, marriage takes priority over plans for a career. She attempts to rebel, is locked in the house and hit by her father and brothers. Desperate, she goes to see a social worker who removes her to a hostel. This creates a permanent gulf between the girl and her family. The social worker felt justified in her intervention as she was acting on an assumption based on her cultural norms, that of the young person's right to self-determination. But what of the client's long-term interests? How far can she survive on her own?

## Example 3

The Muslim parents of a 6-year-old leukaemic child refuse to allow medical treatment for their child, stating as their reason their 'belief in the wisdom of Allah'. Medical staff who are involved accept the parents' position as truly reflecting Islamic belief, without checking out from Muslim colleagues whether this would be in accordance with the teachings of Islam. Valuable time is lost in debating the relative merits of 'respecting one's patients' belief systems' while usually competent therapists, now deskilled by confrontation with an 'unfamilar belief system', stand by helplessly instead of exploring other psychologically based reasons for the parents' attitude.

Confronted with the uncomfortable and disorientating impact of another ethnocultural group, British therapists sometimes respond by attempting to acquire factual information about the cultural practices of their ethnic client families. This can be both limiting and overwhelming, leaving the therapists with a range of static cultural and racial stereotypes. Cultural data can make sense only within the system of cultural meanings of the group (Ballard 1982), through an understanding of how the elements of a culture are integrated into a meaningful whole.

Another common response is to take a 'cultural relativist' position: that all unfamiliar behaviour, just because it apparently conforms to cultural patterns and beliefs, is normal. 'It's the way these people are.' With regard to the question of delusions, Devereux (1980) stresses the difference between traditional belief and subjective experience. It is one thing to believe in the existence of the Devil, a belief shared by other members of one's group; quite another when the belief is transformed into a subjective experience, of a delusional type, as when one hears the Devil's voice and feels controlled by him.

How does one acquire the intellectual tools with which to make sense of the unfamiliar patterns presented by 'ethnic' clients? Existing anthropological literature is viewed with suspicion and mistrust. Sashidharan reminds us of the political context in which anthropology and transcultural psychiatry developed in the late nineteenth and early twentieth century – a time of 'subjugation and colonisation of black people in most of Africa and Asia by European nations' (Sashidharan 1986 : 169). He suggests that when Kraepelin, the father of comparative psychiatry, wrote about 'racial characteristics' of the Javanese (lack of responsibility, linguistic poverty, the absence of deep self-reflection, and so on (Kraepelin 1904 : 166) he was 'clearly articulating the pervasive notions about non-European cultures that prevailed in his day'. Similarly early anthropological studies, at the outposts of the empire, served the interests of colonial administrations. British therapists are heirs to these academic and historical traditions, with their Eurocentric bias. As members of the dominant group in British society, they do not experience directly the frustrations of racial harassment and disadvantage. It is important that these factors be taken into account, in considering the attitudinal shift that needs to occur in current family therapy theory and practice in Britain.

To what extent do our values and beliefs, rooted in the culture in which we were socialized, influence our therapeutic hypotheses and plans for intervention? Do our theoretical assumptions encompass the different role expectations of family members from family systems with different value orientations? In order to be able to mobilize strengths and competencies in families originating from a different cultural patterning to our own, we have to be aware of what these strengths are.

# ETHNOCULTURAL DIFFERENCES IN SYMBOLIC BELIEF SYSTEMS AND VALUE ORIENTATIONS

The ideas, myths and beliefs of the culture influence perceptions of appropriate sex and family role behaviour, the explanation and experience of health and illness, definitions of normality and deviance. This ideational plane (Seltzer and Seltzer 1983) determines what impulses and fantasies can become conscious and which must be suppressed (Devereux 1980). Different cultures provide guidelines for how to be acceptably deviant, within a pattern recognized by the culture (Linton 1936). For example, among traditional Chinese of all social classes, depressive affects are frequently somatized (Kleinman 1980). The tendency for somatization is also reported in other ethnic groups including African (Binitie 1975), Indian (Gada 1982) and Afghan (Waziri 1973). Culture-bound syndromes are described, with origins based on cultural beliefs, for example in the sexual neuroses in young Indian and Chinese adults. In Indian and Chinese belief, semen possesses physical and mental vigour and longevity and frequent loss of seminal fluid is harmful (Rao 1986). These culture-bound syndromes are none the less 'representations in the individual of symbolic themes concerning social relations', and 'articulate both personal predicament and public concerns' (Littlewood 1986 : 49). Littlewood also suggests that the western social context of parasuicide has close parallels with non-European culture bound reactions.

Value orientations that are culturally determined organize the individual's view of the proper relationship between self and context – the surrounding world. Lin (1986), in contrasting fundamental differences in conceptions of human beings and their relationship to their environment, reflected both in idea and practice, compares inherent assumptions of western and Chinese belief. I have paraphrased his discussion in Table 12.1. Highly similar values for Indian society are described by Rao (1986).

The organizing principle for the traditional Chinese family is that of filial piety, where loyalties to one's parents take precedence over loyalties to spouse and children. These ideas are continually reinforced in socialization processes in childhood and form part of the egoideal of the adult (Erikson 1968). In the Chinese People's Republic the principle of filial obligations was upheld in the Marriage Law, 1981, where penalties are laid down for failure to honour obligations to parents and other needy family members (Hare-Mustin 1982).

Value orientations determine structural relationships. It is, therefore, not surprising that family organization following the ideal of the pre-eminence of the group would be along extended family lines. In turn, this form of

Table 12.1   Differences in basic assumptions of 'self'

| Western view of 'self' | Chinese view of 'self' |
| --- | --- |
| 1 A person is a separate unit from his or her family and is expected to feel and act on his or her own accord and take personal responsibility. | A person is a relational being, who feels and acts in harmony with the larger unit (family, clan). |
| 2 The human/environment relationship is characterized by open assertiveness and competition. | The proper human/environment relationship is characterized by harmony and synchrony. |
| 3 The mind and body are separate and dichotomized. | The mind/body relationship is a unitary concept reflected in basic premises in Chinese food and medicine. |
| 4 Self-fulfilment depends on 'doing'; action, assertiveness, mastery and control of the environment. | Self-fulfilment is dependent on 'being'; adjustment to an external pattern of which one is an integrated part. |
| 5 Time orientation towards the future. | Time orientation towards understanding the past in order to perpetuate it; conformity to the proper historical precedent of behaviour will restore health and well-being. |
| 6 Verbal, direct communication highly-emphasized. | Reliance on non-verbal communication, or symbolic figurative expressions. |

family organization would also maintain, and perpetuate, its own value orientations through example and practice.

In contrast, family organization following the ideal of the primacy of the individual will, of necessity, be the nuclear family. This is reflected in current definitions of family competence, and associated research into family functioning. For example Lewis and Looney are clear that the selection of family tasks in the assessment of family competence is based on value judgements of the researchers, use of the term 'competence'. 'A family "ought" to raise children who become autonomous, and it "should" provide sufficient emotional support for stabilizing the parents' personalities' (Lewis and Looney 1983 : 4); also, that a family 'ought to function in a way that provides family members with a balance of separateness and attachment consistent with the greatest probability of individual family members' adaptive success at different phases of life' (1983 : 4). I feel these definitions do not incorporate the concept of the network of binding obligations found in groups with highly structured kinship systems. A competent Asian or Chinese family must also produce children who will look after their aged parents, and both recognize and fulfil their obligations to the wider family in such a way that the family honour is preserved, or better still enhanced. Also, the concept of 'family' is not one bounded by two generations. The significant family to which the Asian or Oriental has important obligations *includes* the grandparents and adult siblings.

## ETHNOCULTURAL DIFFERENCES IN LANGUAGE AND COMMUNICATION

Where language is a difficulty, a proper assessment of the family's needs and strengths becomes very difficult. The reader is referred to Shackman (1983) for a thorough discussion of the subject of interpreters. In my own practice I will not attempt to do an assessment unless the interpreter is someone who understands the theoretical and conceptual base from which I am working (for example another colleague) or is a professionally trained interpreter (such as a court interpreter). Family therapy techniques which require that the therapist be closely in touch with the emotional experience in the room, for example unbalancing techniques, are not , I feel, possible without direct access to the family. There are also difficulties in modes of communication. The western-trained therapist's expectation of clear, direct verbal communication is often at variance with communicational styles where direct communication and confrontation are avoided as they may lead to 'loss of face within the group' (McGoldrick *et al.* 1982). Even where the 'shared language' is English, the therapist may not be familiar with dialect, accents (e.g. Afro-Caribbean), or meanings of words (e.g. 'chastisement' as used by Black Afro-Caribbean families). It is important then for the therapist to be aware of culturally determined communicational forms congruent for the group. If there is any doubt, the therapist must consult with a 'cultural interpreter'.

# THE FAMILY LIFE CYCLE – DIFFERENCES IN DEVELOPMENTAL TASKS IN TRADITIONAL, HIERARCHICAL FAMILIES

## Childhood

Respect and obedience for traditional cultural values are reinforced by the way the child is socialized.

> Childrearing practices in Chinese culture are not based on the notion of assisting the child to separate but rather on staying with, and maintaining, strong family ties with ancestors, current family members, and future generations.
>
> (Yung 1984 : 111)

Multiple care-taking (Asuni 1986; Bassa 1978) is common. Strong attachments are formed from early childhood with grandparents, uncles, aunts and cousins, providing a wider variety of models for age and sex-role identification. Frequent and regular contact, often ritualized, as in weekend family meals for the Asian, Chinese or Jewish child, reinforces the principle that 'self-fulfilment is to be sought for and found within the family, not in a frantic search for love outside it' (Bassa 1978 : 335). Children learn time-honoured strategies for tension diffusion and control of aggression that allows the extended family group to survive as a unit. They also learn, from the example set by their elders, of their place in the family and their expected obligations.

## Adolescence

Adolescents of families where the parents originate from traditional hierarchical societies often find themselves expected to conform to cultural norms of correct behaviour. They find themselves in a marginal position, caught between traditional values at home and a differing set of expectations from the school environment where the values are those of the dominant group. The majority of these adolescents resolve this difference by choosing friends of the same ethnic group (Field 1984) and identification with their own ethnicity becomes an important source of self-respect. They also learn the behavioural repertoires appropriate to the different contexts of home, work and school (Ballard 1982). They are not expected, however, to undergo the experience of leaving home (Haley 1980), after formal education. Many Asian girls, for example, would be expected to live at home until they get married. Separation issues are negotiated in an entirely different context from those in Western European, nuclear-type families. However, where the balance between differentiation and interdependence is not worked out in an egosyntonic manner for the adolescent, behaviour problems can present, often acutely and dramatically.

# Marriage
*Arranged marriages*
It is generally accepted that stage-specific family tasks for the life cycle phase of marriage must include the following:

1 The couple must separate from parents of origin and emotionally invest in their own relationship.
2 The couple must work out a mutually satisfactory distribution of power.
3 They must develop a mutually satisfying level of psychological intimacy.

(Lewis and Looney 1983)

How valid are these ideas for the young couple in an arranged marriage, from a culture where extended family traditions are paramount, such as in a Pakistani family? Let us consider the assumptions that are inherent in the arranged marriage. It is the task of parents of an eligible son first to screen applicants and to prepare a shortlist of girls from suitable families, from which the son makes a choice. Socio-economic considerations, career matching and family compatibility are all important, as well as the girl's reputation for unblemished behaviour. The marriage is indeed a marriage of two families, as the young couple will not have had enough time to develop a relationship of psychological intimacy. 'Falling in love' will have to wait until after the marriage ceremony. The young wife will in the majority of instances be expected to reside with her mother-in-law in a joint household. Here, the mother-in-law will, at least initially, be dominant, and make the major domestic decisions as a matter of right. The new wife's psychological survival in this new household will depend on her ability to establish emotional rapport with her mother-in-law, and those of her sisters-in-law who live in the same household. Early on she will also have to work out power relations with her mother-in-law and sisters-in-law, where a formal hierarchy dependent on age often exists.

The first year of the arranged marriage is also the time when the family network on both sides must provide safe boundaries for the new marriage. It is not uncommon, and quite socially acceptable, for young wives to return to their mothers for a cooling-off period during the first year when adjustment problems to the new family become acute. This usually signals a time when the wider family on both sides can help guide the couple over early marital stresses, or relationship difficulties with in-laws. Elders are empowered to intervene in marital arguments and suggest possible solutions. This buffering system is important in the mechanics of tension diffusion and the control of aggression within the family. The absence of this network often leads to high levels of stress, particularly where individuals are already vulnerable. With these expectations in mind the young wife enters marriage knowing that it is a union of two families, and that her own kinship system provides for her an important source of strength and support.

Attempts to sabotage and undermine this structure, as for example the prescription that the young couple should establish their own boundary which excludes mother-in-law, inevitably lead to conflict and withdrawal from therapy. It ignores the authority structure that is culturally prescribed and comes across to the family as alien and incongrous.

It can be seen that stage-specific family tasks at this life cycle phase in an arranged marriage must include the family's capacity to integrate the new bride into its fold. The two most important elements are

1 The development of mutually supportive relationships between the new wife and important figures in the female network.
2 The availability of the wider family on both sides for ongoing negotiations should the need arise.

These tasks are not found in nuclear family systems developed in a Western European context, where young couples are expected to be self-sufficient and to be responsible for their own decisions.

*Mixed marriages*
Intermarriage breaks the old patterns and continuity of a system, while opening the way to new and creative changes. Intermarriages can also produce symptomatic children who cannot reconcile the diversity in the parental background and become caught in the family and parental conflict over which cultural traditions, values and loyalties are more important (Lau 1984; Cohen 1982). Ethnic characteristics can be viewed by the other partner or the in-laws as negative personality traits, especially different styles of emotional expression and communication. Cultural differences in expected roles of husband and wife and how power is distributed and exercised, as well as kinship obligations of the spouse, may not have been sufficiently appreciated and worked through by the partners of a mixed marriage. McGoldrick and Preto (1984) argued that important factors, influencing the degree of adjustment required in ethnic intermarriage, included the following:

1 The extent of difference in values between the cultural groups involved.
2 Differences in the degree of acculturation of each spouse.
3 Religious differences.
4 Racial differences.
5 Sex of spouse, and whether work connections exist, which aid adaptation to this culture.
6 Socio-economic and class differences.
7 The couple's preparation for marriage and knowledge of each other's cultural context.

8 The degree of resolution of emotional issues regarding the intermarriage in both families prior to the wedding, i.e. the couple's permission to marry.

## The aged

In traditional societies elderly people are expected to be cared for by their families and old age confers dignity and respect. In Britain, however, the 'ethnic aged' may be subjected to a variety of stresses not found in the emigrant communities. There may be losses of friends and personal networks in the face of a reduced flexibility in coping responses. The aged person who is the head of household may find him or herself confronted by systems that he or she does not understand. For example, elderly people may not be used to social workers and their statutory powers, particularly if they come from a rural environment, and furthermore their authority is reduced by having to depend on the translation abilities of junior family members fluent in English. Confused elderly people in hospital are also likely to become even more disoriented in alien surroundings unresponsive to their linguistic and dietary needs.

## FAMILY ORGANIZATION

### Asian and African extended families

Despite differences in detail between the post-figurative family systems found in Asia and Africa (Mead 1970), there are important differences, compared to Western European nuclear-family-type systems, in the construction of 'family' as a concept, and the role of the individual within the family. Individuation, personal autonomy and self-sufficiency take second place to interdependence and the need to preserve harmonious family relationships. This has led to the development of family structures that do not conform with Western European norms. Life cycle transitions and discontinuities are managed in the context of different rules with regard to issues of authority, continuity and interdependence. In such families, for example the Asian or Oriental family, relationships are hierarchical between the sexes as well as between the generations (Ballard 1982). Authority is invested in grandparents, or most senior male member; elder siblings are differentiated from younger siblings and expected to exercise authority over them. Breaks are not expected between the experience of the generations and the presence of the aged provides the necessary continuity in the family and a model for the young. Kinship systems are often highly structured, with kinship terms delineating the individual's place, duties and expected obligations in the family. Ballard suggests these 'networks of binding relationships are often the most appropriate focus for an understanding of the family' (Ballard 1982 : 10). Religion may be an important organizing factor as in Islam, where strict guidelines exist for family and sex role behaviour, including segregation between the sexes (purdah).

Extended family groupings are often found in the same household. Even if they do not all live together, contact between family members is still close and frequent. The system of expected reciprocal obligations and clearly worked out role relationships serves as a binding and cohesive force holding the family together. The management of intergenerational conflict in these families must take account of the linear authority patterns, as well as important key relationships with a protective and buffering function not found in Western European nuclear families, such as the mother-in-law/daughter-in-law relationship. An example at this point may be useful.

A social worker reported, as evidence of an Asian (Hindu) father's lack of interest in his difficult and mildly delinquent 15-year-old son, the fact that father wanted him disposed of by being placed in care so that father could go home to India. Further exploration with the family revealed that the father was the eldest son in his family and his presence in India was needed in order to provide his own father, who had just died, with a proper funeral. The delinquent son felt disowned by his family and was testing this by saying that he wanted to change his religion and become a Muslim like his mates; to the family it represented a total rejection of his duties as a son, as this would disqualify him from performing proper burial rites on his own father. The social worker's failure to recognize the significance of the son's role in this family, particularly around the time of the grandfather's death, meant that he was not in touch with issues crucial to the understanding of this family's difficulties, that would have enabled him to feel usefully engaged with the family.

## West Indian family organization

The West Indian extended family functions by different rules compared to the extended family of Asia and Africa. In working-class families blood relationships of either father or mother, more commonly mother, are stressed rather than the husband/wife relationship (Henriques 1949). In the West Indies these consanguineous family groupings exhibit a high degree of stability and continuity over a long period. There is a strong sense of kin beyond that of the immediate family; unlike Asian and African families, functional relationships are not necessarily defined by kinship (Littlewood and Lipsedge 1982). Informal living arrangements, for example long-standing common-law relationships, can often confer on to individuals the rights, responsibilities and authority associated with formal relationships in white or Asian families. For example, the most senior woman in a Black extended family may be grandfather's long-standing co-habitee, who is regarded as the matriarch of the family. Next to her in the hierarchy may follow several godmothers, who may strongly influence executive decisions made by parents on their children.

There is no single type of structure characteristic of Black families. Existing literature on Afro-Caribbean families, mainly from the USA, stresses the heterogeneity in structure and function found in Black families. In response to the turbulent history and deprivations experienced by Blacks in the New World, particular strengths and resiliences have been developed (Hill 1972). These include:

1 role adaptability by family members,
2 strong kinship bonds,
3 strong work orientation,
4 strong religious orientation and
5 strong achievement orientation.

The role adaptability of the single-parent West Indian mother needs to be recognized as a measure of strength. In conditions where West Indian men have felt demoralized, West Indian women have had to assume a strong role as an adaptive response. She has had to compensate for the undermining of the father/husband role, due to lack of education, unemployment and inability to protect his family. The single-parent West Indian mother has traditionally used many supports external to the family, including god-mothers, neighbourhood networks and the Church. Her own family net-work links, and her sense of connectedness with her own family, must be healthy and functioning in order that she can facilitate her children's autonomous growth and mastery of problems. Individuals called 'uncles', 'aunts' and 'cousins' by family members can be important in that they support parental authority and provide role models for identification for children in their formative years. They may have been closely associated with the family for many years despite no formal kinship ties. Where these networks of strength and support have changed, or been lost, in order to help mobilize new coping strategies, the family therapist must be aware of the nature of the losses.

# THERAPEUTIC STRATEGIES FOR CULTURALLY CONGRUENT INTERVENTIONS

I have found the following checklist a useful guide in covering the ethnic dynamic in family assessment (McGoldrick *et al.* 1982):

1 What belief systems or value orientations (including religion) influence role expectations and define and set limits of appropriate behaviour?

2 What life cycle phase is the family at?
3 What is the relevant (significant) family network to be convened? What are the structures relevant to authority and decision-making in the family? What are the kinship patterns? What are the key relationships with important supportive and homeostatic functions?
4 What activities maintain and support structural relationships?
5 What are significant stresses and losses
   ● arising out of the family's own experience;
   ● from environment of origin;
   ● from adaptation to host country?
6 Do the clinical hypotheses take into account the meaning and function of symptoms and behaviour to the family, its cultural group, and the wider cultural framework?
7 Do the therapeutic interventions support the authority structure within the client family, and are they congruent with the family's world-view?

It is important to be aware of the family's *specific* ethnic and religious background (Spiegel 1968), and how the cultural rules influence family organization and authority structures. Within each ethnic group there will be a range of variation from traditional hierarchical families to more modern, egalitarian structures, and the family will need to be located along this continuum. There will also be significant stresses arising out of the family's own historical experience of discontinuities, both in the environment of origin as well as arising out of adaptation to Britain, that will be different for different ethnic groups. For example, Vietnamese refugees in Britain are still not in a position to form self-help groups, unlike other groups, and many still live with recent memories of severe trauma, including torture (Lau 1986). For many Vietnamese adults the continuing separation from their aged parents, who may be dispersed in China or Vietnam, will be incompatible with a genuine sense of security in their adopted country, and will interfere with their emotional capacity to tolerate adolescent demands in their children. Many Asian groups still have strong links with their emigrant communities in the Asian subcontinent. At the time of writing, the majority of the adults and heads of households in Asian families originate from emigrant communities, and conflict over cultural values when it does arise, occurs mainly with adolescent children born in the UK. Ballard (1982) suggests the ethnicity of the second generation differs from that of the parents, in that the tendency is towards the establishment of an overarching Asian ethnic group, while the concerns of the first generation were in terms of the narrow loyalties of the homelands, based on caste and kinship. Marital stresses, particularly in arranged marriages, are difficult to contain away from the extended family network. Each family will have a different pattern of how life cycle transitions were handled that will be unique to the family, but for all families from a particular ethnic group there will be a recognizable range of variation familiar to members of that group.

An assessment needs to be made of existing cultural defences and network and support systems most natural for the family, for example, the Church, neighbourhood and community associations. Where links with the extended family are weak, or where a family is isolated from its ethnic community, the family unit may be more vulnerable to life cycle stresses than the comparable English family. A hypothesis will need to be constructed that takes into account the meaning and function of the disturbing symptoms or behaviour to the family, its cultural group, and the wider cultural network. It is important to stress here that similar issues confront therapists from ethnic minority groups. For example, therapists from the Indian subcontinent may not be sufficiently sensitive to issues of separation in white families with acting-out adolescents. Social workers of Afro-Caribbean origin have been rejected by West African client families, who feel their West Indian social workers do not understand their different family structures and role expectations.

## Use of therapist authority

It is important to use the therapist's authority effectively. Ethnic minority families respond more favourably to therapists who are directive and assertive (Rao 1986; Tseng 1975; Yung 1984) as it conforms to traditional expectations of the learning process, for example the teacher–pupil relationship. Yung (1984) has also described successful problem-solving growth-oriented approaches in structural family work with Chinese families in the USA, in which the therapist is supportive of the parents' traditional beliefs while attempting to modify communication patterns. It is important to maintain generational boundaries that are culturally determined, so as not to alienate the symptomatic individual from the family. The therapist who finds him or herself engaged with the family can then be in a position to reframe the symptomatic family member's response as normal and intelligible in the context of family worries (Lau 1984).

*Example*
Lisa, the 12-year-old daughter of a Greek-Cypriot family, developed worrying anxiety symptoms which included vomiting, crying and 'bizarre' statements to her mother like, 'I feel like I'm a prostitute'. The only event of note that the parents could report was a recent incident in which a classmate had been molested in a local park. Otherwise Lisa was compliant, with no apparent worries or difficulties at home or school. It became clear, however, that if this girl started to behave like her classmates and went out with boys, as girls in her class were beginning to do, this would be regarded as 'impure behaviour'. The parents were insistent that their daughter could not entertain boyfriends until she was betrothed in conformity with traditional norms.

She had previously been extremely popular with her friends, and now was in conflict over such 'normal' requests as going for a walk through the local park with her girlfriends after school as she knew they were likely to meet up with some boys. She had not been able to engage in discussion of any of this with her parents. In working with the family the parents began to understand the stresses their daughter was under and how 'abnormal' her inhibitions were regarded in the cultural context of the school. Lisa was helped to share with her parents how difficult she had found it to be different in her class despite wanting to be a good daughter. If she did what her girlfriends did, she would be 'behaving like a prostitute'. The parents also recognized that the lack of a Greek-Cypriot peer group in the area made it difficult for Lisa to identify with group norms.

## Experiential techniques

Experiential family work aims to help family members experience feelings in their interpersonal context (Byng-Hall 1982) and often introduces new experiences within the session (Madanes and Haley 1977). Sculpting is often effective in mobilizing family members to more productive forms of communication around important affective themes.

*Example 1*
A 15-year-old Asian boy, Aftab, presented in a Secure Unit of a Regional Treatment Centre with a range of 'unmanageable' behaviours including drug abuse, absconding and delinquency. He was described as totally unmotivated and withdrawn by the staff in the Secure Unit. I saw him with his family, who consisted of his mother and adult sisters. Initially there was no communication between Aftab and his family. The women had experienced men in their family as useless and depriving, and in Aftab's youth treated him as a little girl. Taking the family through a series of sculpts at important life cycle phases enabled Aftab's mother and older sisters to see how the anger they had experienced at successive losses and disappointments by various men in the family, for example the father's desertion, had become focused on to Aftab when he started to assert his masculinity a few years ago. The sculpt also enabled Aftab to experience his isolation from the family, to cry, and to reach out to his mother, who took him in her arms. His mother was also enabled in the session to acknowledge Aftab's needs more realistically.

*Example 2*
Gestalt-type techniques can also be used creatively. A Chinese mother found it difficult to mobilize any welfare feelings for her delinquent 14-year-old eldest son, Lee, who she said reminded her of her husband, who had deserted her. I noticed that she was able to enjoy the caresses of her 5-year-old youngest son, who was curled up comfortably on her lap, and

asked her where Lee was at the same age. This enabled her to get in touch with her feelings of loss with regard to Lee, because at the age of 5, Lee was in Hong Kong with her mother-in-law. Lee's mother had been forced by her husband's family to leave Lee, as an infant, with her mother-in-law in order that she could help with the family business in Liverpool. She remembered pining for her 'lost' son, and how this turned to rage when, at a long-awaited reunion with Lee, it turned out that Lee preferred being with his grand-mother, with whom he had spent nearly five years of his childhood.

## Use of cultural metaphors

In transcultural family work, the use of rituals in order to facilitate affective expression has been reported by a number of authors (Levick *et al.* 1981; Scheff 1979). Seltzer and Seltzer (1983) present successful work with Norwegian families using ritualistic interventions – for example funeral and coronation ceremonies, a binding ritual, 'the masking of the witch' – rituals which both concretized and exposed an embedded theme in the family's culture into which they were 'frozen'. Peseschkian (1986), writing from West Germany, uses Middle Eastern stories from his own Bahai Iranian background in a way that engages the growth potential of his families. His stories offer a change of perspective to his families and also present solutions of conflict situations acceptable to the game rules of the culture.

*Example*
A West Indian family was seen in an Observation and Assessment Centre, several years after the mother had died suddenly of asthma. It was obvious that there had been failure to mourn this mother, and the adolescent daughter who had been scapegoated and held responsible for mother's death presented with absconding and delinquent behaviour. Therapeutic attempts to facilitate the mourning process were frustrating, until the widowed father was reported, at a staff meeting, to have been discussing his wife's ghost with a Black kitchen staff member. When this was subsequently explored, the use of this cultural metaphor enabled the family's grief to be approached in a conceptual language that facilitated grief work. They had not felt comfortable talking about ghosts with white staff, or with me, though all family members had held different 'messages' from mother's ghost. Following a successful session in which some of the pain of loss had been openly shared, father said to the children, 'It must have been your mother's ghost asking me to come here today'. He had previously resisted attending sessions.

## Family rituals

Most families have some form of regular family activity which serves the purpose of ensuring continuity and cohesiveness amongst family members.

This special event could be Sunday lunch in an English family, preceded in the morning by church services. For the observing Jewish family, the Friday night dinner provides a focus for a regular family gathering. Many Asian families have a weekend meal in which all extended family members living locally are involved. These regular meeting times are often characterized by a sense of timelessness, of membership being assured by joint participation. Where elements of religious ritual are involved, for example the saying of prayers on the Sabbath, there is a sense of peace and tranquillity which gives added meaning to the event. These family gatherings, however, are also occasions when family dramas can be re-enacted over and over again. For traditional families participation in these family rituals *affirms* one's identity in the family, and the family therapist needs to be aware of its importance. An important approaching family event, for example a wedding in a Greek-Cypriot family, can become a focus for goal-setting. The family may be motivated to work towards resolving its difficulties before the event, so that they could all go to the wedding together, thus preserving 'face' in the community. Religious attendance also falls in the same category: the Black Pentecostal mother with strong church affiliations may feel that her Rastafarian daughter who no longer wishes to go to church with her on Sundays brings unbearable shame to the family.

### Example 1

A 25-year-old Chinese-Vietnamese man, Chan, had spent several months in a psychiatric hospital with depression and psychosomatic symptoms. He was preoccupied with pains in his head and back, and a constant feeling of dizziness. He did not respond to medication of any kind and spent most of his time in bed or wandering aimlessly around the ward. His English was adequate for communication with the staff, who found him impossible to motivate.

Chan was the oldest son in his family, with aged parents and a younger brother still attending school. He had been unable to find employment since arriving in this country and despite showing previous strengths, such as enabling his family to escape Vietnam on a refugee ship, now felt ashamed of not being a good son and provider for his family. He had responded with depressive symptoms and 'illness'. Family sessions which included the aged parents clarified these issues and allowed the old people to communicate their despair and disappointment to him. I suggested to Chan and his family that he was not powerless and there was a possibility for him to return to his rightful place in the family. It was his responsibility to the family to engage in a detailed programme of diet, exercise and occupational therapy which I helped the staff draw up. The diet and exercise regime would strengthen his body, in conformity to Chinese cultural expectations. To formalize the contract, I used a ritual that for traditional Chinese would be considered sacred and binding – I asked Chan to kneel in front of his parents and serve them a cup of tea, and in doing so, commit himself to the programme of rehabilitation that I had proposed. In so doing he could once more restore the link between himself and his family, both past and present. This took place with considerable catharsis of emotions between Chan and his parents. Three months later I heard Chan had responded very well to the programme of mobilization on the ward.

### Example 2

I saw Naranjan and Rajinder, the parents of a 6-month-old baby girl, Tajinder, on a paediatric ward together with a younger sister-in-law, Kuldeep, in response to my request for a family session. The baby, Tajinder, had suffered two recent head injuries. Initially the young mother, Rajinder, was relatively silent and passive. She accepted responsibility for being 'careless' and was anxious to say that everything would be fine; there would be no more accidents to Tajinder, I noticed Kuldeep, the younger sister-in-law, to be much more confident and assertive. She said Rajinder does not talk very much about problems and she was not aware of any difficulties Rajinder had in looking after the children.

The family household in Britain consisted of Naranjan's parents, aged 65 and 50 respectively, and Kulwant (Naranjan's elder brother), Naranjan, Daljit (Naranjan's younger brother), and their families, as well as Naranjan's younger unmarried brother, Paminder, who went to the local technological college. The other siblings were either in India or East Africa. The family jointly owned a business which was managed by the three sons,

*Figure 12.1*   Genogram

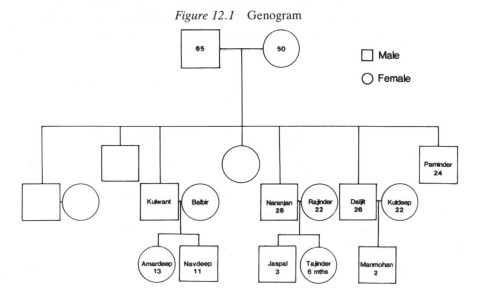

Kulwant, Naranjan and Daljit. The grandparents and Paminder lived with Kulwant and his family. Naranjan and Daljit lived together in an upstairs flat above the shop. The entire family ate together at the weekends.

Naranjan left early in the morning to go to work in the shop with his two brothers. Kuldeep worked in the city, and Rajinder was left at home with her children and Manmohan, Kuldeep's 2-year old. She had found herself overwhelmed with the responsibilities and been unable to share this with her husband and the wider family. There had been some problems around the size of dowry she had brought into the family on marriage; also she felt disliked for various reasons by her mother-in-law. She came from a Ugandan community and her command of English was not equal to her other sisters-in-law, who were brought up in England. She felt under pressure not to complain but to attempt to do a good job. In any case it would have been difficult to complain about her sister-in-law's son's behaviour.

In this context the head injuries were understandable. In the morning she had to change nappies and feed all three children, Jaspal (3), Manmohan (2) and Tajinder (6 months). After this she would go shopping for groceries in the High Street with the children in tow. One day, in the narrow kitchen at the top of the stairs, she had started to put the groceries away when Manmohan pushed against the buggy containing Tajinder, causing it to fall down the narrow flight of stairs adjacent to the kitchen. On another occasion, again after the morning shopping, Tajinder had banged her forehead while rocking violently forward on her rocking seat.

I felt that in order to mobilize family concern from Rajinder's predicament I had to reframe the problem as a family issue. I met with the whole family in their home, and stressed the fact that if another accident occurred it was almost certain that Tajinder would be removed. This would bring shame and dishonour (loss of *izzat* – Ballard 1982) to the family. This was acknowledged by everyone present, and recognized as not merely a problem for Naranjan and Rajinder. The oldest sister-in-law, Balbir, undertook to be more available to Rajinder. The family was then enabled to look at how Rajinder could be more supported in the daily task of looking after three young children.

When I returned in a month's time to see the house there had been obvious improvements. The kitchen had been made safer with a partition wall. Naranjan was more available to his wife in the morning. Kuldeep made sure her son was fed and dressed before she left him with Rajinder. Rajinder was happy, sparkled, and obviously felt supported by the different family moves that had occurred. The strength of the female network of sisters-in-law had obviously been mobilized to ensure that she was not left feeling unsupported, in the interests of family unity and honour.

# CONCLUSION

We see families in crisis, at their most vulnerable. In order to mobilize strengths inherent in family systems different from those in which we were socialized, or to identify important sources of competence, we need to know what they are. That exploration must entail, for the British family therapist from a Western European background, a readiness to see different things, and to make experiential leaps into the unknown. Our failure to do so has meant not only a lamentable lack of adequate provision of appropriate services for ethnic minority families, but also, in many cases, harmful interventions that have led to further isolation of these families through continual reinforcement of negative stereotypes.

# REFERENCES

Asuni, T. (1986). African and Western psychiatry: a comparison. In J.L. Cox (ed.) *Transcultural Psychiatry*. Beckenham, Kent, Croom Helm.

Ballard, R. (1982). South Asian families. In R.H. Rapaport, M.P. Fogarty and R. Rapaport, (eds) *Families in Britain*. London, Routledge & Kegan Paul.

Bassa, D.M. (1978). From the traditional to the modern: some observations on changes in Indian child-rearing and parental attitudes, with special reference to identity formation. In E. James and A.C. Chila (eds) *The Child in his Family: Children and Parents in a Changing World*. New York, Wiley.

Binitie, R. (1975). A factor-analytical study of depression across cultures (African and European). *British Journal of Psychiatry*, 127, 559–63.

Byng-Hall, J. (1982). Dysfunctions of feeling: experiential life of the family. In A. Bentovim, G. Gorell Barnes and A. Cooklin (eds) *Family Therapy, Complementary Frameworks of Theory and Practice*, vol. 1. London, Academic Press.

Cohen, N. (1982). Same or different? A problem of identity in cross-cultural marriages. *Journal of Family Therapy*, 4, 177–99.

Devereux, G. (1980). *Basic Problems of Ethnopsychiatry*. Trans. by B. Miller Gulati and G. Devereux. Chicago, Ill., University of Chicago Press.

Erikson, E. (1968). *Identity, Youth and Crisis*. New York, Norton.

Field, S. (1984). *The Attitudes of Ethnic Minorities*. Home Office Research Studies, Report 80. London, HMSO.

Gada, M.T. (1982). A cross-cultural study of symptomatology of depression: Eastern versus Western patients. *International Journal of Social Psychiatry*, 28, 195–202.

Haley, J. (1980). *Leaving Home: The Therapy of Disturbed Young People*. New York, McGraw-Hill.

Hare-Mustin, R.T. (1982). China's marriage law: a model for family responsibilities and relationships. *Family Process*, 21, 477–81.

Henriques, F. (1949). West Indian family organisation. *American Journal of Sociology*, 55, 30–7.

Hill, R. (1972). *The Strengths of Black Families*. New York, Emerson-Hall.

Kleinman, A. (1980). *Patients and Healers in the Context of Culture*. Berkeley, Calif., University of California Press.

Kraepelin, E. (1904). Vergleichende Psychiatrie, *Zentbl-Nervenheilk Psychiat.*, 27, 433–7. Transl. as Comparative psychiatry. In S.R. Hirsch and M. Shepherd (eds) (1974) *Themes and Variations in European Psychiatry*. Bristol, John Wright.

Lau, A. (1984). Transcultural issues in family therapy. *Journal of Family Therapy*, 6, 91–112.

—— (1986). Family therapy across cultures. In J.L. Cox (ed.) *Transcultural Psychiatry*. Beckenham, Kent, Croom Helm.

Levick, S.E., Jalali, B. and Strauss, J.S. (1981). Onions and tears; a multi-dimensional analysis of a counter-ritual. *Family Process*, 20, 77–83.

Lewis, J.M. and Looney, J.G. (1983). *The Long Struggle: Well-Functioning Working-Class Black Families*. New York, Brunner/Mazel.

Lin, T.Y. (1986). Multiculturalism and Canadian psychiatry: opportunities and challenges. *Canadian Journal of Psychiatry*, 31, (7), 681–90.

Linton, R.N. (1936). *The Study of Man*. New York, Appleton-Century-Crofts.

Littlewood, R. (1986). Russian dolls and Chinese boxes: an anthropological approach to the implicit models of comparative psychiatry. In J.L. Cox (ed.) *Transcultural Psychiatry*. Beckenham, Kent, Croom Helm.

Littlewood, R. and Lipsedge, M. (1982). *Aliens and Alienists*. Harmondsworth, Penguin.

McGoldrick, M., Pearce, J.K. and Giordana, J. (eds) (1982). *Ethnicity and Family Therapy*. New York, Guilford.

McGoldrick, M. and Preto, N.B. (1984). Ethnic intermarriage: implications for therapy. *Family Process*, 23, 347–64.

Madanes, C. and Haley, J. (1977). Dimensions of family therapy. *Journal of Nervous and Mental Disease*, 165, 2, 88–98.

Mead, M. (1970). *Culture and Commitment: A Study of the Generation Gap*. Garden City, NY, Natural History Press/Doubleday.

Peseschkian, N. (1986). *Positive Family Therapy: The Family as Therapist*. Berlin/ Heidelberg, Springer-Verlag.

Rao, A.V. (1986). Indian and Western psychiatry: a comparison. In J.L. Cox (ed.) *Transcultural Psychiatry*. Beckenham, Kent, Croom Helm.

Sashidharan, S.P. (1986). Ideology and politics in transcultural psychiatry. In J.L. Cox (ed.) *Transcultural Psychiatry*. Beckenham, Kent, Croom Helm.

Scheff, T.J. (1979). *Catharsis in Healing, Ritual and Drama*. Berkeley, Calif., University of California Press.

Seltzer, W.J. and Seltzer, M.R. (1983). Material, myth, and magic: a cultural approach to family therapy. *Family Process*, 22, 3–14.

Shackman, J. (1983). *The Right to be Understood. A Handbook on Working with, Employing and Training Community Interpreters*. Cambridge, National Extension College.

Spiegel, J.P. (1968). Cultural strain, family role patterns and intrapsychic conflict. In J.G. Howelles (ed.) *Theory and Practice of Family Psychiatry*. London, Oliver & Boyd.

Tseng, W. (1975). The nature of somatic complaints among psychiatric patients: the Chinese case. *Comprehensive Psychiatry*, 116, 237–45.

Waziri, R. (1973). Symptomatology of depressive illness in Afghanistan. *American Journal of Psychiatry*, 130, (2), 213–17.

Yung, M. (1984). Structural family therapy: its application to Chinese families. *Family Process*, 23, 365–74.

# CHAPTER 13

# SEXUAL INEQUALITY, FAMILY LIFE AND FAMILY THERAPY

*Jennie Williams and Gilli Watson*

## INTRODUCTION

In this chapter we will be addressing family life and family therapy from the starting-point of sexual inequality. Sexual inequality, as a major source of conflict and distress in families, has largely been ignored in family therapy. We explore how and why this has happened, using as a resource the work of women clinicians and academics who have been trying to close the gap between their own experience as women in families, and that represented in patriarchal theories. A theme is introduced and developed throughout the chapter; it is that the social psychological literature concerned with processes that perpetuate inequality between social groups brings a much needed perspective to this field. The reasons are twofold. First, an intergroup perspective enables us to see how family therapy has served an ideological function by supporting the sexual status quo. Second, it directs attention to the types of connections that can be made, and need to be made, between sexual inequality in society and the particular world of the family. Intergroup analyses continually confront us with issues of power, and simultaneously remind us that issues of power have been either ignored or misrepresented by professionals working with families. The task that, therefore, faces family therapy is to do justice to the complexity of domestic power relations, and we make some suggestions about the language that this enterprise will need. Finally we remind the reader that arriving at new definitions of what is problematic in family life brings the challenge of finding new solutions. These solutions, we suggest, need not necessarily be in the form of therapy.

# SEXUAL INEQUALITY: THE STARTING-POINT

So what is sexual inequality? It is, we suggest, when sex determines access to socially valued resources, resources that include access to money, status and power, especially the power to define societal rules, rights and privileges. Sexual inequality does not only mean that women and men live different lives. Women's lives are also systematically accorded less power and status than those of men. Statistics are one way to remind ourselves of some of the ways in which the lives of women and men in Britain are shaped by the fact that biological sex is the basis of social stratification as well as social differentiation.

Recent figures show that the majority of women (51 per cent) have paid work outside the home in addition to their unpaid work within it. Despite the Equal Pay Act the average gross weekly earning of women in 1985 was 65.7 per cent of males (Equal Opportunities Commission (EOC) 1986). Women are over-represented in low status, vulnerable, service occupations. It is also noteworthy that when both a wife and husband are in paid employment, only 8 per cent of married women earn as much as, or more than, their husbands and that the figures in 1980 were the same as those for 1977 (EOC 1986). Women's earnings within families continue to be regarded as secondary to those of men. Surveys of domestic life (e.g. *Social Trends* 1987) consistently find that women remain overwhelmingly responsible for household tasks and child-rearing. In a society that values leisure, men have more free time than women (*Social Trends* 1987). It is also salutary to note from a compilation (National Council for One-Parent Families 1987) of the latest DHSS statistics (1983), that 95 per cent of one-parent families are headed by women, two-thirds of whom are divorced or separated. With 51 per cent of these families dependent on Supplementary Benefit, it is understandable that there is growing reference to the 'feminization of poverty'.

We direct attention to these statistics because they make visible the different material and social psychological worlds of women and men. Described in these stark terms it does not seem surprising to find that sexual inequality has mental health implications. This association is well supported by an extensive literature linking sexual inequality to the mental health of women (e.g. Sturdivant 1980; Howell and Bayes 1981; Penfold and Walker 1984; Williams 1984a; Bravo-Rosewater and Walker 1985), and smaller though growing bodies of work exploring the psychological costs this system exacts from children (e.g. Feldman 1982; Herman and Hirschman 1984) and from men (e.g. Baker-Miller 1976; Solomon and Levy 1982).

This statistical and research evidence serves to remind us that families are the place in which sexual inequality, structured and maintained in the public world, becomes the intimate struggle of the private world. Families are the place in which women and men, whose structural relationship is one of inequality, meet at an interpersonal level. Attempting to solve the conflict embedded in this arrangement is, we suggest, a fundamental characteristic of family life. While these connections have been acknowledged and are influencing the practice of a growing number of mental health professionals, family therapists seem to find it particularly difficult to accept that sexual inequality has a detrimental effect on family life. How has it been possible for family therapists to ignore one of the fundamental structural properties of social and family life and to remain almost totally unaffected by twenty years of impressive work on the consequences of sexual inequality for women and families? Indeed as Goldner (1985b : 22) comments, 'sidestepping [these issues] would appear to be a sign of advanced training in family therapy'. Why has this been the case? In answering these questions we will draw from the recent writings of several women family therapists.

## SEXUAL INEQUALITY: ITS NEGLECT IN FAMILY THERAPY

It has been persuasively argued (Hare-Mustin 1978; James and McIntyre 1983; Layton 1984; Goldner 1985a), that sexual inequality has been ignored because of the dominance of systems theory as an explanatory account of family structure and functioning. It is argued that this theory rendered it impossible to acknowledge the existence of structural inequalities in our society.

Developed in the biological sciences and transferred to the social sciences, systems theory offered an explanation of structure in terms of universal organizing principles within living systems. It was based on assumptions about inherent properties considered to be common to all natural systems, for example, the tendency within systems to organize, and to organize hierarchically. In the application of systems theory to the family, the family came to be seen as another type of 'natural' system subject to the same universal organizing principles. Family structure in this way could be viewed as the result of essentially 'natural' processes. Systems theory offered an explanatory model uncompromised by the difficult issues that are raised when the family is considered in its historical and social context (e.g. Busfield 1982; Oakley 1982; Segal 1983). Indeed it had no language for social process. Within the framework of systems theory the structure of the family could be accounted for by processes internal to it, in terms of, for example, sub-systems boundaries and circular sequences. The result, as James and McIntyre (1983: 22) comment, was the 'collapsing of the family into a theory of structural organisation'. What was distinctly different about the family as a social system was written out in favour of what the family was considered to hold in common with other natural systems.

Systems theory legitimized the disconnection of the family from its complex relationship with social, political and economic systems. The family disconnected in this way could be seen as if it was a free-standing entity, organized on its own terms, independent not only of its current social context but also of its historical context. This encouraged an intense focusing within family therapy on intra-familial processes and a corresponding disinterest in the way in which the family itself represented a particular punctuation of social processes. The family was accepted as 'given' and attention focused not on 'the family in general' but on 'the family in particular', that is on the particular family at hand (James and McIntyre 1983).

One serious consequence, noted by several authors (Hare-Mustin 1978; Goldner 1985a), was that family therapy 'bought' the model of family life dominant in the 1950s. This model 'sold' the family as a haven, and reframed sexual inequality as a harmonious complementary arrangement in which women and men presided over separate but equal worlds. Indeed family therapy not only accepted this construction of family life uncritically, but also assumed that it was *necessary* for healthy family functioning (Hare-Mustin 1978). In this way, by adding weight to the view that it was 'natural' and 'healthy' that women be located in the home, family therapy supported the moves to restore the sexual status quo in the post-war period (Williams and Giles 1978; Goldner 1985b).

The evident compatibility between systems theory and the model of family life popularized after the Second World War is not that surprising. Power had early on been discredited by systems thinkers primarily on the grounds that it was not suited to a systemic theory of circular causality. Inequality had similarly been reduced 'to a matter of perspective' (Goldner 1985b : 22). A model of the family that explained away sexual inequality as harmonious interdependency was therefore convenient to family therapy. Indeed as Goldner comments,

> family therapy ideology would oppose the suggestion that social forces could differentially regulate the nature of participation and the distribution of power within the family such that some family members would be more equal than others . . . the feminist assertion that power in the family life is socially structured by gender simply offends the systemic aesthetic.
>
> (Goldner 1985a : 33)

In buying the post-war model of the family, the family could be fitted into systems theory which assumed a mutuality of interest and harmonious interdependency within systems. The notion that there may be a fundamental conflict of interest between parts of a system, or that a system could function to benefit some of its members more than others, was simply unacceptable. The existence of structured inequalities within families simply didn't fit. The 'family as formed' was therefore accepted and questions about the dysfunctional nature of its social construction were simply not asked. This led to what James and McIntyre have referred to as the reproduction of a fiction:

> that is, that the current family form is unproblematic and appropriate, that problems arising in its functioning have an internal source, are internally maintained and can be internally rectified. . . . This internal rendering prompts the conviction that problems and conflicts can be resolved with a bit of internal tinkering.
>
> (James and McIntyre 1983 : 126)

In this way the social origins of distress are obscured and denied: it is particular families who fail rather than that it is the family itself that contains structural dysfunctions which will lead to stress and conflict.

Family therapy has, therefore, been both unwilling and unable to deal with sexual inequality. The adoption of a 'neutral' asocial theory, within which inequality did not exist, led family therapy to assume that this actually was the case: that inequalities, including sexual inequality, did not exist. The result has been the representation of the family as unproblematic; the unquestioning commitment of family therapists to the contemporary family form with its inherent inequalities; a focusing on technique as solution; and also, we shall argue, the pernicious misrepresentation of domestic power relations.

It is essential that these fundamental limitations in family therapy are addressed, and it is encouraging that this is becoming more widely acknowledged. However, we believe that this undertaking will be successful only when serious attention is given to the processes that maintain sexual inequality. We shall now explain the reasons for reaching this conclusion.


## SEXUAL INEQUALITY: FROM AN INTERGROUP PERSPECTIVE

Throughout this century social scientists have devoted considerable energy to finding solutions to problems created by social inequalities. Although sexual inequality and mental health have not featured strongly in this literature (Williams 1984b) it does none the less contain important implications for the way these issues are addressed within family therapy.

In the first instance, we would like to suggest that the long-standing academic enterprise concerned with inequalities of race, class and ethnicity contains an important object lesson for family theorists and therapists. This lesson concerns the social costs of trying to solve problems created by social inequality without giving due consideration to the underlying intergroup power processes. This has frequently characterized the approach that social scientists have taken to the pressing problems of prejudice, racial discrimination and integration (for a review see Apfelbaum 1978). The most significant consequence of this disregard is that, contrary to intention, proposed solutions typically fail to serve the interests of disadvantaged groups. This approach has led, for example, to the pathologizing of Black people as psychologically disabled by low self-esteem, and to naive and ineffectual ideas about achieving change through educating and mobilizing the guilt of dominant group members (Apfelbaum 1978). Workers in this field were also theoretically unprepared in the 1960s for the emergence of challenges from 'minority groups'; for the impetus for change coming from subordinate groups themselves. The academic response to these difficulties has been to shift the main focus of attention from the manifestations of social inequalities to the processes which establish, structure and maintain asymmetrical intergroup relationships. Of necessity, this has been accompanied by the recognition that these issues cannot be addressed within linear models; inequality is not simply the result of the way that one group acts upon another.

We suggest that the conceptual problems that have dogged the work on inequitable relations between social groups are similar to those we have identified as characterizing the work in mainstream family therapy. In both instances there has been an eagerness to alleviate distress coupled with a reluctance to consider the social processes within which the distress is embedded. In addition, attempted solutions tend to be singularly unhelpful and often punishing to the people most disadvantaged by the situation of inequality. However, as we have already observed, theorists working on asymmetrical intergroup relationships have been struggling to move beyond the impasse which now faces family therapy. What then can be learnt from the more recent developments in this field?

Over the years it has been repeatedly observed that the social psychological dynamics associated with sexual inequality are similar in many important respects to those taking place in other inequitable intergroup relationships. Those, for example, occurring between masters and slaves (Hacker 1951; Chesler 1972) and Blacks and whites (Myrdal 1944; Baker-Miller 1971; Brittan and Maynard 1984). It is on these grounds that the pre-existing work on intergroup relations is now being used to cast light on the inequitable relationship between women and men (Baker-Miller 1976; Williams and Giles 1978). We would like to describe briefly some of the significant processes which have been identified as perpetuating this arrangement. Focusing on these processes will enable two important possibilities to be considered. First, family therapy, theory and practice, has itself been serving an intergroup function by obscuring the existence of sexual inequality and failing to identify the burden it places on family life. Second, those phenomena commonly viewed as family interactions are in fact better understood as intergroup interactions: as interactions between people who are members of inequitable social groups.

# PROCESSES WHICH MAINTAIN INEQUALITY BETWEEN SOCIAL GROUPS

A conflict of interests is embedded in all asymmetrical intergroup relationships: a dominant group, by definition, is in the position to get what it wants at the expense of members of the subordinate group. To maintain this advantage the dominant group needs to use its power systematically to safeguard its position, and keep the subordinate group in its place. This is typically achieved by processes which fulfil two overlapping functions. First, processes which obscure the fact that the intergroup relationship is unfair. Second, processes which make it difficult for subordinate group members to react when the unfairness of the intergroup relationship is not obscured. These processes, their functions, and their implications for family life and family therapy will now be considered.

## Processes which obscure the existence of inequality

Inequitable relationships are most effectively maintained by ideologies that obscure the existence of inequality, and mask the continuous and pervasive conflict of interests between the groups concerned. By ideology we mean 'a socially produced construction of ideas and explanations; a set of procedures and practices which both account for and organise the social system' (Penfold and Walker 1984 : vi). With more or less subtlety, justification for the position of the dominant group is woven into ideologies. This is possible because dominance is invariably associated with the power to define ideology: in our society this power lies almost exclusively in the hands of men. The ideological function of explanations for the social order is well supported by the work of social historians (e.g. Shields 1975; Penfold and Walker 1984). Their analyses show that explanations for the sexual status quo, for example, while apparently evolving over time to accommodate advances in cultural knowledge, none the less are consistently adjusted to ensure that they serve the interests of the dominant group. From this and related work (e.g. Chesler 1972; Williams 1984b; Brittan and Maynard 1984), it is possible to identify some of the common ways in which ideologies help perpetuate sexual inequality. Sexual inequality is maintained, for example, by:

1 Ideologies which justify the existence of sexual inequality by calling it 'natural', 'God given', 'morally correct'.

2 Ideologies which deny that the relationship is one of inequality by calling it 'complementary', 'functional'.
3 Ideologies which ignore or justify violent means of keeping women in their place: 'they need it', 'they deserve it'.
4 Ideologies which name individual or collective reactions against oppression as 'madness' or 'mental disorder'.
5 Ideologies which encourage women to look within themselves rather than to their social position for the possible causes of distress and misery.
6 Ideologies which blame women for the problems created by the existence of sexual and other social inequalities.

Attention will now be drawn to some of the ways in which these ideologies are implicated in family life and family therapy.

*Implications for family life and family therapy*
It is in the work of Jean Baker-Miller (1976) that we still find the most thorough explorations of the effects of sexual ideologies on family life. One of Baker-Miller's particular concerns has been couples who find these patriarchal explanations for sexual inequality acceptable. In these circumstances, she argues, there are likely to be a number of systematic consequences. First, that the needs of both partners will not be mutually satisfied. Second, that this unacknowledged conflict of interests will be the source of some resentment and distress. Third, that the absence of a framework or language which would enable couples to deal directly with these issues, results in attempted solutions that often exact a heavy toll from family members and their relationships with each other.

The attempted solutions which Baker-Miller discusses in some detail should be familiar to family therapists. For example when women assume, or are given, responsibility for the systemic problem of inequality in their relationship, depression is a common outcome. The disappointment and frustration that women feel in inequitable relationships can also result in anger directed towards their husbands, anger which can find expression in contemptuous, disdainful and critical attitudes. However, while psychological sabotage of the male may be understandable in terms of the dynamics of the relationship, it is rarely understood by the protagonists, and leaves untouched the real issue which is based in the situation of inequality. These and many other clinical presentations do not arise from attempts to deal directly with sexual inequality, but from an inability to recognize its existence. The problem, as Friedan (1963) found, has 'no name'; it has been effectively obscured by the ideologies of the dominant group.

That the social and medical sciences have paradoxically made a significant contribution to constructing these ideologies has been argued at length elsewhere (Chesler 1972; Ehrenreich and English 1979; Penfold and Walker

1984) and we shall not labour this point here. However, the specific role of family therapy in this enterprise does require further comment.

It has already been suggested here that family therapy has served an ideological function by denying that sexual inequality, structured and maintained in the public world, is reproduced in the family. Sexual inequality has instead been construed as *complementary*, an arrangement considered to be natural and healthy, and the desirable outcome of mutual negotiation within families. The above discussion (pp. 297–8) now alerts us to further ways in which family therapy may have supported, and itself been shaped, by patriarchal ideologies. It has, for example, been suggested that family therapists have been theoretically predisposed to giving women some responsibility for being kept in their place by violence (Goldner 1985b). Indeed family therapists' attitudes towards women in families often seem to be punitive. It is women who are typically given the responsibility for manifest family problems: this includes the problems created by their own social and familial oppression. Paradoxically these attributions are then often supported by reference to women's pathological use of power.

Within family therapy there has been a systematic preoccupation with, and pathologizing of, women's power in families. Women have been consistently blamed for family dysfunction with reference to their over-centrality, over-intrusiveness, over-protectiveness, over-control, and mind-reading. It is as if women's power is somehow toxic (Layton 1984). This view of women is part of a long tradition of 'blaming the victim' (Penfold and Walker 1984) and is the insidious product of linear thinking and of a punctuation of social process that studiously omits men's power. As Hare-Mustin (1978 : 186) points out, 'traditional therapists who see some women having a greater share of responsibility and power within the home than men overlook the fact that men typically have power and status elsewhere'. The preoccupation with women's power in families ignores what Goldner (1985a) terms 'the dual status' of women: the fact that women's power at home stands in complex dialectical relationship to power in the outside world. Power within the home does not equal power outside it. While they may hold power within the family, women are publicly devalued and dis-confirmed. Indeed we would argue that women's power within the family is more apparent than real, that it is essentially 'delegated power' as managers of systems they do not own. As long as the family has no independent economic existence, women's power within it remains conditional, conditional on that allowed by the owners of families – in most cases men.

Our argument, therefore, is that women in families are not powerful enough: that structured inequality in the public world compromises women's position in the private. Domestic power relations have been misrepresented within family therapy by the focus on 'the power of powerlessness' rather than the abuse of power by the dominant group, and

by highlighting and pathologizing women's power in the domestic world.
The nature of the power relations between women and men, and in
particular, the nature of the power men hold in the public world, have been
kept from discussion.

If these issues, and their clinical implications, are to be addressed systematically, theoretical models are needed that can bring together public
and private worlds. The literature on intergroup relations, while not sufficient in itself, does offer a much-needed perspective. So far, it has provided a
basis for exploring family therapy's ideological functions, and the pernicious
clinical consequences of these theoretical distortions. The literature on
intergroup relations is also useful because it enables us to identify processes
which maintain inequality when ideology fails, that is when subordinate
group members 'see through' prevailing explanations for the sexual status
quo.

## Processes which make it difficult to react against inequality

It has long been acknowledged that subordinate group members are motivated, by their vulnerability, to monitor closely their own behaviour, and
that of people belonging to the dominant social group. Such information is
vital if they are to avoid giving offence or causing anger. Female culture
attests to this motivation to seek some control through knowledge.
Women's magazines, for example, contain a wealth of information about
how to maximize one's options when getting, handling and keeping a man, a
preoccupation which is not mirrored in the content of the popular literature
consumed by men. The close attention women give to these matters can lead
to discoveries about the fallacies of the myths about the superiority of men,
and their vulnerability and weaknesses may be recognized (e.g. Lerner
1983; Eichenbaum and Orbach 1984). Indeed, since the advent of the recent
feminist revival, it seems particularly likely that women may come to view
the received wisdom about the relative values, abilities and competencies of
the sexes with some scepticism. However, 'seeing through' the prevailing
notions that obscure the unfairness of sexual inequality does not necessarily
lead to this arrangement being challenged. When ideology fails, inequality is
perpetuated by other processes; processes which characterize most asymmetrical intergroup relations (Apfelbaum 1978; Penfold and Walker 1984).

When ideology fails women are kept in their place by:

1  Their distribution in jobs and roles which are undervalued, poorly paid
   and often insecure.
2  Their economic dependency on men.
3  Their restricted access to male-dominated social institutions that create

rules, laws and wealth, and which construct the ideologies which justify the sexual status quo.

4 The risk entailed in challenging the status quo, for example, of violence and derogation.

5 Their socialization and the psychological difficulties entailed in challenging internalized accounts of how women and men should be.

6 Processes which make it difficult for women to have a group identity and collectively challenge their social position. This includes the inadequate recording and acknowledgement of women's contribution to history, culture and society; the socialization of women as subordinate group members to distrust their own experiences, understandings and feelings, and to look to the dominant group for explanation; and the physical and psychological isolation that many women experience in families.

We shall now examine some of the significant ways in which these processes are implicated in family life and family therapy.

*Implications for family life and family therapy*
The processes highlighted above make it easier to understand why women, who know that sexual inequality is unfair, don't challenge male dominance. Women 'put up with' their oppression in families because the viable alternatives to their present roles are often equally unattractive, and because trying to change their position within the family is often risky. Women who seek a fairer distribution of power in their relationship with men often meet resistance in the form of conflict, violence and financial hardship; they may find themselves labelled 'bad' or 'mad'. There are also internalized processes which keep women in their place. Lerner (1983) offers a particularly insightful account of some of these subtle, yet important, dynamics.

Lerner describes the process whereby women are enlisted into their subordinate position by powerful cultural injunctions to underfunction. This she summarizes as 'the message is that the weaker sex must protect the stronger sex from recognising the strength of the weaker sex lest the stronger sex feels weakened by the strength of the weaker sex' (Lerner 1983 : 701). Thus within the prescription of male dominance is contained the prescription of female underfunctioning. She argues that within this prescribed complementarity women are being asked to underfunction and protect and stabilize the system in which they operate. She quotes examples of the way in which this underfunctioning is sold to women, for example in the message, 'What is humiliating about being under a man . . . if it is clear to you that he is only on top because you are holding him up?' (Lerner 1983 : 700). Women's competence within this prescription becomes a disloyalty, an aggressive act, a challenge to male competence, fuelled, Lerner suggests, by irrational fantasies of female power and male vulnerability. This management of women's competence through powerful prescriptions to underfunction is one of the subtle ways in which the inequitable intergroup relationship between the sexes is maintained. By setting a prescription to underfunction within a covert message that this underfunctioning is necessary because of the vulnerability of the dominant group, power relations are distorted and subordination ensured.

Women who, for reasons such as those we have outlined, choose not to challenge male power openly, may well try to 'get their way' by more covert means. This requires exercising power without appearing to so that 'he remains powerful and she remains safe' (Smith and Siegel 1985). This use of covert power to influence the relational field while maintaining deference is now well documented (Smith and Siegel 1985; Baker-Miller 1976; Williams 1984c). Included here would be: using helplessness and weakness; applying emotional pressure; and manipulating the emotional tone of situations (Raush *et al*. 1974; Johnson and Goodchilds 1976). These strategies which are part of the female subculture are, as Johnson argues, limited in important ways.

> Indirect and helpless modes of power while useful in the short run leave a woman as the unknown influencer or as known to be weak. Likewise, reliance on personal forms of power can leave women dependent on the relationships that are a part of the power use.
>
> (Johnson 1976 : 108)

Furthermore, as other writers have noted, while deception and manipulation may be judged successful by some standards, they tend not to enhance the self-esteem and mutual respect of the parties involved (Polk 1974; Baker-Miller 1976). Women who have refined these skills are also unlikely to find family therapists an appreciative audience. As we noted earlier family therapists often have punitive attitudes towards the 'power of the powerless'.

The intergroup processes that have been illustrated here are, however, not completely effective in keeping women in their place. This is quite obvious, for example, from the existence of the women's movement. Once ideology fails and sexual inequality is identified as a structural problem with considerable personal and interpersonal costs, change becomes a possibility. The conditions under which this possibility becomes a reality, and the male response to this challenge are again matters of relevance for people working with families, though it is not possible to summarize this work adequately here (e.g. Williams and Giles 1978; Kahn 1984).

For family therapists the immediate challenge is to develop a language which will make sexual inequality tangible, and enable people to read the power relations and processes embedded in the familiar patterns of domestic life. However, if history is not to repeat itself it is important that this language does not serve, or reflect the interests of the dominant social group. In our view this is less likely to happen if family theorists and therapists work from an intergroup perspective. This perspective, as we have shown here, both increases sensitivity to family therapy's ideological functions, and also helps set the family in its social context.

With this perspective in mind we shall now suggest some basic vocabulary and concepts that may help clinicians develop an understanding of domestic power relations.

## TOWARDS A REPRESENTATION OF DOMESTIC POWER RELATIONS

It is important, at the outset, to be clear what we mean by power. First, power is essentially relational. Power does not exist in itself, in isolation from a relational field (Hall 1972). Second, power is not unidimensional, as something that people either have or do not have, power is access to socially valued resources. Therefore, addressing power within relationships is not simply a question of who has the most power in a quantitative sense, but rather who holds, or has access to, what kinds of power. Following this, it may be useful to distinguish the qualitatively different bases of interpersonal power that are brought into play in the struggle to set the rules, and define the nature of the relationship between women and men in contemporary British families.

### Interpersonal power bases

The power bases provisionally listed in Figure 13.1 have been identified by reference to the embryonic literature in this area (Raven 1965; Johnson 1976; Scanzoni 1978; Kahn 1984). They have also been identified in the knowledge that power in our society is both differentiated and stratified on the basis of sex. The nature of these power bases will now be elaborated, and some observations will be made about their characteristics.

| *Women* | *Men* |
|---|---|
| Domestic | Economic |
| Affective | Ascribed |
| Relational | Physical |
| Reproductive | Contractual |
| Sexual | Informational |
| | Language |

*Figure 13.1* Access to power bases

*Economic power*
The major power base in our society is money. Money talks. An illustration of this is provided in a study quoted by Goldner (1985a), in which women were able to get their husbands to take on more domestic work only when their own earnings in the public world approached those of their husbands. From the statistics we cited earlier in this chapter it should be clear that women and men do not have equal access to this power base, and that women's work within the home remains largely unpaid.

*Ascribed power*
This power is accorded to people on the basis of, for example, their sex, class and race. It is not earned, and directly reflects the value system of the dominant social groups. Thus men are the primary holders of this power base. In families it is used to legitimize their position as the 'natural' head of the household, as the person who 'lays down the law' and 'has the final word', whose authority is beyond question.

*Informational power*
Access to information, or possession of skills, not held by the other is a source of interpersonal power. Power derived from this base will vary as a function of the social value associated with the information or expertise that is held. Again this reflects the concerns of the dominant group. Thus, expertise in, or access to, knowledge about the public world holds more value and thereby more power than expertise or knowledge about the private world. Women's knowledge about parenting, for example, carries less value and therefore less power than men's knowledge, for example, about money.

*The power of language*
Language is a power base in that it names experience and reality. That male knowledge and experience are disproportionately represented in language, and male dominance served and perpetuated by language, are claims that have been well substantiated (e.g. Spender 1980).

*Physical power*
The use of, or threat of, physical violence represents a major relational power base. This is predominantly accessible to men because of their greater physical size. Men's violence towards women has also been legitimized in the lack of legislative protection for women from domestic violence, a situation which is only now beginning to change with the very recent preparedness of the police in Britain to intervene in domestic violence. Dobash and Dobash (1980 : 75) remind us of the significance of this power base: 'It is still true that for a woman to be brutally or systematically

assaulted she must usually enter our most sacred institution, the family. It is within marriage that a woman is most likely to be slapped and shoved about, severely assaulted, killed or raped.'

*Contractual power*
The ability to leave the relational field, to 'contract out', is a power base strongly associated with access to money. This is powerfully illustrated in a study quoted by Goldner (1985a) which looked at the economic well-being of partners a year after their divorce. This study found that women's economic well-being had *fallen* by 73 per cent, while that of men had *risen* by 42 per cent. The absence of an independent economic base for women as parents, and the predominance of women in low-paid employment, results in this power being largely accessible to men.

*Relational power*
Connectedness with significant others, either within or outside families, can offer a power base. Friendship alliances, especially gender alliances, and familial alliances, for example, between parent and child, can increase power in negotiations and bargaining. This may especially be the case when there is limited access to other power bases, or when faced with strong opposition.

*Affective power*
Emotion as a power base has been traditionally assigned to women as the care-takers of relationships within the private world of the family. As such it has been devalued and frequently denigrated as an illegitimate source of power. Its use by women has carried the risk of being pathologized, of being seen as manipulative at best, and insane at worst. Such attempts to limit this power base may, as Layton (1984) suggests, reflect irrational fears of women's emotional power or attempts to limit the effectiveness of this strong and legitimate source of power.

*Sexual power*
Sexuality is frequently the focus of major power struggles between women and men (Schwendinger and Schwendinger 1983). As a power base, it holds a high social value in the public world, and is seen as a legitimate source of power for men over women, that is it is men's 'right' to have a sexual relationship with women. For women in families it is largely by withholding this resource that this power base is exercised.

*Reproductive power*
Children are a valued resource and have traditionally represented a power base that women bring to the relational field. With the decline of children as

an economic resource, it is arguable that reproduction as a power base has been diminished.

*Domestic power*

This is a source of power derived from the service relationship, and as we noted earlier, it is a characteristic power base of subordinate groups. Power is largely derived from the threat of, or actual withdrawal of services, though it is limited by the dependence of the holder on the service contract. Domestic power can be exercised by the withdrawal of 'life support' services, for example cooking, cleaning, washing, and so on. However, this power is precariously wielded in a context where there is a risk of being replaced: of losing employment, home and financial support. None the less, the female subculture does suggest that the judicious use of domestic power does have some potential for influencing the relational field.

The power bases that have been briefly described here constitute some of the major sources of interpersonal power. The power from these bases lies in the extent to which their presence or withdrawal alters the relational field by influencing the process and outcome of negotiation. These power bases do not have equal value. Power bases derived in the public world hold more social value than those derived in the private world, and as such they offer greater access to influence and control. These power bases are not equally accessible to women and men. Women typically have access to power bases that hold low social value. They are derived from the woman's position within the private world of the family and as such are 'hidden' sources of power. Men typically have access to socially valued power bases derived from their direct relationship with the public world. Hence sexual inequality is both embedded in and perpetuated by inequality of access to differentially valued power sources.

## Interpersonal power processes

Once there is a vocabulary with which to talk about the bases of power, it is easier to look more closely at the ways in which power bases are used interactionally. Power processes are the ways in which power bases are used to influence the pattern and course of family life, for example, decision-making, negotiations and conflict regulation. It has already been stressed that power processes within the family have been misrepresented within family therapy. To rectify this, there needs to be a continual awareness that the power relations between women and men in families take place within the context of structural inequality between the sexes in society.

In this chapter we have identified a number of important ways in which the intergroup power processes maintaining sexual inequality shape the lives of women and men in families. These processes help determine not only the kinds of power bases that men and women have at their disposal, but also whether and how these resources are used. Intergroup processes affect the capacity of family members to recognize that sexual inequality creates problems for themselves and their relationships, and also whether women use their power bases to survive within or to challenge openly their oppression in families. Family therapists need to develop a greater sensitivity towards these and other interpersonal power processes and their intergroup parameters, and the mental health costs that are associated with exercising power in these ways. Professionals for whom this is a new venture may well gain insight and inspiration from some of the existing literature in this area (e.g. Baker-Miller 1976; Bell and Newby 1976; Scanzoni 1978; Baker-Miller and Mothner 1981; Lerner 1983).

## IMPLICATIONS FOR PRACTICE
### Taking power into the room

The analysis of power relations that has been outlined here brings the public world into the realms of the private. It allows and encourages us to ask different questions. We are invited to look at families and their problems from a different perspective. It becomes important, for example, that we know how a particular family copes with living in a world where men and women are not accorded equal power and status. There are several questions that we would ask in the first instance. How has this family divided out its tasks, especially those of earning money and of child-care? How much flexibility did they feel they had in making these decisions, and how satisfied are they with them? Whom does this arrangement benefit most? What are the costs of this arrangement? How is it explained, for example, is it seen as 'natural' or 'normal'? Second, we would want to know about the power bases available to the family. Who has access to what kinds of power bases? How are these power bases evident in negotiations and conflict? At what point does money talk? When are children brought in as relational power? Is violence a 'covert veto' (Morgan 1985)? What does it mean for a family that one person may be able to 'leave the field' because of his or her direct access to money? In what way are complementarities within the family based on these power bases, and what flexibility is there within them? Is the structured asymmetry between the sexes in society mirrored in this family?

These are some of the questions we should find ourselves thinking about if we are seriously concerned to see family problems and distress in the context of sexual inequality. How therapists might work with the answers to these questions is clearly an important issue. However, at this juncture we believe that issues of practice are secondary to those of theory. The pressing need at the moment does seem to be for therapists to relinquish or revise ways of thinking about families that are the legacy of patriarchal theories. There are no reasons for believing that this is an easy task (Douglas 1985), nor that it can be accomplished overnight. Furthermore, until these changes in thinking have been achieved, it is hard to imagine that as therapists we can offer families in distress constructive help, and it is all too easy to recall our theoretically rationalized potential for being destructive. However, as family therapists are unlikely to interrupt their practice while these changes are taking place, we offer some guidelines.

Working with an understanding of domestic power relations is not about asking families to solve sexual inequality in the public world, nor is it about 'fixing' sexual inequality by encouraging role reversals within the family, such as asking Dad to do the hoovering while Mum cleans the car. It is about work with families that is concerned with the ways that sexual inequality structures, constrains and delimits them as women and men in families; the ways that unresolved power issues are associated with their differential access to power bases; and with finding better solutions to their particular difficulties without ignoring the constraints imposed on their lives by structural inequalities in society.

## Taking therapy out of the room

An understanding of power relations allows us to take the private world of the family into the public world constraining it. It enables us to work outside the consulting room in 'de-privatizing' the family: to resource and empower the family in its relationship with the public world. This includes working to influence the position of women and men within families in terms of, for example, access to child-care facilities, funding for single-parent families, family centre work (see Chapter 14 and De'Ath 1986). Family therapists also have the potential to make a constructive contribution to social policy by challenging ideologies that reproduce the isolated, under-resourced family, and the sexual inequality contained within it. There have already been good precedents in this area (Walker 1985).

## CONCLUSION

Within this chapter we have highlighted the need to understand intergroup processes in order to appreciate the impact of sexual inequality on family life. We have argued that the family has been misrepresented within family therapy in the use of systems theory which has not permitted the interrelationship between the family and the social structure to be addressed. We have argued that, as a result, family therapy has misunderstood and pathologized women's position in families.

It has been our contention that family therapy cannot operate without an understanding of domestic power relations. Simply ignoring or denying power does not remove inequality, but permits it to flourish. We have suggested that power can be made tangible, and that understanding power relations can become part of general assessment work with families. None the less, we share Goldner's (1985b) reservations that resistance to addressing issues of structural change may result in sexual inequality being given token treatment within the field of family therapy. Work on power relations within families is not a simple matter of facilitating 'role reversal', nor is it a matter of asking families to solve sexual inequalities structured into our society. It is about helping families to acknowledge the existence of sexual inequality and its effect on their lives. For clinicians, the fundamental challenge is to bring the public world into the room and not reproduce the myth of the family in isolation.

The family is undergoing major changes as the numbers of single parent and reconstituted families increase (Oakley 1982). The economic constraints for families are becoming all too evident. Family therapy needs to acknowledge the economic basis of family life and be willing to debate this fully. It may be, as we have suggested here, that this will take therapists out of the consulting room to legitimate interventions that resource and empower family life in relation to the public world.

If family therapy is not to repeat the errors of analysis, which have led to a misrepresentation of family distress and of women's position within the family, it will need to abandon its intellectual isolation and make connections with other literature. We trust that this chapter has indicated some of the ways that these connections can be established.

# REFERENCES

Apfelbaum, E. (1978). Relations of domination and movements for liberation: an analysis of power between groups. In W.G. Austin and S. Worchel (eds) *The Social Psychology of Intergroup Relations*. Monterey, Calif., Brooks/Cole.

Baker-Miller, J.B. (1971). Psychological consequences of sexual inequality. *American Journal of Orthopsychiatry*, 41, 767–75.

—— (1976). *Toward a New Psychology of Women*. Harmondsworth, Penguin.

Baker-Miller, J.B. and Mothner, E. (1981). Psychological consequences of sexual inequality. In E. Howell and M. Bayes (eds) *Women and Mental Health*. New York, Basic Books.

Bell, C. and Newby, H. (1976). Husbands and wives: the dynamics of the deferential dialectic. In D.L. Barker and S. Allen (eds) *Dependence and Exploitation in Work and Marriage*, London and New York, Longman.

Bravo-Rosewater, L. and Walker, L.E.A. (eds) (1985). *Handbook of Feminist Therapy*. New York, Springer.

Brittan, A. and Maynard, M. (1984). *Sexism, Racism and Oppression*. Oxford, Blackwell.

Busfield, J. (1982). Gender and mental illness. *International Journal of Mental Health*, 11, 46–66.

Chesler, P. (1972). *Women and Madness*. New York, Doubleday.

De'Ath, E. (1968) Working with families, people, practice and politics. *Association for Family Therapy Newsletter*, 6, 3–4.

Dobash, R.E. and Dobash, R. (1980). *Violence Against Wives*. London, Open Books.

Douglas, M.A. (1985). The role of power in feminist therapy: a reformulation. In L. Bravo-Rosewater and L.E.A. Walker (eds) *Handbook of Feminist Therapy*. New York, Springer.

Ehrenreich, B. and English, D. (1979). *For Her Own Good: 150 Years of Experts' Advice to Women*. New York, Anchor.

Eichenbaum, L. and Orbach, S. (1984). *What do Women Want?* Glasgow, Fontana.

Equal Opportunities Commission (1986). *The Fact About Women is . . .* Information sheet available from Statistics Unit, EOC, Overseas House, Quay Street, Manchester.

Feldman, L.B. (1982). Sex roles and family dynamics. In F. Walsh (ed.) *Normal Family Processes*. London, Guilford.

Friedan, B. (1963) *The Feminine Mystique*. Harmondsworth, Penguin.

Goldner, V. (1985a) Feminism and family therapy. *Family Process*, 24, 31–47.

—— (1985b). Warning: family therapy may be hazardous to your health. *Networker*, Nov.–Dec., 19–23.

Hacker, H. (1951). Women as minority group. *Social Forces*, 29, 60–9.

Hall, R.H. (1972). *Organisations: Structure and Process*. Englewood Cliffs, NJ, Prentice-Hall.

Hare-Mustin, R.T. (1978). A feminist approach to family therapy. *Family Process*, 17, 181–94.

Herman, J. and Hirschman, L. (1984). Families at risk for father–daughter incest. In P.P. Rieker and E.H. Carmen (eds) *The Gender Gap in Psychotherapy: Social Realities and Psychological Processes*. New York, Plenum.

Howell, E. and Bayes, M. (eds) (1981). *Women and Mental Health*. New York, Basic Books.

James, K. and McIntyre, D. (1983). The reproduction of families: the social role of family therapy? *Journal of Marital and Family Therapy*, 9, 119–29.

Johnson, P.B. (1976). Women and power: toward a theory of effectiveness. *Journal of Social Issues*, 32, 99–110.

Johnson, P.B. and Goodchilds, J.O. (1976). How women get their way. *Psychology Today*, 10, 68–70.

Kahn, A. (1984). The power war: male response to power loss under equality. *Psychology of Women Quarterly*, 8, 234–47.

Layton, M. (1984). Tipping the therapeutic balance – masculine, feminine or neuter? *Networker*, May–June, 21–7.

Lerner, H.G. (1983). Female dependency in context: some theoretical and technical considerations. *American Journal of Orthopsychiatry*, 53(4), 697–705.

Libow, J.A. (1985). Gender and sex role issues as family secrets. *Journal of Strategic and System Therapies*, 4, 32–41.

Libow, J.A., Raskin, P.A. and Caust, B.L. (1982). Feminist and family systems therapy: are they irreconcilable? *American Journal of Family Therapy*, 10, 3–12.

Morgan, D.H.J. (1985). *The Family, Politics and Social Theory*. London, Routledge & Kegan Paul.

Mustin, R.T. (1978). A feminist approach to family therapy. *Family Process* 17, 181–194.

Myrdal, G. (1944). *An American Dilemma*. New York, Harper & Row.
National Council for One-Parent Families (1987). *Information Sheet*. Available from 225 Kentish Town Road, London.
Oakley, A. (1982). Conventional families. In British Family Research Committee (eds) *Families in Britain*. London, Routledge & Kegan Paul.
Penfold, P.S. and Walker, G.A. (1984). *Women and the Psychiatric Paradox*. Milton Keynes, Open University Press.
Polk, B.B. (1974). Male power and the women's movement. *Journal of Applied Behavioral Science*, 10, 415–31.
Raush, H.J., Barry, W.A., Hertel, R.K. and Swain, M.A. (1974). *Communication, Conflict and Marriage*. San Francisco, Jossey-Bass.
Raven, B.H. (1965). Social influence and power. In I.D. Steiner and M. Fishbein (eds) *Current Studies in Social Psychology*. New York, Holt, Rinehart & Winston.
Scanzoni, J. (1978). *Sex Roles, Women's Work, and Marital Conflict*. Lexington, Mass., Lexington Books.
Schwendinger, J.R. and Schwendinger, H. (1983). *Rape and Inequality*. London, Sage.
Segal, L. (ed.) (1983). *What is to be Done about the Family?* Harmondsworth: Penguin.
Shields, S.A. (1975). Functionalism, Darwinism, and the psychology of women. *American Psychologist*, 30, 739–53.
Smith, A.J. and Siegel, R.F. (1985). Feminist therapy: redefining power for the powerless. In L. Bravo-Rosewater and L.E.A. Walker (eds) *Handbook of Feminist Therapy*. New York, Springer.
*Social Trends* (1987). London, HMSO.
Solomon, K. and Levy, N.B. (eds) (1982). *Men in Transition: Theory and Therapy*. New York, Plenum.
Spender, D. (1980). *Man Made Language*. London, Routledge & Kegan Paul.
Sturdivant, S. (1980). *Therapy with Women: A Feminist Philosophy of Treatment*. New York, Springer.
Walker, L.E. (ed.) (1985). *Women and Mental Health Policy*. London, Sage.
Williams, J.A. (1984a). Gender and intergroup behaviour: towards an integration. *British Journal of Social Psychology*, 23, 311–16.
—— (1984b). Women and mental illness. In J. Nicholson and H. Beloff (eds) *Psychological Survey 5*. Leicester, British Psychological Society.
—— (1984c). *Feminism and the Interpersonal Dynamics of Couples*. MSc Dissertation. University of Exeter.
Williams, J.A. and Giles, H. (1978). The changing status of women in society. In H. Tajfel (ed.) *Differentiation between Social Groups: Studies in the Social Psychology of Intergroup Behaviour*. London, Academic Press.

CHAPTER 14

# FAMILIES AND THEIR DIFFERING NEEDS

## Erica De'Ath

## INTRODUCTION

The family and family life seem always to be under scrutiny, being seen simultaneously as both the cause of, and the solution to, a wide range of social problems. While sociologists and anthropologists have long described the near universality of the family as the basic socializing unit of a community, it is only in recent decades that the family has attracted the status of 'theory', 'therapy' or 'policy'.

After the Second World War a new emphasis was placed on the importance and value of family life. Financial support was introduced in 1943 with a universal tax-financed family allowance system as part of the Beveridge social insurance proposals (Beveridge Report 1942), housing, health and education services were developed (Middleton 1971) and the task of the welfare, children's and mental health services was to move away from the punitive measures where families were often separated and children taken into public care and to create a new tradition embodied in the Curtis Report (1946) and the Children Act, 1948, to keep the family together by providing advice, assistance and support to families and individuals seeking help (Jordan 1974; Packman 1975).

It is, therefore, hard to realize that in 1970, 'no political party in the UK . . . identified itself with the social and economic interests of the family' (Wynn 1972). This apparent lack of interest in the family has changed markedly. In 1977 the Conservative Party Conference declared that they were 'the party of the family' (Thatcher 1977), and the 1978 Labour government Budget was called 'a family budget' (Callaghan 1978).

Although 'the family' has become a focus of interest and debate in an increasingly political arena over the last ten years, many family therapists have attempted to remain aloof from issues which are beyond the immediate family interaction no matter how much they contribute to the family's inability to cope.

Family therapy is often described as the treatment of family systems, and concerned with the way that families function. But what exactly do we mean when we talk of 'the family' and of 'functioning'? Respect for family life is guaranteed under the European Convention on Human Rights (Article 8) but many people might regard the very word 'family' as relating to an ideal institution rather than a tangible reality. As far as the state and family life is concerned non-intervention, at least in 'normal' and 'functioning' families, appears to be considered a value in itself. Indeed, as the Review of Child Care Law (DHSS 1985b) states, it is generally accepted that the state should not intervene between parent and child simply because it could provide or arrange something better than the parent can provide but only if the parents are falling so far below an acceptable standard that their children are suffering harm as a result. Although research can identify links between inadequate housing, low income and uncertain health with such problems as school truancy (Essen and Fogelman 1979) there is a danger that those families who cannot raise their children appropriately, find a job, provide an income sufficient to support their family, or whose children engage in delinquent activities, are seen as having some form of personal failing, character weakness or lack basic training which can be rectified by the intervention of psychiatrists, psychologists, social workers, probation workers or other similar welfare professionals.

Britain may not have a formal or explicit family policy but the majority of our legal, fiscal and social welfare legislation is based on the notion of the traditional 'normal' nuclear family. By this is meant a family where the father is in full-time work and the mother is at home looking after two dependent children. While the majority of children do still grow up with their natural parents this image of the traditional nuclear family now applies to only 5 per cent of households, because of numerous other factors such as unemployment, women working, divorce, and an increase in single households of both the young and elderly (Rimmer 1981).

Family life as lived by real people is simply what you find behind the door. Individual families are affected by where they live, what they eat, their jobs or their lack of them, who they are and what they think about themselves, their values, their attitudes and their beliefs. All families will also be affected by local and central government policies which will influence the range, type and quality of services and facilities available to them – housing, education, health and social welfare or recreational, and their ability to choose and purchase alternatives. It is the interactions between these factors which make family life easier for some families than for others. It also means that those working with families need to be sensitive to the different ways in which a family is able to cope with stress, crisis and behavioural or interactional problems because of the influence and impact of those other systems.

Family life is a process of change and development, not a static affair. All families pass through a series of stages or transition points and many have to cope with a variety of crisis events. No matter how similar such events may appear, families will respond in different ways according to their capacity to cope, and in many families that will be related to their capacity to adjust to change, and their belief in their ability to control their own lives and actions, and to make their own decisions and choices.

The purpose of this chapter is to consider how family therapists can accommodate the fact that there are many different types of families with many differing needs. Just as there is no 'blue-print' for the perfect family there is no one theoretical system of family therapy that can be applied to families who seek or are referred for help. The concept of a family as a system, of a group of people interacting and bound by certain rules or fixed habits of behaviour, is common but there is a wide variety of methods used to attempt to change the functioning of a family. The success of these different models will often relate to the therapist's ability to understand the differing needs of all family members and the wider networks and systems of which the family and its individual members are a part.

# EVERYDAY FAMILY LIFE

Being a parent has probably never been easy but each generation seems to produce accounts of how 'everyday family life' is more difficult than it used to be. Perhaps this reflects not so much the actual difficulties but the differences from one generation to another, not only of expectations, but also of the roles and relationships between family members and generations, the reality of daily routines and circumstances, and the changing nature of family patterns and structures.

Unfortunately we are often slow to analyse research in terms of what impact the particular findings may have for a wider field of social analysis, education, training and services. For example, in 1960 a survey of wives at home with young children noted, 'Clearly the nature of women's roles is changing, and the situation at present is one of conflict and stress' (Gavron 1965). It was nearly twenty years later that the link between clinical depression and a woman's daily experience was demonstrated (Brown and Harris 1978), and almost a decade after that study we are only just beginning to find ways of alleviating some of the experiences relating to that stress (Pound and Mills 1985; Koziarski *et al.* 1986). The voluntary sector has generated many imaginative community projects, family centres, home visiting and befriending schemes to help alleviate the isolation and stress experienced by so many young mothers but professional interest has been disappointing, attracting little interest and even less funding.

The 1970s became dominated by the concept of the 'cycle of deprivation' (Joseph 1972) and the war against poverty (Jordan 1974). While Sir Keith Joseph promoted preparation for parenthood as a means to equip parents better to meet their responsibilities for their children, others argued that it was futile to expect changes in parental behaviour without comparable changes in the social situation (Holman 1973). Indeed, it was not retraining that parents needed but 'large-scale fiscal measures to speed up slum clearance and housing schemes, to improve local amenities, to boost family income . . . to improve the job market' (Wilson 1974 : 253).

Concern with how families function and how they may function better provided the focus for two DHSS seminars. Sir Keith Joseph stated that 'there is little argument that the way families function is vital to the health of our society' (DHSS 1974 : 8). Eminent speakers spoke of the need for 'skills in interpersonal relationships, in communication, in coping with stress, and in shaping behaviour . . . [and for] certain permitting circumstances' (Rutter 1974 : 20) and made recommendations on how to provide support systems for families in relation to work, school, the neighbourhood and the home (Bronfenbrenner 1974 : 100–4).

In a study funded by the DHSS, looking at the needs of children Mia Kellmer Pringle emphasized the long-term influence of family relationships on children's psychological development. The quality of family life not only 'gives a sense of security, of companionship and belonging to each of its members; it also bestows a sense of purpose and direction, of achievement and of personal worth' (Pringle 1975 : 60). Another study ten years later, also funded by the DHSS, looked at the needs of parents, at the skills involved, and provided a national overview of what is available in the field of preparation, education and support for parents (Pugh and De'Ath 1984). This book aimed to encourage the many people who are working with parents and their children, whether as professional or voluntary workers, to re-examine what their own contribution might be to the network of supportive and educative services. It also highlighted how many parents find their confidence undermined by professional 'expertise' and argued that we should value and build on the abilities, skills and knowledge that parents bring to their role.

Family life cannot be seen in isolation from the wider patterns and changes in society. It is here that the diversity of family life and the differences between generations are most marked. Family structures are changing as divorce, co-habitation and remarriage are experienced by growing numbers of adults and children. Family patterns are changing as parents have fewer children, but as the older family members live longer there is an increase in the number of four or even five generations alive at the same time. Roles within families are changing in response to the greater equality of women and changing employment patterns; in some families the men may remain at home due to unemployment while the women are in paid work. Current trends in marriage indicate that the vast majority of women (92 per cent) and men (86 per cent) will marry (Rimmer 1981) and that even after a marriage has broken down many marry again within five years.

One of the most significant changes in family life over the last twenty years has been the rise (almost 600 per cent) in divorce. One in three marriages is now likely to end in divorce and 60 per cent of those will involve children under 16 (OPCS 1985). For many parents and children the transition is not helped by the adversarial nature of the divorce courts, which often increase conflict over custody, access and financial support rather than encouraging parents to agree arrangements jointly for the children (see Chapter 11). One of the main arguments used by supporters of family courts and conciliation services is the awareness that many adults take into future marriages unresolved conflict and bitterness which may jeopardize the remarriage (Parkinson 1986). As second marriages currently seem twice as likely to end in divorce as first marriages (OPCS 1986), a minority of children may be involved in two or more divorces and a growing number of step-relatives and half-siblings. At any one time there are approximately 1 million single-parent families with the care of 1.5 million children. A quarter of these families will be widowed mothers or lone fathers. The vast majority will be separated and divorced mothers, with some single mothers. Some will remain lone parents, some may experience a number of changes with one or more co-habitees over a period of years, many will remarry after a period of co-habitation and become a stepfamily.

We have no statistics to tell us how long children spend in any one of these stages of family transition, how many children are involved, what effect it has upon them or their relationship with their natural parents or step-parents. A recent estimate suggests that about one-fifth of babies born in 1982 are likely to experience a separation of their parents before they reach school-leaving age (Richards and Dyson 1982). Geographically there are important variations with a particularly heavy concentration of lone parents in certain inner-city areas, which has obvious implications for provision of services at a local level. While some people seek to denigrate the single and separated parents (Boyson 1986) there is a danger that remarriage and stepfamilies may be seen as part of the 'solution' to single-parent households. Not only is there a lack of research evidence to support this view but also it has been argued that many children do better remaining in a single-parent family than in having to make further adjustments to a third form of family life, the new stepfamily (Richards and Dyson 1982).

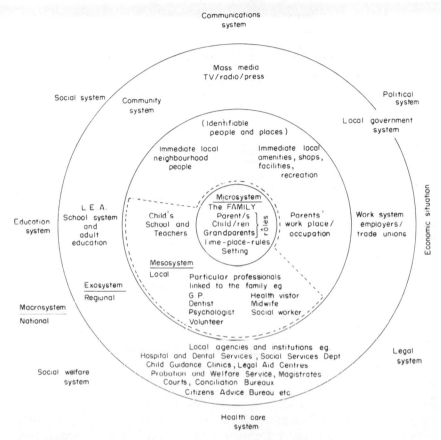

*Figure 14.1* An Ecological model of the system network of any one family. Dotted line indicates extent of normal involvement of family therapists beyond the family system

In trying to identify what we might mean by 'everyday family life' it is clear that family structures and patterns in general have changed over the last forty or fifty years and continue to change for individual families. It is also clear that all families are located in a wider society which is variously described as a suprasystem or the ecological context. Unfortunately most family therapists and others from the helping and caring professions work only within narrowly defined boundaries, as Figure 14.1 indicates. This becomes critical if we accept that some symptoms of family dysfunction are indicators of a dysfunction in systems beyond those boundaries.

Caplan (1976) argues that since most systems of support rely upon intactness, stability and integration within the family the implications for social planning and services must be to promote those very factors through income maintenance, housing, transport, health and welfare services and

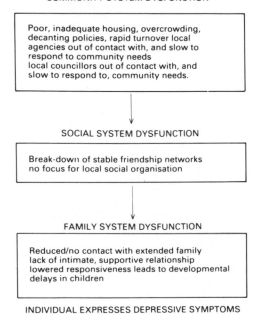

COMMUNITY SYSTEM DYSFUNCTION

Poor, inadequate housing, overcrowding,
decanting policies, rapid turnover local
agencies out of contact with, and slow to
respond to community needs
local councillors out of contact with, and
slow to respond to, community needs.

SOCIAL SYSTEM DYSFUNCTION

Break-down of stable friendship networks
no focus for local social organisation

FAMILY SYSTEM DYSFUNCTION

Reduced/no contact with extended family
lack of intimate, supportive relationship
lowered responsiveness leads to developmental
delays in children

INDIVIDUAL EXPRESSES DEPRESSIVE SYMPTOMS

*Figure 14.2*   Depression as system dysfunction

promotion of community and family facilities. Ryan (1986) describing depression as an indicator of dysfunction of community, social and family systems (see Figure 14.2) also highlights the importance and potential of a combination of formal and informal modes of intervention. Again, this model refers to factors outside the control of an individual medical practitioner, psychiatric worker, teacher, social worker or family therapist. Far from ignoring that fact or remaining aloof or overwhelmed by its implications, Ryan outlines one way in which change can be initiated at the levels at which dysfunction ocurs: within community, social and family systems. Before discussing such possibilities for working with families in the future it is important to recognize that different families may have different priorities as well as different patterns and pressures.

## THE NORMALITY OF FAMILIES

The majority of families who 'present symptoms' to clinicians, or seek advice and guidance from the helping professions, are suffering from distress, dis-ease and an inability to cope rather than a disease needing medical treatment. The current economic and social difficulties being experienced by millions of children, young people and adults are likely to increase the amount of marital and family crises. Unfortunately, as I have argued elsewhere (De'Ath and Haldane 1983; De'Ath 1983; De'Ath and Hill 1984), our health, education and social services devote little attention to equipping people with the knowledge to anticipate problems or the skills to solve or manage them. Instead we require clients to identify themselves through a problem, casting them in an inadequate or passive role rather than as people able to identify some of their immediate needs and seeking ways in which to meet those needs.

A glance at the range of contexts in which the principles of family therapy and a systems approach are incorporated highlights some of the difficulties facing an individual therapist or worker in trying to meet the differing needs of any family or family member (Treacher and Carpenter 1984; Campion 1985). In fact, one of the most important factors for any therapist or worker is to establish clearly the kind of help and advice that is being sought by the family, and the referring agency, and whether such help or advice can be appropriately given (Gorell-Barnes 1984; Murgatroyd and Woolfe 1985). There are several studies which demonstrate that the kind of help people want, or the priority they attach to particular needs, is not what they are offered (Mayer and Timms 1970; Lerner 1972; Rees 1979; Merrington and Corden 1981). It may also result in the investment of considerable social work resources and therapeutic effort with inconclusive outcomes (Mattinson and Sinclair 1979; Sainsbury *et al.* 1982). Families in poverty, who have a child with a handicap, single parents or stepfamilies, and families whose children have been taken into care, all are particularly vulnerable. As one mother described it, 'Nobody had neglected or ignored her. Unfortunately, however, they had offered counselling when practical advice was what was needed' (Russell 1978 : 8).

The Short Report (1984) noted that the majority of children in care are not recognizably different from other children and they are not in care because of their behaviour or characteristics but because of circumstances beyond their control in their family circumstances: homelessness, a single parent unable to cope, marital breakdown, unemployment of parents, illness. How can family therapists work effectively with such families either before or after their children have been taken into care? Recent research has again highlighted the discrepancy between what parents had identified as a priority when seeking help and what had, in fact, been offered. Parents who had sought help to avoid abusing their children had been denied short-term or respite care until they had either abandoned the child or reported or threatened non-accidental injury (Vernon and Fruin 1986), while other parents report that 'Nothing helpful in their eyes had been offered and some were left with a very real sense of despair' (DHSS 1985a : 9).

The last decade has also seen a significant change in attitude, support and

responsibility towards children and teenagers with handicaps and disabilities, encouraging living in ordinary family environments rather than in large
institutions. This affects not only those families with a child of their own to
care for but also the many foster and adoptive families who have been
recruited to help move some of the children and young people out of large
impersonal institutions. What does family therapy have to offer to these
families who are likely to have a number of problems to overcome in the
years ahead but are not problem families? Not only do such families have to
adjust to a new family member with very particular and special needs but
also they often encounter doubts, scepticism and prejudices from friends,
social workers, doctors and other professionals who may question their
reasons and capacity to take on such a responsibility (British Agencies of
Adoption and Fostering 1985).

In order to explore briefly some of the different priorities and needs that a
child, parent or therapist might have I shall take four different examples of
families who invariably experience some difficulties during transition stages
of family life or who frequently come to the attention of the professional
social welfare or health agencies. This is not meant to be an exclusive list and
some factors relate to specific transition points or stages of family life. It is
meant to act as a prompt for family therapists to consider the differing needs
that may compete for time and attention when they are working with a
family.

## SINGLE-PARENT HOUSEHOLDS

Single parents and their children have so many different needs that it is
unrealistic to think that any one worker or therapist could meet them all.
What is needed is an awareness of those different needs and concerns, an
understanding of how to offer appropriate support for the well-being of the
children and parent, and the ability to talk with the family and negotiate a
plan of action.

First, parent concerns are likely to be practical issues in the first instance
(whether their status is as a result of separation, divorce, bereavement or
choice) clarifying income, housing and child-care arrangements. For many
single parents there is a danger that poverty and practical problems take
precedence over personal needs such as the isolation, loneliness and possible stigma of being a single parent.

Second, child concerns will be a mixture of personal, parental and
practical and may express themselves in different ways at different times:
adjusting to the loss of the non-custodial parent and fearing the loss of the
custodial parent; visiting arrangements with the non-custodial parent and
grandparents; anger about the new family arrangement or change in circumstances, especially if there has been a change in household, school,

neighbourhood or friends. Many children are not informed of what is happening or what decisions have been made and often worry quite unnecessarily.

Third, family therapist concerns will vary according to the agency, role and function:

1 *Strictly practical arrangements*: welfare benefits and allowances; negotiating with housing, child-care or education agencies; exploring community and self-help networks.
2 *Personal and therapeutic issues*: the changing structure of the family from two parents to one; roles, rules and boundaries of family members specially when there is a non-custodial parent or co-habitee; child management; recognition of separation and loss; acceptance of new status as a single-parent household.
3 *A policing role*: sometimes an uneasy combination of both the above; trying to secure the best possible circumstances for the family in terms of housing, income and child-care support, while also making an assessment of the personal capabilities of the parent; identifying and implementing appropriate therapeutic intervention or making recommendations on the long-term needs or placement of a child.

Parents are not always aware of the different roles and functions of professionals and it is not easy for them to separate the practical needs from the personal. It is insensitive to imagine that a parent can focus solely on the personal and therapeutic issues such as developing a closer emotional relationship with a child, or dealing with feelings of loss and separation when the electricity has been cut off, the giro is late and there is no food in the house. It is equally insensitive to focus on all the areas where a parent may appear inadequate, for example household hygiene or educational or psychological stimulation of the children, without giving credit to the fact that so far she or he has kept the family together in what may be extremely difficult practical circumstances.

# FAMILIES WHERE A CHILD HAS A HANDICAP

An indication of the need for simple and practical help for parents of children with special needs is evidenced by the demand for the booklet *Help Starts Here*, published by the Voluntary Council for Handicapped Children. Over 600,000 copies have been distributed since 1976.

Clarifying what parents actually want is further reinforced by Davis (1985) describing a home-visiting scheme, run by the Tower Hamlets Child

Development Team, originally designed to teach operant conditioning to parents. Instead he found parents wanted to talk about social, personal, marital, financial difficulties or about coping in general. Sessions just listening to parents were invariably associated with improvements in the child's behaviour without any explicit attempt at direct intervention.

First, parent concerns are frequently dominated by the current management of the child and of his or her health, education, physical and cognitive development. Anxieties are also related to the future in terms of practical and financial arrangements when they get older and die. Voysey (1975) identified four typical problem areas for parent encounters with professionals: creating the desired impression; 'breaking through' the mutual ignorance of the other's definition of the situation; controlling information; and obtaining information. Her research also identifies parental concerns regarding the effects on family life; on the relationship with the disabled child; on normal child members; on the marital relationship; and on non-family member activities.

Second, the child with the handicap may be concerned not only with his or her particular disability but also with the way in which the family and others behave towards him or her because of it. Frustration and anger, self-pity and powerlessness, a desire to please and fear of failing may be experienced several times all in one day.[1]

Third, the family therapist may want to focus on:

1 *Practical issues*: allowances; obtaining physical aids; arranging access to health or educational facilities, or respite care.
2 *Personal or therapeutic issues*: the parents coming to terms with their 'loss' of a normal and healthy child; looking at the impact of this child on their marital relationship and their expectations and relationship towards any other children; allowing themselves to take 'time out' from their child by using respite care.
3 *Management issues*: very specific techniques related to managing the child, for example behaviour modification or Portage programmes.[2]

## STEPFAMILIES

Few people have been trained to work with stepfamilies or to appreciate the differences between natural families and stepfamilies. Listening to what stepparents, stepchildren and all the family members have to say may be crucial to determining how family therapists can possibly respond to what will probably be a variety of diverse and complex needs, both emotional and practical.

First, stepfamilies are formed through many different permutations of relationships – single, separated, divorced or bereaved adults – one or both ot whom brings a child or children from a previous relationship. Their concerns will be many and varied, some relating to their own age and stage of the life cycle, to that of their new partner, and to the age and stage of family life of all existing children, whether living with them, visiting or apart. Stepfamilies are different from natural families but not necessarily better or worse. All are born from loss, and partners and children have different histories. Stepparent concerns are frequently related to all learning to live together – adapting to new family structures, roles, responsibilities and expectations, clarifying rules and discipline, sorting out money, perhaps coping with access visits and maintenance. Habits of a lifetime, for both adults and children, may be challenged and new patterns of behaviour negotiated.

Second, children may have to adapt to a vast range of changes, not only a new parent figure but possibly stepbrothers and sisters, a new house, school, neighbourhood, grandparents, friends and neighbours. A child where both parents have remarried may simultaneously be the eldest in one family and the youngest in the other. Each family may have its own rules and the child has to remember which is which. This may generate anger, frustration, confusion, or an acceptance that different people have different needs and expectations. Children in their teens may resent the renewed emphasis on family life which conflicts with their own desire for peer group activities.

Third, the family therapist may have particular responsibilities in meeting with a stepfamily; working with stepfamilies is not easy because of the complexity of the issues and the potential number of people who influence and interact with the family:

1 *Practical issues*: in post-divorce families difficulties over access and child maintenance often result in a referral relating to child behaviour at home, on access visit or at school; or court welfare reports are required to review practical aspects of such arrangements.
2 *Personal and therapeutic issues*: divided loyalties can be the cause of much tension within stepfamilies (between spouse and the children, between the new family and the old one, between spouse and grandparents); unresolved issues from the previous relationship; anxieties about making the present marriage successful; divisions of roles and responsibilities within the family; whether to have a baby of the new marriage.
3 *Parenting issues*: problems in stepfamilies are more likely to relate to parenting issues between adults and children than to the marital couple relationship (Anderson and White 1986); whereas child-rearing is normally a central and spontaneous activity in a first time marriage stepparents may feel they have to make a special effort to like their stepchildren and exhibit 'conscious parenthood', a rational rather than emotional effort to be a 'good parent' (Burgoyne and Clark 1984). If they then have children of their new marriage the bond of natural parentage may

generate a different parental behaviour (whether more sensitive to the needs of the stepchildren, or non-custodial children, or more differentiated in favour of the natural children) and cause tension within the family, particularly with the adult and children relationships.

# DISADVANTAGED FAMILIES

It is frequently observed that therapists and helping agencies replicate the powerlessness and helplessness of the families they try to work with (Jenkins 1983: Reder 1983). The therapist is often tempted to take over and do what he or she can for each individual family rather than attempt to raise the level of self-esteem and self-confidence to mobilize the strength both of the families and their local communities, and aim to change not only each family's own ability to help itself but also that of the surrounding community.

First, parents are likely to be living on welfare benefits or low income and living in substandard or inadequate accommodation; fuel costs may be high, nutritional and health care awareness may be low. The lack of choice and control over their own lives and those of their children, the powerlessness that they experience may encourage them to be passive and apathetic – doing no more than they are required to do, or angry and demanding – insisting you find them better accommodation, more money, clothes and bedding for the children.

Second, children will often reflect the modelling of their parents – they may be listless, passive, uncommunicative, have difficulty in expressing their view or concern, little sense of personal responsibility or consequences of their actions. Equally they may be restless, unable to concentrate, with a range of physical, emotional or developmental delay. Children who have spent a considerable part of their early years in bed and breakfast accommodation are particularly at risk since they have had no chance to experience living in a family household.

Third, the morale of such families is usually low, making it difficult for a family therapist, especially if there are expectations for dramatic change in material circumstances and apathy towards household or child management or the value of personal relationships.

1 *Practical issues*: clearly alleviating the practical discomfort and disadvantage is a major factor particularly where a family is living in cramped, overcrowded, physically deteriorating and unhealthy accommodation.
2 *Personal and therapeutic issues*: allowing parents an opportunity to explore their own needs as individuals and as a couple; building up self-esteem and self-confidence; identifying what they do well and enjoy as a

couple and as a family with a view to enabling and empowering them to take more control over the shaping of their own lives.

3 *Community issues*: disadvantage is often the result of misconceived or unintended consequences of government or local authority social, housing, educational and welfare policies. Treating one family at a time will not resolve or alleviate their problems. As well as enabling and empowering family members to take more control family therapists have the opportunity to make known the implications and consequences of social policy in order to prevent further hardship and disadvantage for other children, young people and their families.

4 *Inter-agency issues*: some families attract the attention of many professional helpers (Roberts 1979), the therapist must therefore be aware of which other agencies the family is involved with, and consider how to work effectively together, intervene in any unhelpful multi-agency relationships and ensure that the needs of the family are given priority so that inter-agency involvement does not contribute to their disadvantage and become part of the family's problems (see Chapter 9; Adams 1979; Dimmock and Dungworth 1983; 1985; Reder 1986).

## WHAT DO FAMILIES NEED TO FUNCTION?

As already stated, families need 'certain permitting circumstances' (Rutter 1974 : 20) to function adequately. The question we need to ask as family therapists is, 'To what extent should the provision of material needs and concern with housing, education or social policy be considered therapeutic?' Essentially there are two separate issues related to the immediate short-term needs of a family to function sufficiently well to ensure that family members do not do too much harm to each other, and the long-term aim of trying to create within the family a nurturing relationship to allow for the parents to behave as, and for the children to become, caring, coping adults. The Infant Studies Intervention Project at UCLA, an intense programme with two staff members assigned to individual families with high-risk infants and offering a combination of home visiting, clinic sessions and counselling, still felt that for many cases the most useful intervention would have been a coordinated network of community services to help meet the families' economic, legal, housing, social and psychological problems (Bromwich 1981).

Clearly we can begin by recognizing the diversity of family life and the importance of listening to how families both define their family situation and what they feel their needs are. We can acknowledge that coping skills and strategies can be both enhanced and depressed by other systems which impinge on their family life. Finally, we must acknowledge that there are numerous other people who may have an effect upon family members, whether other professionals, extended family members, peer group, support or self-help groups. In short, we must acknowledge the range of internal and external influences upon a family and its individual members and the limitations of one family therapist upon their life as a whole.

If we look again at the whole context in which a family lives, as depicted in Figure 14.1, it is noticeable that family therapists tend to work with a very limited part of the overall systems network that impinges on any family. I am not the first to point out that one of the challenges for family therapy is

> to consider it in the widest possible context – not simply in the context of particular settings, or particular client groups, but in the context of social policy and the politics and economics of the social services.
>
> (Jordan 1981 : 269)

At the moment we appear to fail to acknowledge the importance and relevance of a systems perspective to our work with families as having direct implications for social policy. As a result, we will continue to serve families suffering the consequences of such policies and may well fail to provide them with any useful means of altering or alleviating their situation. It is not enough to limit our knowledge, skills and expertise as family therapists to be helpful with specific problems when we are in a pivotal position to be able to document the impact and consequences of certain policies for the development of future children and their families. Disadvantaged and poor people have to cope with problems and stresses that would tax even the most accomplished and adequate members of our society. As others have argued:

> The combination of poor housing, low incomes, uncertain health, insecure employment (coupled often, no doubt, with limited knowledge of parenting skills) offers a prescription for low achieving, poorly behaved, disenchanted or alienated young people. It represents a 'prescription for anti-welfare' for children.
>
> (Wedge 1984 : 14)

Our apparent disinclination to become involved in issues relating to such 'anti-welfare' policies encourages the view that the problems confronting those families referred to us lie within themselves, that their inability to function effectively and their inadequacies are of their own making and it is our role as 'experts' or professionals to re-educate or re-form them. It is noticeable that in the government response to the debate on the Social Services Committee on Children in Care, Mr Ray Whitney, then parliamentary under-secretary for the Department of Health and Social Security, stated:

> Whatever may be the structure of the Court system, the state of the law, the level of liaison and control of all the various agencies involved, in the end, the effectiveness of that whole system must rest to a very large extent on how one adult can work with the child and his family.
>
> (*Hansard* 1986)

Responsibility for the effective functioning of families deemed to need intervention or support appears to rest solely on the worker, whether a family therapist or another of the 'helping' professionals. It is hard to reconcile that statement with the facts that many children come into care not because of specific behavioural or emotional problems within the family but because of the unemployment, homelessness, poverty or illness of their parents. Unless the environment in which these families live is changed, no matter how skilled individual practitioners may be with the families on their case load, there will always be more families in need of 'treatment' and more children coming into care.

Families have not been so reticent in seeing the inappropriateness or inadequacy of both policies and provision and have sought to make their views known and to tell us about what they need. The creation and development of self-help groups over the last twenty years is testimony to the fact that many parents are not satisfied with the services provided or the manner in which they are delivered. Parents of children with handicaps who found some professionals were insensitive to their need for understanding and support or whose 'expert' advice had little practical relevance in securing special equipment or facilities set up their own groups and organizations. Not only did such parents wish to become better informed in providing and caring for their child but also they wished to increase the amount of research to investigate the causes of such handicaps, to alleviate some of the suffering through better designed equipment and to improve the training of those professionals who were there to help the parents and children.

The success of collective action by parents is often seen as a middle-class activity, with examples of playgroups and National Childbirth Trust classes being cited as educated and affluent women providing services more in keeping with their middle-class life-style. While this may have been true of the early days of the consumer movement it is no longer an accurate reflection of the many community and self-help initiatives designed to help parents and families function more actively and effectively for themselves and their children (De'Ath 1985).

During the 1970s groups were set up by parents who were angry at the way in which social policies and welfare provision discriminated against them and sought both to rectify the legislative anomalies and also increase awareness of their needs with the relevant professionals. Gingerbread provides a network of over 400 self-help groups for single parents and offers advice on a range of issues from welfare rights to adjusting to family life with only one adult figure. OPUS (Organizations for Parents Under Stress) links together all those Parents Anonymous groups for parents who have or feel in danger of abusing their child. OPUS runs training courses for the many parent volunteers who offer a twenty-four-hour crisis line, home visiting and befriending service and in some towns a drop-in centre. Stepfamily also offers a telephone listening service, having found that so many stepfamilies required advice and support which was sensitive to their needs and which appeared to be lacking in those professionals they had turned to for help.

Many of these self-help organizations exist because the group of parents coming together to form them know what their needs are and that they aren't being met elsewhere. They describe such needs as

1  The practical means to bring up a family, adequate housing and income, suitable facilities or physical aids and equipment.
2  Information and factual advice on welfare rights and benefits (approximately 4 million families live on Supplementary Benefits).
3  Information, advice, guidance and skills in child management, household management, social and life skills (not just when they are in crisis but when they need to know).
4  Informal advice and support from others who are or have been in a similar situation, self-help groups, family centres and community networks.
5  How to cope, rather than insights into why they are not coping, and recognition of what they do manage to achieve rather than an emphasis on all they do not manage to do.

Increasingly the development of family centres is challenging the notion of individual treatment sessions and discrete activities with individual children or families (Phelan 1983; Hasler 1984; Cannan 1986; Smith 1986). Many centres, both in the statutory and voluntary field, are exploring ways of working with all local families, whether in a supportive, preventive or interventionist way within their own local community and attempting to address their needs as citizens, neighbours, parents and children, as well as the specific aspects of their own family structure or dynamics (Thamesdown's Voluntary Service Centre 1984; Warren 1986; Adamson and Warren forthcoming; Holman 1988).

## WHAT CAN FAMILY THERAPISTS DO?

Although family therapy is reputed to have begun hesitantly in the 1950s (Walrond-Skinner 1976), work with parents and children together occurred long before that. First, family therapists need to remind themselves of some of the pioneering work with families such as the Peckham Health Centre of 1926 (Pearse and Crocker 1943) or the Parent and Child Centre in Birmingham established in 1934 (Davies 1980). Second, they should examine what is known about family support activities developing now (Pillai *et al.* 1982; De'Ath 1987). Third, they should reflect on what constitutes the content of a family therapy session; 'the topics are to do with the fact of family life not the presence of a labelled disturbed family member' (Dare 1979 : 2).

Family therapists need to be clear about both their role and responsibilities. There will always be a need for specialists offering 'treatment of family systems' and working primarily in hospital departments and clinics, what Caplan (1971) has called the secondary level in a community approach to preventive psychiatry. However, if we are truly concerned with enabling families to function then we need to address how we can contribute to the other two levels – primary prevention and administrative action.

Primary prevention relates to reducing the risks to future families by increasing the skills and opportunities for healthy family functioning. This might be done in a number of ways, not least of which would be trying to determine what it is that makes a family function in a healthy way (Lewis *et al.* 1976), and what makes some children and families identified as multiply disadvantaged achieve 'success' where others fail (Pilling forthcoming). It is a question not only of increasing our own knowledge but also of finding ways in which this may be passed on through educational and life skills programmes to children and young people, both to help them enjoy living in their own family and to grow towards maturity and become responsible and capable parents if and when they choose to have their own family.

Adding to the wealth of knowledge of family functioning is not sufficient, it is the appropriate sharing of that knowledge which is the key to primary prevention. This includes encouraging informal support networks, providing realistic information and opportunities for parents and young people to seek informal advice on problems as and when they arise as children grow older. As well as gaining access to information young people and their parents also want to develop the skills to cope with the issues, whether they are related to discipline, behaviour, development, school or access arrangements. Skills of negotiation and communication become particularly important as children reach and pass through adolescence when family life can be sorely tested as understanding and rules relating to sex, drink, drugs, smoking, behaviour, money, clothes, hair styles, and other everyday events have to be clarified and agreed.

Family therapists can attempt to meet some of the differing needs of the families they work with both by offering their own skills, knowledge and experience to the community and by being aware of what the community is already developing and providing for itself. If change does, indeed, need to be initiated at the levels at which dysfunction occurs within the community, social and family systems, it makes sense to pool resources and seek to develop an integrated programme of formal and informal support and provision for the local estate or area (Ryan 1986). The development of self-help groups and family centres has widened the opportunities for community-minded family therapists to work with parents, families, children and young people within the community and away from clinics.

First then, family therapists could consider acting as consultants, supervisors or trainers to those providing drop-in centres, crisis phone lines, self-help groups, or one-to-one befriending schemes. This can be an extremely important contribution if offered in the spirit of partnership and sharing of skills and expertise since working in informal or self-help setting can be very stressful (Fogell 1986).

Second, family therapists could contribute directly to such services by running parent advice sessions, offering crisis therapy, writing straightforward information leaflets or serving on the management committee.

Third, family therapists need to keep up to date with the community and support networks locally in order to be able to give such information to the families they work with; for example, having a list to hand of the current contact, address and telephone number of groups such as Gingerbread, Stepfamily, Contact a Family, Homestart, MENCAP, Child Poverty Action Group and Parents Anonymous, as well as a list of family centres, drop-in centres, community centres and child-care facilities.

This is not always easy but increasingly there are networks to enable professionals to be informed if they choose to do so. Umbrella organizations exist to help make such information available: Child Care, Family Centres Network, Personal and Family Services Group (National Council for Voluntary Organizations), National Self-Help Support Centre, Voluntary Council for Handicapped Children, Voluntary Organizations Liaison Council for Under-Fives, and others (see De'Ath and Webster 1986).

Administrative action is perhaps the most difficult for many family therapists to see as a legitimate area for their activity or concern. As outlined earlier, however, if the legal, educational and welfare system is so designed that it inhibits rather than enhances the work there is surely a duty, especially if employed within the public service, to highlight this factor on purely pragmatic cost-effective grounds. Awareness of unintended consequences of government policies that cause unnecessary and unwarranted hardship and that necessitate a further charge on the public services, once again on pragmatic and cost-efficiency grounds need to be identified and documented for relevant ministers, civil servants and policy-makers. In addition, suggestions for alternative policies and practice based on experience, knowledge and specialized expertise are welcomed even if not always acted upon. The development of services within the voluntary sector which are subsequently incorporated into professional practice and government thinking are a testimony to this.

If family therapists see themselves as a professional body they need to consider whether they have a responsibility to comment on existing or proposed child-care or family welfare policy and practice issues. The current

Conservative government has introduced a wide range of changes in legislation and practice that affects the family life and functioning of virtually every single child, young person and family in this country. Many such policies and legislative changes were made available in draft form as consultative documents, reports, guidelines and working papers. Some professional bodies have always felt it part of their duty to respond to such documents and others are beginning to do so.

The Association for Family Therapy (AFT) in Britain has a small Family Law and Policy Group. In 1984 this group submitted a response to the Booth Committee in relation to conciliation services and to the Parliamentary Select Committee (Social Services) Short Report with regard to children in care. There has been little activity since that time and I am not aware of any requests from the membership of AFT that comments or submissions should be made on policies that have arisen subsequently; for example, the Review of Child Care Law, the Social Security Act, the Bed and Breakfast Regulations (the increasing use of bed and breakfast accommodation for families with young children), the DHSS Child Abuse Guidelines, the Law Commission papers on Custody and on Guardianship, the Lord Chancellor's Review of Family Courts. It is not clear whether family therapists as an association feel it is inappropriate to respond to such issues but clearly it is a possible form of administrative action they could choose to take if they seriously wished to acknowledge the systemic world in which families live and function.

As individuals, family therapists can look at their own practice in meeting the differing needs of the families with whom they work. Most families understand the concept of making the best possible use of scarce resources. Joining with the family to pool resources and knowledge and to set short-term and long-term objectives and priorities is usually more constructive than their passive acceptance of your 'expert' knowledge which they may perceive as valid but currently irrelevant or inappropriate. Examining the structural determinants within the family and the constraints imposed by factors external to the family so as to emphasize the strengths within the family rather than focus on the weaknesses can also lead to insight by family members as well as clarifying what actions they already take, how these are inhibited or enhanced by others, and what they might do to change things. The family definition of their situation, their awareness of their own cultural and social patterns, their perception of male and female roles, and of the notion of authority and accountability within their family, all will affect their needs and, in turn, the ability of therapists to hear, understand and respond appropriately.

# MEETING THE NEEDS OF FAMILIES IN THE FUTURE

Looking at current developments in social and welfare policy it seems likely that the four groups of families highlighted earlier will continue to seek advice and guidance from the helping professions.

Divorce rates show no sign of diminishing; indeed current figures suggest that one in twenty-two children will see their parents separate by the age of 5 years old, with one in five by the age of 16 years (Haskey 1983). The numbers of single-parent households are therefore unlikely to decline. The increase in the separation of parents with younger children may give rise to a higher frequency of remarriage and of subsequent re-divorces. In 1985 one in six divorces was for a second or later marriage; since 1978 such re-divorces have almost doubled (OPCS 1986).

As medical intervention increases there may be greater numbers of children enabled to live despite having severe mental and physical handicaps. The emphasis on care in the community and the closure of residential institutions may put additional stress on to families if there is inadequate respite care or financial provision to alleviate the demands of providing constant nursing and supervisory care. The continued economic crisis and changing social and welfare legislation suggest that there will continue to be large numbers of families living in long-term poverty.

Many family therapists will already be familiar with the above pattern of family life in the 1980s and aware that many families presenting with problems will have one or more of the above traits. What family therapists should consider is whether this is a chance phenomenon or whether there may in fact be a direct link. If family therapists believe that the families they see are unable to function adequately because they find the fact of single parenthood, divorce, stepfamily relationships, physical or mental handicap, or long-term poverty places constraints and stresses on their family life such that it is difficult to function without support, advice and permitting circumstances, what do family therapists intend to do about it?

Family life is held to be a central tenet of our social and welfare policy. The ability to cope and function adequately is seen to be affected by a number of personal and family characteristics but also by social and environmental constraints. Basic living conditions and community support are seen as part of the permitting circumstances necessary for family functioning. Although the nature of family patterns, structures, roles and expectations may be changing most children still grow up in a family and most people want to marry, many for a second or even third time.

In summarizing the key issues for family therapists in working with the differing needs of families in the future I have placed these in three groups. The issue remains what, if anything, family therapists can do to alleviate or reduce the stress on families in the future.

## Issues for practitioners

1 The need for more and better knowledge of diverse family types and their differing needs.
2 The ability to work in partnership with families, joining with them in identifying and defining the priority of needs and ways of meeting them.
3 A willingness to examine factors outside the family that constrain and influence their ability to function adequately and to take steps to alleviate or redress those.
4 A willingness to share professional and personal skills and resources with the community; a 'barefoot doctor' approach to encourage the development of self-help and community support within the neighbourhood.
5 In addition to sharing generalist skills as above, a willingness to share specialist professional knowledge and skills when appropriate. For example providing consultation, supervision, training or direct services to those offering informal support in areas such as child abuse, marital counselling, post-natal depression, separation, divorce and bereavement.
6 Offering specialist professional knowledge and skills as a community preventive and educational service to parents and families – a service they can use as and when they need it and not limited access through professional referral systems.

## Issues for the health, education and social welfare systems

1 Ensuring that family life education and opportunities to develop coping life skills are available to all as part of our general and continuing education provision.
2 Acknowledging that values, attitudes and skills are learned and shaped by our environment and can therefore be altered, improved and added to.
3 Acknowledging that family life is a continuous process and skills and knowledge need to be developed all the time to adjust to change and meet new needs. This requires access to information and opportunities to learn from others, both professionals and other families, to share skills and experience and make the best use of scarce resources.
4 Families require 'permitting circumstances' and conditions for learning and functioning; any support or intervention services need to be appropriate, accessible, amenable and available.
5 Families need to be enabled to make choices, take responsibility and be independent if they are to function adequately and this requires appropriate levels of support within the family and community.

6 Working in new ways with families requires adequate and appropriate training and supervision of all practitioners working with children, young people, families and in linking with the informal self-help and community support networks.

## Issues for policy-makers and politicians

1 Families cannot function adequately unless they have basic 'permitting circumstances' such as appropriate housing and sufficient income to keep warm, feed and clothe themselves.
2 Families need choices in child-care, respite care, employment opportunities and personal development if they are to function successfully as citizens.
3 The balance between the privacy of the family and the needs of the state for healthy and responsible citizens requires commitments from both sides.
4 Interventionist policies which appear to present an 'all or nothing' approach reduce choice, enforce powerlessness, inhibit change and development, increase stress and dysfunctional patterns in families, reduce the capacity to change and greatly limit the ability of the helping professionals to achieve improvements in family functioning.

## CONCLUSION

As the literature on family therapy grows it appears that the promise of effective intervention in a wide range of problems and in diverse agency settings has been met (Treacher and Carpenter 1984). However, the social context of the family can no longer be ignored. The differing needs of families relate not simply to the problems they present, or the procedure and agency through which they are referred. The ability and capacity for families to function are related to the interactions they have with immediate systems in the neighbourhood and with the schools, health, housing, social and welfare agencies and other services. Such interactions are shaped, determined and constrained by the wider economic, political, social and legal systems.

Family therapists understand that an individual's ability to function does not exist in isolation but is influenced by, and in turn influences, other persons and other systems in his or her environment. It is time that family therapists recognized that they also do not exist in isolation but are influenced by and could in turn influence more significantly those systems which inhibit and can enhance the lives of the families with whom they work.

## NOTES

1 Other children in the family may be ambivalent to both parents and the handicapped child, experiencing not only anger and resentment at the constraints put upon 'ordinary' family life but also eagerness and perhaps guilt to help.
2 The Portage Home Teaching Scheme originated in Wisconsin, USA, in 1972 and was first introduced in England in 1976. The Portage Home Teaching Model has three key features: use of direct contact people (parents, friends, neighbours), structured teaching methods, and positive monitoring and recording procedures. See Cameron, S. (1982) (ed.) *Working Together: Portage in the UK*. Windsor, NFER-Nelson.

## REFERENCES

Adams, R. (1979). Agency and family therapy. *Journal of Family Therapy*, 1, 211–19.

Adamson, J. and Warren, C. (forthcoming). Family centres. In A.P. Wolton and W.C. Elliot (eds) Oxford, Pergamon.

Anderson, J.Z. and White, G.D. (1986). An empirical investigation of interaction and relationship patterns in functional and dysfunctional nuclear families and stepfamilies. *Family Process*, 25, 407–22.

Beveridge Report (1942). *Social Insurance and Allied Services*. Cmd 6404. London, HMSO.

Boyson, R. (1986). Quoted in *Guardian*, 10 October at Church Society Fringe Meeting, Conservative Party Conference, Bournemouth.

British Agencies for Adoption and Fostering (1985). *Whose Handicap? Finding New Families for Children with Mental Handicaps* (video). London, BAAF.

Bromwich, R. (1981). *Working with Parents and Infants: An Interactional Approach*. Baltimore, Md, University Park Press.

Bronfenbrenner, U. (1974). Children, families and social policy: an American perspective. In DHSS, *The Family in Society*, London, HMSO.

Brown, G.W. and Harris, T. (1978). *Social Origins of Depression: A Study of Psychiatric Disorder in Women*. London, Tavistock.

Burgoyne, J. and Clark, D. (1984). *Making a Go of it: A Study of Stepfamilies in Sheffield*. London, Routledge & Kegan Paul.

Callaghan, J. (1978). Women's Labour Conference, Southport, 14 May.

Campion, J. (1985). *The Child in Context: Family-Systems Theory in Educational Psychology*. London, Methuen.

Cannan, C. (1986). Sanctuary or stigma? The roles of the family centre. *Community Care*, 22 May.

Caplan, G. (1971). *An Approach to Community Mental Health*. London, Tavistock.

—— (1976). The family as a support system. In G. Caplan and K. Killilea (eds) *Support Systems and Mutual Help: Multidisciplinary Explorations*. New York, Grune & Stratton.

Curtis Report (1946). *Report of the Committee on the Care of Children*. Cmd 6902. London, HMSO.

Dare, C. (1979). Editorial, *Journal of Family Therapy*, 1, 1–5.

Davies, M. (1980). The pre-school child in difficulty: a systems viewpoint. *Journal of Family Therapy*, 2, 101–14.

Davis, H. (1985). Developing the role of parent adviser in the child health service. In E. De'Ath and G. Pugh (eds) *Working Together with Children with Special Needs: Implications for Preschool Services*. Partnership Paper 3, London, National Children's Bureau.

De'Ath, E. (1982). Interventions with families: preparing the way for teaching parenting skills. *Journal of Family Therapy*, 4, 229–46.

—— (1983). Teaching parenting skills. *Journal of Family Therapy*, 5, 321–36.

—— (1985). *Self-Help and Family Centres: A Current Initiative in Helping the Community to Care*. London, National Children's Bureau.

—— (1987). A multiple approach to family support. In T. Goldberg and I. Sinclair (eds) *The Family Support Exercise*. London, National Institute of Social Work.

De'Ath, E. and Haldane, D. (1983). *The Family in a Political Context*, AFT Occasional Paper 1, Aberdeen University Press.

De'Ath, E. and Hill, M. (eds) (1984). *Towards a Coherent Policy for Disadvantaged Children*. University of Dundee, Extra-Mural Dept.

De'Ath, E. and Webster, G. (1986). *Families and Self-Help: A Resource Pack*. London, National Children's Bureau.

DHSS (1974). *The Family in Society: Dimensions of Parenthood*. London, HMSO.

—— (1985a). *Social Work Decisions in Child Care: Recent Research Findings and their Implications*. London, HMSO.

—— (1985b). *Review of Child Care Law: Report to Ministers of an Interdepartmental Working Group*. London, HMSO.

Dimmock, B. and Dungworth, D. (1983). Creating manoeuvrability for family/systems therapists in social services departments. *Journal of Family Therapy*, 5, 53–71.

—— (1985). Beyond the family: using network meetings with statutory child care cases. *Journal of Family Therapy*, 7, 45–68.

Essen, J. and Fogelman, K. (1979). Childhood housing experiences. *Concern*, 32, 5–10.

Fogell, C. (1986). Dilemmas for staff working in informal settings. *British Journal of Social Work*, 16, supplement, 103–9.

Gavron, H. (1965). *The Captive Wife: Conflicts of Housebound Mothers*. Harmondsworth, Pelican.

Gorell-Barnes, G. (1984). *Working with Families*. London, Macmillan.

*Hansard* (1986). Children in care adjournment debate, 24 February, para. 700–31.

Haskey, J. (1983). Children of divorcing couples. *Population Trends*, 31, 20. London, HMSO.

Hasler, J. (1984). *Family Centres: Different Expressions – Same Principles*. London, Children's Society.

Holman, B. (1973). Poverty: consensus and alternatives. *British Journal of Social Work*, 3, (4), 431–46.

—— (1988). *Putting Families First, Prevention and Child Care*. London, Macmillan.

Jenkins, H. (1983). A life-cycle framework in the treatment of under-organised families. *Journal of Family Therapy*, 5, 359–78.

Jordan, B. (1974). *Poor Parents, Social Policy and the 'Cycle of Deprivation'*. London, Routledge & Kegan Paul.

—— (1981). Family therapy – an outsider's view. *Journal of Family Therapy*, 3, 269–80.

Joseph, K. (1972). The parental role. National Children's Bureau Annual Conference 1972. *Concern*, 11.

Koziarski, M., Hodgson, S. and Nical, A.R. (1986). Family therapy in a community mother and toddler project. *Journal of Family Therapy*, 8, 207–24.

Lerner, B. (1972). *Therapy in the Ghetto*. Baltimore, Md, Johns Hopkins University Press.

Lewis, J.M., Beavers, W.R., Gossett, J.T. and Phillips, V.A. (1976). *No Single Thread: Psychological Health in Family Systems*. New York, Brunner/Mazel.

McKay, A., Goldberg, E.M. and Fruin, D. (1973). Consumers and a social services department. *Social Work Today*, 4, 486–91.

Mattinson, J. and Sinclair, I. (1979). *Mate and Stalemate*. Oxford, Blackwell.

Mayer, J. and Timms, N. (1970). *The Client Speaks: Working-Class Impressions of Casework*. London, Routledge & Kegan Paul.

Merrington, D. and Corden, J. (1981). Families' impressions of family therapy. *Journal of Family Therapy*, 3, 243–61.

Middleton, N. (1971). *When Family Failed: The Treatment of the Child in the Care of the Community in the First Half of the Twentieth Century*. London, Gollancz.

Murgatroyd, S. and Woolfe, R. (1985). *Helping Families in Distress: An Introduction to Family Focused Helping*. London, Harper & Row.

OPCS (Office of Population Censuses and Surveys) (1985). *OPCS Monitor*, Reference 85/1, 5b and 7. London, HMSO.

—— (1986). *Population Trends*, 45, Table 15, p. 55. London, HMSO.

Packman, J. (1975). *The Child's Generation: Child Care Policy from Curtis to Houghton*. Oxford, Blackwell.

Packman, J., Randall, J. and Jacques, N. (1986). *Who Needs Care? Social Work Decisions about Children*. Oxford, Blackwell.

Parkinson, L. (1986). *Conciliation in Separation and Divorce*. Beckenham, Kent, Croom Helm.

Pearse, I. and Crocker, L. (1943). *The Peckham Experiment: A Study of the Living Structure of Society*. London, Allen & Unwin.

Phelan, J. (1983). *Family Centres: A Study*. London, Children's Society.

Pillai, V., Collins, A. and Morgan, R. (1982). Family walk-in centre – Eaton Socon: evaluation of a project on preventive intervention based in the community. *Child Abuse and Neglect*, 6, 71–9.

Pilling, D. (forthcoming). *Escape from Disadvantage*. London, National Children's Bureau.

Pound, A. and Mills, M. (1985). A pilot evaluation of newpin – home-visiting and befriending scheme in South London. *ACPP Newsletter*, 7, 13–15.

Pringle, M.K. (1975). *The Needs of Children*. London, Hutchinson.

Pugh, G. and De'Ath, E. (1984). *The Needs of Parents, Practice and Policy in Parent Education*. London, Macmillan.

Reder, P. (1983). Disorganised families and the helping professions: 'who's in charge of what?' *Journal of Family Therapy*, 5, 23–36.

—— (1986). Multi-agency family systems. *Journal of Family Therapy*, 8, 139–52.

Rees, S. (1979). *Social Work Face to Face*. New York, Columbia University Press.

Richards, M. and Dyson, M. (1982). *Separation, Divorce and the Development of Children: A Review*. University of Cambridge, Child Care and Development Group.

Rimmer, L. (1981). *Families in Focus: Marriage, Divorce and Family Patterns*. London, Study Commission on the Family.

Roberts, W. (1979) Family or agency – where to intervene. *Journal of Family Therapy*, 1, 203–9.

Russell, P. (1978). Help starts here. *Concern*, 28. London, National Children's Bureau.

Rutter, M.L. (1974). Dimensions of parenthood: some myths and some suggestions. In DHSS, *The Family In Society: Dimensions of Parenthood*. London, HMSO.

Ryan, P.J. (1986). The contribution of formal and informal systems of intervention to the alleviation of depression in young mothers. *British Journal of Social Work*, 16, supplement, 71–82.

Sainsbury, E., Nixon, S. and Phillips, D. (1982). *Social Work in Focus: Clients' and Social Workers' Perceptions of Long-Term Social Work*. London, Routledge & Kegan Paul.

Short Report (1984). House of Commons, Second Report from the Social Service Committee, Session 1983–84, Children in Care, vol. 1. London, HMSO.

Smith, T. (1986). Family centres: prevention, partnership, or community alternatives? In A. Macfarlane (ed.) *Progress in Child Health*. Edinburgh, Churchill Livingstone.

Thamesdown's Voluntary Service Centre (1984). *Local Partnership in Action: A Look at Family Projects in Swindon*. Thamesdown VSC, Swindon.

Thatcher, M. (1977). Conservative Party Conference, Blackpool.

Treacher, A. and Carpenter, J. (1984). *Using Family Therapy*. Oxford, Blackwell.

Vernon, J. and Fruin, D. (eds) (1986). *In Care: A Study of Social Work Decision-Making*. London, National Children's Bureau.

Voysey, M. (1975). *A Constant Burden: The Reconstitution of Family Life*. London, Routledge & Kegan Paul.

Walrond-Skinner, S. (1976). *Family Therapy: The Treatment of Natural Systems*. London, Routledge & Kegan Paul.

Warren, C. (1986). Towards a family centre movement: reconciling day care, child protection and community work. BAPSCAN Conference, March, Scotland.

Wedge, P. (1984). Disadvantaged children: the scale of the problem and the scope of solutions. In E. De'Ath and M. Hill (eds) *Towards a Coherent Policy for Disadvantaged Children*. University of Dundee, Extra-Mural Dept.

Wilson, H. (1974). Parenting in poverty. *British Journal of Social Work*, 4, 241–54.

Wynn, M. (1972). *Family Policy*. Harmondsworth, Penguin.

# CHAPTER 15

# FAMILY THERAPY RESEARCH

*Arlene Vetere*

## INTRODUCTION

This chapter describes some family therapy research in Britain. My task is not easy. First, North American family therapy researchers present us with an exciting if somewhat overwhelming selection of research studies from which we might sample happily and endlessly, and second, examples of sound British family therapy research are scarce. This scarcity is a little puzzling. Attendance at the Association for Family Therapy conferences and research workshops over the past few years has revealed an active interest in family therapy research among British clinicians, who share many researchable ideas. It may be that British clinical researchers are less likely to publish or even to get their research off the ground. I shall consider some of the reasons for the lack of published family therapy research in Britain later in the chapter, a more notable lack since family therapy itself has been a working medium for British clinicians for nearly two decades.

Family therapy research is an umbrella title for distinct types and methods of investigation. Since there is not space to consider them all, I address three major areas: family therapy outcome research, family therapy process research, and family therapy training research. Wherever possible, British examples are used to give a flavour of the themes taken up by researchers, along with the associated methodological difficulties. But it is just as important to look at some of the reasons why research does not happen, and, to put the horse before the cart, to question whether we need research at all, who pays for it and who consumes it? The chapter will end with a look at some future directions for British family therapy research and ways in which practical, low cost research can be effected.

# FAMILY THERAPY OUTCOME RESEARCH

## Introduction

Outcome research dominates the field of family therapy research. Economic and local political pressures to evaluate the effectiveness of family therapy may in part account for the abundant North American outcome literature of the 1970s, and although outcome studies slackened off in the early 1980s we now have the phenomenon of reviews of the reviews of family therapy outcome research (see Gurman and Kniskern 1981: Gurman *et al.* 1986). In Britain, though, such outcome research lags behind practice and training in family therapy. Where clinical practitioners reach forward to embrace ever-new family theories and family intervention techniques and to teach aspiring family therapists, we find there is no sound empirical base for such practice in Britain. In particular some major systems of intervention, for example strategic and paradoxical techniques, have not been rigorously evaluated at all, except in a descriptive or anecdotal fashion.

In this section I shall look at two examples of British work which exemplify the two main types of outcome research: research which compares a family therapy intervention with traditional clinical practice and research which compares one form of family therapy with another.

## Expressed emotion (Leff, Kuipers, Berkowitz, Eberlein-Vries and Sturgeon 1982)

The study of Leff and colleagues (1982) describes family therapy as part of a multimodality treatment package for schizophrenic patients at high risk of relapse. Their research is based on the understanding that schizophrenia has a complex aetiology, which includes a genetic component, but that acute stress (for example life events) or chronic stress (such as long-standing family problems) can cause or exacerbate schizophrenic symptoms in vulnerable individuals.

Their study developed out of the work of Brown and colleagues at the Medical Research Council Psychiatry Unit in London, where it was noted that relapse was more common among those schizophrenics discharged to live with close relatives than those living alone and that 'close emotional ties' were not always beneficial for schizophrenics (Brown *et al.* 1966). Brown and Rutter (1966) developed a method for rating the relatives' attitudes to the patient from recorded interviews, i.e. expressed emotion (EE, as 'close emotional ties' came to be known). It was found in two prospective studies that a high rating for hostility, over-involvement or critical comments (high EE) in the relative with the closest contact with the schizophrenic individual was strongly predictive of relapse in the nine months following discharge from hospital (Brown *et al.* 1972; Vaughan and Leff 1976). Further studies indicated that the effects of highly arousing environmental conditions, such as contact with high EE relatives, could be moderated by both avoiding such contact and by taking anti-psychotic medication (Leff *et al.* 1973).

The study of Leff and his colleagues (1982) aimed to reduce the relapse rates of high-risk schizophrenic patients in a controlled trial of a 'psycho-social' intervention. Forty patients met the research diagnostic criteria of schizophrenia on the Present State Examination (Wing *et al.* 1974). Twenty-four patients were from families high in expressed emotion, as assessed by the Camberwell Family Interview (CFI), and had more than thirty-five hours face-to-face contact with their family per week. All patients were discharged from hospital at the beginning of the intervention and all were maintained on neuroleptic drugs. Only a few were discharged with residual active symptoms, thus there was a good match of family risk variables between the groups. The predicted probability of relapse based on the work of Vaughan and Leff (1976) for each patient over a nine-month period is approximately 50 per cent. Relapse was assessed with the Present State Examination (PSE). Both high and low EE families were randomly assigned to a control condition of routine out-patient care or an experimental condition, yielding four groups. The low EE families were included to assess the effects of the education programme and did not take part in the individual family therapy sessions, whereas the high EE families received the whole intervention package.

The family treatment package consisted of an education programme, a relatives' group and family therapy. The education programme ran over two sessions and provided information to the family members on the nature, course and treatment of schizophrenia. A knowledge interview was conducted with the families before and after the education programme and at nine months follow-up to assess the retention and assimilation of knowledge about schizophrenia. The rehabilitation of the schizophrenic patient was the main focus of the discussion in the relatives' group. Both high and low EE families were invited with the expectation that low EE family members would vicariously teach high EE family members alternative ways of coping with a schizophrenic relative. The family therapy sessions aimed to reduce EE in the relatives and/or face-to-face contact with relatives since both have been found to be detrimental to rehabilitation in previous studies. The treatment sessions took place in the family home and varied in the techniques used and in the number of sessions offered each family, with a range of 1–25 sessions and a mean of 5.6 sessions.

The PSE and EE assessments were repeated at the nine month follow-up. The discussion of the results will be limited to those twenty-four patients with high face-to-face contact with high EE relatives. The results provided empirical support for the 'psychosocial' intervention along with medication in reducing relapse rates. (Other studies of psychosocial intervention and neuroleptic medication have consistently reported findings of reduced relapse rates in schizophrenia, for example Falloon *et al.* 1982.) One patient relapsed in the experimental group (9 per cent) whereas six patients relapsed in the control condition (50 per cent); the latter figure is commensurate with Vaughan and Leff's predicted relapse rate. However the psychosocial intervention group had reduced EE levels in only six out of twelve families and reduced levels of contact in only five out of twelve families. The follow-up EE ratings for this group showed a decrease in critical comments about the schizophrenic patients, but no statistically significant reduction in rated emotional over-involvement. The findings from the knowledge interviews indicated that family members were increasingly optimistic about the outcome of schizophrenia and had altered their perceptions of the patient in a favourable direction, perhaps accounting for the reported decrease in critical comments (Berkowitz 1984). It is difficult to evaluate the impact of the family therapy sessions since the techniques varied from 'dynamic interpretations to behavioural interventions' with no conceptual basis for their use, thus making replication difficult. (Compare the Falloon *et al.* 1982 study's consistent use of a clearly described behavioural method.) Leff (1983) reports that at a two-year follow-up only one out of seven experimental patients who were able to be contacted had relapsed. In summary, this study demonstrates the beneficial effects of a family-oriented intervention and drug treatment with schizophrenic patients at high risk for relapse and also provides evidence for a beneficial effect of social intervention independent of compliance with medication.

The findings need to be interpreted with some caution since a number of problems remain outstanding. The Cook and Campbell (1979) criteria for internal and external validity of therapy outcome research will be used to guide our discussion. The study has strengths in the area of internal validity, for example the random assignment of families to treatment conditions, a good match of family risk variables between the groups, use of a control group and low attrition. The weaknesses in internal validity need some unpacking, for example use of routine out-patient care as a control condition is particularly thorny for outcome research, since it is difficult to establish whether it matches the experimental group in terms of expectancy of outcome and credibility of the procedures and it does not control for hours of contact. The study did not employ outcome measures from multiple sources, relying on psychiatric measures of functioning. Strachan (1985) discusses the need for outcome measures of social functioning, measures of hypothesized intervening variables of family functioning and process measures of change. The effective ingredients of the psychosocial intervention package need to be unpacked; for example an experimental design which contrasts family education with family therapy will facilitate understanding of their relative impact on family functioning and possible interactive effects. The researchers themselves (Berkowitz 1984) and various reviewers (Barrowclough and Tarrier 1984; Waring *et al.* 1986) have commented on the need in future research to separate out the effects of the three components of the treatment package and to distinguish between the specific and non-specific effects of treatment. The use of multiple t-tests in the statistical analysis of the results is somewhat questionable as ANOVA methods may be more appropriate. Finally, caution is to be exercised since the primary follow-up period of nine months is fairly short for such a chronic condition as schizophrenia and the numbers of families involved are fairly small.

The strengths of the study in the area of external validity are commendable. The therapists were experienced practitioners and there were no artificial constraints on the therapy. The study took place in an NHS setting and clients' homes and the participants were genuine applicants for out-patient therapy. The schizophrenic patients were assessed with the PSE and the families were assessed with the CFI, both standardized instruments. A high level of ethical concern was maintained since clear contracts were negotiated between the families and the schizophrenic patients and the researchers/therapists. The aims and procedures of the study were clearly described to the participants. The weaknesses in external validity include lack of process analyses of what the family therapists actually did during sessions, lack of specification of the treatment mode (thus making replication difficult), different family session lengths and lack of blind diagnoses and ratings, although second opinions were sought in marginal cases.

In conclusion, this is a practical, clinically oriented research project which illustrates a number of advantages for the clinician-researcher, such as feasible use of the clinician's time and physical and financial resources, and which provides short-term benefit to a group of schizophrenic individuals at high risk for relapse. Small-scale studies (dear to the clinician's heart), such as replicated single case and multiple baseline across treatment conditions designs, can be employed in future work to identify the active ingredients of the family intervention package. Such designs can incorporate multiple measures of psychiatric and social functioning, which Strachan (1985) argues need to be included in further research. Finally the project demonstrates the positive role that family members can play to help keep the schizophrenic patient well. The importance of communicating this to families may produce a shift in the negative, blame oriented attitudes to families that some therapists are charged with holding (see Grunebaum 1984 and Terkelson 1983 for further discussion). Rather than emphasizing the family's possible role in causing schizophrenia or, as the EE studies suggest, exacerbating an existing condition, the preventive, rehabilitative role of the family can be explored, releasing family members from guilt and providing therapists with a positive framework within which they can meet and work with families.

## Bennun's project (1986)

Bennun's (1986) project is a comparative study of the efficacy of the Milan method of family therapy with a problem-solving family therapy in NHS settings in Exeter (see Selvini-Palazzoli *et al.* 1978 for a description of the former method; see Jacobson and Margolin 1979 for a description of the latter method). Twenty families were assigned over a three-year period to either of the treatment conditions. Initially Bennun intended to study families with an alcoholic member, but later expanded the study to include families with a depressed member and later still all referrals. The two groups were unmatched other than ensuring that equal numbers of alcoholic and depressed presenters were allocated to each group. Twenty-seven families were interviewed to secure the sample of twenty.

The maximum number of treatment sessions for both groups was ten. Five therapists treated the families, although Bennun conducted all the Milan treatments and two of the problem-solving cases. The remaining four therapists treated two families each within the problem-solving format.

Outcome was measured at three levels:

1 Symptomatic change in the identified patient was assessed with a variety of appropriate behavioural measures, for example the Severity of Alcohol Dependence Questionnaire (Stockwell *et al.* 1983), the Beck Depression Inventory (Beck 1967), the Fear Questionnaire (Marks and Mathews 1979), and so on.
2 Family system change was assessed by family members using a modified form of the Personal Questionnaire (Shapiro 1975) which yields change scores on a four-point ordinal scale.
3 Family members rated their satisfaction with the treatment on a five-point scale, along with their report of whether their initial concerns had increased, decreased or remained the same.

Symptomatic assessment was carried out during the first interview, after the fifth session and after the final session. Systemic assessment was carried out at the beginning of every second session. Family satisfaction was assessed at the end of treatment. Follow-up took place over the telephone six months after the final session. Unfortunately only thirteen families were able to participate in follow-up of whether they still experienced the initial referral symptoms and whether they had subsequently sought other help.

Bennun reports the results separately in terms of symptomatic and systemic change. All participating families appear to have achieved favourable symptom change from pre- to post-treatment. No attempt was made to test for significant differences within and between treatments because of the small sample size and the spread of presenting problems. However, the family system change data derived from the Personal Questionnaire method were in a comparable form across treatment conditions, so it was possible to test for statistically significant differences between treatments. Those families who took part in the Milan treatment effected significant changes at the systemic level, compared to those families receiving problem-solving therapy. Ratings of family satisfaction were reportedly high. The follow-up data remain incomplete.

Bennun critiques his own study, paying particular attention to the selection of outcome measures, the sample size, the therapists involved and the definition of change employed. The criticisms of design and method raised here will be those pertinent to the NHS-employed 'scientist-practitioner', and they will be discussed within the Cook and Campbell (1979) criteria used earlier in the chapter.

The study has strengths in the area of external validity, for example the use of an NHS setting; the therapists were NHS employed; the families were genuine referrals for out-patient therapy and were selected as representative of the types of families who commonly obtain these forms of treatment; and there were no artificial constraints on the therapies. The weaknesses in external validity revolve around the deployment of therapists and the monitoring of the therapy. The Milan treatment group was treated by one therapist, whereas the problem-solving group was treated by five therapists. Thus we cannot be sure how therapist effects interacted with treatment effects and whether so-called non-specific treatment effects biased the outcome for the Milan group. Process analyses were not reported as to whether the Milan and problem-solving therapists behaved in sessions according to their theoretical allegiances, although Bennun reports that the Milan treatment was observed and supervised through a one-way screen. Levels of therapist experience were not reported so it is not possible to assess whether this variable affected outcome.

The internal validity of this study is less strong, for example families were not randomly assigned to the two treatment groups, the treatment groups were not compared with equivalent control groups, and although no attrition occurred during the course of the treatment the sample of twenty families was highly selected and perhaps highly motivated. The lack of control groups in this study does not permit the evaluation of the effectiveness of the Milan method *vis-à-vis* other more traditional individually oriented forms of intervention, no treatment and/or a placebo control. Clinician-researchers might object to the inclusion of a no-treatment control group on ethical grounds, but as the psychotherapy outcome study reported by Sloane *et al.* (1975) demonstrates, high levels of ethical concern can be maintained with careful monitoring and treatment on demand for these groups. The Milan method still awaits systematic investigation of its effectiveness. Future studies need to define and operationalize the Milan therapy concepts and examine their effectiveness across different client groups and against other traditional forms of psychotherapy and family therapy. Lebow's (1981) discussion of the need for a multivariate schemata for conceptualizing such research enterprises, and the Gale and Chapman (1984) checklist of requirements for outcome research.

Of particular interest is the presence of families with a depressed member. It would be interesting to determine whether family therapy *per se* is the treatment of choice through preventing further relapse or contributing to lowered incidence of depression in other family members, or cognitive therapy for depression (Beck *et al.* 1980) which has been shown to be effective (Teasdale 1985). This brings us back to the perennial outcome question of determining the specific effect of a specific treatment on a specific problem.

Gurman and Kniskern (1981), Gurman *et al.* (1986) and Lask (1980) have noted that most outcome research relies on a single evaluative source for the assessment of change, that is 'symptoms' as medically defined, rather than system changes. Commendably Bennun sought information on family improvement from multiple sources within the family: the presenting family member, family assessment of family system change and family members' self-report of satisfaction. Assessment of symptomatic change was tailored in part to the salient concerns of the presenting individual although the other family members were not assessed individually for the impact of family therapy on their functioning (see Alexander *et al.* 1976). However the assessments of systemic change were not carried out blind by an independent coder. As in Dowling's study (to be reviewed later), Bennun participated in the research as therapist and formulator of the PQ items, thus experimenter bias cannot be ruled out as a source of error. The question of bias raises the problem of determining from whose point of view we assess outcome, for example individual family members, the therapist, independent assessors, the research funder, and so on, and whether these different perspectives can be cross-correlated to yield comparable assessments.

Bennun tackles the current controversial issue of whether outcome is to be assessed at the individual symptomatic or family systemic level and goes some way to answering the question by assessing across system levels. I agree with Bennun that logically symptomatic change cannot occur in the absence of systemic change so that the thrust of therapy is towards the social context of the symptomatic behaviour. Bennun is to be commended for addressing this controversy, particularly as the assessment of family system change is still problematic. Our notion of change is determined by our theoretical model, but many family system concepts, such as enmeshment, have yet to be rigorously defined let alone operationally defined! (See Gale and Vetere 1987 for further discussion of this problem.)

A study like Bennun's can be instructive despite its limited methodological adequacy. Gurman and Kniskern (1978) pointed out that the 'worship of therapeutic technology' obscures the importance of tailoring outcome criteria to the needs of a particular family or to the theoretical orientation of the therapist. This study addresses both these points and goes a long way to meeting the minimal adequacy criteria for outcome research as outlined by Wells and Dezen (1978), i.e. specification of the independent variables; utilization of a range of reliable and valid outcome measures; use of these measures to demonstrate change from either pretreatment to termination or pre-treatment to follow-up (or both); and use of appropriate methods of statistical analysis.

Along with the empirical verification of family therapy, there is a place for discovery-oriented research using the techniques of orientative sampling (London and Thorngate 1981). London and Thorngate recommend extensive sampling of the individual case, especially over time. The orientative sample functions to sensitize the researcher to salient variables and leads to a useful mapping of the population without prior assurances of its representativeness. (See Vetere and Gale 1987 for a fuller discussion of its use in family research.)

The careful study of family therapy in uncontrolled designs is valuable, as illustrated by, for example, the work of Bentovim and Kinston (1978) and Kinston and Bentovim (1978). Following the work of Malan (1976), they developed a time-limited focal therapy technique for use with families where the child was the 'identified patient'. Change in family functioning was measured on an individualized case basis using the method developed by Malan to assess psychodynamic change in individuals.

# FAMILY THERAPY PROCESS RESEARCH

## Introduction

Family therapy abounds with theories and techniques which have one startling fact in common, a lack of research which tests the clinical theories. Given the enormous resources expended on family therapy outcome research, even more noticeable is the lack of research which systematically describes and evaluates the *process* of therapy. In particular, one problem for outcome research is the need to establish whether therapists are doing what they say they are doing. Outcome research, as we have already said, evaluates the effectiveness of therapy; it does not have tools for reliably describing the sequence of events that constitute that therapy. Thus it becomes clear that research linking process with outcome is needed, if we are to identify those specific processes which enhance therapy.

Process research attempts to measure, either directly or indirectly, client, therapist or client-therapist variables during a therapeutic session. Thus any aspect of the experience and behaviour of therapist and family members during the family interview could be tackled. Pinsof (1981) provides an excellent descriptive and extensive review of family therapy process research and its methods of measurement, such as self-report studies of therapists' behaviour, direct observation studies of therapist and family members' behaviour, and so on. He outlines some conceptual and methodological limitations of the extant research, such as the use of new and unstandardized questionnaires and coding schemes; too many researchers doing only one study with a consequent lack of replication; research groups developing interests and instruments with a singular lack of awareness of each other's work, and so on. It is interesting to note that Riskin and Faunce (1972) levelled similar criticisms at family interaction researchers. Thus it would appear that not only do research groups' interests and techniques not cross-fertilize but also the criticisms of Riskin and Faunce did not cross discipline boundaries and influence family process researchers.

Reviewers often seem to assume that published studies represent the state of the art; it would be interesting to survey research which fails, is produced for internal consumption, is contained in unpublished theses, and so on. Pinsof's list of reasons why process research is not reported is daunting. He lists, among others, the problems for clinicians of doing research, the challenge of methodology, the tradition of psychotherapy process research's individual orientation, the lack of adequate microtherapy theory in family therapy, and the present economic and political climate. We might add to this list of reasons that the field has in large part been ignored by academic psychologists (Vetere and Gale 1987).

Pinsof considers it premature to try to delineate rigorous evaluative criteria for family therapy process research and suggests that each study be reviewed on its merits. As the field has not expanded considerably since 1981 (see Gurman *et al.* 1986), the same approach will be adopted for the process study considered here, that of Dowling's (1979) research at the Family Institute, Cardiff.

## Dowling's study (1979)

Dowling (1979) reports a comparative study of five therapists' in-therapy behaviour in various combinations of co-therapy pairs. While co-therapy remains a popular technique in family therapy practice, there is little empirical evidence that co-therapy contributes either to improved outcome or is an economic use of resources. Earlier researchers (for example Rice *et al*. 1972) examining the importance of co-therapy in terms of outcome, used self-report data of therapists' own styles of therapist behaviour as perceived by their co-therapist and therapists' subjective ratings of outcome. Dowling's project was the first observational study of co-therapy behaviour. Co-therapy here refers to a team of two therapists who conduct treatment *in vivo*.

The study aimed first, to examine the extent to which therapists' behaviour is consistent when working with different co-therapists, second, to develop profiles of the behavioural patterns of the different co-therapy pairs, and third, to assess whether co-therapy pairs function in a complementary manner. Dowling and her colleagues developed a family therapist coding system, adapted from the Developing Interactive Skills Category System as used by the British Air Transport and Travel Industry Training Board, which consisted of fifteen mutually exclusive categories for describing in-therapy verbal behaviour (see Dowling 1979 for a full description of the fifteen categories). Sampling from an hour-long audio-tape from each of the beginning, middle and end of the co-therapy treatment of nine families (only one interview was obtained for two of the nine cases), Dowling used the coding scheme to examine what family therapists do. For example, the therapists spent one-third of the therapy time (twenty-three hours) intervening in the family system, mainly using the five categories of enlarging, integrating, pointing out, eliciting and proposing, whereas such categories as open (self-disclosure), disagreeing, bringing-in, defending/attacking and shutting out were rarely used.

The question of whether the five therapists were cross-situationally consistent in their therapeutic style was assessed by computing Kendall's coefficient of concordance for their consistency in the ranking order of their use of categories across co-therapy pairs. Dowling found a high degree of stylistic consistency despite the presence of complementarity of function, that is therapist X 'proposes' less with therapist Y who 'proposes' more, but 'proposes' more with therapist Z, who uses this category less often.

The five therapists were asked to use the fifteen category scheme, which the rater had used, as a self-report questionnaire and rank order the categories to describe the profile of an 'ideal' co-therapy partner. The most desirable categories were pointing out, bringing-in, proposing, open, enlarging and disagreeing. Dowling argues that the presence of three rarely used categories (bringing-in, open and disagreeing) in the above list lends support to the notion of the complementarity of function, as therapists may seek behaviours in a co-therapist that they do not exhibit themselves. The therapists were in high agreement over the characteristics desired in their co-therapists.

Again using the category scheme as a self-report device, Dowling attempted to examine whether the therapists preferred specific behaviour patterns for specific kinds of families. Although unable to answer this question, it was found that certain categories were ranked as highly desirable for all families: supporting, bringing-in and eliciting, while disagreeing, defending/attacking and shutting-out were considered least desirable. It is interesting to note that disagreeing is seen to be desirable for an 'ideal' co-therapy partner, yet undesirable in the preferred co-therapy behaviours for specific families.

Dowling was interested in the accuracy with which therapists perceive their own behaviour for its implications for practice and training. Dowling assumes that the more accurately therapists perceive their own behaviour, the more reliable will be their observations of the family and that family therapy trainees can be taught to monitor their own behaviour. She hypothesized that the experienced therapists (levels of experience were not specified clearly) would have accurate perceptions of their own behaviour. Each therapist's observed use of the categories from the audio-taped data was compared with their self-report data on therapeutic style and no correlation was found between the two data sets for four out of the five therapists. Dowling herself was the only therapist to obtain a significant Spearman rho correlation, which she attributed to her greater familiarity with the category scheme through using it to rate her own and other therapists' behaviour.

In summary, this study found that the participating therapists had a consistent co-therapy style and agreed about the types of behaviours thought to be desirable or undesirable in a co-therapist. However, Dowling did not find that the therapists were able to describe their own behaviour accurately, which raises some doubts about the accuracy of the self-report data or of the validity of the scale, which was originally devised to describe interactions between flying instructors and their students.

There is a major methodological stumbling block to the interpretation of these findings in the fact that Dowling not only participated in her study as a co-therapist, but also was the sole coder. The potential sources of error derive from the lack of intra-rater reliability and inter-rater reliability in the use of the coding scheme, the definition of the scoring unit for the audio-tape data, the clarity and reliability of the coding scheme itself, the small number of therapists involved, their levels of experience and possible bias resulting from Dowling's multi-role involvement in the study. For example the finding that the therapists' perceptions of their own behaviour did not correlate with their rated audio-taped behaviour might reflect coder bias or lack of clarity in the coding scheme itself, so that different therapists are interpreting the various categories differently. Certainly Dowling's suggestion that the therapists receive prior training in the use of the coding scheme is important, but the category scheme itself needs to be assessed further for its reliability in discriminating family therapists' behaviour and for its lack of ambiguity in interpretation.

Dowling combined a self-report measure which attempted to capture the experiential reality of the co-therapy process with the direct application of a coding system to co-therapists' behaviour. Such a combination of the subjective and objective domains is rare in family therapy process research. (See the work of Gottman 1978 and Orlinsky and Howard 1975; 1978 as notable exceptions.) Although it is not clear to what extent the findings are due to real differences and similarities in the therapists' behaviour or to the poor reliability of the data, the study represents an important attempt to describe co-therapists' behaviour in an objective manner. This study is a brave attempt to look at what therapists actually do in therapy.

Process research is still in its infancy. Many of the coding techniques in use have been developed in other contexts and may not be suitable for critical aspects of family therapy process, for example many behaviours occurring simultaneously. Cromwell *et al.* (1976) and Straus and Brown (1978) have commented on the limited reliability and validity of the available measurement instruments. It remains puzzling, though, why family process researchers have not availed themselves of the instruments developed by family interaction researchers. (See reviews of family interaction research by Doane 1978; Jacob 1975; Riskin and Faunce 1972.)

Some recent developments in individual psychotherapy process research may hold promise for family therapy process research, for example the Interpersonal Process Recall (IPR) technique used by Elliott and his co-workers (1986) which elucidates the subjective experience of therapy. IPR uses a recording to stimulate participants' recall of their experiences during therapy. As soon as possible after recording the tape is reviewed with the help of a trained 'enquirer' who uses a series of non-directive questions and probes to stimulate recall of moment-by-moment thoughts and feelings. Such a technique can be used to investigate the so-called non-specific effects of family therapy, in particular the impact of the therapist's style on the family members and its implications for outcome. Another example is Comprehensive Process Analysis (Elliott 1984) which developed out of IPR research. Events in therapy thought to be crucial to change, 'significant events', are investigated in depth. This approach is essentially qualitative and involves the development of a model by observers of the pathways to the events reported as helpful by clients. The model can be used in single case designs to investigate the relevance of significant events to outcome.

# FAMILY THERAPY TRAINING RESEARCH

Kniskern and Gurman (1979) commented that research on family therapy training had not kept pace with other developments in the field, and to their knowledge there were no empirical studies of the process or outcome of family therapy training. It seemed there was no evidence to support the assumption that training in family therapy increases clinical effectiveness. Since that time writers have clarified the methodological difficulties of such research, for example the lack of a standard stimulus situation, such as a recorded first interview with a family, for assessing conceptual and behavioural skills, the lack of an instrument for measuring family system thinking, the lack of empirical information about which therapist skills (conceptual, behavioural, experiential) correlate with effective outcomes and whether acquisition of these skills leads to more effective therapists (Tucker and Pinsof 1984; Gurman *et al.* 1986). We still lack comprehensive empirical evaluations of family therapy training programmes, although Tucker and Pinsof's study is a welcome move in that direction.

Although these developments across the Atlantic are exciting, we shall stay with the British theme of the chapter and discuss the work of Walrond-Skinner (1979), conducted at the Family Institute, Cardiff. A useful framework for discussion is provided by Street's (forthcoming) *systemic* model of family therapy training programme development. Street observed that most reports of family therapy training leave the reader to infer the model of programme development employed. He adapted the Gottman and Markman (1978) scheme for the evaluation of a psychotherapy service, which emphasizes the evaluation of specific components of that service using small-scale studies. They advise abandoning the grand factorial design which attempts to answer most aspects of the outcome question. Thus Street presents a flow chart of eight stages of family therapy training programme development, which include selection of trainees and the context of training, the therapy model to be taught and by what methods, assessment of both training and trainee efficiency/effectiveness, and a training cost-benefit analysis with feedback procedures for the redesign of the programme. Each of these objectives can be explored and assessed by means of small-scale studies which influence in an interactive and iterative manner future development of the training programme. For example the decision as to which therapeutic method is to be taught is influenced by the leads to theoretical model studies, which in turn influence the selection of training methods, and so on.

Within the terms of Street's model, the study of Walrond-Skinner's (1979) study illustrates how the objective of assessing training efficiency leads to studies of student changes during training, which in turn influence how trainees' efficiency is assessed. Her repertory grid study of personal change in family therapy trainees challenged the apparent dichotomy between 'reflective' and 'behavioural' methods of training. Broadly speaking 'reflective' or insight-oriented supervision takes place after the therapy session, is non-intrusive, emphasizes the personal growth of the trainee, and so on. 'Behavioural' supervision is 'live', whereby the trainer guides the trainee, is intrusive, emphasizes executive skills in therapy, and so on. Walrond-Skinner speculated in her research that personal growth might occur in the latter behavioural mode even though it is not encouraged specifically. Family therapy training programmes teach general system theory conceptualizations of families and their patterns of behaviour (see Tomm and Wright 1979). It is assumed by Walrond-Skinner that changed construing of families is reflected in associated personal change; thus she presents us with a truly systemic view of the impact of training on the individual.

Fourteen social work students on three-month and six-month family therapy training courses (experimental group) and six family therapy untrained social workers who had professional contact with families (control group) took part in the study. The control group was included to assess whether ongoing professional contact with families contributed to personal growth and did not take part in the training. The course focused on the teaching of executive therapeutic skills (in the style of Cleghorn and Levin 1973) using the 'behavioural' mode and 'live' supervision. Personal growth was not a focus of teaching. Each group was assessed before and after training with both repertory grids and a questionnaire. The repertory grids were modified to include dyadic relationships as elements, for example relationships with family of origin, supervisor, client families, and so on. Trainees were asked to construe each dyadic relationship in terms of how they related to the other and how they perceived the other as relating to them. (See Fransella and Bannister 1977 for a discussion of repertory grid technique.) The participants' professional selves were analysed in terms of how they viewed the relationships between their actual selves, their ideal selves, and their social selves (their perceptions of the agencies' expectations of them) in relation to client families. Walrond-Skinner acknowledges the difficulties of defining the self and personal growth and adopted the above tripartite system as a means of focusing on personal change in the participants' subjective world.

Three areas of potential change were explored. If personal growth occurs during training, it is hypothesized that the gap will close between the perception of first, the actual and ideal self, second, the ideal self and the social self, and third, the actual self and the social self. A greater integration of professional and personal self identity is hypothesized after training. Analysis of the pre-training repertory grids revealed little convergence between the three aspects of the self, the isolation of the ideal self and that personal and professional relationships were carefully distinguished.

Analysis of the post-training repertory grids revealed internal integration between the ideal self and the social self for the fourteen family therapy
trainees, whereas the control group demonstrated no significant closing of
the gap. After the three-month training course, there was no lessening of the
gap between how they perceived themselves actually functioning and how
they would like to function, yet after the six-month training, the gap had
started to close. This finding has implications for the length of training.
Furthermore, Walrond-Skinner investigated how much personal growth
took place after training. The two groups were assessed for their cognitive
complexity, that is capacity to construe behaviour in a multidimensional
way, as indicated by changes in the students' construct systems when viewing
video-taped family therapy sessions. The six-month training period produced
changes in the direction of increased cognitive complexity, whereas the
control group showed no significant changes in their cognitive complexity.

Finally, changes in the students' perceptions of various family therapy
situations before and after training were assessed with an eighteen-item
questionnaire. The questionnaire sampled such items as toleration of hostility, affection and sexual attraction, fear of damaging families and being
damaged, and so on. Significant positive change was recorded for eight of
the eighteen situations in the trainees' group compared with no significant
changes in the control group.

Overall the findings indicate that personal change, as measured with
repertory grids, took place, even after a brief behaviourally oriented
training programme. These findings were corroborated by Dowling and
Seligman (1980) in their survey of the 'consumer satisfaction' of thirty-eight
Certificate of Qualification in Social Work (CQSW) students who had
participated in family therapy training at Cardiff. Twenty-five of the thirty-
eight respondents rated their own personal growth as 'very relevant'.
Walrond-Skinner's study did not attempt to evaluate the effectiveness of the
training. It would have been interesting to follow-up the students to see what
changes in their construing of their professional selves occurred as a function
of subsequent family therapy practice. Such work might give some indication as to whether self-awareness of this nature facilitates family therapy
practice. In this respect, the Dowling and Seligman (1980) and the Dowling
*et al.* (1982) studies' follow-up of the 'consumer satisfaction' of thirty-eight
CQSW students who had completed a family therapy training course found
that the mean percentage of family therapy practised since qualifying was 23
per cent and the mean percentage of family therapy practised in the present
post was 30 per cent. Although family therapy is increasingly accepted in this
country, such low reported rates of practice raise implications for the
potential professional frustration of the respondents and the need for
organized peer support. The only other empirical assessment of personal
change in family therapy training comes from the Tucker and Pinsof (1984)

study. They expected three attributes of the students to change with training: theoretical perspective, use of therapy techniques and self-actualization. Self-actualization was assessed pre- and post-training with the Personal Orientation Inventory (Shostrom 1974) and no significant differences were found in the trainees' scores. The authors argue however that the trainees were a highly self-actualized group initially since their pre-scores fell within the self-actualized range!

Walrond-Skinner's study, like the others reviewed in this chapter, demonstrates the feasibility of small-scale studies for clinicians. For example repertory grids can be analysed within statistical packages available for use on microcomputers, which are increasingly to be found in many departments. The use of Street's model of family therapy training programme development encourages research activity directed to specific questions, for example Street and Foot (1984) developed a micro analytic approach to the training of observational skills using concepts derived from structural family therapy (Minuchin 1974). Despite some methodological constraints, they demonstrated that inexperienced family therapy trainees could be tutored in both structural concepts and in how to translate them into specific observations, efficiently and quickly. At the same time, Street's model of training programme development is systemic, with built-in feedback between the stages of the model. This allows for the continuous monitoring of training, making changes where necessary, rather than waiting until the training is complete before evaluating it. Gurman and Kniskern (1981) pointed out that evidence of family therapy effectiveness is of little use if it is not translated into training programmes to ensure sound future practice. It would appear the time has come to integrate the empirical study of training programmes with the empirical study of family therapy outcomes.

# SOME FUTURE DIRECTIONS

## Introduction

How do the few studies reviewed here inform future directions for research? For example Dowling's study reported the development of a category scheme for describing aspects of co-therapy process. Category systems by themselves are static, as they do not always allow us to reconstruct the process of behaviour from summated data. Analysing the categorized co-therapy behaviours within lag sequential analysis programmes (Gottman and Bakeman 1979) to capture better the flow and patterns of therapy would provide an important leap forward in process research. In this section the focus will be on attempts to link process with outcome research and on the role of small-scale designs in family therapy practice. Special attention will be paid to the problems of doing such research.

## Integrating family therapy process research with outcome research

There have been few direct attempts in the family therapy literature to relate process to outcome. Apart from the early work of Alexander and Parsons (1973) and Kinston and Bentovim (1978), there has been little systematic investigation of the relationship between interactional changes among family members and therapy outcomes. Alexander and Parsons linked family interaction to outcome measures in their comparative study of family therapy with the families of delinquent teenagers. They observed that short-term behaviourally oriented family therapy led to a reduction in maladaptive interaction patterns, and concomitant increases in positive reciprocity and clarity of communication compared with the other groups. Kinston and Bentovim (1978) in their study of brief focal family therapy used a focal hypothesis which included both symptomatic and family system change as the reference point for therapeutic outcome.

These early studies are important markers for any future work which attempts to explore whether family interaction changes during therapy have significance for outcome. For example Seeman *et al.* (1985) report tentative findings of a positive correlation between measures of early family interactional change (measured after six weeks of family therapy) and favourable treatment outcome, as assessed from both families' and therapists' points of view. These results are tentative because early interactional change in therapy was also associated with more favourable initial status. Thus early change may be influenced by a number of factors, not least family members' motivation and level of initial functioning. Replication of this study needs to be undertaken before the implications for optimum treatment length can be explored. It is interesting to note that few markers of family interaction style have been found to predict treatment outcome. Gurman and Kniskern (1981) review research which indicates that family styles characterized as low on authoritarianism, coercion and competitiveness and open to disagreement, seem to have a moderately beneficial mediating effect on outcome. A number of family constellation variables and family demographic variables have been studied as prognostic indicators of treatment outcome. For example the Montreal group (Woodward *et al.* 1981) attempted to distinguish good and poor outcomes of brief systems-oriented family therapy using seventeen demographic predictors and six criteria. The study was part of a long-standing research project aimed at delineating measurable client, therapist and treatment characteristics that are predictive of family therapy outcome. Few measurable differences between the outcome groups were found in the Woodward *et al.* study. The authors recommended further specification of salient family therapist and treatment characteristics.

One puzzling aspect of the Woodward study was the lack of a guiding theoretical framework for the selection of the demographic predictor variables. Theory allows us to examine the impact of the variables on treatment outcome in an orderly manner. While not denying the value of exploratory work, there are many theories of family behaviour available to guide similar future work, for example Kantor and Lehr's (1975) distance regulation theory and Nye's (1982) choice-exchange theory. Theory development proceeds apace, yet the testing of theory in clinical domains lags well behind. Gale and Vetere (1987) outline the importance of family theory to research and practice and call for the diversion of research time and energy to the testing of theory in clinical settings.

## Small-scale studies

Single case designs are well suited to unpacking the 'effective ingredients' of large-scale group designs. The EE research of Leff *et al.* (1982), discussed earlier in this chapter, is a good example of the need for further clarification of the differential and/or interactive contributions of the three treatment modes to an effective outcome. Reversal designs and multiple baseline designs (see Kazdin 1982 and Kratochwill 1978 for full descriptions of the methods) are the most commonly used in clinical settings, although Rabin (1981) and Crane (1985) note that they are used infrequently in family therapy research outside of the behaviour modification literature on families. Why might this be?

Single case designs use the 'subject' as their own control. Thus it is essential to establish a baseline of stable responding before introducing the intervention, for the purposes of comparing treatment and no-treatment conditions. Unfortunately it is not always possible to achieve a stable baseline partly because of the impact of self-monitoring and increasing self-awareness on the family members' behaviour. Single case designs also demand clearly specified dependent measures of family members' behaviour which can be operationally defined, reliably measured before, during and after the intervention and are sensitive to change. As Crane (1985) points out, such measures are not easily found, not least because many family theoretical concepts have not been operationally defined. Reversal designs demand a treatment withdrawal condition which can powerfully demonstrate the impact of the intervention on the family members' behaviour. The ABAB (where A = baseline, B = treatment) design is one example. However many clinicians object to such designs on ethical grounds and query the possible harmful effects of changing the treatment strategy. Multiple baseline designs overcome the need to return to baseline and the possible irreversibility of treatment effects, but they are less powerful in demonstrating causality than the reversal designs. Systematic replication of single case studies, in the manner advocated by Sidman (1960) can increase the generalizability of the results.

The above reasons may account only in part for the unpopularity of small-scale research in family therapy practice. There is evidence that some practitioners not only do not produce and publish research, large or small scale, but also do not consume such research, that is they are not influenced by research findings (Barlow *et al.* 1984; Watts 1984). Busy and committed practitioners working in socially legitimate ways with needy client groups may believe research to be a self-indulgent form of escape from the sharp end of clinical work. Indeed many prospective researchers fall by the wayside. Gale (1985) cogently points out that the 'manufacturing' model of research is inappropriate. Research is not a bolt-on module to be picked up for one or two sessions a week; it is a way of life. The systemic nature of the impact on a researcher's life is such that it 'affects work, domestic arrangements, leisure time, self-esteem, frustration, tolerance [and] capacity to devote attention to others' (Gale 1985 : 194).

In whose interests is it then that clinicians do research? What sort of research suits whose purposes? It is clear that not only do clinicians need a *reason* to do research but also the research strategies need to be useful to them. One way of bridging the gap between research and practice has been suggested by the scientist-practitioner model (Barlow *et al.* 1984). Evaluation is built in to this approach since assessment and formulation with clearly stated goals not only aids therapy but also represents the first stage of evaluation. Small-scale designs are compatible with this model.

To return to the Bennun and Leff studies, we might wish to consider whether those family groups who did not improve actually *worsened*. Group designs with their pre- and post-measures ignore the *course* of treatment, whereas single case designs permit the investigation of progression through treatment with their emphasis on continual monitoring and recording. Feedback is built into the treatment process so both family members and therapists can see the effects of an intervention. Single case designs can be used to demonstrate the effects of specific interventions in family therapy, for example preventing the 'identified patient' (parental child) from interfering in parental care-taking, by using Minuchin-style structural mapping in a predictive way. Formal quantitative methods for describing pattern and progress in clinical interactive data are being developed, for example lag sequential analysis (Gottman and Bakeman 1979).

Gurman and Kniskern (1981) note that we know more about the kind of family therapist style that increases the chances of negative therapeutic effects, than about the components of treatment which induce deterioration! Using small-scale designs we can investigate the role of deterioration and by varying treatment components within a model of family therapy practice we might shed some light on drop out and premature termination rates. Some therapies prescribe relapses (Haley 1976) as mediators of treatment; if deterioration effects have temporal significance this will affect chosen length of follow-up. Outcome researchers in general need to cite the number of cases of improvement and on how many criteria, of no change and of deterioration. The two outcome studies described here went some way towards this. In particular, Bennun's use of an individually tailored outcome measure (PQ methodology) facilitates investigation of differential outcome effects, since it was related to his theoretical perspective and the needs of individual families.

## CONCLUSION

In this post-Griffiths era of increased clinical accountability, structural reasons for doing research, motivated by questions of who pays and who benefits, become more pertinent. The Griffiths Report's recommendations (1983) for the improved management of the NHS have prompted the need to justify clinical time and resources in pursuit of a more efficient and effective health service delivery system. This must not be allowed to obscure the ethical responsibility held by all clinicians to ensure that their therapies benefit their clients and do not make them worse.

The studies described here were selected to give a flavour of the themes taken up by British family therapy researchers. They have demonstrated how low-cost, practical studies can be undertaken within the constraints of clinical settings, particularly if clinicians are willing to embrace the scientist-practitioner model of service delivery. These studies have been helpful also in paving the way for future research by highlighting both the need for single case studies and for research which links process to outcome.

## REFERENCES

Alexander, J. and Parsons, B.V. (1973). Short-term behavioral intervention with delinquent families: impact on family process and recidivism. *Journal of Abnormal Psychology*, 81, 219–55.

Alexander, J., Barton, C., Schiavo, R.S. and Parsons, B.V. (1976). Therapist characteristics, family behavior and outcome. *Journal of Consulting and Clinical Psychology*, 44, 656–64.

Barlow, D.H., Hayes, S.C. and Nelson, R.O. (1984). *The Scientist-Practitioner: Research and Accountability in Clinical and Educational Settings*. New York, Pergamon.

Barrowclough, C. and Tarrier, N. (1984). 'Psychosocial' interventions with families and their effects on the course of schizophrenia: a review. *Psychological Medicine*, 14, 629–42.

Beck, A.T. (1967). *Depression: Clinical, Experimental, and Theoretical Aspects*. New York, Harper & Row.

Beck, A.T., Rush, A.J., Shaw, B.F. and Emery, G. (1980). *Cognitive Therapy of Depression*. Chichester, Wiley.

Bennun, I. (1986). Evaluating family therapy: a comparison of the Milan and problem-solving approaches. *Journal of Family Therapy*, 8, 225–42.

Bentovim, A. and Kinston, W. (1978). Brief focal family therapy when the child is the referred patient – I. Clinical. *Journal of Child Psychology and Psychiatry*, 19, 1–12.

Berkowitz, R. (1984). Therapeutic intervention with schizophrenic patients and their families: a description of a clinical research project. *Journal of Family Therapy*, 6, 211–33.

Brown, G.W. and Rutter, M. (1966). The measurement of family activities and relationships: a methodological study. *Human Relations*, 19, 241–63.

Brown, G.W., Birley, J.L.T. and Wing, J.K. (1972). Influence of family life on the course of schizophrenic disorders: a replication. *British Journal of Psychiatry*, 121, 241–58.

Brown, G.W., Bone, M., Dalison, B. and Wing, J.K. (1966). *Schizophrenia and Social Care: A Comparative Follow-up of 339 Schizophrenic Patients*. Maudsley Monograph 17. Oxford, Oxford University Press.

Cleghorn, J. and Levin, S. (1973). Training family therapists by setting learning objectives. *American Journal of Ortho-Psychiatry*, 43, 439–46.

Cook, D.T. and Campbell, D.T. (1979). *Quasi-experimentation: Design and Analysis Issues for Field Settings*. Chicago, Ill., Rand McNally.

Crane, D.R. (1985). Single-case experimental designs in family therapy research: limitations and considerations. *Family Process*, 24, 69–77.

Cromwell, R.E., Olson, D.H.L. and Fournier, D.G. (1976). Tools and techniques for diagnosis and evaluation in marital and family therapy. *Family Process*, 15, 1–49.

Doane, J.A. (1978). Questions of strategy: rejoinder to Jacob and Grounds. *Family Process*, 17, 389–94.

Dowling, E. (1979). Co-therapy: a clinical researcher's view. In S. Walrond-Skinner (ed.) *Family and Marital Psychotherapy: A Critical Approach*. London, Routledge & Kegan Paul.

Dowling, E. and Seligman, P. (1980). Description and evaluation of a family therapy training model. *Journal of Family Therapy*, 2, 123–30.

Dowling, E., Cade, B., Breunlin, D.C., Frude, N. and Seligman, P. (1982). A retrospective survey of students' views on a family therapy training programme. *Journal of Family Therapy*. 4, 61–72.

Elliott, R. (1984). A discovery oriented approach to significant events in psychotherapy: Interpersonal Process Recall and Comprehensive Process Analysis. In L. Rice and L.S. Greenberg (eds) *Patterns of Change*. New York, Guilford.

—— (1986). Interpersonal Process Recall (IPR): a psychotherapy process research method. In L.S. Greenberg and W.M. Pinsof (eds) *The Psychotherapeutic Process: A Research Handbook*. New York, Guilford.

Falloon, I.R.H., Boyd, J.L., McGill, C.W., Razani, J., Moss, H.B. and Gilderman, A.M. (1982). Family management in the prevention of exacerbation of schizophrenia: a controlled study. *New England Journal of Medicine*, 306, 1437–440

Fransella, F. and Bannister, D. (1977). *A Manual for Repertory Grid Technique*. London, Academic Press.

Gale, A. (1985). On doing research: the dream and the reality. *Journal of Family Therapy*, 7, 187–211.

Gale, A. and Chapman, A.J. (1984). The nature of applied psychology. In A. Gale and A.J. Chapman (eds) *Psychology and Social Problems: An Introduction to Applied Psychology*. Chichester, Wiley.

Gale, A. and Vetere, A. (1987). Some theories of family behaviour. In A. Vetere and A. Gale, *Ecological Studies of Family Life*. Chichester, Wiley.

Gottman, J.M. (1978). Couples interaction scoring system (CISS): coding manual. Unpublished manuscript. Dept of Psychology, University of Illinois, Champaign, Ill.

Gottman, J.M. and Bakeman, R. (1979). The sequential analysis of observational data. In M. Lamb, S. Suomi and G. Stephenson (eds) *Methodological Problems in the Study of Social Interaction*. Madison, Wis., University of Wisconsin Press.

Gottman, J.M. and Markman, H.J. (1978). Experimental designs of psychotherapy research. In S.L. Garfield and A.E. Bergin (eds) *Handbook of Psychotherapy and Behavior Change: An Empirical Analysis*, 2nd edn. New York, Wiley.

Griffiths Report (1983). *Report of the NHS Management Inquiry*. DHSS. London, HMSO.

Grunebaum, H. (1984). Comments on Terkelson's 'Schizophrenia and the family' – II. Adverse effects of family therapy. *Family Process*, 23, 421–8.

Gurman, A.S. and Kniskern, D.P. (1978). Research on marital and family therapy: progress, perspective, and prospect. In S.L. Garfield and A.E. Bergin (eds) *Handbook of Psychotherapy and Behavior Change: An Empirical Analysis*, 2nd edn. New York, Wiley.

—— (1981). Family therapy outcome research: knowns and unknowns. In A.S. Gurman and D.P. Kniskern (eds) *Handbook of Family Therapy*. New York, Brunner/Mazel.

Gurman, A.S., Kniskern, D.P. and Pinsof, W.M. (1986). Research on marital and family therapies. In S.L. Garfield and A.E. Bergin (eds) *Handbook of Psychotherapy and Behavior Change*, 3rd edn. New York, Wiley.

Haley, J. (1976). *Problem-Solving Therapy*. New York, Harper Colophon.

Jacob, T. (1975). Family interaction in disturbed and normal families: a methodological and substantive review. *Psychological Bulletin*, 82, 133–65.

Jacobson, N. and Margolin, G. (1979). *Marital Therapy*. New York, Brunner/Mazel.

Kantor, D. and Lehr, W. (1975). *Inside the Family: Toward a Theory of Family Process*. San Francisco, Jossey-Bass.

Kazdin, A.E. (1982). *Single Case Research Designs: Methods for Clinical and Applied Settings*. New York, Oxford University Press.

Kinston, W. and Bentovim, A. (1978). Brief focal family therapy when the child is the referred patient – II. Methodology and results. *Journal of Child Psychology and Psychiatry*, 19, 119–43.

Kniskern, D.P. and Gurman, A.S. (1979). Research on training in marriage and family therapy: status, issues and directions. *Journal of Marital and Family Therapy*, 5, 83–94.

Kratochwill, T.R. (1978). *Single-Subject Research: Strategies for Evaluating Change*. New York, Academic Press.

Lask, B. (1980). Evaluation – why and how? (A guide for clinicians). *Journal of Family Therapy*, 2, 199–210.

Lebow, J. (1981). Issues in the assessment of outcome in family therapy. *Family Process*, 20, 167–88.

Leff, J. (1983). A follow-up of the London schizophrenia project. Paper presented at the Society of Psychotherapy Research, Sheffield, England.

Leff, J.P., Hirsch, S.R., Gaind, R., Rhodes, P.D. and Stevens, B.C. (1973). Life events and maintenance therapy in schizophrenic relapse. *British Journal of*

*Psychiatry*, 123, 659–60.

Leff, J., Kuipers, L. Berkowitz, R., Eberlein-Vries, R. and Sturgeon, D. (1982). A controlled trial of social intervention in the families of schizophrenic patients. *British Journal of Psychiatry*, 141, 121–34.

London, I.D. and Thorngate, W. (1981). Divergent amplification and social behavior: some methodological considerations. *Psychological Reports*, 48, 203–28.

Malan, D. (1976). *The Frontier of Brief Psychotherapy*. New York, Plenum.

Marks, I. and Mathews, A. (1979). Brief standard rating for phobic patients. *Behaviour Research and Therapy*, 17, 263–7.

Minuchin, S. (1974). *Families and Family Therapy*. London, Tavistock.

Nye, F.I. (ed.) (1982). *Family Relationships: Rewards and Costs*. Beverly Hills, Calif., Sage.

Orlinsky, D.E. and Howard, K.I. (1975). *Varieties of Psychotherapeutic Experience: Multivariate Analyses of Patients' and Therapists' Report*. New York, Teachers College Press.

—— (1978). The relation of process to outcome in psychotherapy. In S.L. Garfield and A.E. Bergin (eds) *Handbook of Psychotherapy and Behavior Change: An Empirical Analysis*, 2nd edn. New York, Wiley.

Pinsof, W.M. (1981). Family therapy process research. In A.S. Gurman and D.P. Kniskern (eds) *Handbook of Family Therapy*. New York, Brunner/Mazel.

Rabin, S. (1981). The single-case design in family therapy evaluation research. *Family Process*, 20, 351–66.

Rice, D.G., Fey, W.F. and Kepecs, J.G. (1972). Therapist experience and 'style' as factors in co-therapy. *Family Process*, 11, 1–12.

Riskin, J. and Faunce, E.E. (1972). An evaluative review of family interaction research. *Family Process*. 11, 365–455.

Seeman, L., Tittler, B.I. and Friedman, S. (1985). Early interactional change and its relationship to family therapy outcome. *Family Process*, 24, 59–68.

Selvini-Palazzoli, M., Boscolo, L., Cecchin, G. and Prata, G. (1978). *Paradox and Counter Paradox*. New York, Jason Aronson.

Shapiro, M. (1975). The assessment of self-reported dysfunctions: a manual with its rationale and applications (II). Unpublished manuscript. London, Institute of Psychiatry.

Shostrom, E. (1974). *The Personal Orientation Inventory*, 2nd edn. San Diego, Calif., Educational Industrial Testing Service.

Sidman, M. (1960). *Tactics of Scientific Research*. New York, Basic Books.

Sloane, R.B., Staples, F.R., Cristol, A.H., Yorkston, N.J. and Whipple, K. (1975). *Psychotherapy versus Behavior Therapy*. Cambridge, Mass., Harvard University Press.

Stockwell, T., Murphy, D. and Hodgson, R. (1983). The severity of alcohol dependence questionnaire: its use, reliability and validity. *British Journal of Addiction*, 78, 145–55.

Strachan, A.M. (1985). Family approaches to schizophrenia: recent developments. In F.N. Watts (ed.) *New Developments in Clinical Psychology*. Letchworth, British Psychological Society in association with Wiley.

Straus, M. and Brown, B.W. (1978). *Family Measurement Techniques*. Minnesota, University of Minnesota Press.

Street, E. (forthcoming). Family therapy training: a systems model and research review. *Journal of Family Therapy*.

Street, E. and Foot, H. (1984). Training family therapists in observational skills. *Journal of Family Therapy*, 6, 335–45.

Teasdale, J.D. (1985). Psychological treatments for depression: how do they work'? *Behaviour Research and Therapy*, 23, 157–65.

Terkelson, K.G. (1983). Schizophrenia and the family: II. Adverse effects of family therapy. *Family Process*, 22, 191–200.

Tomm, K. and Wright, L.M. (1979). Family therapy skills. *Family Process*, 18, 227–50.

Tucker, S.J. and Pinsof, W.M. (1984). The empirical evaluation of family therapy training. *Family Process*, 23, 437–56.

Vaughan, C.E. and Leff, J.P. (1976). The influence of family and social factors on the course of psychotic illness. *British Journal of Psychiatry*, 129, 125–37.

Vetere, A. and Gale, A. (1987). *Ecological Studies of Family Life*. Chichester, Wiley.

—— (1987). The family: a failure in psychological theory and research. In A. Vetere and A. Gale (eds) *Ecological Studies of Family Life*. Chichester, Wiley.

Walrond-Skinner, S. (1979). Education or training for family therapy? A reconstruction. In S. Walrond-Skinner (ed.) *Family and Marital Psychotherapy: A Critical Approach*. London, Routledge & Kegan Paul.

Waring, E.M., Carver, C., Moran, P. and Lefcoe, D.H. (1986). Family therapy and schizophrenia: recent developments. *Canadian Journal of Psychiatry*, 31, 154–60.

Watts, F.N. (1984). Applicable psychological research in the NHS. *Bulletin of the British Psychological Society*, 37, 41–2.

Wells, R.A. and Dezen, A.E. (1978). The results of family therapy revisited: the non-behavioral methods. *Family Process*, 17, 251–74.

Wing, J.K., Cooper, J.E. and Sartorius, N. (1974). *Measurement and Classification of Psychiatric Symptoms*. Cambridge, Cambridge University Press.

Woodward, C.A., Santa-Barbara, J., Streiner, D.L., Goodman, J.T., Levin, S. and Epstein, N.S. (1981). Client, treatment and therapist variables related to outcome in brief, systems-oriented family therapy. *Family Process*, 20, 189 97.

# INDEX

In the following index, 'family therapy' is abbreviated to 'f.t.'

*Index compiled by Peva Keane*